EBORACUM

The Fortress

Graham Clews

Order this book online at www.trafford.com/08-1027
or email orders@trafford.com

Most Trafford titles are also available at major online book retailers.

Editor: Marg Gilks

Cover Design/Artwork: Laura Diehl

Note for Librarians: A cataloguing record for this book is available from Library
and Archives Canada at www.collectionscanada.ca/amicus/index-e.html

Printed in Victoria, BC, Canada.

ISBN: 978-1-4251-7363-0

*We at Trafford believe that it is the responsibility of us all, as both individuals
and corporations, to make choices that are environmentally and socially sound.
You, in turn, are supporting this responsible conduct each time you purchase a
Trafford book, or make use of our publishing services. To find out how you are
helping, please visit www.trafford.com/responsiblepublishing.html*

*Our mission is to efficiently provide the world's finest, most comprehensive
book publishing service, enabling every author to experience success.
To find out how to publish your book, your way, and have it available
worldwide, visit us online at www.trafford.com/10510*

 www.trafford.com

North America & international
toll-free: 1 888 232 4444 (USA & Canada)
phone: 250 383 6864 ♦ fax: 250 383 6804 ♦ email: info@trafford.com

The United Kingdom & Europe
phone: +44 (0)1865 487 395 ♦ local rate: 0845 230 9601
facsimile: +44 (0)1865 481 507 ♦ email: info.uk@trafford.com

10 9 8 7 6 5

Dedication

Eboracum, The Fortress, is dedicated to the grand and ancient City of York, which as little as sixteen hundred years ago was known as *Eboracvm* by its Roman occupants. It is the place where I was fortunate to have been born. It is often said: The history of the City of York is the history of England.

Other Books by The Author

Jessica Jones and The Gates of Penseron (2006)
Eboracvm, The Village (2007)

Contents

Notes

Certain words or place names have been *italicized*
the first time they are used.
Please refer, respectively, to Appendix II or III
for the modern definition or place name.

Refer to Appendix IV,
page 421, for use of Roman number VIIII.

Foreword

Regarding the first novel, *Eboracvm, the Village*, I consistently heard two suggestions that would have improved the book. The first was that a map or two would have been of great help in tracing the events that took place around Eboracum. The second was that some sort of guide be given readers to help them grow comfortable with the many unfamiliar names and places, which take a chapter or two to get sorted out.

I have cured the first problem by including such a map in *Eboracvm, the Fortress*. As to the unfamiliar names and places, I must simply ask the reader to tough it out. As a help, though, I offer the summary below. I would point out that I was stuck with any name that is "double barrelled" or, to put it another way, has three or more syllables. These are the names of real people taken from the pages of history, and there seemed to be no other course than to use the names as I found them. The ones that (for the most part) have two syllables or less are invented characters. Even so, I have tried to keep their Celtic and Roman origins accurate.

As to the place names, the first time they are used in the book I have placed them in italics; the modern name can be found in Appendix III. A quick summary of the real historic characters follows.

HISTORIC CHARACTERS

Cartimandua: ruler of the tribal area known as Brigantia, and a "client queen" of Rome.

Galgar: this is the only real name I did shorten, because history seems to have "Latinized" it into Galgacus, which simply did not sound right for a Caledonii king (or primary chieftain), and the leader of the combined tribal army in what is now Scotland.

Gnaeus Julius Agricola: (senator and general): Governor of Britannia from A.D. 78–85.

Quintus Petilius Cerialis: (senator and general): Governor of Britannia from A.D. 71–74.

Vellocatus: second husband of Cartimandua, and former shield bearer to Venutius.

Venutius: first husband of Cartimandua, and likely a Brigantian king in his own right.

GENERAL

A final comment: there is a certain amount of profane language in the book. Some people might find it coarse. If such words offend, then I apologize; I do not, however, make apology for their use. It is not gratuitous. The reader will find that such language is employed almost exclusively by the soldiers and warriors in the book, and then merely for emphasis. I spent sixteen years in the Canadian Armed Forces (Reserve) and, quite bluntly, this is the way soldiers talk. My research finds that soldiers and warriors two thousand years ago cussed just as colourfully. To use their actual words, however, would mean nothing, so modern equivalents have been substituted.

A glossary of place names can be found in Appendix III.

North England and Scotland
Roman Place Names and Tribal Territories

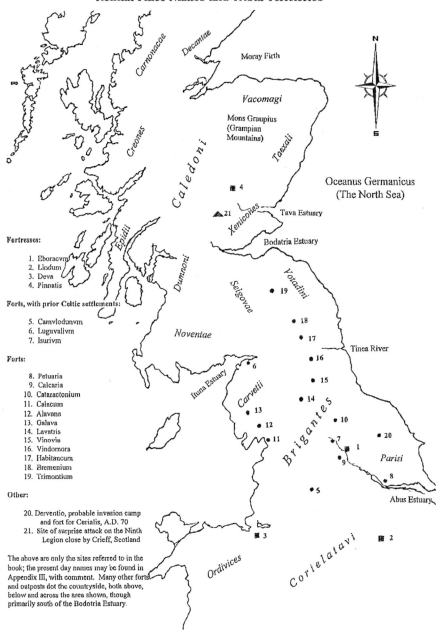

Carnonacae
Decantae
Moray Firth

Vacomagi

Mons Graupius
(Grampian
Mountains)

Creones

Caledoni

Taexali

■ 4

Oceanus Germanicus
(The North Sea)

▲ 21

Xenicones

Tava Estuary

Epidii

Bodatria Estuary

Dumnoni

Votadini

Selgovae

● 19

Fortresses:

1. Eboracvm
2. Lindum
3. Deva
4. Pinnatis

Noventae

● 18

● 17

Tinea River

Forts, with prior Celtic settlements:

5. Camvlodunvm
6. Luguvalivm
7. Isurivm

● 16

Forts:

Ituna Estuary

● 6

● 15

8. Petuaria
9. Calcaria
10. Cataractonium
11. Calacum
12. Alavana
13. Galava
14. Lavatris
15. Vinovia
16. Vindomora
17. Habitancum
18. Bremenium
19. Trimontium

Carvetii

● 14

● 13

● 12

● 10

Brigantes

● 11

● 7

■ 1

● 20

● 9

Parisi

● 8

Other:

20. Derventio, probable invasion camp
    and fort for Cerialis, A.D. 70
21. Site of surprise attack on the Ninth
    Legion close by Crieff, Scotland

● 5

Abus Estuary

The above are only the sites referred to in the
book; the present day names may be found in
Appendix III, with comment. Many other forts
and outposts dot the countryside, both above,
below and across the area shown, though
primarily south of the Bodotria Estuary.

Ordivices

■ 3

Corielatavi

■ 2

Prologue

Britannia, A.D. 78

I: CAMULODUNUM

The hound was a dark, ridge-backed beast that trailed the pack as if distracted. It loped rather than ran, from time to time lifting its grey muzzle to sniff the air. It was clearly puzzled by something missed by the other hounds that raced ahead in pursuit of a terrified stag. Elena, her face flushed as much by wine as excitement, decided to hold back on the reins. Her horse quickly fell away as the hunt thundered on and, a moment later, she smiled. The ridge-back raised its head, bayed once, and sped off toward a stand of trees that capped a hill off to her right.

The animal had barely disappeared into the undergrowth when loud, excited howls erupted, followed by angry squeals, the crack of snapping branches, and the thud of fleeing hooves. Elena readied her spear and gained the edge of the woods in time to see the squat shape of a large boar disappear through the bracken, the hound nipping at its heels. She urged the horse forward, her body one with the animal as it leapt over winter deadfall and wove between the trees.

Grunting and screaming its rage, the huge boar lumbered at a surprising speed, its awkward gait fuelled by panic. It soon cleared the trees and raced across the open pasture, making for the dense forest barely a hundred yards away. The hound leapt alongside, ripping at the animal's flanks and savaging its rear, but unable to bring it down. Elena broke clear, grinned, and dug hard with both heels. The distance quickly narrowed, but she realized the boar would find shelter before she could close.

1

The creature reached the first of the trees, and both animals vanished from sight. Growls and a further scuffle followed, along with a sharp yelp. The boar appeared again, farther back in the forest, the hound limping unsteadily behind. Elena raised the spear and urged her horse toward the same path, vaguely aware the two animals had stumbled on other prey.

A bear rose angrily from its hollow, head toward the depths of the forest and the retreating hound; the pounding of the horse's hooves made it quickly turn. With a roar the beast stretched tall on its hind legs, adding terror and size to its gaunt, winter-starved bulk. Squealing, the horse skewed sideways and lost its footing. Elena plunged over the animal's neck and landed hard on the gnarled roots of the nearest tree. She sensed rather than heard bone crack. One arm twisted up painfully behind her, she screamed her agony as she rolled across the dirt, coming to rest against the bear's hairy leg.

Gasping at the stabbing pain, horribly aware of the warm fur against her cheek, Elena looked up at the towering figure of the bear. "Shit!" she squealed, and the rush of panic instantly dulled the pain. The creature seemed to be weaving—or was it her mind? Its head was bent forward, the eyes staring blankly downward as if it were confused. For a moment neither moved, then the animal blinked, shook its massive muzzle, opened its jaws, and roared.

Elena edged backward but the pain returned, stabbing hard at her shoulder. She couldn't help it—again she screamed. The bear hesitated, then swung its head sideways, its attention elsewhere. The grunting and pawing of another struggle filled her ears, followed by a long, spine-chilling squeal of pain. The horse was down, clearly badly hurt, and trying to gain its feet. A broken leg…

The bear glanced down again, as if uncertain. Elena forced back the panic and kept eye contact. Foolish though the gesture felt, she bared her teeth and growled. The animal raised its head, grunted, and again glanced toward the fallen horse. It hesitated, then, with a final look down, swung toward the larger prey. Not daring so much as a sigh of relief, Elena fumbled for her knife.

The forest echoed with the terrified squeals of the horse and the bear's snarls. Then, except for the heavy, grunting shuffle of the bear itself, everything grew strangely quiet.

At that moment, as if the gods had been deliberately waiting, the baying of the hound filled her ears. Cursing the pain, Elena raised her head. The ridge-back, bless its fool heart, hurtled through the trees, skidded to a halt, and set to nipping and snapping at the bear. The gaunt animal fell back on all fours, vainly swiping at its tormentor with massive claws. Then, as if disgusted, it again raised itself on its hind legs, let go a long, angry roar, and dropped once more to the ground. Ignoring the hound as if it were no more than a wasp, it ambled off through the trees. As she stared at the beast's wobbling hind end, Elena was suddenly struck by how much smaller the animal looked.

She sighed and dropped her head back on the damp earth, staring up at the spring canopy of fresh leaves high above, and the bright, life-giving sparkle of sunlight. Her breath gusted out in an enormous sigh of relief, on which rode two words: "Thank you..."

"So?"

Gaius rose to his feet and joined Agricola, who stood farther out in the pasture, holding the reins of both their horses. "She'll live," he grunted as if Elena's injuries were of no consequence, though he was both relieved and annoyed. Damn the woman. And damn Cartimandua as well! The day was hardly begun, yet the barbarian queen was again plaguing his life with her endless interfering.

"With what injury?"

Gaius sighed and shrugged. "Her arm's broken above the elbow, and the other shoulder's dislocated. She's—"

A scream came from between the trees and both men turned. Elena was on her knees, her left arm bound in a makeshift splint, her head bent forward in obvious pain. Catey stood behind her, gripping both shoulders. One of her men held Elena's right arm, stiffened at the elbow, and now in a forward position. She flinched as he moved the limb carefully downward, bending it across her chest.

"So now it's just a broken arm," Agricola observed dryly. "Anything else?"

"Cuts, bruises, and injured pride," Gaius said as his anger, or perhaps his embarrassment, got the better of him. "She should have remained at the lodge with Catey. The pair of them were into the grapes before the slaves had the food off the table this morning. Now look at them." He gestured.

Elena was trying to climb to her feet, Cartimandua vainly attempting to help without inflicting further pain. Elena shook her head at the effort of it all, and sank limply back down to her knees. "Dammit!" Gaius muttered under his breath as he heard the barbarian queen order a litter. He turned to face Agricola, and found him grinning with amusement.

"And of course neither of us had a drop, did we?" the older man drawled.

"That's not the point."

"I suppose not. But what is? Gaius, the woman almost grabbed a bear by the balls. You should be thankful she's still alive." Agricola chuckled. "Now that would have been something, wouldn't it? How many men can claim their woman has done that, and got away with it? Not many. It's usually us they've got by the plums."

"*And* they get away with it," Gaius muttered, now uncomfortable with his sudden outburst. But the woman should have been more careful. She might have been killed! And as for the wine, he and Agricola had hardly touched it, and he handled his drink far better than Elena anyway.

"I doubt she'll be riding on with us tomorrow," Agricola murmured, raising his eyebrows as if seeking confirmation.

"I doubt she'll be going anywhere soon," Gaius agreed, then realized where the governor was pointing his spear. "That's not a problem. It's not as if she's my wife."

"Yes, of course she isn't." Agricola snorted derisively, then shrugged. "I suppose it really doesn't matter if she's there or not. Your daughter will be, though?"

"Both the girls will be there. And the boy."

"That's good, then. When there's a change of command, the garrison likes to see the new legate's family on parade," Agricola said. "Lets them see exactly who they're getting."

Gaius grinned. "They'll see who they're getting soon enough."

II: EBORACUM

"This place is a disgrace. I've seen better marching camps! The ramparts are sagging, the palisades are rotting, and the buildings look as if they've been thrown up, not put up!" Agricola clasped one hand to his forehead as if wounded, and sighed. "When I last saw this woodpile, it was newly cut from the wild. It was crude. It was hastily built. It was beleaguered by barbarians on all sides. But let me tell you this, it looked like a Roman fortress!"

He glared tight-lipped at the Ninth Hispana's corps of officers, daring any to so much as breathe a sigh of denial. The silence held, broken only by the creak of shifting leather that echoed softly off the plastered walls of the headquarters building. Which, Agricola noted, had large cracks where they met the ceiling.

"It was neat, it was clean, and above all, it was well-ordered," he continued, raising his voice. "Which means the soldiers inside were neat, clean, and well-ordered!"

Feet shuffled, and a barely audible murmur reached Agricola as he glared down from the *tribunal* at the east end of the building. No benches had been provided, which placed the men below at a disadvantage. That had been Gaius's suggestion. He stood off to one side of the great cross hall, arms folded across his chest, his eyes scanning the fifty-odd faces staring up at the governor. Agricola wondered how many of them he recognized.

"This regiment is rumoured to be a bad luck unit," he said, careful to keep his voice raised. "It was damn-near annihilated by the bitch Boudicca. It suffered five hundred casualties at what the barbarians call Bran's Beck. And it's been skulking behind these walls for the past four years. In a few words, that's the way of it, right?"

Feet shuffled again, and while nobody saw fit to agree, nobody appeared ready to disagree.

"I said, right!" Agricola barked.

A low, reluctant murmur of agreement followed.

"That is nothing but pure, raw, unadulterated pig shit!" the governor of Britannia sneered. Agricola shook a finger at them. "The Ninth had an unblemished record before that. Its record was, in fact, magnificent. Magnificent, that is, until it left the south of this miserable province, and marched north. It served well under Plautius. Before that, it earned battle honours in Macedonia and Hispana. It served faithfully in Africa. Dammit, this legion was birthed before Julius Caesar himself, and it fought well for Caesar when asked. And it fought well in its last major battle, here in the north, at *Stannick*! There was no bad luck that day. There was only skill, training, hard slogging, and damned good soldiering. I want to see that again!"

"Your new legate will no doubt ensure I get what I want." Agricola drew back a pace, allowing the low shuffle to again fill the hall before pressing on. Lowering his voice, he gestured across the hall to Gaius, who seemed to stand taller, one hand moving upward to square his helmet as the other picked at the folds of his cloak. "Many of you know him. General Sabinius has served with distinction from Judaea to Germania. He served two tours of duty with the Ninth. He was the man responsible for building the fortress here at Eboracum. And the general—" Agricola again paused to rake the room with a glare intended for every man present. "The general no doubt has a few words to add to mine."

With an abrupt nod, he stepped down from the tribunal and strode stiffly toward the main entrance without so much as a sideways glance. But he paused in passing Gaius and placed one hand firmly on his shoulder as he turned back to the assembly.

"Despite heavy fighting, despite heavy casualties, those soldiers of the Ninth at Bran's Beck did hold their position," Agricola said, his voice deliberately heavy with emotion. "They stood fast and they stood ready; they stood ready to fight to the last man." His hand rose and fell in a hard slap on Gaius's shoulder. "And here—here stands the man who led them."

Agricola turned his face toward Gaius and, still holding the pose, winked. "Your helmet's still not square," he whispered. "I've seen tarts do less primping."

"And here stands the man who led them!" Gaius almost snorted in disgust as the words ran through his mind. His mouth felt suddenly dry as

the steady clomp of hobnailed boots trailed Agricola from the room, leaving an empty silence that was a sound in itself. Every last man was waiting for him to speak, and there was no putting it off.

And here stands the man who almost balled the whole thing up, he thought, suddenly aware his cheeks were uncomfortably warm. But Agricola's words held no sting, he decided; it was simply his conscience recalling decisions that could have been better chosen. There were men here who almost certainly felt the same way. Men whose eyes followed him as he made his way to the tribunal.

The sea of faces was at first a blur, and Gaius licked his lips, forcing himself to calm down and focus. Several faces were familiar, yes, but damned few. Then, as the jumble in his mind began to clear, he saw a few more, though he could name only one or two. Four commissioned officers, tribunes, stood off to one side, each looking disturbingly young. Those he couldn't expect to recognize. But the others were centurios, experienced men, nearly all promoted from the ranks. Most had seen long service in the Ninth, and should have been familiar.

Even so, there should have been more of them here, whether he knew them or not. Only two-thirds of the legion's field officers were present, he knew that. Two cohorts were seconded elsewhere, and a dozen or more detachments had been taken from others, but that only partly explained the shortage. More than a few vacancies were due to administrative inertia. And that, Gaius knew, ground down a legion's spirit as surely as a lost battle.

Gaius almost sighed in relief as his eyes found a face he could name. The man had been a *decanus* at Bran's Beck, where he'd entrusted his own son, Marc, to the veteran's care. "Octavius! Good to see you've been promoted."

The man's hard features lit with pleasure. "Thank you, sir. How's the boy?"

"Er, he's fine. Hale and healthy," Gaius replied, deliberately vague. Another face seemed eager to be recognized and he smiled as the man's name popped into his mind. "Aelius. Good to see you. Still with the first cohort?" The centurio nodded as if suddenly tongue-tied. "Flavius," he said to another familiar face. "I see the underworld still hasn't claimed its due. How's the leg?"

Several glanced sideways at Flavius, and laughed at his reply: "It let me down, sir. The damn thing healed, and kept me in the legion."

As if a fog had cleared, Gaius saw a dozen more he could have named. The tension in the long cross hall eased noticeably, at least for him. "Pluto would have spit you out anyway."

Several other men started to speak, but Gaius raised one hand to signal that the easiness should, for the moment, be set aside. For the first time since stepping onto the tribunal, he felt comfortable as the familiarity of command settled once more on his shoulders.

"The governor did not utter a word that was untrue," he began, his voice even but firm, "but here is where it ends. When the wax melts on the tablet, it leaves a clear, even surface. That is the way it will be with the Ninth. What we now write on that surface is how you will be judged. And you, I, we all have a clear, even beginning.

"This year starts with not only a newly appointed *legate*, but also a new *primus pilus*. Many of you will remember Titus Aurelius Urbicus." Gaius paused, allowing time for the words to register. The grins, the sideways nods, all showed that nearly every man there knew Titus; many had fought under his command. More than a few called out their approval. Gathering confidence, he spoke the next words harshly, keeping his face devoid of expression. "He will not be a happy man when he arrives!" Again he paused, allowing the silence to hang. One or two eyebrows lifted in query. Then he smiled. "The poor man is almost fifty. He thinks he's coming here to take over as *praefectus castrorum*!"

Following an unusual change of command ceremony, conducted in the absence of the previous legate due to ill health, Agricola departed for the West. The governor's campaign against the tribes beyond *Deva* was not expected to be prolonged, but the fighting would be hard. He ordered yet another cohort of the Ninth to follow, with the promise it would be returned before the end of summer. What was left of the legion would concentrate on "keeping the bung in the barrel of Brigantia" until the following year, when the Ninth and Agricola's old regiment, the Twentieth Valeria Victrix, would once again join forces.

"Only this time," Agricola murmured to Gaius, only half in jest, "the Ninth will damn-well wait for me, before they do battle!"

Gaius had simply grinned, recalling a previous governor under whom both men had served, Petilius Cerialis. The general had launched an impetuous attack on the barbarian fortress at Stannick with only half his army in place. That the assault proved successful seemed only to have fired Agricola's irritation.

The night of Agricola's departure, Gaius sat down in the privacy of the commander's residence and, for first time since arriving at Eboracum, made an effort to tend to his own interests. It was difficult. The huge building felt like an empty barracks block. His daughter Aelia was off in her quarters with Elena's daughter, and young Tuis had gone to his own room hours ago. The only one missing was his woman Elena. Irritating as she could be, the huge residence felt empty without her.

A new commander was expected to maintain appearances, and a woman helped. Elena, especially, should have been there—Eboracum had been her home. He'd been looking forward to bringing her back as much as she had been eager to return. And there was a further advantage: her presence should prove useful in dealing with the local tribes.

Gaius sighed. Just when they were almost there again ... He wondered, not for the first time, what perverse interest the gods were taking in his affairs. It was something they did far too often in this place, and never for the better. This time, he admitted, Gaius Sabinius was not the target of their arrows—not directly. They had been aimed at Elena, who was lucky to be alive. And as with so many past events in Britannia, the aging barbarian queen Cartimandua had been involved. An odd sense of familiarity haunted him.

"I thought you'd prefer an unwatered red, sir."

Gaius looked up. Metellus had padded into the room, a tray in one hand and a jug of wine in the other. A single goblet sat on the tray, along with an assortment of glistening pastries, dried honeyed fruit, and cubed cheese. The slave set the tray on a small table alongside Gaius's chair, then carefully filled the goblet.

"It went well today?"

"No better or worse than expected," Gaius muttered, his mind still at Camulodunum. He'd made several promises before leaving there—

no, they were really decisions—and all had been pushed on him by Elena. He was as certain as death that she'd been prodded by Catey. Both women had played ruthlessly on his sympathy as Elena's bruises swelled her limbs to twice their size, and the cuts and scrapes grew livid. Yet in fairness, the first two decisions he'd wavered on for far too long, and were overdue: those regarding his son Marcus and Elena's boy Rhun.

It was the third promise that irked, however, and it had been one hastily made. He still wondered why he'd capitulated. Was there more to it than Elena was admitting? He'd been on the verge of a flat refusal when Catey's husband had come right out and asked as a favour, and how do you refuse a man who freed you from prison—even if the escape proved to be a farce? Vellocatus, curse him, was far too cunning for his own good. But to arrange a transfer for that arrogant, strutting, yappy little stoat...

Gaius leaned back in his chair with a long, resigned sigh and waved one hand that sent Metellus in search of writing material. The distant howl of a wolf drifted over the fortress wall as the slave returned. The lamps were topped, the wine goblet refilled and a second added for the tired scribe. As Gaius began to dictate, Metellus, tongue between his teeth in concentration, smiled and unconsciously nodded his approval.

Chapter I

Vetera, Lower Germania, A.D. 78

Rhun enjoyed a certain ritual on returning from patrol; it was almost a rite, now grown to the point of superstition. And as the squadron of auxiliary cavalry rode through the fortress gate and onto the *via principalis* on a fine March evening, there seemed no reason to change. He turned to Turren, the troop's *optio*, and gave the usual order to "take them in." Then, edging his horse into the shadow of a huge stone granary, he watched the riders clatter by on their way to the stables.

The men of the XII *Turmae*, Second *Ala* Tungrorum rode in two ranks on stocky horses that were hardly more than large ponies, yet Rhun's chest filled with well-concealed pride as, eyes narrowed, he assessed each man and his mount. When the last trooper had ridden past he nodded his satisfaction and, face expressionless, swung in behind. He trailed the last two horses as far as the stable block, where Turren waited patiently.

"All in order, sir?"

"All in order," Rhun replied, and today it was. The patrol had been an easy one, as most were. The frontier was at relative peace, and not even the armies of Rome had fought each other of late.

"Should I see your horse is stabled, then?"

"That's good of you, Turren," Rhun replied, careful to remain expressionless as the ritual played out. "Would you care to join me for a drink?"

"I'd be delighted, *decurio*," Turren replied, his mouth tight yet ready to twitch, as if fighting the need to remain serious.

"I'll be in my quarters, then." Rhun solemnly handed Turren the reins and dismounted, stumbling as his legs took his weight. He stamped both feet to restore balance, then strode past the stables toward the barracks block.

As commander of a squadron, which at full strength numbered thirty souls, Rhun had his own quarters at one end of the building. The doorway lay close by *Vetera*'s stone walls, yet far enough back to catch the rays of the dying sun. It was a fine evening, and he left the door open as he walked inside, giving the spartan sitting room barely a glance.

Shedding sword, belt, and mail armour with a sigh of relief, he hung each in turn on a row of wooden pegs set shoulder high in the wall. The leather tunic followed, but the grubby undershirt was too much effort; he simply tugged it free of the waistband and let it fall over his leggings like a field hand's smock.

A shelf had been built into the wall across from the door, and it held nothing but a motley row of drinking vessels. Rhun studied them all as if undecided, and finally chose the usual two: a plain pottery mug and a brass tumbler elaborately etched with swirls and whorls. He set both on the low pine table in the middle of the room, then moved to a wooden chest, where he carefully studied a row of dusty wine jugs. Selecting an Iberian biturica, he removed the bung, sniffed the contents, and nodded approval. He set the jug between the two cups then, with a gaping yawn, sprawled on one of the chairs, set both feet on the table, and waited.

Turren was not long in arriving. He entered the room with no word of greeting, walked directly to the table, lifted the jug, and turned to face Rhun. "Should I pour, Decurio?"

"By all means, Optio." Groaning with the effort, Rhun climbed to his feet, lifted the brass tumbler, and thrust it forward.

Turren filled the vessel to the brim, then followed suit with the mug, raising it high after setting the jug back on the table. Rhun clinked his tumbler against the clay lip of the mug, then tasted the wine. It was, as always, a good vintage. He took pride in having no other, claiming it as his only weakness.

"Life's too short to drink cheap wine," he began solemnly.

"Too brief to serve the army," Turren added.

"So piss on Rome, and let's go home," both men chanted together. "To the land of the Catuvellaunii!"

The rims clinked again, and for a moment the only sound was the soft liquid slurping of wine. Rhun sighed his appreciation and, in a sing-song voice, completed the ritual: "And to the green hills of Bri-gan-tyaaa!"

Another sip, then both men sat down, each swinging his legs onto the table.

"That last part does not rhyme, you know," Turren said.

"So you keep saying." Rhun wriggled farther back in the chair. He peered over the rim of the beaker, slowly breathing in the fragrance of the wine. "So tell me, would you really go home, if you had the chance?"

Turren raised his wine and grinned, an expression mostly lost in the thick, greying moustache that drooped from the corners of his mouth. "So you keep asking."

"And?"

"And the usual answer: I don't know. It's been almost twenty years. I'm not even sure where my home is." Turren's head dropped, his eyes narrowing as he stared into the wine. "Five more, and I suppose I'll have to decide."

Rhun stared at his optio, struck not for the first time by the notion that he could be looking at himself in twenty years. It was not a good thought. Not that Turren looked that old; in fact, he seemed to be aging well for a man who had to be at least forty. The Briton was lean and fit, and his tanned face was relatively free of wrinkles. *So what, then?* Again, not for the first time, Rhun found himself brooding at the prospect of the future: stuck in Lower Germania, perhaps for a lifetime.

At least *his* career was a hundred miles ahead of Turren's, who only a year past had earned the rank of optio. Which, Rhun had to admit, wasn't bad for a Catuvellauni prisoner taken in battle. And which, in turn, made his own ranking nothing but a mystery—though he had his suspicion of its origin.

So, why did such thoughts leave him depressed? A mood that had, of late, become an unwelcome part of the ritual.

"Sir!"

Rhun drained the brass cup, his eyes shifting to a vaguely familiar face blocking the sunlight from his doorway. The man was some sort of headquarters clerk, and looked smugly pleased about something. Was he eager to pass on someone's bad tidings? Or was he just being pleasant? Rhun shook his head in disgust. "What?"

"The legate wanted to see you the moment you returned."

"Now?"

"He said as soon as you got back."

"Shit!"

"Sounds like you've pissed in someone's *puls*," Turren muttered.

Rhun ignored the comment, other than to curse, and heaved himself once more to his feet. He began tucking the shirt back into his pants. The legate himself! What did the man want? Hopefully he was being summoned to some kind of special orders group. Should he get dressed again? The chain mail? No, he was done for the day, and it had been a long one. Dressed the way he was should be good enough. What had he done wrong, anyway? The wax-scratcher offered no answer. The way the army worked, it could be anything.

The legate himself! The man sat in his headquarters building, so far removed he might have been one of the gods. Maybe the chain mail was better. Rhun reluctantly reached for the leather tunic. "I'll be there shortly."

Rhun strode through the outer entrance of the legate's residence—the man was not, after all, at the headquarters building—his mind dredging up past sins. They were few, and not one should have pressed hard against the legate's shield. Even so, with the nagging guilt that haunts a man of clear conscience, he turned left and headed for the reception room.

A tall, hulking trooper stood outside, slouched against the wall as if propping it up. His head was lost under a mop of shaggy black hair, and his face, but for a large nose and dark eyes, was all but hidden by a full beard. Were it not for his armour and weapons, which were, Rhun noted, in good order, the creature might have been dragged from a cave. As he passed by, the man nodded balefully, like a bleary-eyed bear.

Rhun's nerves were drawn tight as a bow string as he stepped inside the reception room. Slamming one foot on the stone floor, he drew himself to attention and cried, "Sir!"

"Rhun..." The commander of the XV Primigenia Legion casually acknowledged his presence without looking up, and motioned to a chair.

Rhun saw that a second man was already seated, an auxiliary cavalryman like himself. This one was also a decurio, but not, apparently, a particularly disciplined one. The trooper sat with his feet stretched before him, ankles crossed; an arm hooked around the back of his chair appeared to be all that stopped him from sliding off the seat.

"Thank you, sir," Rhun replied stiffly. He took the only other chair, across from the ill-disciplined stranger. The man stared back through half-lidded eyes, a knowing, lopsided grin on his face. He seemed amused—very much so. Was there some sort of trouble? Or—the thought left Rhun cold—was he being mocked?

The decurio was much older, perhaps the same age as Turren. He looked the sort of man to search out trouble, and not give a soldier's damn where he found it. His face was tanned the colour of leather, except for a livid scar running down one cheek. His brown hair was drawn back in a ponytail, and his wispy, greying beard and long moustaches were in sore need of a trim. The nose was as battered as his face, large and bent by more than one breaking. If Rhun were to lay odds, he would have placed the cause on brawling. Yet the man's mail tunic, which still retained the old shoulder pieces, was clean and well oiled, and the metal on his scabbard glittered, as did the hilt of his sword, though that might be simply from use.

"What do you know of the Ninth Hispana's legate?"

The commander's question came like an arrow from a forest, and Rhun turned to face him, lost for an answer. "Where is the Ninth?" he asked cautiously. "Last I heard, it was in Brigantia."

"Still is."

Rhun shook his head, baffled by the question. "Then that's the only thing I know about it, sir. I certainly don't know who the commander is."

"Well, I do!" The legate grunted his annoyance and gestured first to a dispatch pouch that lay open on the table, then to the lounging trooper. "And so, it seems, does this ill-trimmed specimen. And if *you* don't know who the legate is, I'll tell you. He's the bugger who's been given leave to rob Lower Germania of its best cavalrymen. A full regiment's been commissioned from this province, which means I've been struggling to find fifteen squadrons of cavalry. Now it appears yours has been specifically included in the tally."

"Mine?" Rhun blurted, surprised. He'd been at Vetera a mere fifteen months, and fully expected to remain on the frontier for years. Perhaps forever. Certainly for the foreseeable future. Then it sank in that the legate said the transfer was to the Ninth Hispana, which was stationed at…Rhun's body sagged. Was he being transferred home, back to the Roman province where he had once lived? Where he had been born!

As the shock faded, his emotions boiled into anger. Memories flooded his mind: his father, his brother, his sister, all of them either killed or lost; and his mother…

Damn them! His mother! And they wanted him back there?

No hope, no peace of mind would come with such a return. The province of Britannia was no longer his home. As far as he was concerned, and the thought struck like a bolt of lightning, no such place existed anymore, literally, or in his mind.

But why send him there? Why would a Brigante tribesman be transferred back to the land of his people? The army had a hard and fast rule: native auxiliary troops do not serve in their own province. It had been done in the past, certainly, but only when dictated by necessity or, of course, politics. The rule was a wise one. Vetera itself bore proof of its wisdom. Less than a decade past, this same fortress had been razed by local Batavi auxiliaries. The town on the far side of its walls still bore the black scars of rebellion. And for their betrayal, a good many now served in Britannia, while more than a few Britons now served in Lower Germania.

Which made Rhun wonder. Were those men going back too, or would they be spread among the other squadrons? Surely they would remain, culled out and kept back. In fact, would *he* be held back? If his squadron was being sent somewhere, that didn't necessarily mean he was going with it!

Rhun felt concentration pinch the skin between his brows. What had the legate said? A full regiment was being formed? Fifteen squadrons? Rhun shook his head. That didn't make sense. Had he heard correctly? He turned to ask, but the legate was droning on about lack of troops, and wondering where, in a bog's bottom, he was going to scrape up replacements.

"It's Agricola, of course," the legate grumbled. "He wants his legions at full strength to ensure success in Britannia. Then he'll return to Rome piled with glory, and expect honours and a triumph of—"

"Sir?"

"What?"

"Did you say fifteen squadrons?"

"Yes, and most of them from my command. I'll have to rob regiments scattered from—"

"You said a full regiment. There are sixteen squadrons in a full regiment."

"I can count, trooper!" the legate barked. "The one troop difference is the reason this insult to Rome's discipline now disgraces my building!" He pointed to the strange decurio. The man's grin broadened, as if the insult was a compliment. "There, believe it or not, sits the leader of the sixteenth."

"Where ... ?" Rhun began, his eyes turning to the decurio, who was now absorbed in the state of his fingernails.

"From farther east, along the *Rhenus*. And you saw that oaf slouching outside the door when you came in?"

Rhun thought for a moment. "Built like an ox? Same bovine look?"

"That's the one. It's this man's second-in-command." The legate leaned back in his chair with a sigh. "If you think this piracy has my piss boiling, you should see what the commander of the Tenth Gemina wrote when he had to give them up."

The decurio stirred, and spoke for the first time. "The man's superstitious."

"He is?"

"We saved his life once."

The legate gestured once more toward the dispatches. "And proved valuable to the previous commander, I gather. Plus a few other odds and ends in between that seem to have turned out well. Horseshit luck, no doubt."

"My squadron *is* considered lucky." The decurio managed to shrug his indifference without sliding off the chair. "It's not true, of course. You make your own luck. The fact is, we're good at what we do. We're from Brigantia."

Rhun's eyes widened, but he couldn't resist a retort. "I see you're also modest. How did you arrange a transfer back?"

"He was asked for by name," the legate interrupted. "Same as yourself. The requests…" He hesitated and glanced down at the dispatches as if they were poison. "Dammit, I suppose they're really orders, not requests. The Ninth's legate may have phrased it that way, but it's sealed by Agricola in the name of Vespasian. Nonetheless, the dispatches, as far as they pertain to the pair of you, do offer the privilege of refusing the transfer." He glanced up, eyebrows raised in question. "You might want to consider that option if you don't—"

"I'm not going to do that," the decurio said emphatically. "I'm going."

"You never mentioned the commander's name, sir." Rhun leaned forward, his mind racing over the possibilities, all of them slowly ebbing until only one remained. His belly felt suddenly sour inside.

"I didn't, did I?" The legate selected one of the dispatches, studying it at length as if the name was not already scribed on his mind. "Ah, here it is. He's a Sabinius. Gaius Sabinius Trebonius." He looked up. "Do you know him?"

Rhun slumped back on the seat. Oh yes, he knew Gaius Sabinius Trebonius! He knew him only too well. The legate Sabinius—how did the rotten bastard ever get that rank?—was the man who had destroyed his home, raped his mother, forced her into slavery, and tore his sister and brother from them both. Sabinius was the same man who had ordered the killing of one of his closest kin, Nuada, even as he, still half child, had tried to defend her. The man had also seen to the slaughter of her husband, Cian. Oh yes, he knew the man. And one day, he had promised himself, one day they would meet. And when that happened—

"I said, do you know him?"

Rhun looked up to find the legate staring. He coughed to clear his throat, surprised to find his voice cracking as he fought back his anger. "Y-yes, sir. I know him."

"And you're going to accept the transfer?"

"I-I … " Rhun was surprised to find he wasn't sure. Such a posting would almost certainly bring him face to face with the man. Was he ready for that? And what, in fact, would he actually do? The revenge he'd sworn on the Roman loomed suddenly real. Acceptance of the transfer could prove a death sentence for them both.

"He'll go!"

The words came from the decurio. Rhun turned, his face flushed with annoyance. "I'll be the one that decides!" he snapped.

"No, you won't. I will. It's for your own good, you stupid bugger." The decurio's lopsided grin was almost a laugh, and his eyes danced with merriment. "I more than once changed your nappies when you were a bairn, boy. You did as you were told then, and you'll do as you're told now. You'll take the transfer."

Rhun and the legate stared in amazement, but only Rhun found himself able to speak. Even then, the words faltered as the decurio's tanned and battered face grew vaguely familiar. "Y–you're … "

"Aye, lad, I'm your da's brother, Cian. Now stop gawking, and start gathering your kit."

Chapter II

Rome, A.D. 78

The Sabinius city house was not ostentatious, even though it had been built in one of Rome's better neighbourhoods. It sat, in fact, in one of the best, halfway up the southwest slope of the Palatinus hill, overlooking the Circus Maximus. Its size, by comparison with others in the narrow street, was neither large nor small. Its gardens, hidden behind tall walls, were merely average, but as well kept as any on the "Mons." The building had been selected by its owner for that very reason: it blended with its surroundings—a good, average house that attracted no attention at all.

For the past half a decade or so, Senator Julius Sabinius, Gaius's older brother and sole sibling, had himself tried to do exactly that: attract no attention at all. And now he lay outside the city in a small cemetery not far off the Tusculanan Way, having finally achieved his goal.

Julius's death had left his brother Gaius a wealthy man, and not without a certain amount of inherited influence. Yet his new circumstance had also produced vexing changes.

Gaius had not been a rich man before his brother's death, but he had been quite comfortable—more or less. While he was seldom short of funds, the purse strings had always been carefully watched. Once or twice brother Julius had offered loans that were never pressed for repayment, and this had sometimes troubled his conscience. Yet even now, Gaius failed to realize those loans had served as balm to Julius's own conscience, for his brother's political blundering had more than once hampered his career. That blundering had in fact led Gaius early in life to the anonymity of the legions, which had grown to be a family of their own.

Gaius found his sudden wealth brought with it a multitude of responsibilities, many of a social nature. He quickly discovered that society on the Mons held far more pitfalls than appeal. Outside the military, Gaius was essentially a private man; a soldier, more at ease in the company of other soldiers, where a good blade was worn on the hip, not between the shoulder blades. So, when Agricola offered him command of the Ninth Hispana Legion, it was too ripe a plum to resist.

In taking the post, Gaius realized he was turning his back on many problems; most, however, were readily postponed or, better still, placed under the care of his daughter Aelia. Those that couldn't would not fester, and the minor ones he was well rid of anyway—such as where, exactly, did he fit in the harsh pecking order of Rome; what social obligation should he host, refuse, or attend; who should be invited, who should not, and who cared anyway?

The night at Eboracum when he sat down with Metellus and dictated orders, two of those problems had been dealt with at once. One was the return of Elena's son Rhun to Britannia, which seemed a reasonable enough gift for the woman; the second was the transfer home of her husband's brother, which was damned unreasonable. The mouthy little stoat should have spent the rest of his life in Germania … though Gaius grudgingly admitted the man's record there had proven excellent—when the little fart wasn't up to his neck in trouble. He'd given in, though it was against his better judgement.

Once that was decided, only one matter really stood unresolved— a matter much closer to home which, of late, had grown acute. He'd put it off until assuming command at Eboracum, where, he admitted, distance made the decision easier.

The problem had reared its head soon after he'd inherited his brother's estates, arriving at his door claiming neglect and indifference. Its name was Marcus, and he wanted to move in with his father. The excuse that he could no longer bear living under the same roof as his mother sounded reasonable; the trouble was, the boy had too much of his mother in him!

Gaius had reluctantly agreed, setting one condition: his son must do a term of service in the legions. Marcus, in turn, felt he'd already seen far too much of the legions as a child, most particularly in Brigantia. He was quick to show the scar on one thigh to prove it, in a deliberate jab at his father's conscience for nearly getting him killed over there—which in both men's minds was completely true.

Harsh words followed, and he was on the point of tossing the boy back to his mother when, spurred by a twinge of guilt, he agreed to a compromise. Marcus Sabinius Trebonius would join the *Praetorian Guard*, if his father was able to secure him a tribune's commission. Much to his surprise, Gaius found he had the influence to do so.

The sun had almost reached its zenith, which for Marcus Sabinius was prime time for the first meal of the day—the tongue was no longer thick, lingering headaches had all but vanished, and food finally held its first trace of appeal. That particular morning the meal was in the atrium, for it was a bright, mild day in early spring. Two dishevelled youths were also present, both left over from the previous night's bacchanalia.

The food was served by the household slaves, nearly all of whom were young and female, a condition that had cost Marcus a good deal of coin. Gaius had left the estate overseer with explicit instructions to the contrary, and the price of bending the man's principles was one more reason for his son's shortage of funds. His constant lack of coin cut deep into what might otherwise have been an idyllic existence.

"The trouble is, he doesn't provide enough," Marcus complained, absently fondling the rump of a naked slave as she set a platter of dried figs on the table. "I may have to look for another blood-sucking moneylender. The one I'm using is proving unreasonable."

"Your father wasn't happy last time," noted the dark-haired youth sprawled on the couch to Marcus's left, sipping a late morning goblet of uncut wine on the excuse that it would cure his headache. "Made all sort of threats, I recall."

"Agh, talk of better things, Marius!" Marcus groaned, and thrust his own goblet toward the slave for more of the same. "There's got to be something I can sell that he won't miss."

"I thought the Praetorians paid well," murmured the second youth, a fair-haired fop with an ashen complexion, who was intent on the figs.

"Not enough. Plus it's not due, and it's already spent!" Marcus raised himself on one elbow and drained half the glass. "I had no idea the guard would prove so expensive. I don't think the pater did, either. The monthly cost of the messing alone is … "

Marcus paused as one of the few male slaves waved to catch his attention. The lad was a slim, handsome youth with fine features and a mop of curly blond hair that had obviously been dyed. You have to cater to all your guests, Marcus had explained more than once to those with raised eyebrows, quickly adding that he didn't bend in that direction himself. On the other hand, if the inquirer himself wanted to lean just a little, then …

"What is it?

"A soldier, master. At the street door. He wants to see you."

"Who is it?"

"I don't know. He's from the guards."

"Tell him to piss off," the youth called Marius said, airily waving his free hand.

"Shit," Marcus muttered, and pushed himself up to sit on the couch. "Better not. Did you tell him I was here?"

"No need, I can see for myself," a deep voice boomed from the far side of the atrium. An officer in full uniform including a crested helmet crossed the quadrangle, his hobnailed boots clattering painfully loud on the tiled floor.

"Agh!" Marcus clutched at the ache in the side of his head.

"Young sir!" The soldier slammed to attention, his weathered features twitching as they fought a mocking grin. "I come bearing orders from on high."

"How high, praefectus?" Marcus mumbled, climbing insolently to his feet, for no other reason than he didn't like looking up at the man. Lucius Silva, the legion's praefectus castrorum, was an officious turd at the best of times.

"From the Praetorian legate himself!" Lucius seemed inordinately pleased as he presented Marcus with a sealed scroll. "You will also observe, young sir, that appearing on the illustrious document is Vespasian's seal of approval."

"The emperor?" Marcus said, his voice almost a squeak. "Why would—"

"Shouldn't worry yourself, young sir; it's nothing personal. The emperor's seal on a gentleman's transfer from the Praetorians is simply a matter of form." Lucius gazed benignly at Marius; his mouth curled at the corner, with little attempt to hold it steady. "It seems that today it is not I who has to piss off, but our young tribune. An overseas adventure, I believe."

"Overseas?" Marcus asked weakly, and the hand holding the scroll fell as his arm went limp.

"Nothing new to *you*, though, young sir. You're an old hand in Britannia, I believe." Lucius gestured to the dangling hand. "It's all in there."

Marcus lifted the scroll as if it were made of lead and fumbled with the seal, his head pounding. The military had no more right to dispatch him to Britannia than to send a harlot to the Vestals! He was a Praetorian tribune. His father had arranged as much, and they had clasped wrists on it: he would join the Praetorian legion for a service of three years; he would live a suitable, officer-like life that would do credit to the family; then ...

Marcus abandoned that line of thought as his eyes skipped over the wording. Tribune Marcus Sabinius ... by the order of His Imperial ... will report immediately ... take ship at Ostia ... overland to ... the commanding officer ... at *Deva*! What cesspit of Rome's army had been constructed at Deva?

"There's a full-size fortress at Deva, of course," the praefectus supplied as if reading his thoughts, though the man's eyes had followed Marcus's as they scrolled down the page. "The Twentieth Valeria Victrix is stationed there. Fine regiment. Been in Britannia since the invasion. Senator Julius Proculus is the legate. Newly appointed." The smile turned to a leer as Lucius removed his helmet and set it on a side table cluttered with wine jugs. He found a reasonably clean goblet and filled it. "I took the time to find that out for you, young sir. Very fair man,

Julius. Strict disciplinarian, mind you. But as I said, very fair. Treats everyone the same."

Marcus fought to rein in his growing anger. Two words had stood out above all. One was Britannia. The other … "When is immediately?" he demanded.

"Oh, probably no real hurry. Tomorrow. Maybe the next day. Never looked into that. All I wanted to do was to make sure the record shows the order was handed to you. Let's see, when was that?" The praefectus glanced at the sundial. When he continued his voice was heavier. "A half-hour short of midday. I did call earlier this morning, but the blond studlet told me his master was not to be disturbed." He gestured to the young male slave. "Personal acquisition, is he?"

"No, damn you. I keep him for …" Marcus glanced at his two guests, both of whom glared angrily back, and his voice faded to a whisper. "Should there ever be a need. Where do I—"

"The orderly room has your travel documents. I imagine they'll still be there tomorrow."

"My travel party. What arrangements do I—"

"Ah, tribune. It is not a party. You are going to the frontier. You are going as a junior tribune, not a legate. You are permitted one slave and up to three horses. One of those horses will be a pack animal, and one will be for the slave. You are not to be slowed down by a walking slave. No slave, no extra horse."

"One slave?" Marcus shouted, his anger growing. The son of a man of *senatorial rank*, and only one slave! The order was ludicrous. Why, his father … Marcus swore under his breath. His father, he recalled, had served as senior tribune of the Ninth and kept only one slave. Or at least he'd kept only one until purchasing that barbarian whore and her daughter. That prompted another thought. "I—"

"And the slave will be male."

"Shit!"

"There will be a travel allowance you can draw on," Lucius continued before he drained his wine, obviously relishing his role as harbinger of bad tidings. "You can obtain more detailed—"

"Yes, yes, I know," Marcus grated, and though the praefectus's authority far exceeded his own, he turned his back, pretending to study the scroll. "That will be all. Go."

"Oh, aye, young master Sabinius. Very good, young sir." Marcus could hear the praefectus's broad grin in the tone of his voice. Instead of leaving, the man sauntered to the side table and topped up the goblet. "Lots of proud history, the Twentieth. You'll enjoy it. Makes men out of boys."

"What would you, a palace guard, know about that?" Marcus blurted, then cringed inwardly. It was the wrong thing to say to a praefectus.

Instead of growing annoyed, though, Lucius grinned and grew garrulous, his words flowing like grain from a torn sack. "Ah, but not always, my boy, not always. Served in Britannia with the Twentieth, you know. Grew up in it, in fact. Was there—what?—twenty years ago, under old Seutonius. Held the rank of decanus at the time. We knocked that red-haired bitch Boudicca off *her* roost, I can tell you! Good man, Seutonius. And what a battle! They'll be talking about that one for a hundred years." Lucius sipped at the wine, then smacked his lips. "Outnumbered ten to one, we were. At least. Actually, I think it was closer to twenty ... "

The ripe, tangy sea-smell of drying kelp filled Marcus's nostrils as he and his slave neared the narrow neck of ocean separating Britannia from Gaul. The tart odour had been present even before the port of *Gesoriacum* came into view, yet he hardly noticed, too preoccupied with recent injustices, and a righteous anger that increased with each milestone that tolled off the distance from Rome.

The gross iniquity of the gods ate into his belly. But it was his father who'd dispatched him to the forsaken ends of the empire, he reminded himself, not the gods. Or did they all work hand in hand? For as much as he'd tried to have his orders cancelled in the brief time remaining, every path seemed oddly blocked.

His mother, Helvia, had been the first to refuse him. He knew all too well that she was on intimate terms with more than one senior officer, and a senator or two could likely be added to the list. Yet she'd been callously indifferent to her son's problems, claiming to have no influence, which was an outright lie; that she was extremely busy, which was a farce; then pointing out that it took money she didn't have to arrange such things, which was true. She'd finally told him to stop his whining and she would see what could be done— words that, for a brief moment, ignited a spark of hope in an otherwise bottomless pit of gloom.

The fact that he'd as good as abandoned his mother when his father's fortunes improved never crept into his mind. Nor did Helvia mention it. She simply shrugged, promised to see what could be done, and gone on with her life.

There had been time for her to see to it, Marcus complained when the final day arrived. There had, in fact, been ample time for a lot of things, for the praefectus had lied through his yellow teeth. When the man passed him the order, two weeks remained before his departure, not a day. And that same order allowed almost eight weeks to reach Gesoriacum, which was liberal enough, as it turned out, though it hadn't seemed so at the time.

If he'd had the money, he would have taken every allowed day, too, save those spent on the first leg of the journey—travel orders placed him and the three horses on a galley for *Massalia*. Marcus was seasick for most of the voyage.

The ride across Gaul from Massalia might have been leisurely, had it not been for what waited at the other end, and the company he was forced to keep, and the food dished out at every station, and a litany of other complaints, most involving his fellow travellers. The civilians using the highway were generally crude and boring, while those from the army were always rankers, all in a hurry to reach the next Roman station. Perhaps the worst part was that not one of them showed the respect due a Praetorian tribune.

Yet any journey was the safer for numbers, so he reluctantly put up with it. And there was a certain sense of security to be found in the slave he'd chosen, on the advice of the estate overseer: a hulking brute of a field hand named Urs—a dumb, almost bovine creature who followed instructions with a slow precision and kept his mouth shut and his thoughts to himself.

Marcus would have liked to dawdle, even stop, and once or twice did so; but any inn that caught his fancy was expensive, and more often than not lay in a town or village that was garrisoned anyway. As to the military lodgings, as far as Marcus was concerned, they were poorly placed. The engineers had been far too efficient. They built the things a good day's ride apart, so if a soldier wanted a bed without paying for the privilege, he had to keep moving at a brisk and steady pace.

The port of Gesoriacum appeared on the horizon as a dark, saw-toothed clutter of buildings, the fort itself most prominent. For once Marcus found himself ahead of his fellow travellers, who always seemed to cluster together in their hurry to reach the next outpost. He'd travelled the final leg in the company of a bevy of traders, each with an empty cart, and every last one eager to fill it with goods ferried across from Britannia. The squeal of ungreased axles pricked his foul mood into a brooding anger, and he'd taken the lead as the finality of the sea crossing loomed near.

The slave Urs quietly urged his horse forward until it was a respectful pace or so off his master's right shoulder, the pack animal trailing behind him. There he remained, ignored until finally summoning the nerve to cough.

Marcus turned, his brows furrowed in annoyance. The pair had hardly spoken during the past weeks, and when they did, it was for one to give orders and the other to grunt his understanding. The fellow's name suited his hulking, bear-like appearance. The brute had been acquired some years before, the overseer had informed Marcus, adding that the man was of limited intelligence, and quite docile. The slave did understand a basic Latin, however, which was just as well, for his native dialect was unintelligible. Urs had been brought in from Lower Germania, which meant they journeyed toward the slave's homeland. This was no concern to Marcus; the man was marked, and the port lay a long way from his home. Besides, the creature was as dull as a rusty blade and, judging from his pace, just as slow out of the scabbard.

"What is it?" Marcus growled, turning his eyes back to squint up the road to the low gaggle of buildings on the horizon.

"We near the coast, master," Urs observed slowly, pointing ahead to the grey strip of sea that lay beyond the dark outline of the port.

"My, you've a keen eye," Marcus sneered.

"Thank you, sir," Urs replied, the sarcasm apparently lost as he pulled thoughtfully at the tangled mass of his beard. "Will we be crossing it, then?"

"Yes, and when we do, you'll see the horses are well secured for the journey. I don't want damaged hides or broken bones."

"Of course not, sir," Urs said, and for a few moments sat quietly in the saddle as the horses plodded along the hard road. Then, as if unsure such a question was proper, he asked, "Might I ask where it is we are going, once we get there?"

"Yes, you might," Marcus said, and perversely said nothing more.

Urs, with the bare trace of a sigh, again seemed to take the words at face value. "Where are we going, sir, once we get there?"

Marcus sighed in turn, and again looked briefly at his slave. The question wasn't an unreasonable one, he supposed, considering they were crossing to a new land. And, on analysis, it wasn't impertinent, either. It was just plain annoying. He shrugged. "Deva. It's a fortress on the west side of the province."

"I see. Thank you, sir." Urs nodded as if grateful for the information and tugged slightly at the reins, slowing his horse until it was again trailing behind his master.

Marcus frowned, mildly uncomfortable with the exchange. Yet as he mulled over the slave's words, he could find nothing there to fault the man. Had there been a trace of something in the fellow's eyes, though? A small glint? A spark of slyness? The fellow was terribly slow, and other than protection on the long journey, of little domestic value. Perhaps a profit might be made by selling the brute at the dockyards, and picking up another when he reached Deva. Prices were sure to be lower in Britannia, and further coin might even be gained if there was one less body on the passage across …

Marcus poked about the docks at Gesoriacum, intent on selling Urs, but no one showed interest in acquiring a hulking slave that a Praetorian guard was obviously trying to dump, nor did they want one without proof of previous ownership. And further along the sharp edge of that blade, even should the big Briton sell, everyone he talked to said the prices were just about as high in Britannia, and the goods apt to be of poor quality. As the day wore on with no takers, Marcus grudgingly rationalized that a slave was a slave, so what was the difference? Besides, simply doing nothing helped him ignore any vague sense of unease—and for Marcus, doing nothing was a practical, short-term solution to any concern.

The next morning, intent on presenting his orders to the harbour master to obtain transport to Britannia, he passed along docks congested with men and horses. A cavalry regiment from Germania was crossing, which did not bode well for securing a quick passage. Marcus wandered into the harbour master's office on the heels of the regiment's commander, a man whose deep, angry complexion warned of a badly frayed temper.

The praefectus leaned over the counter, hurling invective at two clerks, both of whom edged cautiously away from the other side. When he finally paused for breath, Marcus blithely reached past the man's shoulder and set his orders on the countertop. "One of you two see to that. Myself, three horses, and a slave, for *Dubris*."

The commander, a hard, beefy man of middle years with weathered cheeks burned by both sun and irritation, whirled and swept glaring eyes over Marcus, who felt a rush of blood to his cheeks. Under the man's contemptuous gaze, for the first time since joining the guard, Marcus was conscious of another image: that of a smooth-faced youth of barely twenty years, plumped in the finery of the Praetorians, and as much at home on the frontier as a peacock in a cock pit.

The veteran commander seemed to agree. "Fuck off!"

Marcus stood dumbfounded, once more gaping at the commander's broad back. Feet shuffled behind him, followed by a muffled cough that could only be a stifled snigger. He didn't dare turn to look. His eyes caught the amusement in those of the nearest clerk. The man was laughing at him! Damn him! An insignificant scroll scratcher, and the prick was laughing!

Summoning his courage, Marcus stepped half a pace forward and slapped his palm down on his orders. The praefectus flinched and turned rigid. "I'll be back. See this is looked after when the horse humper is finished." Marcus uttered the words quickly and, before anyone could move, whirled and disappeared through the door. Heart pounding, he clattered down the steps and hastened along the dockside in search of Urs, fervently hoping the "horse humper" wasn't following.

He caught sight of the slave by one of the warehouses, his shaggy thatch a good half a head above any others that crowded the docks. Urs seemed to be haggling with a short, corpulent creature who, despite being well dressed, had the oily look of either a merchant or a whoremaster. Both men fell silent as Marcus approached.

He didn't acknowledge the stranger, but spoke only to Urs. "It will likely be a while. A regiment of barbarian cavalry is crossing. I don't know when—"

"Master, I saw as much. I have been asking. This is Nikomedes. Perhaps he can help."

"How can he help?" Marcus, irritated at the interruption, nonetheless deigned to look at the man.

Nikomedes shrugged and nodded toward the sea. "If you are in a hurry to get there ... "

Marcus buried his annoyance and pondered the words. He wasn't in a hurry at all. In fact, he didn't care if he ever got to Britannia. On the practical side, though, what else was he going to do? He certainly had no desire to linger in a stinking seaport, especially this one, even though the weather was downright halcyon. There could also be a cost to lingering, and his funds were running short. Perhaps the price of an early departure might balance against what would be spent in waiting. Shaking his head, Marcus shrugged his indifference. "Not particularly."

Nikomedes simply leered, as if sensing a fellow trader. "Do your orders specify military transport, sir, or do they give the option of civilian?"

"Huh?"

"If there are no naval ships available, civilian ships are often used."

"I ... "

"We went by civilian transport to Massalia, sir," Urs urged in an oddly eager tone.

"There you are, then, tribune. I could have the horses loaded well before noon, and the tide ebbs soon after."

"Which will cost me?" Marcus asked. The notion of a quick departure, on seas that were for the moment calm, suddenly brimmed with appeal.

"Five thousand *denarii*."

"Shit!" Marcus threw his hands skyward in a classic bargaining posture, though the gesture was completely sincere. There simply wasn't that much money to be had. "That's three months' pay."

"But sir, think of—"

"Nikomedes forgets that the army pays well for passage on civilian ships, sir," Urs interrupted, his voice a growl as he placed a hand, not too gently, on the trader's shoulder. "Especially officers. I think all he's *really* asking for is a pittance as favour for speeding your journey."

Marcus stared at Urs, astonished at the slave's flow of words, and for the moment was unable to speak. Nikomedes winced under the grip of the huge fingers, and whispered, "Of course, sir. There is naturally a deduction for that. That would leave a net figure of, what, perhaps two thousand?"

The grip tightened. Marcus, confused, vainly tried to push Urs and his words to the back of his mind, and make sense of his finances. "Two hundred."

"A thousand!" Nikomedes tried to pull away from the tight grip on his shoulder, then relaxed as the fingers eased.

"Five hundred," Marcus countered, staring at Urs rather than the trader. Where, in the dark pits of Hades, had the brute suddenly found his tongue? "And that's final. Five hundred is two years' pay for a foot soldier!"

"Five hundred, then," Nikomedes quickly agreed before the fingers again tightened, adding half under his breath, "Which is less than two weeks' pay for a centurio."

"A senior centurio," Marcus shot back, acutely aware of his own drop in pay on leaving the Praetorians.

"Take the horses over to the *Catalina*." Nikomedes pointed Urs toward a fat merchant vessel moored on the far side of the harbour, away from the naval galleys. "Oh, and besides the five hundred, I'll need a payment voucher from the harbour master to collect the difference." With that, the plump trader waddled off along the dock toward his ship.

Marcus stood beside Urs, unable to move, his mind tumbling with questions as he tried to absorb what had just happened. At the top of the list was the sudden acuity of his dumb, lumbering slave. He realized, with a start, that a not-so-subtle shift had occurred in their relationship, though exactly what it was, he couldn't be sure.

"Urs," he began slowly, staring up into the big man's eyes. For the first time, he realized that they were grey—a hard, iron grey, and hooded. "Urs, you are a slave."

Marcus said nothing more for the moment, as his mind suddenly returned to the exchange of words on the last leg of their journey. With a sense of foreboding, he remembered the slyness—and it *was* slyness—that had crept into the man's eyes when told where they were going. Or had it been astonishment? Or even satisfaction? Marcus raised one hand as if gathering his thoughts, then, very firmly, said, "Urs!"

"Sir?"

"Urs, do you happen to know where Deva is?"

"More or less. Well, not exactly. I do know it's somewhere north of *Glevum.*"

"I see," Marcus said, and mumbled "shit" under his breath. "Which means, I suppose, that you do know the whereabouts of Glevum."

"Yes, sir. It's at the head of the *Sabrina* River."

Marcus closed his eyes, almost afraid to ask. "And how do you know this, Urs?"

"That's where I was first taken before being sold into Germania, sir."

"Aaagh!" Marcus placed a hand on his forehead, his mind swimming. He couldn't help asking one more question, which was totally redundant, yet it fell from his mouth before he could stop it. "Then you are a Briton?"

"Yes, sir, a *Silure.*" The slave's eyes widened in surprise. "You didn't know?"

Marcus groaned. At least the man had the sense not to add, "My, you've a keen eye, sir." For that, he would have had him flogged! Yet there was no denying the error: he was taking a semi-savage slave, twice his own size, back to the land of his birth, a place even more savage than the man himself. And as to the savage part, Marcus was suddenly not so sure. When he looked harder at Urs, the dullness of eye was not nearly as bovine as it had seemed back in Rome. In fact, both eyes looked more like those of a wolf. Damn that overseer!

Marcus glanced numbly about the bustling dockyard, trying to gather his wits. He couldn't rid himself of the slave, not without virtually giving him away, and that was out of the question. Money was short as it was, yet he'd be damned if he would arrive at Deva without a slave. He was just plain stuck. And when you're stuck, like it or not, you deal. Marcus turned to the slave, his jaw clenched tight as he fought the urge to scream at the man, or see him beaten.

"Urs, we are going to Britannia. You know that if you run and get caught with no attestation of freedom, you will be put to death?"

Urs's response was a slight setting of the jaw, which told Marcus that at least the message was not falling on deaf ears.

"I know that once we have crossed the sea, at the first opportunity, you are considering..." Marcus paused, then emphasized the word. "You are *considering* escaping to your tribe, and hiding there."

Urs swallowed hard, but admitted nothing.

"If you do, I know your tribe," Marcus continued. "I will come for you. I will be *obliged* to come for you, and I will find you. And even if I am unable, others will do so. You will be hunted down and, more importantly, so will any wife and child you may have when you are caught. Urs, such an existence, for as long as you live, is not freedom." The slave licked his lips as if about to say something, but Marcus quickly gestured for silence, not wanting to hear words that could not be ignored. "There is another way."

The grey eyes grew suddenly sharp. Marcus realized, again with a start, that he had indeed underestimated the slave's intelligence. Even so, with what he was about to propose, it was probably better. The man was more likely to see the wisdom of it.

"Tribunes are posted, at the most, for three years," Marcus continued, sincerely hoping his father had not committed him for near that many; shit, he'd already served more than one with the Praetorians. "It's been known to go longer than that, but I can assure you, that's time enough for me. And once done, I will be sent home. To Rome. Simply put, I see no point in dragging a Silure slave all the way back to Rome if he's served me well in his homeland. I would be willing to grant freedom to that slave."

A spark gleamed briefly in the otherwise expressionless grey eyes. *He's thinking,* Marcus realized, and the flow of words, when they finally came, showed that he'd indeed underestimated the man.

"I am not yours to give."

"True, but I can arrange it with the man who owns you—my father. Which will be much easier to do if his son has been well cared for." Marcus shrugged, deciding to tread on boggier ground. "If necessary, I will buy you first, then free you."

"But you would have to find the money, sir." Urs's look said he placed little faith in that happening. "How would this slave be assured that his *true* master might honour his son's commitment?"

The man's language jarred Marcus, and the idea that he now seemed to be bargaining with his own slave was overwhelmingly irksome. Nonetheless, he fought his annoyance and continued. "It will take time. I am sure a commitment can be obtained from your true owner within the year. Certain of it, in fact. Even so, if I cannot get one, I will write a remission myself at the end of my tour. It would never be questioned."

Urs nodded, his lips pursed. "And what if you are slain?"

Marcus fumbled for the answer to that one, for the possibility had occurred to him a thousand times, but not in this particular context. He gave the matter a moment's thought, and offered the only words that might be believed. "It is your task to see that doesn't happen."

"Three years is a good trade-off." Urs thrust his arm forward, staring hard into Marcus's eyes. "But will you clasp a slave's arm on it?"

With the greatest effort yet, Marcus kept his temper. He reached out, and each man grasped the other's wrist.

Marcus approached the harbour master's office in the vain hope the praefectus had finished his business and gone. He ran headlong into the man at the top of the steps as he was leaving.

"Coming back for a second try?" the cavalryman asked, his demeanour less surly. He lifted both arms and stretched, yawning as he peered about the busy harbour. Marcus deduced that the man's problems had finally been solved.

"No longer an issue," he mumbled, and made to edge past.

"Horse-humper indeed!" The man shook his head as if in disbelief, but his eyes held no malice as he gazed down at Marcus. "Well good luck, boy. With my lot ahead of you, you'll be looking at the arse end of horses for another month."

"Doubt it. In fact, I'll be waiting for you tomorrow at Dubris. I just need to pick up my orders."

"Cocky young pup, aren't you?" the praefectus said, then, as if unable to believe it was true, asked, "Really?"

"Really."

"Money! Never fails. Pampered, primped-up Praetorians!" The praefectus grunted the words, then shrugged philosophically. "Let me give you a word of advice, though, my flush, intrepid tyro. When you do get across, toss the fancy armour before you even get to where you're going. The army fights over there. It doesn't prance and parade for the ladies." Sighing his disgust, the cavalryman started down the steps. "Oh well, as I said, good luck. You, boy, will especially need it."

"I don't doubt it, but I had lots last time I was there."

The praefectus stopped and stared back at Marcus. "You've been over there before?" His eyes narrowed in doubt. "Where are you posted?"

"Deva."

"Was that where you were before, boy?"

"No. *Ebor*. It's up north, in Brigantia." Marcus lifted the hem of his tunic, revealing the white scar on the inside of his thigh, a good handsbreadth in length. "Got that fighting Venutius."

"You gotta be older than you look." The praefectus's weathered face split with a grin. "North is where this 'horse humper' is posted, lad. *Isurium*. What's the lay of the land up there?" He stuck out a beefy hand. "Cornelius Griphus, Fourth Regiment, Augusta Gallorum."

"Isurium?" Marcus, enjoying the sudden attention, pretended to ponder the question as he briefly clasped the cavalryman's wrist. "Nothing special. Mixed garrison, cavalry and infantry. It was just completed when I left. Good site, though. Open, and slopes down to a river. There's a fair-sized barbarian village. It was there before we were." He shrugged, deliberately showing his disdain. "The locals like to think it's a town. Sits fifteen, twenty miles north of Ebor, on the west side of the *Abus*. Lots of trees. Good farmland. Nice, if it wasn't stuck in the arse end of nowhere. I got sliced about ten miles farther on, when we ran head-on into Venutius's army. We were..."

Marcus's voice faded, his eye caught by a young decurio staring at him from perhaps fifty paces away. As soon as Marcus spotted him, the man shifted his attention. Marcus watched for a moment, for the trooper's face seemed familiar in a vague sort of a way. He was above average height for a Gallic cavalryman, who were tall enough to begin with. The fellow had that irritating look of military competence: a straight-backed assurance that showed in the way he ordered his men with a minimum of bluster. He wore his uniform in the crisp, neat, yet worn and casual manner of the professional. He seemed quite young for his rank.

"Who's the decurio?" Marcus asked.

The praefectus followed his gaze, then shook his head. "Can't remember his name. The regiment is newly raised. His troop came out of Vetera, if I remember. I can find out, if you want."

Marcus absorbed the information. The man was likely a Tungri if he was from Lower Germania. There was no reason the fellow should be familiar. "Doesn't matter," he muttered, and returned to his story. "Anyway, we were heading north. Neither side knew the other was..."

Chapter III

Eboracum, A.D. 78

Rhun travelled to Ebor by way of *Londinium*. The regiment then moved north in column, splitting up at the fortress of *Lindum*. A small detachment rode directly to *Derventio*, using the route through *Petuaria* that crossed the Abus estuary by ferry. Rhun's squadron remained with the larger force under the command of Cornelius Griphus. The reduced regiment continued on a longer trek that crossed firm, higher ground to the northwest, and descended on Ebor through a cluster of hovels called *Calcaria*.

Dismay gradually overcame Rhun, the farther the regiment travelled. On the one side of the blade, the vast forests, the lush fields, and the wind-rippled fens were as green and ripe as in his memory, perhaps even more so. But on the other side, the small settlements through which they rode were no longer the warm, cosy nests of his childhood. For the most part they consisted of crude, mean, hovel-filled crossroads and poorly built farmsteads. The exception, when encountered, seemed to be owned by someone of position or wealth or, naturally, was an outpost where Rome had firmly planted her roots. And as to the people themselves…

At a small village where they paused to water the horses, Rhun saw an old man mending his nets, close by the riverbank. For a heart-stopping moment the familiar image of Sencab, with his long, greying beard and shaggy, ill-kempt head of hair, flooded his mind. It couldn't possibly be him, of course; they were miles from Ebor. Yet even so,

Rhun was drawn to the aged man.

Despite the warmth of the day, the fellow wore a short, armless jerkin of leather with moulting patches of fur clinging to the outside. He crabbed sideways in fear as Rhun drew near, stopping a few yards upwind. The man's clothing was grimy and torn, his beard and hair matted with tiny clumps of what looked at best to be dirt. The raw odour of crudely tanned leather caught in Rhun's nostrils, along with the pungent smell of his body.

This old man clearly belonged to the lowest order of the village *kin*, a slavelike creature with no *honour price* whose scruffy appearance and bad odour might be expected, Rhun rationalized. Yet Sencab had been of the same order, and he had once followed Sencab like a puppy, listening to his nonsense, lapping up his wisdom, and doing his best to emulate the old man. Though Sencab and the man who crouched before him might have been twins, Rhun felt no sense of affection for the bent and frightened figure.

Puzzled, and with an odd, empty feeling inside, he climbed back on his horse. He spent a good deal of the remaining journey brooding, for no reason he could discern. And at Ebor itself, the space between the rivers that had once been home, the disturbing void seemed to widen. Nothing was familiar. Almost in shock, Rhun realized he had not been prepared for that at all.

The huge fortress had obliterated all sign of the village—he'd expected that. But the tall, friendly forest that had once sheltered his home with a lush wall of foliage had been brutally cut back, leaving nothing but bare land. A massive wooden dock now clung to the north bank of the Abus, shrinking the vast river to half its size; and the Fosse, the lesser stream that protected the northeast approach to the stronghold, struck him as little more than a murky rill.

Of course, he'd been barely in his teens then, no more than a sprout. Everything must have seemed larger, especially the fortress. The stronghold had briefly been his prison: a dark, ominous structure where he paid scant attention to anything but his misery and an all-consuming rage. His own mother had been there then, trying to ease the shame and anguish of defeat by twisting his mind against his own people. What had she been made to endure, what had she suffered, to even attempt such treachery? Elena had been a strong woman, he remembered; steadfast, with a mind and a wit that gave even his father pause.

His father! Was his father even alive?

Rhun shook his head to rid his mind of the past, and forced his attention to the disorder rampant on every side. The regiment's makeshift camp sprawled across a huge training field east of the fortress, and bustled with activity that matched the clamour of the Ostian docks. Strings of horses were tethered in a massive crisscross of lines, dark leather tents had risen like mushrooms, and between it all, Tungri cavalrymen moved like locusts on a field of grain. The sight eased his mood.

"My bunch is between you and the river, just in case you lose your way."

Rhun turned to find Cian had wandered up the slope, leading his horse by a rope halter. The animal had been curried, and its coat shone as if oiled. The tack was clean and polished, and Cian himself was brushed up as if ready to fall in on parade.

"You on punishment detail?" Rhun asked, then, because it might possibly be true, said, "Who did you shit on this time?"

"Show more respect to your elders." Cian grinned, then gestured eastward toward the Fosse. "I'm going to see something. Wanna come?"

"What about the men?"

"Luga's settling the troop. He *has* done it once or twice before." Cian sounded suddenly impatient. "You coming or not?"

"Where to?" Rhun asked, then he understood; his uncle's farm had once been on the far side of the smaller river. "Yeah, I'll go get my horse."

When he returned a few moments later it was to find Cian mounted and staring intently across the Abus. His eyes were on a column of cavalry, the lead element already plodding carefully onto the bridge. The river, which at Ebor lay on the far reaches of the tidal flow, was on the ebb, and had been so since noon. Even so, the water remained high, rushing hard against the stone piers.

"River's not at its lowest yet," Cian observed.

"It's not that high," Rhun said, and grasped the pommel to swing onto the saddle. "Or are you hoping the damned thing's going to collapse?"

Cian ignored the comment and leaned forward, one hand rising to shade his eyes. He squinted, then leaned back again, his lips pursed. For a moment he said nothing, then, with a shake of his head, murmured, "I think that's your legate."

That evening the squadrons messed in the open field east of the fortress. Rhun and Cian settled themselves on a single horse blanket, side by side, enjoying mugs of watered wine and steaming piles of boiled beef and barley. Cian was in a sombre mood. Little remained of the old farm. The site was still clearly marked, but the small lodge and the animal pens had vanished, replaced by an open-sided shed of sawn lumber, used only to store tillage equipment. The pastures had been widened and turned to crop, farmed by someone who saw no need to actually live on the lush stretch of land. Perhaps it was farmed by the legion itself.

"They probably gave it to some arse-kissing Roman tax collector who doesn't know a plow from a piss pot," Cian grumbled.

"There's a good crop of barley starting," Rhun offered, then realized that wasn't the thing to say. "What does it matter? You don't want to farm anyway. You never did like it. You told me so. Too much hard work."

"A man's gotta eat," Cian said defensively.

"He's gotta shit, too," Rhun replied, "but that doesn't mean he has to spend his life digging sewers."

"That's not the point. It was *my* land. And Nuada's as well. It would have been the kids' one day, too. I don't … " Cian's voice faded as he caught sight of a boy, barely into his teens. The youth had paused in front of the command tent in the middle of the bivouac area, obviously asking directions, for one of the troopers was pointing their way. The lad looked completely out of place in the crowded camp, dressed in a short, belted tunic of white linen and open sandals. Cian shook his head. "What, in Dagda's darkest dreams, do we got here?"

"Whatever it is, it's lost," Rhun muttered, his attention returning to the plate of beef, his first taste of fresh meat since landing in Britannia.

The boy ambled closer and halted perhaps five paces away, where he stood staring, a huge grin on his face.

"What you want, boy?" Cian growled, but the lad's full attention was on Rhun, and he ignored the question.

Rhun glanced up, puzzled. The boy's face wore a silly, simpering grin, and he decided the lad was probably simple. Yet the youth continued to stand there, hands at his side, as if expecting something. The boy finally spoke, using the Brigante tongue with a distinct Roman accent. "Are you Rhun?"

"Yeah. Who wants to—" Rhun stopped short, his heart thumping as if struck by an axe. The face coaxed up a deeply buried memory, and suddenly the smiling features crystalized. "You! You're ... ?"

"Tuis," the boy whispered. "You are Rhun?"

They stared at each other. Cian climbed quickly to his feet, his voice a roar. "Tuis, me lad. Tuis! Remember me? Your uncle Cian?" He picked the boy up in a great bear hug and swung him around in a circle, laughing and yelling at the top of his voice.

Rhun slowly rose, stunned. When Cian finally set Tuis on his feet, both of them red-faced and panting with pleasure, he could only stare.

"Give the boy a squeeze, you great, gormless turd," Cian gasped, and pushed the pair together.

"Tuis," Rhun mumbled, as he first hugged his brother to his chest, then held him at arm's length so he could see him the better. "How? What are you doing here?"

"I'm here with father," he said.

"Father!" Rhun cried, and grasped Tuis by the shoulders as he and Cian glanced at each other in shock and disbelief. "Da's here?"

Tuis blinked and grasped his head in anguish, looking back and forth between the two men with a face that was suddenly so miserable, he looked ready to cry. "Aagh, Rhun, I'm sorry. No. No he's not ... " his eyes dropped to the ground as if he were shamed, and both hands slid slowly down his cheeks. "No. It's just that I've got used to ... "

"Got used to what?" Rhun demanded, with a sick, sinking feeling as to the answer.

"I-I got used to calling him father."

"Who?" Rhun cried, staring angrily down on his brother.

"Gaius. The legate."

"What!" Rhun pushed his brother angrily backward. He stood shaking his head as if the action could clear it of Tuis's words, then, his face twisted with bitterness, he held both arms out in supplication. "How could you? After what he did to Mam? And to Nuada?"

"He adopted me, Rhun. And he's been good to me," Tuis said defensively. "And he's been good to Mam as well."

"Adopted you!" Rhun seethed, his voice shaking with anger. "And Coira? I suppose he *adopted* her, too?" he said sarcastically.

Tuis seemed baffled by the outburst. "He offered to, but she refused. She said she'd rather just stay as a companion, as long as there was a chance Da was still alive."

"A companion!" Rhun's voice rose to a screech. "What the fuck does that mean?"

"It means she's a friend to his daughter, Aelia," Tuis cried, his own voice rising. "They're kind of like sisters."

"Sisters!"

"Calm down, Rhun," Cian said, and laid a hand gently on Tuis's shoulder. "How about your mam? How's she doing, lad?"

"Not too badly. She's recovering at Camulodunum with Cartimandua."

"Recovering?" Rhun cried. "From what? Did the bastard have her beaten?"

"No." Tuis again looked at his brother, this time in puzzlement. "Her horse shied from a bear when they were hunting. A couple months ago, on the way up here. She broke an arm pretty bad and put her shoulder out. Catey said she should stay at Camulodunum until she got better. Mam knows her from when they were both here at the fortress. I think they were sort of friends. D—Gaius and I just got back from seeing her. She's coming here soon." Tuis shrugged. "Coira and Aelia too, I suppose. They went back a while ago, and stayed on to help."

"Catey!" Cian sounded almost amused. "Seems friendly enough, Rhun." He looked down at Tuis. "I don't suppose you ran into a man called Vellocatus?"

"Of course. He's Catey's husband. He's nice," Tuis replied. "He took me hunting."

"So all's honey and old times," Rhun interrupted, remembering another old score. "Dammit, Cian, what about Nuada? This is the bastard that killed your wife."

Tuis shook his head in confusion. "What are you talking about?"

"The legate. He killed Nuada. Right there in front of that stinking granary at Stannick."

"That's not how Mam tells it," Tuis said sharply, and he turned to his uncle, shaking his head in denial.

"Did you actually see him kill her, Rhun?" Cian demanded, an odd, questioning look on his face. "You told me he did, but did you see it?"

Rhun clenched his jaw and narrowed his eyes in anger, but before he could say more, Cian spoke again. "It's important to me, Rhun. Did you actually see him kill her?"

Rhun stared at his uncle, fighting his anger. He shouldn't be angry at Cian, he knew that, yet he was. And why? Because of the vindictive Roman, that was why! The man had haunted him every day of his life since the fall of Stannick. The man had been right there outside the granary when the Batavi auxiliary had come crashing inside. Rhun's mind drifted back to the memory. Nuada had killed that one with her spear. She'd charged from inside the granary, screaming her anger…

"Did you actually see him kill her?" Cian again demanded.

Rhun shook his head sharply, grudgingly. "Not exactly. She killed a Batavi auxiliary and ran outside—"

"So maybe he didn't."

"He was right there on his horse. And Mam was with him, too. And there was a sword in his hand and it was all covered in blood!"

"Still up on his horse? And your mam was there too?" Cian muttered half to himself, then, surprisingly, broke into a smile. "And she killed some poor, numb-brained Batavi! I'll be buggered."

"Mam said she did for two, before a third one got her," Tuis volunteered.

"Rhun, I never heard any of this before." Cian shook his head in disbelief, the smile widening.

"Yeah, well, I never dug too deep into it before. And it wasn't a pleasant sight," Rhun grated. "But he was there. I saw that. If it wasn't him that killed her, it was one of his men. On his order."

"You always said it was him that killed Nuada," Cian spoke softly as he took a step backward, looking first at Tuis, then at Rhun. "You also said my Emla and Murgen were taken, and sold into slavery. By the same *bastard*, as I recall."

"They were," Rhun replied, his voice softening to match that of his uncle as he spoke of his two young cousins. "He was right there with them, and then they were gone. I'd been smashed on the head, dammit. I can't remember every last detail."

"Da took Emla and Murgen," Tuis said, his head moving back and forth between the two men in pace with their shouting, which was beginning to attract the attention of Rhun's men.

"See, he did sell them!" Rhun cried, then turned on his brother. "And Tuis, you call that prick 'da' once more, and I'll tan your arse so hard it'll burn through your britches—or whatever it is you're wearing under that piece of Roman garbage."

"I was talking about our own da, you turd," Tuis retorted, his jaw thrust forward. "And I'll dig your eyeballs out before I let you lay one lousy hand on me."

"Don't talk to me like that, you little—"

"Rhun!" Cian yelled, and grabbed him by the arm. "Use your thick skull, and listen."

"So you're in with him too," Rhun began, then stopped short and gaped at Tuis. "Our own da?"

"Yeah. Mam took Emla and Murgen, and gave them to Da. It was Aunt Nuada's last wish before she—she crossed over." He glanced at Cian, and offered a helpless shrug. "Da was living with her before that. They both thought you and Mam were dead."

"How did she manage to get them to Da?" Rhun asked numbly.

"Gaius let her take them."

"And she came back?"

"She would have had to," Cian said, and laid a hand on Rhun's shoulder. "He still held you and the other two children."

"That's not true. Gaius told her she could take us both with her," Tuis offered blithely, "and Coira, too. But only if Coira wanted to go." He looked disarmingly up at Cian, and again offered a shrug as if by way of explanation. "I know, 'cause he teases Mam about it once in a while, and she doesn't deny it."

"Teases?" Rhun muttered, both arms falling limply to his sides. "Shit!"

"I think," Cian said slowly, "both you and I have to talk to your Mam, Rhun."

The order arrived while it was still dark, carried by one of the night guards from the Ninth's headquarters building. It was relayed through the regiment's command tent, causing Rhun to be dragged from his blanket two hours before dawn broke. It seemed an escort was required for two dispatch riders, each carrying reports meant for Deva. Rhun was specifically named for the detail, with instructions to take a half-dozen men as support. The two riders would be turned over to a further escort to complete their journey at—Camulodunum!

"Where you will rest your mounts for a day before returning to Eboracum." Rhun read the words aloud, then held the order out to Cian, should he want to stumble through them himself.

"Sounds like someone thinks you should go see your mam," Cian mumbled sleepily, as he'd also been dragged from under his blanket by his nephew.

"Do the dispatch riders always need an escort?" Rhun asked, puzzling over the words scratched in the dull wax surface.

"Of course they do," Cian said through a yawn. "It says so, right on the stupid order."

Rhun led the small troop of riders through the gates of the fort at Camulodunum as night was falling, after a hard ride from Eboracum that began before dawn. There were the two dispatch riders and Cian, plus Turren and four other men, chosen from a score or more who had wanted to come along for the ride. No trouble had been expected; none had been found. But the ride had been long, and neither he nor Cian had trouble finding sleep when their heads hit the straw less than a half-hour later.

Cartimandua's lodge, for it was hardly a palace, sat a half-mile from the fort, surrounded by defences of its own. They were weak, lacking the deep ditch and the solid rampart of the Roman fort. But the walls were tall, Rhun noted as he walked inside with Cian the next morning, and rimmed by a walkway that offered a decent fighting platform, provided nobody was too serious about a heavy siege. The log uprights, while still good, were aging, and showed signs of rot where they met the ground, despite a thick layer of tar. He suspected that once the Roman fort had been built nearby, any improvement to the lodge's defences had lost priority.

The pair were not challenged, for the gate was open and unguarded. The lodge stood less than a hundred paces inside, and reminded Rhun of Venutius's, at Stannick. It was a long, plain, rectangular building with a steeply sloped roof covered in reed thatch. A series of upright beams that framed the walls supported the structure, similar in size to the pilings at Eboracum that held the huge dock clear of the water. The gaps between had likely been filled with planks and wattle, Rhun guessed, but they were coated with a pale, tinted plaster. He wondered if that was courtesy of the fort commander, for the same material coated the walls of a hundred officer's quarters, from Vetera to Rome.

There were few people about the compound. A smith clanged his hammer outside a crude shop, the forge a dull glow as he shaped a shoe for a stocky animal that was more pony than horse. The animal gazed balefully at them as they made their way to the lodge door, seemingly the only living creature to pay attention, except for one other Rhun noticed only as they approached: a girl, sitting close by the entrance of the lodge. At first he thought she'd been placed there to ensure no one entered; then his eye caught something nestled in her lap. When he drew nearer, he saw it was a large, uncoiled scroll. The girl could read!

Rhun and Cian stepped onto the low threshold, each nodding a greeting. "We'd like to speak to Cartimandua, lass," Cian said in his own tongue.

The girl didn't answer. She gazed up at Rhun, studying his face with a pair of deep brown eyes that reminded him of a doe. A tiny smile bent her lips. "You're Rhun."

For a moment he was startled. Surely his sister had not changed that much in a mere half-dozen years or so. Coira and he had been—what, fourteen then? She'd been a tousled, yellow-haired girl with flashing eyes that were—blue. He shook his head at his foolishness, and stared back. The age fit, certainly, but her hair was dark, almost black, and her smooth features were calm, serene, and—well, they were also beautiful.

An elbow dug hard in his ribs. "This speechless oaf *does* go by the name of Rhun, miss," Cian said. "I'm his wise Uncle Cian. And you are?"

The girl smiled and rose to her feet, her soft eyes reflecting amusement. "Aelia. I did not expect to see either of you until we reached Ebor. Come inside. Are you hungry?"

"Could eat a bear, and it doesn't have to be dead." Cian grinned as they followed her into the dim interior of the lodge.

"How do you know me?" Rhun asked, his eyes on the smooth, rolling sway of her *stola*, and the occasional glimpse of ankle.

"Coira. And of course, your mother," Aelia replied without turning.

"Then you must be … "

"A Sabinius. Gaius is my father."

Again Rhun felt the elbow in his ribs. He turned to find Cian smirking and mouthing the name "Gaius." His uncle shook his head and thrust both hands out, thumbs down. Rhun made an obscene gesture with his fingers.

"Are Coira and my mother here now?" he asked.

"You just missed Coira; she went hunting with Vellocatus," Aelia said, leading them through an oak-raftered hall that formed the centre of the lodge. Several menials were clearing the prior evening's shambles from the long tables; a boy shovelled stale ashes into a large copper pail, and a trio of well-fed hounds sniffed the rushes for leftover scraps. The air was heavy and ripe with stale odours.

"Your mother is likely in Cartimandua's quarters. Come, I'll take you there."

One end of the lodge was closed in by a wall, and Aelia disappeared inside. A low murmur of voices drifted through the curtained door, and a moment later she reappeared and ushered them through.

Rhun stopped short, startled by what he saw. The huge room was full to the point of clutter, with both furnishings and women. Camulodunum lay in the hills, and the morning outside was chill. But here, inside, it felt almost too hot. A cheerful fire blazed in a hearth built of rock and mortar, and the room itself was paved with large flagstones, neatly cut and provided once again, Rhun assumed, by Rome. It was the furniture, though, that held his attention.

Long, padded couches lined the walls, interspersed with single chairs, padded footstools, carved tables, and cabinets. Glassware, goblets, plate, and an array of sculpted marble crowded every flat surface. The floor was scattered with statuettes, each gazing inward, and smaller figures, cast in bronze and silver, had been set carefully on a forest of fluted columns.

Thick, tawny bear hides were strewn on the floor, and all the walls but one had been hung with loose, brightly coloured cloth. The exception was across from the fire. It had been plastered and painted in the manner of the Romans, only the figures were bearded Britons and their women.

"Shi-it," Cian breathed, and added a low whistle. Rhun agreed. The effect was overpowering.

A dozen or more women were in the large room. Most were working, one pair sorting and piling clothes, several more in a corner sewing, and others simply moving about, cleaning and organizing the clutter. Two women bustled around a female figure that lay face down on a slab-like table set by the fire, her head cradled on both arms. Vials of oil sat nearby. At the sight of the two men, one of the women straightened and began wiping her hands on a towel. The second fussed with the white sheet loosely draped across the figure's torso, as if making certain everything was covered that needed covering.

Rhun, after a quick glance, hardly noticed. His eyes were fixed on the woman who had risen from the chair next to the table. Her hair was the colour of honey, cut short and curled in the Roman style. One arm rested in a sling, and one side of her face held the faintest remnant of a bruise. Anyone other than Rhun would have found the woman attractive. Yet all that came to mind was that his mother, tall as she was, seemed much smaller than he remembered. Other than that, well, she was his mother: her name was Elena and there were questions.

The woman on the table stirred and rose on her elbow, one hand clutching the loose sheet so it covered at least a minor portion of her breasts. She squinted deep, greyish blue eyes at Rhun, blinking to focus. Her hair, once raven, was heavy with grey and had yet to be combed; it fell over her eyes, and she shook her head to shift it. Rhun judged her to be old, at least fifty or more from the fine web of wrinkles on her cheeks, but she must once have been quite beautiful.

"You've grown since I last saw you," the woman observed, after a glance that swept him from head to toe. "I trust your disposition has also changed. When you weren't sulking like a spoilt bairn, you were squalling and scratching like a wild cat." When he said nothing, she added, "So, boy, have you changed?"

Rhun decided that the woman might once have been a queen, but that didn't mean he had to like her. He simply inclined his head and said, "Ma'am."

"Good," Cartimandua snapped. "Then say hello to your mam. The foolish woman seems to think she's missed you."

Rhun realized that there was very little of which a man could be certain anymore. Cian had been the first of it: finding him alive was shock enough, but a decurio in Rome's army! He often wondered how that sat with his uncle's conscience. That was a door yet to be opened, for he still battled with his own traitorous thoughts. Perhaps one day they might open it together.

But then, to hear his own mother confirm that her—her what? Owner? Slave master? At best, her lover—had been trying to save Tuis and him from the slaughter at Stannick—that was, in some odd manner, devastating. It might have been best, perhaps, if he'd died there too, for the unease he felt would have died with him. Like Nuada, who had not been killed by the bas—by the Roman after all, the same Roman who now fornicated with his father's wife.

There is a lot of time to think when riding a horse, and all the way back to Ebor, Rhun brooded. Several facts remained that he was unable to rationalize, no matter how hard he tried. The first was that his mother not only appeared satisfied with her arrangement with the Roman, she also seemed willing. And the second, and that cut deeper, was that she'd stood idly by while Tuis was adopted by the man! Rhun was as certain as the day dawned that if she'd dug in with both heels, that travesty could have been stopped.

And her excuse for why she'd never returned him to his own father was yet a third. He'd heard too many lies in his lifetime to believe that one.

Chapter IV

Deva, A.D. 78

Marcus arrived at Deva to find the Twentieth Valeria Victrix fighting in the hills to the southwest, engaging the Ordovice tribe in a final campaign before marching north. Nearly all the legion's attached auxiliary troops were tasked there, along with half the strength of the Twentieth itself. Two cohorts from the Ninth had also been drawn in, along with a further two from the Second Adiutrix stationed at Lindum. But above all, the mixed force was campaigning with no help whatsoever from tribune Marcus Sabinius Trebonius.

His father had recently returned to Eboracum, following a brief commander's conference called by Agricola before returning to the field. Marcus had missed him by less than week, and for that he was thankful. It was a confrontation he was willing to postpone indefinitely. There had been no correspondence before or after his departure, and more than once he wondered if his father even knew he was in Britannia. Undoubtedly the cunning bastard did, but if not, he'd likely not be long in finding out.

And what then? He would doubtless be left to rot on the Twentieth's vine, remaining there for only the gods knew how long. His father, he knew, naively hoped it would *mature* him. He was mature enough, without serving three years—or was it …? Marcus, to his utter frustration, couldn't determine exactly how long he *had* been committed to serve. Time spent in the Praetorians should count, yet if you took— what was it now?—fifteen months from three years, the sum left was a lifetime. For the hundredth time, Marcus cursed his father.

Julius Proculus, the legion's legate, was also in the field with Agricola when Marcus reported for duty, which was a small relief. The man was no doubt feeling like a third wheel on a chariot, for the governor was known for taking a firm grip on the reins of any junior's command. The senior man remaining at the fortress was the praefectus castrorum, a dour-faced veteran nearing the end of his career. After a critical appraisal, which included the comment, "Get rid of the tarty wardrobe, tribune," the praefectus took the usual course of action: keep the buggers busy. Which suited Marcus, boring as his duties proved to be. The weather improved, becoming nearly balmy, and he began ticking off the months—the faster they passed, the sooner he could get on with the rest of his life.

Then, on one of the few dark, rainy days of that early summer, the Twentieth's legate returned, bringing with him two of the legion's cohorts that were due for rotation.

"So, you grow tired of Deva, tribune?"

Marcus glanced down at Julius Proculus, seated behind a table in the headquarters building within earshot of half a dozen clerks, and anyone else who cared to listen in. The legate's thin face, not handsome to begin with, was twisted in a glare that made it downright ugly.

"Sir, all soldiers complain about the routine of headquarters duty," Marcus replied, cursing inwardly as his mind settled on the cause of the legate's comment. He'd spent the previous night in the mess, trading grievances with Valerius Saturninus, another of the legion's junior tribunes. Valerius had returned from the field with the legate, and a dry throat and a tongue eager to talk with one of his own kind. Valerius must have betrayed their words, Marcus decided, which had been pure bluster. *Every table-bound scroll-scratcher complained about not serving in the field, fighting for glory. None of them mean it, though!*

"Ah, I see! So you long for field duty. Is that it?" Julius asked, as if pleased he'd divined the answer.

Oh, shit! Marcus searched for a neutral response that wouldn't sound overly eager. "I, er, I suppose that..."

"Speak up, man, speak up."

"Of course, sir," he mumbled, hearing muffled titters behind him.

"How noble. And this—" Julius gestured to an ugly mountain of lists, orders, vouchers, and dispatches that awaited his attention "—this naturally bores you, I suppose?"

"N-not exactly, sir. It's just that from time to—"

"This," the legate's voice rose as he stabbed a long, thin finger at the pile, *"this* is what an officer's work consists of, tribune. It's as important as the battlefield where we fight. Without all this, the army wouldn't be here. It would starve. It would have nothing to fight with. It wouldn't know where to go, how to get there, or when to arrive. The empire turns on this-this—" he looked up at Marcus and sneered "—'bum-fodder,' I think I heard you call it, last night. Tribune, if you don't know how to command it, then you command piss-all. Yet you think it's below you, best left to minions such as I."

Marcus stifled the urge to agree, and instead offered the expected response. "No, sir!"

The legate glanced at a scroll that lay on the desk, his eyes narrowing. Marcus recognized his orders to report for duty. A note had been attached. "I see you are a Sabinius."

"Yes, sir."

"No doubt related to my counterpart at Eboracum." Julius's thin lips split in a humourless grin. "Two new legates for two old legions. Interesting times. So, are you related?"

"He's my father," Marcus said, deciding the grin offered hope.

"Hmm, never met him before coming here. Seems a nice enough fellow." The legate's jaw tightened, and the grin turned to a grimace as his eyes took in the mountain of documents. He again studied Marcus's orders, slowly nodding his head. With no warning, he roared a name. "Marius!"

A clerk rushed quickly to the table, a wax tablet and stylus at the ready.

"Centurio Crispus. Is he in the building?"

"I'll get him, sir."

"Do it. But first, find me the specifications for the next outpost north of *Calacum.* I can't remember the name of the godless place."

"Sir." The clerk bobbed his head and disappeared.

Julius returned his attention to Marcus, a grim smile on his face.

"I'm afraid Governor Agricola already has all the help needed to slay the wild barbarian, young Sabinius." The legate's tone was almost pleasant. "I'm sure we can find something of interest for you, though. We do try to accommodate our young officers."

Marcus felt a brief sense of relief, though he was unsure about the legate's smile; it had a touch of slyness about it. And his tone...

The clerk returned with a large bundle of scrolls, dropped them on the table, and scurried off to find the centurio, Crispus.

"Here, catch." The legate tossed the bundle across the table. "Plans for one fort, standard size, infantry and cavalry combined, for the use thereof. Go and build the damned thing."

"S-sir?"

"As we speak, the third and sixth cohorts are finishing the road to Calacum. You would know that, of course, because it's all there in that pile of 'bum-fodder' you've grown bored with." Julius gestured to the litter of documents. "You'll find that the fort at Calacum was pretty much finished this spring. Pay close attention to it as you ride by, so you can build another one just like it. To the northwest. Lots of hills, I believe. And you may be in luck. The site has already been selected and surveyed." He pondered for a moment, then shrugged. "Though I'd place odds that the barbarians have removed the stakes."

"S-sir?" Marcus managed to stutter a second time.

"Oh, yes. You will take the eighth cohort. It's due to leave in two days. I'm sure the men are glad of the change. And it's good experience. For you, I mean, not the men."

"T-take, sir?"

The legate ignored the question, his eyes falling back to the desk. He sighed as if in pain, then cursed, then began sorting through the mountain of documents. Marcus stood clutching the bundle of plans, his jaw open in disbelief. One of the looser scrolls slid from his grip and dropped to the floor. He bent and picked it up, staring numbly at the meaningless symbols and figures scrawled across its surface. The lines slowly came into focus, and they had the look of an Archimedean nightmare. Childhood memories flooded his mind, of his father proudly trying to explain such charts. The thought started his blood boiling.

Marcus rose unsteadily to his feet, then jumped as metal-studded boots crashed against the floor behind him, followed by an ear-splitting *"Sir!"*

He whirled, almost dropping the entire bundle. For a moment Marcus was unsure if he was staring at a man or a minotaur; whatever it was, it was a solid, hulking mound of muscle from its bull-like neck to its brawny calves, with sharp black eyes that glittered like those of a snake. It had deliberately crept up and startled him.

"Crispus, do you know Tribune Sabinius?" the legate asked mildly.

"No, sir!" The man's eyes shifted to appraise Marcus from head to foot. His expression offered no hint of opinion.

"Tribune Sabinius, this is Crispus, the senior centurio of the eighth cohort," Julius continued. "You will go with him, and be in nominal command. Do you know how that works, tribune?"

"Er, nominal means 'sort of not really,' sir?"

"Nominal means that you *are* in command, tribune—until you fuck up. Then Centurio Crispus will gently correct you, and you will continue in command until you again fuck up. But you are always, always *in* command. Get it? It's a most excellent form of training."

"Yes, sir."

"The fort you are going to build is called ... " Julius frowned and turned to the centurio. "Do you remember the name of the fool thing, Crispus?"

"*Alavana*, sir."

"Yes, of course. Ala-whatever. Now, do either of you have any questions?"

Marcus had a thousand of them, but none he felt he could ask, especially in front of the centurio and what seemed to be a regiment of snotty, eavesdropping clerks.

Crispus, however, appeared thoughtful before replying, "No, sir." Then, in a deliberate, measured tone, he added, "Does the legate have any for the centurio, sir?"

Julius scratched his chin as he considered. "No, not really. Tribune Sabinius has my, ah, full confidence. He's eager to be out in the field rather than wasting his many talents in petty administration. I suppose we'll have to struggle along without him." He grinned like a hungry wolf. "I'm sure he'll gain more experience with you, Crispus. You will both work well together, I'm sure. You will, in fact, work together *all* the time. Understood?"

Crispus assumed the same wolfish look and roared, "Understood, sir!"

To Marcus's surprise, the centurio then turned, crashed one foot on the stone floor, and demanded in a parade square bark, "What are your marching orders, sir!"

For the briefest of moments Marcus was nonplussed, but he'd been around the military a good part of his younger life and, despite outward appearance, knew the drill. Which, from the smug hint of a smile on Crispus's impassive face, the centurio did not realize. The man was expecting him to publicly founder!

Mustering what bravado still lingered, Marcus turned to the legate. "You said the cohort departs two days from now, sir. I assume it will be at first light?"

Julius seemed taken aback, but he muttered, "Correct, tribune."

"Thank you, sir," Marcus said, and turned to Crispus. "See to it, then, will you? I'll want the details first thing in the morning: order of march, attachments, enemy assessment, supply state, and such. You know, the usual thing." In the brief silence that followed, Marcus could not resist pouring oil on the fire. He thrust the plans into the centurio's hands. "Here, you'll need these. Carry on!"

Crispus stared at the bundle of plans, eyes wide as he realized he'd just been dismissed. His mouth tightened, and the booted foot again crashed on stone. "Sir!"

Marcus also jumped to attention and turned to face the legate. One arm thumped across his chest in salute, and before anyone could say a word he roared "Sir!" and fled the building.

The fort at Alavana would be built west of the main road north, a route that one day would be permanently surfaced all the way to the fort at *Luguvalium*. Marcus was surprised by the amount of progress, despite the hard campaigning. Calacum stood almost ninety miles north of

Deva, and the road itself, while not yet paved with stone all the way, was well maintained. Only the final ten miles to Alavana proved to be nothing more than a cart track.

The site lay at the bottom of a lush valley cut by the *Luna*, a broad stream that wound from the great hills of Cumbria to empty into the *Moricambe* estuary. The fort would be strategically placed to monitor tribal movement between those same hills and the coast. All of which, Marcus decided, meant the fort would attract more barbarians than bears to a beehive.

Work on the structure began immediately, and Marcus soon learned what the word "nominal" meant to the Eighth's senior centurio. Before the first shovel could break soil for the marching camp, before the sweating ranks of soldiers could dig dirt for the ramparts, Crispus approached, his body erect and arms swinging. He snapped to rigid attention, a stance that both men knew was a sham. As did everyone else in camp, Marcus realized, for the farce was carried out, precise and correct, in front of anyone who cared to look. This was not the way matters were dealt with in the field; this formality, he knew, was reserved for the parade ground.

"Where do we stake the walls, sir?" Crispus asked.

"You can see to that, centurio."

"Sir, that tasking is normally overseen by the primus pilus. He is not here, sir. That makes it your responsibility."

Several junior centurios had gathered, clearly there to amuse themselves, and Marcus felt his cheeks grow warm. "Then I delegate it to you, centurio."

"I would be delighted to do that, sir, but I have specific orders from the general that *you* are to do it. Would you like me to send for the surveying party?"

Marcus grumbled his assent, red-faced, as he thought over how the centurio intended to play his game. It appeared that two rules were being laid down: if a tasking is backed by a direct order from the legate, there will be no choice but to obey; all taskings will be backed by a direct order from the legate.

Muttering under his breath, Marcus scoured the area for any sign of the previous survey. There was none. He scanned the riverbank, paced the slope and, when no encouragement was forthcoming from Crispus, arbitrarily made his selection. Nobody said a word, and the work itself didn't take long. The surveyors dutifully squared off the four corners of the fort, and when it was done Marcus stepped back and decided the result was not bad.

The fort appeared smaller than others he'd seen, but that was because he was looking at nothing more than a rectangle of four long cords stretched between four corner stakes. They were definitely square, for the two lengths of cord that diagonally crossed the centre were the same length, and taut as bow strings. Marcus knew enough to thank Pythagoras for that. All in all, he decided, it looked quite good.

He was wondering what to do next when a shadow loomed at his shoulder. He turned to find Crispus studying the staked out foundation, his chin resting in one hand. The bull-like head nodded as if in satisfaction and, for the space of an eye blink, Marcus felt quite pleased.

"Nicely squared off, I see," Crispus observed, then his eyes slid toward the river. "Do you not think the west wall is a little close to the water, sir? I wonder if it might wash away, should there be a flood?"

"No, I don't think so ... " Marcus began, but stopped as he saw the centurio's eyes move farther up the rise.

A meaty finger rose to point. "That dirty line up there, sir. Isn't that the floodwater mark? I'd warrant this itty stream makes quite a river of itself when the spring runoff comes."

The second attempt, when completed, earned the comment, "A bit close to the trees, don't you think, sir?"

"So?" Marcus shot back, wondering what he'd missed. "They'll be cleared."

"And handy they'll be, too, because we can use them. And the ones farther behind, as well. Hundreds of them, where the slope goes sharply upwards—they'll be handy, too. In fact, we'll be able to roll them easily downhill to the fort once they're trimmed."

"Yeah ... "

"And when they're all gone, a man will be able to stand up there and enjoy a wonderful view of the river, and the valley, and ... " Crispus turned on his heel as if in disgust and stomped off to where the men were digging the camp. "And the full inside of the flaming fort. All of it within range of an arrow."

The third attempt remained where the stakes were driven. That probably would have been torn up too, Marcus decided, if Crispus could have found the smallest excuse. But the marching camp had been completed by then, the tents pitched, the horse lines strung, and the equipment was being unloaded. The day was wearing on, and even a senior centurio couldn't stand by while his men sat frustrated and idle. The point had been made.

Construction proceeded at a snail's pace. Marcus seethed, for the delay was due entirely to the useless repetition of work, for which he blamed the centurio. The men found it all amusing at first, but by the end of the week, even the laziest was showing signs of frustration. Marcus was shocked to find the grumbling directed his way, rather than at the cause of it all: the dithering pettiness of Crispus. The man could not be satisfied.

The first stage of construction was the rampart. As with every other tasking for his damned fort, it seemed Julius Proculus had specifically ordered his junior tribune to supervise its construction. Crispus's snide comments followed every step, delivered only after construction was either complete or well under way.

It started with the laying of the dirt base (Would it not be better if we used logs and tree limbs to make the earth bind, sir?), followed by the size of the berm itself (Do they often build them that fat and low, sir?). Then there were the parapets (I hear, sir, that poplar rots very fast in wet ground.) and the temporary granaries (I'd wager a month's pay that that enormous hole is dug well below the high water table). Even staking out the horse lines was a disaster (I wonder, sir, when it rains, if the shit will run downhill?).

Marcus, for the most part, kept his temper and his words to himself. When he did blow, he generally found himself talking to the centurio's back, and standing foolishly by himself in front of the men. And if Crispus did deign to listen, it was with a deaf ear, or deliberate ignorance. When moving the horse lines a second time, Marcus looked the centurio in the eye and snarled, "Centurio, shit always runs downhill. And one day, I promise you, it will."

"Only if you leave the horse lines where they are, sir," Crispus blithely replied, then turned and walked away—whistling.

The old adage about which way shit did run, Marcus gradually realized, was no longer true for him. As summer wore on, it did nothing but run uphill. When Crispus didn't ask questions after the fact, he displayed a snide, sarcastic ignorance as Marcus issued one flawed order after another.

When he detailed patrols and assigned rosters, it might be "I never realized we had so many men, sir." Or, after he'd made up and signed off on the supply requisitions, it might be "I'll be damned, I didn't know a transport wagon could hold that much." And in ordering construction of the fort's barracks: "By the gods, sir, does Pedanius realize he has men living in two places at the same time?" But the most irritating and constant words that set Marcus's teeth to grinding were "So that's how they do it in the Praetorians, is it, sir?"

The fort at Alavana took a month longer to complete than scheduled, and by the end of it Marcus felt drained. The only saving grace was the slave Urs. The man both understood and accepted his master's predicament, displaying no outward scorn or lack of respect. At the end of each exhausting day, the huge fellow managed to have hot water ready, a meal waiting, and a measure of wine poured—watered though it was. This was after toiling most of the day himself, working alongside the gangs building the fort. The great, hulking slave seemed to possess the only face on site that came close to be being friendly, or at the very least, not hostile.

A garrison of auxiliary infantry moved into the fort at the end of August, along with two squadrons of cavalry. And much to his disgust, Marcus received new orders to continue farther into the Cumbria hills, and build a second fort a day's march to the northwest. Someone had already given the site a name, though the gods knew who dreamed them up, Marcus thought as he read it: *Galava*.

Crispus and Marcus, in an unspoken understanding, realized the construction of the new fort had to be organized along different lines. Both knew the considerable delay in completing Alavana would place completion of Galava close to winter. And each was aware that the men were, to put it mildly, no longer amused by the "young tribune's" fumbling. No doubt realizing that the troops were growing just as pissed with him as they were with Marcus, the centurio produced a timetable for the fort's construction a few days before the march to Galava.

Marcus studied the schedule as the cohort prepared to move out, for there was little else to do. To his surprise, he found himself picking out faults in the details. He thought of several changes, small though they might be, that could speed construction, or lighten the logistics. He made notes, deriving no small satisfaction in any improvement—after all, if the centurio had produced his timetable at Alavana, it would have saved them all a deal of trouble! He felt a perverse delight in the fact that, should he be proven right, Crispus would be proved wrong.

The cohort arrived at Galava late in the afternoon, following a forced march that started before daybreak. The wagons, under heavy escort, trailed in after the main column. Crispus immediately had his "nominal" commander dispatch two patrols of cavalry to scout the area, and place double the usual number of pickets.

Marcus, who had arrived at the head of the vanguard, found himself curiously eager to start, and began at once to implement his changes. "I want the marching camp placed on the same site as the fort," he told Crispus as they stood gazing down the length of an enormous lake that filled a long green valley, running north to south. The site was magnificent, far better suited to a villa than a legion outpost. "If we do that properly the first time, it will save digging dirt twice."

"Of course," Crispus agreed readily, his eyes taking in the terrain. "It's usually done that way," he added, completely expressionless. "The men detest having to do the same thing twice."

"Then why didn't you say so at Alavana?"

"Because you were building the fort at Alavana, sir, just as you are building the one here."

"But it was you who gave orders where to dig the marching camp."

"No, sir, we had a brief discussion about the siting, then you went off to stake out the fort by yourself. You told me to see to the marching camp, as I recall. In fact, when I asked where you wanted it, your exact words were 'Any fucking place you please, centurio.'"

"Then why didn't you site the *fucking* camp in the best *fucking* place to build the *fucking* fort?"

"Oh, I did—sir," Crispus said, his face still blank

"No you didn't, I did," Marcus shot back, then his mind slowly absorbed what the centurio was telling him, which simply added to his exasperation; he wondered if the familiar routine was starting over again. "On the third try, I might add."

"If you say so, sir."

"And I still think where I put it was exactly the best place, dammit," Marcus said stubbornly, and turned his back on the lake, carefully studying the contour of the land to the north. "As for this one," he continued, pointing to where the ground swept upward, a good way back from the lake, "see that line of driftwood up there? It will have to be sited a good hundred paces beyond. That's the high water mark, and we don't want the wall swamped every spring."

Chapter V

Eboracum, A.D. 78

Rhun wore his chain mail armour, polished leather boots, a belted sword, and his helmet, even though he knew he'd be carrying the latter when he'd entered the legate's quarters. The cavalry camp was still in a state of organized chaos when he and Cian had returned, and he knew that arriving in a tunic and leggings would have been excused, but for some inexplicable reason, he wanted to show the man that he was dealing with a soldier, even if it was one who, for the moment at least, wore a Roman uniform.

Tuis opened the door to the legate's residence as if he lived there, and it struck Rhun, almost by surprise, that his brother actually did. The gods, Rhun decided as he followed Tuis through the large entry hall and into the atrium, could be perverse sods when they wanted.

The light was fading and torches had been lit on all four sides of the sheltered courtyard, each angled upward in its own metal bracket. Two large braziers originally meant to hold coals had been stoked with split birch, and blazed cheerfully in the centre. As Tuis stepped forward, a lean, bearded Briton rose from one of the chairs placed close by the fires. He was perhaps ten years older than Rhun, neatly dressed, and wore his long, fair hair tied in a ponytail. His fingers had been idly strumming a small harp, which he set carefully beside the chair.

"Criff, this is my brother," Tuis announced.

Both men nodded a greeting, and Criff said, "Met your mother again a while back. Fine woman. How is she?"

"Well enough," Rhun said, his voice neutral, unsure what to make of the man. His features were pleasant enough, but the watery blue eyes seemed lacking in strength—or were they full of guile? Or perhaps just plain innocence? Whatever it was, they seemed unwilling to meet his own for more than a few moments at a time.

"That's good. I saw her after the accident. She was in a good deal of pain. She's a strong woman, though. It takes more than a bear to set her back." Criff's smile was certainly friendly enough. "Catey almost had to tie her down to make her stay, but she's the better for the rest."

"Ah yes, Catey." Rhun smiled in turn. *The sharp-tongued woman with a penchant for the luxuries of Rome.* "The old queen, Cartimandua."

Criff grinned. "She'd flay you alive for the 'old,' though one day she'll have to accept it. After all, she's m—"

He broke off as a door slammed somewhere in the building. A clatter of boots followed, echoing along a planked walkway, and a Roman officer in full dress stepped from the shadows. He wore a gleaming breastplate decked with an array of honours, *pteruges* of red leather, shoulder flashes of the same material, and a cloak edged with purple and pinned at the shoulder with a gilded, eagle-shaped clasp. Rhun found the effect surprisingly intimidating.

Despite the impressive uniform, the man's most distinctive feature was a long, jagged scar that ran across the top of his skull. It glowed pale through his short-cropped hair in the light from the flickering torches. As a child, Rhun had seen Venutius's warriors inflict that wound, not far from where they now stood. He slowly brought himself to attention.

Gaius stopped, hands on hips, and stared. "Trooper."

"Sir." Rhun stiffened and stared straight ahead, his eyes focused somewhere above the scar. He wondered at the man's attire. Was the full dress uniform to remind him of his place? Or did legates always wander about their residence that way? Surely it wasn't to impress, as he himself had chosen to do. That was too much to accept. Rhun resisted the urge to shake his head to clear it, and instead took satisfaction in the fact that he stood half a head taller than the Roman. Last time he'd seen the legate, the man seemed a giant.

"Damned inspections," Gaius muttered, gesturing absently to a chair by the brazier as he fumbled to undo the clasp on his cloak. "Take a seat, if you wish."

Rhun glanced sideways from the corner of his eye, and saw that only three seats were set close by the brazier. Two were now occupied by Tuis and Criff. He braced his back and said, "I'm fine, sir."

Gaius raised one eyebrow. "Suit yourself, then." He tossed the cloak on the back of the empty chair and turned to Tuis. "Find Metellus, son, and tell him we could use something to eat. Something to drink, too. Then perhaps you might leave your brother and me alone."

Tuis nodded, smiled at Rhun, who was scowling at the legate's use of the word "son," and departed. Criff took the hint a few moments later, casually retrieving the harp as he left. Now there were three empty chairs, and Rhun felt foolish as he stood at attention next to the crackling brazier. Gaius didn't help matters by slumping down on the nearest chair with a great sigh, fumbling with the straps on the left side of his chest armour.

"You had a good journey from Germania?" he asked, lurching to one side as he freed the ties, then started on the shoulder pieces.

"Very good, sir. The sea was calm and the weather good, for the most part."

"Nothing worse than a choppy sea, especially that short crossing to Gaul. Caesar himself found as much." Gaius grunted as the shoulder pieces came free; he set them down beside the chair. Without bothering to undo the right-hand set of straps, he slid the armour off sideways, and set it on top.

The tunic of soft red leather he was left wearing struck a chord in Rhun's memory. There had been another one of the same colour years ago, when the Roman had been captured at Stannick. As if reading Rhun's mind, or perhaps it was the subtle shift in his expression, Gaius said, "Yes. Your mother stole one just like it from me once."

"My sister had a small jacket out of it," Rhun said, which in turn brought the memory of Coira, but he was damned if he was going to say more.

The slave Metellus appeared with a large tray holding a wine jug, three silver goblets, and a platter loaded with cold meats, oysters, cheese, an assortment of breads and pastries, and a small bowl of the ever-present *garum*. Rhun had once despised the thin sauce, for the Romans used it to flavour almost everything they ate. Sheer necessity, however, had forced him to use it, and it was now addictive. His mouth watered as the slave set the tray on a small table close by the brazier. The man remained long enough to fill two of the silver goblets.

"Is Criff not coming back?" Metellus asked, glancing first at Rhun's unbending stance, then at his master.

"I don't believe so," Gaius replied as the slave handed him one of the goblets.

Metellus handed the other to Rhun, threw a few more birch logs into the braziers, then asked before turning to go, "Was there anything else?"

"No, that's all." Gaius dismissed the slave with a wave of his hand and settled back in his chair, sipping the wine. He stared owlishly over the rim of the goblet.

Rhun found himself at an even greater disadvantage: a drink in one hand, a stiff back, and a legate who seemed intent on making him feel ill at ease. With his next words, however, Gaius showed he didn't consider the problem his own. "I see that you've retained a certain amount of your—what might we call it, intractability?"

"Sir?"

"You can stand there all night if you want, but it's your pride and your back that will pay for it." Gaius tipped his head and allowed an oyster to slide off its shell and down his throat. He washed it down with another sip of wine, then returned his gaze to Rhun. "So, did they tell you where you're to be posted?"

"Isurium."

"Did they tell you for how long, and why?"

"No, sir."

"Well, I can tell you it won't be for long. And as to why, Agricola, once the western tribes are subdued, intends to secure the north. A system of forts will be built, extending all the way to Luguvalium. Do you know where that is?"

"It's an outpost high up on the west coast. There's a large estuary there, I believe."

Gaius nodded his approval. "I'm pleased to see you've taken time to study the ground. Your squadron will take an active part."

"I see," Rhun said, his voice neutral. He decided now was as good a time as any to try the wine.

"How do you feel about that?"

"I'm sure my men will carry out their duties as well as they did in Germania," he replied, perhaps too glibly, for it was an outright lie. Some of his men would carry on as usual, but there were more than a few who were very doubtful, including himself. And as for his uncle, well, Cian was not his responsibility. He raised the goblet and took another pull on the wine; it was quite good.

"Rhun, Rhun!" Gaius said, slowly shaking his head. "You return home with a squadron full of Britons surreptitiously traded for those in your troop who wanted to remain in Germania. You then tell me they'll carry out their duties as well as they did in Gaul! How can I believe anything else you tell me after that?"

He paused as if waiting for comment, and when Rhun offered none, said, "I would guess that, at best, the loyalty of every one is torn, including yours. And at worst, they're merely waiting for the right time to desert—also including you. Would you not say that's how the sword is poised?"

Rhun's jaw tightened, but still he said nothing. He wondered how, in the name of Dagda, the legate knew he'd bartered away more than half his squadron while still in Vetera, in exchange for homesick Britons. And done quite well by it, too. Cian had suggested the scheme, for he'd done it himself before leaving his own regiment. The strategy healed two wounds with one balm: those men traded off had women and children in Germania, and no wish to leave; and those traded in turn were Britons, good men all, who simply wanted to return home.

"Why don't you stop standing there as if there's a spear rammed up your arse, lad, and sit down," Gaius said, breaking the impasse, and gesturing to one of the chairs.

As Rhun reluctantly eased himself onto the chair, he continued. "Agricola *will* pacify Brigantia, including the Carvetii. He will use all force necessary, and it's important you realize that. Rhun, I want you to think before you answer this question: do you doubt at all that this will happen?"

For several long moments Rhun remained silent, his mind racing over all he'd seen the past seven years, including the disciplined armies now mustered in Britannia. When he finally replied, his voice was a mumble. "If that is what is planned, I do not doubt it will happen."

"Agricola will not stop there, you know. He will pacify the land beyond Brigantia, for the Caledonii are as troublesome as your own people, and in the long run pose far more threat. The governor will subdue them if it means going to the very ends of this island. Now, again, do you doubt this will be done?"

Rhun paused far longer, his mind absorbing the scale of such an undertaking. When he gave his answer, it was an honest one. "If Rome decides to commit the resources, then yes, there is no doubt it will be done."

"Let me assure you, short of disaster elsewhere in the empire, those resources are committed. Which brings me to my point: do you believe that resistance by the tribes will prove fruitless?"

Rhun sighed, for the question cut deep at his innards. The force of the legate's logic left him drained, yet also angry—both with Rome, and the Roman sitting across from him. Without realizing it, Rhun had leaned forward, elbows on his knees, his head bowed. The effort of a reply was, for the moment, beyond him, but Gaius persisted.

"Rhun, will resistance prove fruitless?"

He mumbled a response, which was more a nod of the head than anything else. Gaius appeared relieved.

"I am not trying to jam a *pilum* point-first down your throat, boy," he continued. "Or up your arse, for that matter. I'm simply trying to satisfy myself that you understand the situation. I also have to determine on which side of the shield your loyalty rests; for in the end, you are a soldier, a junior officer in the Imperial Army of Rome."

"And as such, expected to fight my own people. Kill them," Rhun muttered bitterly. With a sudden, stark clarity he truly understood why Rome did not permit "barbarian" units to serve in their homeland.

"Pour yourself some more wine, before you crush that goblet." Gaius refilled his own and handed the jug to Rhun. "And no, I don't expect that. Nor does the empire—at least, not under Agricola. He's a fair man, and I like to think I am, too. There may be alternatives. I gave the matter much thought before bringing you home, you know." He paused for moment then grinned, as if to himself. "And your mother gave the matter much voice, believe me."

Gaius propped his feet comfortably on the third chair and leaned back, carefully eyeing Rhun as he continued. "How or why you came to be here is not the point. It's what you do next that matters. The army of Venutius fell apart after Stannick. The reprisals that followed were not harsh, at least not compared to what happened under Seutonius. But punishment must be meted out to halt further insurrection. Slaves were taken, yes, but that's the way of war. Stannick was reduced as a fortress, and that was the end of it—then."

Rhun was curious, remembering half-heard words around the hearth as he listened to his father before the final battle. "Did Venutius ever get his help from the north? Or from the Carvetii?"

The question brought a smile. "Some if it was forthcoming but, as often happens with the tribes, it came too late. The Carvetii were always there. After all, they're more or less Brigantes anyway. The trouble was, even their people didn't get to Stannick in time. Nor did the support from farther north. We attacked before Venutius expected. In fact, we led him to believe it would happen later than it did." Gaius shook his head at the memory. "I discovered your father was one of the people to whom we fed such information."

Rhun bit his lip and nodded his understanding, but did not push for details. Instead, he asked, "And the old man himself?"

Gaius frowned, as if displeased with the question. "Your mother saw him just before the battle at Stannick. He was trying to warn those inside the fortress, which is where you were. It was worthy of him. Elena said he was tired, but otherwise unhurt."

Rhun nodded his understanding, but could not prevent a grim smile. "I wasn't speaking of my da. I meant Venutius. Was he taken?"

"His body was never found, nor has he been heard of since. And no single person seems to have taken his place. But there's a mood of rebellion with all the tribes, as far north as we care to ride. There is one woman from the Carvetii, however, who *is* gaining a following. She's called Morallta, I believe."

"Great Fury," Rhun translated, and felt a small glow of satisfaction;

he was almost sure he knew who the woman was. And, he thought ruefully, so had his father—in more ways than one. "A good name, for someone who intends to lead and fight."

Gaius nodded agreement. "Strangely enough, her warriors are well trained. Not the usual rabble you find throwing themselves on our spears. In the end, though, the result will be the same. It may simply take longer." He fell silent, sipping at the wine as if pondering how much longer.

"You said there may be alternatives," Rhun said.

"Yes, though there's only one I prefer." Gaius's dark eyes sharpened as he spoke. "It occurs to me that there is a role you can play in Brigantia, without fighting your own people. Your success would reduce casualties on both sides, but mostly on that of your people."

Rhun simply stared, already half a step ahead of the legate.

"Your squadron will be assigned duties separate from the rest of the regiment. You don't fight, you merely teach the inevitability of defeat." Gaius leaned forward, peering intently at Rhun's face. "If that's what you believe is truly going to happen, trooper, then you *must* let your people know. It's almost a duty."

When Rhun still said nothing, Gaius added, "There is also a value that you yourself would display. You are your own testimony: a tribesman who can become a part of something far greater. And you know what that is, Rhun. You have seen it everywhere: in Germania, here in the south, in Rome itself. A better life. A safer, ordered life. A life in which a man may serve with honour."

Honour! That was the heart of it, Rhun thought, and a matter unresolved. How do you gain honour serving those who conquer your own people? "You said alternatives. That's only one."

"Yes." Gaius set the goblet to one side and again leaned back, pressing his fingers together as he stared at Rhun. "There's the obvious, of course: regular duties, remain part of your regiment. The others are equally simple. Back to Germania, though I imagine the fact you are here shows that's not an option. And finally, I can arrange service in the southern part of the province."

Rhun did no more than nod his understanding.

"There is a further one, though it would take more time. I can have all the Britons in your squadron released on condition they settle in the south. Those in your uncle's troop, as well. But ponder this: your men are no longer who they were. They are trained, disciplined cavalry. They must be, or they would no longer serve the army of Rome. To what life will they return? And if they pledge their swords elsewhere, or if they run ... "

There was no need to finish the threat, but it didn't matter. The legate's option held no appeal. It was the mention of Cian, though, that gave him pause. "My uncle. Why was he brought back? In fact, how did he get recruited in the first place?"

"Ah, your uncle." Gaius sighed, and seemed to grow reflective. "I'm surprised he's still alive. Your father was named Cethen Lamh-fada, as I recall. Cethen of the Long Arms. I have often wondered if his brother's full name was Cian of the Big Mouth." He smiled at the notion. "He was identified after the fighting at Salvi's Creek, although I believe your people called it Bran's Beck. It wasn't difficult. Cian shouted your father's name to the guards, the gods, and anyone else within hearing. He claimed he was your da's brother, and I owed him much, including his life."

"And you did?"

"No." Gaius grinned again, almost sheepishly. "It was your da to whom I owed it, though in fairness, it was he and Venutius who placed it at risk. I must admit, young Rhun, the gods have played their games with your family and me." He shook his head as if in despair. "It was, however, your mother's pleadings that led Cian to the auxiliaries, rather than slavery. His teeth were a bit long for a new recruit, but he did prove a good soldier."

"My mother pleaded?" Rhun said doubtfully.

Again Gaius grinned. "When she wasn't screaming about the debt that was owed." He rose, stretched, and gave a satisfied belch.

Rhun stood too, taking the move as prelude to dismissal. When Gaius said no more, he said, "Speaking of family, sir, I see your son is posted here as well." Rhun noted, with some satisfaction, that the words seemed to strike a hidden target.

"He's here?" Gaius said, obviously surprised. "How do you know that? I didn't know myself whether—when he would arrive."

Rhun noted the slip and wondered. "I believe I saw him on the docks at Gesoriacum. He appeared well, though I never spoke to him. It wasn't my place. I assumed he would be assigned to your command."

"No, no." Gaius smiled, clearly pleased with the information. "He's posted to the Twentieth."

"One of the first legions posted to Britannia," Rhun murmured, and glanced across the atrium, again unsure if it was time to go.

Gaius saw his indecision. "You had better return to your men," he said, but his face furrowed in a frown. "You will no doubt want time to decide. Talk matters over, perhaps."

"Thank you, sir," Rhun said, but there was still more on his mind. "Cian, sir. Are the alternatives you mentioned open for him, too? He served well in Germania."

"Yes, I know. The fool would have been twice as decorated if he wasn't such a brainless bastard when not fighting the enemy." Gaius shook his head. "I've given much thought to that matter, as well. And yes, the options are there for him."

"I'll let him know, sir."

It was only as Rhun left the east gate of the fortress, plodding down the path that led back to the regiment's camp, that he realized the legate had not mentioned a word about the escort duty to Camulodunum. The Roman was a strange man. That would have been the first question asked by one of Rhun's own people.

When he finally returned to his tent, it was dark. His mouth was dry from too much wine, his brain fogged for the same reason. Cian was asleep, but he pulled him from his blanket and dragged him to the edge of the communal fire, where the embers still glowed an ash-coated crimson. Rhun tossed a log on the dying coals, and rolled over a second so they both could sit.

"This isn't going to take long, is it?" Cian grumbled as he set his rump on the rough bark and yawned.

"I don't know, Cian; it may," Rhun said as he settled alongside. "I've a lot to tell, and I'm confused. I need advice."

"Well, lad, I'm the man to give it; I've got lots to offer." Cian yawned again, long and hard, before finishing with a sigh. "And why not? Nobody ever takes any."

Chapter VI

Galava, A.D. 78

Cethen Lamh-fada was not a happy man. When his mind scanned forty years of existence, something it did far too often these days, it was to ponder on where the time had gone, or to simply brood on its waste. Surely, by the great red beard of Dagda, there had to be more to life than simply staying alive until you died.

He unwrapped his wineskin from the pommel and moodily raised the spout to his lips. Letting the reins hang loose, he cocked one leg across the saddle which, for the moment, eased the pressure on his backside. The horse, a fine chestnut gelding of middle years with a white blaze and the name of Gadearg, plodded on, taking no advantage of the lack of pressure on the bit.

Trailing behind the animal, side by side in column of two, were over a hundred similar riders, though few were as well mounted. And alongside, seemingly lost in her own thoughts, was an auburn-haired woman whose attractive features were deeply tanned by the late summer sun. As did everyone else in the column, she carried two spears, a sword that hung loose from a baldric, and an oval shield with a falling, flaming javelin painted across the face. A mail tunic covered the upper part of her body, hiding the curve of her figure, but a pair of tight doeskin britches revealed long, slim legs, finely muscled and firm in their grip on the saddle.

The woman finally spoke after a good half-mile of forested track passed by in silence, and the column entered a meadow cleared for pasture. "You're brooding again."

Cethen looped the wineskin tie back around the pommel and half turned, peering at Morallta through half-lidded eyes. "Why is it," he began, but paused to yawn before finishing. "Why is that when a man thinks, he's brooding, but when a woman broods, she's thinking?"

"I don't brood."

"Then neither do I." Cethen's thoughts ran idly through the last half-day of their trek through the forested Cumbrian hills. "You were saying just as much as me, you know, which was nothing. So you were brooding just as much as me."

"It was you who was off with the faerie," Morallta said testily, "and I'm not going to argue it. There are more important things we need to think on."

"There always are," Cethen sighed, and slouched lower in the saddle.

"We can't go on like this, you know."

"What?" Startled, Cethen turned again, this time giving Morallta his full attention. The woman never spoke of personal matters, for there was hardly need. At best theirs was a pact of convenience; at worst, it was two people living side by side in a wary truce. Their small lodge was hardly a lovers' nest, though when passion did flare, which was not often, it burned fast and hot. Which was, he supposed, another matter that of late didn't sit well on either side, though for different reasons. "I thought we were plodding along well enough. As well as we ever have."

"Not us, fool," Morallta snorted. "I mean the tribes. They pull together less now than they ever did under Venutius, damn him." Her face twisted with anger at the memory. "The fool! Asleep, with a Roman army climbing his walls! If the idiot had been only half as vigilant as his enemies!"

"If!" Cethen grunted, picking up the word. It brought back far more memories than the failure at Stannick. Something similar had been said the last time he'd seen Elena, outside those same walls; and *her* reply held more than a trace of regret. He repeated the words, as much to himself as to Morallta. "'*Ifs* are nothing more than wishes. The gods made life an *is*, not an *if*.'"

"That's either very profound, or you're brooding again," Morallta said curtly. "And I don't much give a damn which. There's sign the Romans will move north again, and every chief with half a following argues over who will lead the tribes."

Cethen sighed again, uncocked his leg, and eased forward in the saddle. He glanced over one shoulder at the column of riders, now making its way across the valley floor. The ranks were about as straight as a coiled adder. Morallta looked too and said nothing, which meant she really was brooding, damn her, and he knew what about.

"You won't come forward on leading them yourself, yet you're unwilling to join with any one of 'em." Cethen shrugged. "You're no different than the rest. Eventually, all but one has to roll over and bare his throat, or we'll all go down in pieces."

"That's what the Romans count on," Morallta said sharply, then a moment later added, "And it won't be me who rolls. There's nobody better to lead, and the tribes know it. Damn Venutius anyway."

"What's he got to do with it?" Cethen asked. "The old bugger's long dead."

"And he hid the torque before he died. If I had it, they'd rally. As they did for him," Morallta snarled, slamming one hand down on the pommel. "The Romans didn't get the cursed thing, we know that much. And everyone down to the lowest skivvy and his hound has looted the ruins at Stannick looking for it, and found nothing. Without the damned thing, it's like racing a lame horse."

"Everyone else will have a lame horse as well," Cethen offered.

"Which is their concern, not mine." Morallta frowned as movement at the far end of the clearing caught her attention.

Cethen followed her gaze. Three riders lashed their horses along the valley floor, tearing across the open sweep of grassland at a dead gallop. "Trouble," he muttered.

"There better be," Morallta snapped. "I'll not tolerate flaying an animal like that for no good reason." She raised a hand to order the column forward, and kicked her horse to an easy gallop.

"Roman patrol," the lead rider of the three called, reining her animal up sharply in a bone-jarring, stiff-legged halt.

"Where, how many, and what are they doing, Innsa?" Morallta demanded, not slowing her own horse, forcing the three riders to wheel and catch up.

"About two miles away, following the stream north where it runs by Curnan's place. About twenty, maybe a few more. They look like they're patrolling," Innsa shouted, her face eager.

"If we hurry, we can cut down the ravine below Bear's Head Rock and get there first," the second of the three called from behind.

"What do you think?" Cethen asked.

"It has been a while," Morallta cried, her face flushing with excitement as she dug in her heels.

"Yeah." Cethen muttered, all too aware of the woman's aroused senses as he fumbled with his shield. Shaking his head, he kicked hard at Gadearg's belly and the gelding leaped forward. The leather tie bounced loose, and the wineskin tumbled to the ground with a wet splat. Glancing backward, he saw it trampled by the next horse in line. Cursing, he struggled to free his helmet from the other horn of the pommel, this time taking more care.

They cleared the bottom of the ravine in line, and ran headlong into the Roman patrol a mile from Curnan's farmstead. There would be no lying in wait; there would be no ambush. Morallta, Cethen, and the lead ranks of the column burst into the open, and the enemy patrol pushed forward, clearly intending to fight. But as more and more riders emerged from the ravine, the decurio reined short in dismay, then wheeled and bolted; his men did the same, in a mad muddle of horses and riders.

Cethen smiled grimly as the Romans turned in panic, and he glanced sideways, even as he lashed down on the chestnut's rump. Morallta's face had flushed a deeper red. Her spear dropped forward as she slammed both heels into her horse's belly. Her mouth was open, her breath short, and her features ecstatic as the animal leapt forward. The tip of the spear quickly found the pit of a Roman back. There was no stopping her, Cethen knew; the woman might well have been in rut...

The chase took on the feel of a stag hunt. The fleeing Romans raced downhill toward Mor-loch, following the wide, fast-flowing stream that ended there. Heedless of rocks and deadfall, they splashed through the shallows and swarmed through the trees scattered on either side. In no time at all, they were thundering past Curnan's mean cluster of huts, and back into the forest.

The Roman horses were fast, faster than most that pursued them, but Cethen's people knew the land. More than one Roman rider found himself caught short before the forest gave way to level, open ground. The lead horses burst from the trees and raced forward in a clamour of thundering hooves and shrill screams.

Cethen and Morallta were moments behind, caught in the mad, slashing tangle of their own riders and the Roman stragglers. Lathered horses pounded over the flattened grass and on through the last of the thinning trees. The blue waters of Mor-loch glinted in the distance, but something new now lay in between. Cethen squinted at the obstacle maybe three, four hundred paces ahead—a set of earthworks, Roman earthworks that only yesterday had not been there.

"Morallta, stop!" he yelled, his eyes sweeping the low, unfinished rampart that swarmed with Roman foot soldiers like a nest of angry ants.

"Keep going! Keep going!" Morallta screamed, brandishing her bloodied spear.

Cethen glanced sideways, alarmed at the order. The woman's eyes were glowing, dammit, and she was actually smiling! Cursing, he dug both heels hard into Gadearg's belly.

The supply wagons lumbered in with their escort two hours before dusk, and found the marching camp near completion. The ditch was halfway dug, and the dirt piled up behind as the rampart's base; the stakes carried by each soldier for the make-do palisade were laid in neat ranks inside the enclosure; the horse lines were paced off and drawn up; and a half-dozen tent lines were pitched in the centre. Marcus walked through it all with a certain satisfaction, Urs trailing behind with a pickaxe on one shoulder and a shovel on the other.

The slave's keen eyes were the first to spot a single rider bursting from the forest almost half a mile away. It was one of the pickets, desperately flailing his horse. Urs opened his mouth to shout, then just as quickly changed his mind and closed it again.

The first cry of alarm came soon after, from the top of the incomplete rampart. By then the forest was erupting with horses, their riders' cries faint against the wind blowing in from the lake. As if time had slowed, the soldiers inside the camp scrambled for weapons, all order seemingly gone. Few wore helmets and chest armour, and more than a few were farther than ten paces from their weapons.

Marcus stood in the centre of the enclosure, stunned. The riders were from one of the two auxiliary patrols, they had to be, though hardly a dozen were left, each one lashing his mount toward the camp. Right behind—no, mixed in with them was what must surely be a full cohort of barbarian cavalry. It streamed down the slope like an enormous pack of hounds, as if herding the panicked auxiliaries onto the unfinished rampart. And the whole lot of them, he realized in horror, were thundering straight toward him at an alarming speed.

Vaguely aware of Crispus shouting orders somewhere off to his left, Marcus turned as if in a dream to find his shield. Urs, his face impassive, already had it in hand. As he thrust it forward, the slave glanced over his master's head. Marcus turned. The first of the patrol was already through the shallow ditch and over the half-finished rampart: a yelling, screaming tangle of men, weapons, and horses. Centurios stood screeching orders as dozens of desperate *decani* tried to beat their squads into line.

Mind numb, Marcus drew his sword, vaguely aware that the short blade was nearly useless against cavalry armed with spears and shields. The camp was a storm of dust and confusion. Men were trying to form ranks; Marcus moved to join the nearest, but a barbarian horseman loomed out of nowhere, spear poised. He braced himself, instinctively raising the shield, but a pickaxe flew past his head and struck the man's arm. It was enough to jar his aim, and the barbarian galloped past into the confusion. A second rider followed, this time a woman, and more by luck than skill, Marcus parried her spear. It deflected into the shoulder of a man who had moved up alongside Marcus. He hoped it wasn't Urs.

A third thundered straight for where he stood, but the man's spear pointed elsewhere. Though the rider posed no danger, Marcus stabbed desperately with the near-useless sword. The blade slid into the horse's belly, surprisingly fast, where the muscle met the haunch. It sank more than half its length, only to be ripped from his hand as the animal thundered by. The beast squealed and skewed sideways, kicking high with its hind legs. Its rider, whose spear had found the back of a screaming soldier, was flung from the saddle.

Marcus followed the rider's fall, his fuddled mind bent on recovering his weapon. The blade had flown from the animal's belly to land in the dirt close to the barbarian rider, who was struggling to his knees. Quickly grabbing the hilt, Marcus raised the sword in both hands and plunged the point down hard where the man's leather armour met his helmet. He stared numbly as the body sprawled forward.

The roar of voices broke through his fogged mind and he whirled, weapon ready. But the fight had moved on—it appeared to have moved on completely. Dazed, he looked about and saw other men doing the same. There seemed to be no fighting anywhere, nor was there any trace of the barbarians. The attack had passed so quickly it was difficult to believe it had happened at all. But the groans of the wounded and a scattering of still, silent bodies, gave the truth of it. The harsh echo of Roman voices quickly replaced the silence, and the camp started to regain an appearance of order.

The barked commands finally died as the men formed up in ranks, and the compound fell strangely quiet. A single, distant voice floated across the ramparts, howling in triumph; the sound echoed chillingly across the waters of the lake, and back across the slope. The barbarian cavalry, instead of vanishing into the forest, had formed two long, even ranks facing the camp. Centurios again began screaming orders, but Crispus roared for silence, angrily kicking at the corpse of the barbarian killed by Marcus. There were few such bodies in sight.

"They'll not try anything else." The centurio glared at the ranks of barbarian horsemen. "We outnumber them, and we're ready. Finally."

"It's never stopped them before," Marcus murmured as he edged quietly alongside. "They go at it like madmen, until someone smashes a boss in their teeth."

"How would a tadpole like you know?" Crispus growled, his eyes unmoving.

"Because I've fought them before," Marcus said, an edge to his voice.

"Yeah. Where? In your worst nightmare?"

"On the other side of these hills." Marcus gestured vaguely eastward. "Venutius."

"Sure," Crispus grunted, the word heavy with disbelief. His eyes remained fixed on the cavalry as two riders moved to a position in front of the line.

Marcus saw the centurio bite down on his lip, as if wondering whether the barbarians would attack after all, and he smiled to himself, despite his annoyance. "Yeah, sure! Only once, I admit, but we took a lot of casualties. We ran into his army head on, when it came down to attack Isurium. I got sliced in the leg."

"Salvi's Creek? In the square?"

"Uh-huh. Or Bran's Beck, depending which side you were on."

"I assumed you were on ours."

"Arsehole," Marcus whispered under his breath, then said, "I was."

"Well, I'll be damned," the centurio muttered, then, after a long silence, saw fit to add, "By the way, nice work with the barbarian rider. Next time, though, keep a grip on your sword."

"I tried."

"Not hard enough. You've got to allow for both the force and the direction of the blow. Ride with it, and be quick. Oh, and one other thing."

"What's that?" Marcus sighed.

"Arseholes are not only useful, they put up with a lot of shit."

Crispus said no more, his eyes on the enemy cavalry. The two riders had halted in front of the quiet ranks, one with a raised sword. A sharp order cut through the eerie silence. Each barbarian spear, which had been held upright, suddenly fell forward. A low rumble rippled through the Roman lines, and one or two centurios growled warnings. But the spears were quickly lifted again, twirled three times in a full circle, and suddenly stopped, all together, again rigidly upright. The voice again rang out, and a long, jeering cheer drifted up to the camp; the raucous noise seemed especially loud in the fading light.

"They have to be deserters," Crispus muttered.

The rider with the sword raised a hand to remove a plain, domed helmet, revealing a glorious head of dark auburn hair. It fell over her shoulders in a manner clearly calculated to show her sex. Even at that distance, Marcus could see the woman was striking.

"Not unless Rome's changed her recruiting policy," he murmured, then grinned. "It might not be a bad idea."

"Good luck, tribune. I fight with what I can handle," Crispus muttered. "That one's equipped with talons."

"It's what else she's equipped with that fascinates me," Marcus replied.

A third order rang out, and the two ranks swung into column. It was as neatly done as any auxiliary unit, on any parade square. Several riders galloped ahead, probably to ride scout, Marcus decided. It was all very impressive. The woman turned too, but not before pulling back on the reins, causing her horse to rear, its forelegs pawing the air as she released a final scream of triumph. With a last wave of the sword, she dug her heels into the animal's belly and galloped to the head of the column. In no time at all, it had vanished into the trees.

"Fucking women!" Crispus grunted.

Marcus thought that over and added, " … is what I'd much rather be doing."

The fort was finished soon after summer, when the autumn frosts touched the peeled logs of the palisade with a slippery coat of rime. The structure was less than a month behind schedule, the entire delay due to the time taken to build the fort at Alavana. The defences were complete, including the four massive gates set in each wall. The headquarters building had been roughed in and weatherproofed, as had the granaries and the commander's residence. The long barracks buildings were framed, and only the bathhouse and a few workshops remained to be finished, a task that would likely be left to the garrison itself, depending on further orders.

Marcus, Crispus and the other centurios moved into the commander's residence once it was framed in, though it was devoid of furnishings and would remain that way until the auxiliary praefectus arrived. Other than the commander's own rooms, which Crispus and Marcus took over, the structure was in a constant state of clutter.

As October wore on, a week or two before they expected relief to arrive, Marcus found himself alone with Crispus in the building's atrium. They sat on the sunny side of the weed-filled square, their backs to the portico's support posts, enjoying a brief respite from the ever-present wind, and a rare but comfortable conversation. The centurio had changed over the past months. The man had been a bastard while building the fort at Alavana, and more than once Marcus had been on the point of challenging him. Only a shred of common sense and, he had to admit, fear had stopped him. After the astonishing attack by the barbarians, though, the bull-like veteran had become almost human, even helping to write the report describing the brief fight. Of course, Marcus reasoned, the man should have, damn him. For Crispus, when the blade finally slid home, was the one standing naked with no shield—the "young tribune" was only in *nominal* command.

The ambushed auxiliary patrol had lost more than a dozen men. The mad charge through the camp had cost just as many infantry, along with a good forty wounded. Two had since died, and more than one would be useless for anything but staff duty. Only three enemy dead had been found, the most devastating number of all. Crispus seemed to take the figures as a personal failure, for the disparity *always* went the other way.

Marcus sighed, took a pull on the wine jug that sat between them, and handed it to Crispus. "We'll have to start partitioning the barracks soon, just to keep them busy."

"Still no report on exactly when we're being relieved?" the centurio asked, though he usually read the incoming dispatches before Marcus did.

"No, but I suppose there are worse places to be," Marcus said, and meant it. The unfinished outpost held far more appeal than a crowded fortress commanded by a supercilious legate who thrived on humiliating junior tribunes.

"Are you requesting new orders?" Crispus asked.

"I thought we'd be going back as soon as the garrison arrives,"

Marcus said. "Why?"

"Why?" Crispus shrugged, and took a swig from the jug before replying. "If I was as young as you, I'd let the legate know I was keen. Eager to do what Rome commands. That sits well with senior officers, and this one seems pissed at you. It wouldn't do any harm."

"Fair enough, but what *good* would it do?"

Crispus shrugged. "Well, we've done two forts, and a fine job of both." He stopped and belched before finishing. "Even though the first isn't set in the best place it could be, but the legate wouldn't know that."

"Arsehole."

"Try life without one," Crispus said amiably, and took another swig. "Anyway, we did run a bit late, but the legate expected that. I think he wants you whipped into shape or beaten into submission." He grinned. "I'm still working on the submission, but the 'whipping into shape' is hopeless."

"As I said ... " Marcus held a hand out for the jug. "You still haven't answered the question."

"It leaves a good impression. That never hurts. You're going to get new orders anyway, so let him know you're ready and willing." Crispus shrugged, and amusement crossed his face. "Sometimes orders get fouled up or forgotten. It's not a good career move to arrive back at base without any, just because another unit's shown up where you are. Be keen, ask for your orders before you get them. The purple-stripers always expect more than they ask for. I learned that the hard way, when the Iceni revolted."

"You did?" Marcus, his curiosity roused, dropped his hand; the jug seemed to be staying right where it was.

"Uh-huh," Crispus said seriously. "It was Seutonius. The old bugger gave us a speech you wouldn't believe, just before the final battle with the Iceni bitch. Supposed to get our blood heated up, though sometimes I think they give speeches just to be read out later for the record. Anyway, he said we were outnumbered twenty to one, and told us every man had to do his part."

"So what happened?" Marcus shifted around to look at Crispus, intrigued.

"So, in the middle of the battle, he found me sitting under a tree wiping blood off my sword. Madder than a gored bull, he was. Wanted to know what I was doing on my bum when men were still fighting."

Marcus frowned. "What were you doing?"

"I told you, wiping my sword. You see, I'd already done what was ordered. *I'd* killed my twenty!" Crispus roared with laughter, and almost dropped the jug.

"Crispus, that was terrible," Marcus said.

"I know lad; thanks," he said, chuckling. "But the point is, they always want more than they ask for. Write and tell him we're done."

Marcus opened the dispatch, read it, then read it again. Seething, he rushed from the headquarters building in search of Crispus. He found him at the smithy, watching one of the armourers put an edge on his blade.

"Look what you made me do!" Marcus cried, holding the scroll aloft.

"Calm down, lad," Crispus said, edging him out the door. It was raining, and both men stood with feet planted in the mud, the drizzle running down their faces. "Now, what is it?"

"This. This is what it is!" Marcus thrust the dispatch in the centurio's face, forcing Crispus to squint. "Your advice stinks. It stinks."

"Easy, I can't read the damned thing when it's shoved halfway up my nose."

"Then let me do it for you." Marcus pulled the dispatch back and read it aloud, though it was hardly necessary; one glance had been enough to scribe it in his memory. "You will take the eighth cohort and proceed to garrison Luguvalium until relieved. You will retain *nominal* command. Further orders will follow."

Crispus grabbed the order and stared at it, mouth open. The rain had made the ink run, but neither seemed to care. At any other time Marcus might have relished the expression on the centurio's face, except he knew an equally miserable expression was also etched on his own.

Chapter VII

Eboracum, A.D. 78

Elena swayed lazily in the saddle as the horse plodded downhill toward the fortress. The stronghold sat squat and solid on the far side of the river, the peeled timber palisade topping the rampart in a long, orderly line that epitomized Rome herself. Ebor was no longer as she remembered it, and as the small column neared the river, the change grew more apparent. The towers, the walls, the buildings inside, no longer glistened with the yellow of new-cut wood. The earthworks had eroded in places, leaving dirty furrows torn through the sod. And at one point, down by the southeast corner toward the Fosse, the slope had given way entirely, exposing the base of the palisade itself.

A dozen work parties were busy all along the wall, however, and she could see that sections of the berm had already been repaired; farther on, close by the westernmost tower, a small stretch of the palisade appeared to have been completely replaced. Elena would have wagered ten denarii to two that similar crews toiled on the other three walls. She smiled, knowing Gaius's penchant for order.

Buildings, not many, had sprung up outside the walls, which was why they now called the place Ebor*acum*. Most appeared to be either shops or places to store trade goods, and these were set close by the river, but a few more, houses from their appearance, had been built southeast of the fortress. Elena looked on these with mixed feelings, for their presence meant permanence. Again a smile tugged her lips, this one rueful, as she recalled Cethen's insistence that one day their people would drive Rome away from here.

A bittersweet sadness welled up inside her, for it was as certain as the sun's rising that his dream would never happen. Beyond that, Elena mused as the fortress loomed closer, there was probably little else of which she was certain—though at least her brood was together again, for the first time in years.

Within two weeks of his return, the Fourth Augusta Gallorum had deployed. Rhun's troop, along with Cian's, were the only cavalry units remaining at the fortress, other than the four squadrons on the Ninth's own roster. The legate had yet to push for an answer to his odd proposal, but when the last of the regiment rode north, Rhun knew the choice had to be made. Or, as Cian put it, the time had come to extract one's finger, and decide.

The shadow of the fortress walls was not the place to do that. A fresh batch of recruits had marched overland from Petuaria and set up camp on the practice grounds close by the two troops. The constant shouts of decani, the endless thumping of marching feet, and the crash of wooden swords on wooden shields was torture to both ears and nerves. The weather was fair, and the sky almost cloudless. It took little urging from Cian to move the two squadrons across the Fosse and along the bank of the Abus to where his home had once stood.

Both troops were at full strength, the legate had made sure of that, and sixty men rode past what remained of Cian's old farmstead. Only the creak of leather and the soft clink of metal broke the silence as they neared the river and dismounted. Their cinches eased, the horses were turned loose, their reins left to drag in the long grass. Someone lit a fire close by the riverbank, and in less than a half-hour, Rhun's men lay sprawled on the grass, chewing on a makeshift meal and washing it down with a thin local beer.

Every one but Cian. Suddenly sombre, he ambled off in the direction of his old home.

A large oak stood close by the river's edge. When he finished eating, Rhun climbed to his feet and casually set his back against the trunk, nursing his beer in both hands. Any choice on the legate's proposal, he realized, was not his to make, nor was it Cian's. The verdict, for that's what it really was, affected them all, and though he and his uncle now served Rome, it would be decided by them all, in the old tribal manner. This was not like a battlefield order or a drill field command; it was a private pronouncement requiring nothing more than a man's judgement.

Though Cian was not back, Rhun looked about the circle of expectant faces and uttered one word. "Well?"

The first question came from Turren, and was clearly on everyone's mind. "What are you going to do? Your mind must be made."

"It is, but I'll tell it later," Rhun replied. "Your decision should not depend on mine."

"Of course it should," Branaught, a squad leader from Rhun's own troop, called out. "It's your troop, and you should tell us what you're going to do. If you've decided to stay, that might be good reason for us to stay as well."

"Or good reason to leave," someone said, and everyone laughed.

"Returning to our old way of life in the south—can we count on that promise? Can the legate be trusted?" The question came from one of Cian's men, a Catuvellauni trooper called Pisear. His home had once been within sight of Londinium.

"I believe so, though your circumstance might be different." Rhun frowned as he tried to recall Gaius's words. "I'm not sure the offer was extended to all Britons, or only the Brigantes. I'll have to make sure on that point. But what I am sure of is this: if he gives his word on the matter, it will be honoured."

"Pisear, you can't go south. You forget why you're here to begin with!" The man seated next to him belted him on the shoulder, then turned to explain. "His own da forced him to join up. He caught him humping his new wife. It's the only natural talent the lad has, besides fighting."

"Then if he humps as often as he fights, there'll be lots left over for the rest of us," someone else quipped, and again everyone laughed.

Both squadrons were in good spirits, which pleased Rhun. That meant most of them likely had their minds made up, and were not unhappy with the way of it. The reason for the gathering had to be talked out, though, whatever the final choice.

"Tell us more about how he expects to use us," Luga suggested, a dark frown showing his uncertainty.

Rhun nodded, pondering the reply. Now they were talking about it out loud, he realized a good deal of the answers remained unknown. In discussing the taskings with both Cian and the legate, it had become obvious that nobody had a firm grasp on what was expected. And there were other unspoken matters. Could the legate really be trusted? It seemed the only one ready to vouch for that was his own mother—and yes, he supposed, himself, too. Rhun shook both thoughts from his mind.

"I think, by now, we all understand the Romans," he began, ignoring the hoots and jeers that followed. "In order to conquer, they would rather negotiate and divide than fight. Either way, whoever they point their sword at ends up wearing the yoke. And since we are the sharp edge of that sword, it means that when they do fight, *we* conquer for them. Anyone disagree?"

Again the chorus of hoots and jeers, capped by Luga's slow, drawling wit: "Do we still get paid if we lose?"

"Never happened before, big man," Pisear said, then grinned and asked, "Does anyone know?"

"Yeah, we do, but you've gotta be alive," Rhun replied, and smiled as he went on. "For me, there is only one premise: do I believe the Romans will win here? If the answer is yes, which I believe it is, then that raises a second premise: can I serve the Roman army without harming my own people? Because—"

"That's two premises. Make up you mind," Branaught said.

Rhun ignored the interruption. It struck him, as the words were about to fall from his mouth, where the crux of his indecision lay. Perhaps it hadn't been set firm in his mind before, but as he urged his troop and Cian's to decide for themselves, he suddenly realized he was about to voice the real reason for his own choice. "Because," he continued, and held his arms out, palms up, as if offering an excuse, "in all honesty, I like what I'm doing."

A chorus of hoots, louder than any others, greeted the words, along with more than a few choice comments. Rhun laughed and raised a hand, calling for quiet.

"Look, most of you do too, if you had to admit it," he said defensively. "And I suppose by saying how I feel, I've told you which way I'm going. If I don't have to hurt my people, if I can avoid meeting them in battle, if I don't have to kill them, then I'll stay with my squadron." Rhun looked down on their upturned faces and grinned. "If I still have one."

"So it turns a full circle, doesn't it? We can't stop the Romans so we help them; yet if we help them, then they can't be stopped." Cian had returned in time to hear the last of it, and slumped to the ground near Rhun's feet. His face was sombre as he grabbed his pack and rummaged for the food he'd brought, but not before placing a small, finely worked carving on the grass in front of him. It was a man on a horse, cut from deer antler. The hind leg was charred, but it was otherwise whole.

He looked up, and found everyone staring. "I carved it for my kids, years ago," he muttered, eyes shifting back to the contents of his pack. "It's all I found worth keeping."

Cian's return seemed to cast a cloud on the gathering and Rhun wondered, as he had a thousand times, what was right; but he'd started, so he had to finish. "So there you have it. We've served in Germania, and you know the way of it. Over there, Rome's enemies had better odds than my own people, and even those were grim. If there's a chance of using my shield to help my own people survive, I'll do it."

"So you are going to stay," Luga said, scratching at his thick black beard.

"That's what I said, Luga. If I have the tasking promised, then there'll be one squadron of Roman cavalry who are trying to persuade our people, instead of killing them. Look how it was in Germania. Who ever gave a pig's ear for an enemy who's trying to kill us?"

"They'll still be trying to kill us," Turren pointed out practically.

"If I've tried my best and the hotheads still want my head, then my conscience sits well. I'll oblige them in turn," Rhun replied, his voice touched with irritation, for he wasn't sure it would sit well.

"It still smells of treachery," someone said, and several voices echoed the words.

"What do you think, Cian?" Luga asked.

"I've given up on thinking." Cian glanced up from his beer mug, where he'd been trying to soften a spelt biscuit in the lukewarm suds. "It hurts the head. But if you do think you must think, there's not much point anyway, not in the long run. We all wind up just as dead in the end. Anything in between is passing time, and that's often not worth the bother."

"Whoa, who smeared shit on your saddle?" Branaught snorted.

"Nothing lasts, Bran, including us." Cian set the mug down, picked up the carving, and stared moodily at the soot-streaked figure. "Nothing!" He tossed it in the air, about a foot or so, and caught it; then his face grew taut, and he lifted his arm to throw it at the flames.

Rhun's hand snaked out and grasped his uncle's wrist. He deftly pried the figure from his fingers, and Cian didn't resist. "I'd like to keep it," he said. "It has good memories. I had one like it, once. Got it from you. If I ever find it again, you can have this one back—uncle."

"Your gloom's all very fine, Cian," Conn, one of the Brigantes in his uncle's squadron, persisted, "but what are *you* going to do?"

Cian shrugged. "Stay here and keep my nephew's bum wiped, I suppose. And you?"

The question was the heart of the matter, and in no time everyone was arguing—as Rhun had expected. It would likely continue for the rest of the afternoon, long after each one's choice had been made. There seemed no sense in remaining, for he could already tell what the answer would be. He looked over at Cian and his uncle grunted and climbed to his feet. Moments later, they were riding back to the camp.

A single rider approached as they broke free of the trees that sheltered the river Fosse. The horse tore across the field at a breakneck pace, only to be pulled up short by a sharp jerk on the reins that set the animal back on its haunches. The large bay's blood was racing; it pranced and skittered across the grass as the rider sat easy in the saddle, grinning from ear to ear.

"I see you finally made it to Ebor," Rhun said dryly.

"Good eyes."

"Nice horse." Rhun glanced down at the animal's withers and saw no trace of lather; the gallop had been a brief show of bravado. "The legate know you've got him?"

"Of course." Coira turned the reins until the horse fell in between the other two, and nodded to Cian. "Uncle."

"Good to see you," Cian said.

"I missed you both at the camp, but Gaius told me what you were likely doing. You were taking a long time, so I had a horse saddled and spent an hour or two on the practice field while waiting." Coira looked brightly at each of the weathered faces and flashed a smile. "So how did it go?"

"The legate sent you?" Rhun asked, unable to resist the jibe.

"The legate sends me nowhere." Coira's voice held more than a trace of irritation. "I came because I returned from Camulodunum with mother. And my brother is here."

"Then I'm glad you command your own destiny," Rhun said in a tone that made Cian lean forward and stare as if unsure he'd heard correctly.

"I do. As much as anyone does," Coira snapped and, ignoring Rhun, turned and spoke to Cian. "My brother was at Stannick, and almost died there. You know that; he knows that. And Aunt Nuada did die. As did thousands of others." She reached across and touched one of the two spears slung upright against Cian's saddle. "Many of our people died on the wrong end of these. I don't want to see that happen again." She slapped both shafts angrily, making them rattle. "And I don't believe the Romans will be defeated, any more than you do. So if it does start again, then it happens all over again. You can help stop it."

"It's not that simple," Rhun mumbled, deliberately remaining surly. He couldn't explain why, but he just didn't feel like warming to his sister's enthusiasm. Even so, he was surprised at the vehemence in her voice.

"Simple?" Coira sneered, and turned to face him. "Of course it's simple. Look at you. You've spent the past six, seven years with the Romans. Cian, you spent it with their army. You both did well by it. You proved yourselves." She gestured back across the Fosse. "All those others back there—many may be Britons, but they all take the empire's pay. They've learned much. They're the best, and Rome made them— and you—what you are." She paused and tapped her temple with one finger. "But above all, Rome has made you less ignorant than you were. You don't have to love her, any more than I do; but I don't see how you can go back to the way you were, any more than I could."

As if to emphasize the truth of her words, the soft thump of a drumbeat drifted across the river, breaking the sudden, almost painful, silence. A sleek galley swept into view, its oarsmen rowing her steadily upriver toward the dock. The bow cut cleanly through the dark current, a foamy white wake falling away on either side. As the vessel drew near a sailor standing in the prow waved, and all three absently returned his casual salute.

The vessel was an impressive sight, yet in a strange way it was also a peaceful one. It no longer held the threat of an invading enemy, as did the one almost a decade past, when the legate first came to Ebor. His sister was correct, Rhun thought reluctantly. Much had changed, and with all of them. He watched as the galley drew level, and suddenly chuckled. Would this one crash into the dock?

"So that's it, then?" Coira persisted, and when Rhun turned to her with a look of amusement, she added, "It's not a laughing matter."

"And that, for certain, is the truth of it," Rhun said, and perversely changed the subject. "So Mam come with you?"

"Yes." Coira's voice was iced.

"Then we can tell her that despite your rhetoric, the *matter* had already been decided."

"Despite?"

"Yeah, Cian's troop is going to take the legate's offer."

"And you're not?" Coira cried, her tone angry yet incredulous.

"Didn't say that." Rhun shrugged, drawing out an almost compulsive urge to irritate his sister on what was, he'd stubbornly decided, a very private decision. "I'd already settled on taking the offer. It was only Cian's mind that was maybe not made up."

For a moment Coira held her silence, as if trying to hold her temper. Finally she spoke, her words terse. "You can be a real turd!"

Rhun shrugged once again, and grinned. "Yeah, I know. Nice to have company."

Chapter VIII

Luguvalium, A.D. 78

The storm struck around midday, driving hard in their faces as the cohort made its way north. The gods seemed unable to decide whether to hurl ice-cold rain or frozen sleet. Both blew in on the teeth of a hard, gusting wind that bit at the flesh and clung to the uniform in a thick skin of freezing slush. The rain and ice pelted down in turn, one endlessly following the other, as the column marched slowly toward the fort, arriving long after darkness had fallen.

It first appeared that Luguvalium had been abandoned. The scouts had ridden ahead, as blindly as the rest of the column. They were still at the gate when the vanguard arrived, sitting their horses, baffled at the sight of barred doors.

"Break it down," Crispus barked, and in the same breath ordered the cohort to stand to, in battle order.

Orders rang out along the column, lost in the howling wind. Before they could be carried out, a single figure appeared at the top of the gate, demanding to know who stood below. Without mincing words, Crispus told him. Several more faces soon appeared above the wooden palisade, pale and soaked, a row of ghosts suspended in the wind-driven sleet. After an interminable time and a good deal of muffled argument, the gate finally swung open.

"Never mind the headquarters building," Crispus muttered, as his horse moved forward of its own accord. "Straight to the commander's residence."

"Yes, *sir!*"

Shivering, Marcus gave his tired mount a quick jab of his heels, but it was already plodding after Crispus's. The long, dark ranks of soldiers tramped through the gate, shields raised and spears thrust forward. Underneath the walkway that spanned the tower, the icy gusts faded as if a door had been slammed, and the darkness grew darker. One of the gate guards loped alongside Crispus, the entire force almost lost under the shadows of the long, low buildings.

"Which side of the head hut is the commander's residence?" Crispus demanded.

"On the *sinistra*," the guard shouted.

The centurio nodded, and when the road ended in front of the headquarters building, he reined his horse to the right. The residence sat less than fifty yards away, another dark, unguarded shadow. Marcus tossed the reins to the man as he slid stiffly from his horse, then turned and removed a leather pouch from his saddle pack. With a nod from Crispus, both men marched toward the entrance with hands on the hilts of their swords.

A figure appeared in the doorway before they could demand entry, that of a veteran nearing his time. "What is going on, you—" The man stopped short when he saw the two officers.

Crispus did not bother to keep the anger from his voice. "Crispus Martinus, senior centurio, Eighth Cohort, Twentieth Valeria. And Tribune Marcus Sabinius. We are here to take command. Where is the senior officer?"

"Er, I…"

"Here." Marcus stepped into the shelter of the building and removed a scroll from the round leather casing. He thrust it under the man's nose. "Are you Aulus Licinius Clemens?"

The man nodded, glancing from Crispus to Marcus, his hard, weathered face tightening with concern. He said nothing as his eyes scanned the scroll, which was impossible to read in the dim light.

"Those are our orders, if you care to inspect them," Marcus added unnecessarily, impatient to get the man moving.

The head of the column turned onto the main street and marched steadily past the unlit building, close to eight hundred soaking feet splashing rhythmically through the heavy slush.

Aulus stared at the dark column of shadows as if stunned. "I was told to expect reinforcements. Nobody said anything about being replaced. The orders I received didn't mention—"

"We need to get these men housed and fed. Immediately," Crispus barked, and gestured over his shoulder with one hand. "I understand you are under strength. Which barracks are empty?"

"Er, none of them, really…" Aulus stumbled backward into the reception hall, where a group of men and women lounged around a large brazier, its charcoal casting a warm, inviting glow. All silently watched the newcomers, their sullenness palpable.

"How many men do you have on strength?" Crispus demanded.

"Er, about…" Aulus frowned and scratched his head "…just over two hundred." He glanced at the men warming themselves by the coals, and one raised a hand with four fingers extended.

"Two hundred and four, I suppose," Aulus said, then, as if offering an excuse, "I'm only temporarily in command."

"So we understand," Marcus said, and tapped the scroll. "The praefectus died two months ago." His curiosity got the better of him. "What was it? Hostiles?"

Aulus shook his head and grunted. "Lockjaw. He stepped on a piece of rusty iron in the stables."

"You're less than half strength. Why is there no barrack room?" Crispus demanded. "I need these men housed, and now."

Shouted orders drifted in from outside as the last of the column filled the street, where the rain had turned once more to a heavy sleet. The troops had been bitching mightily as they waited outside the fort, and Marcus worried how much longer it might be before matters turned ugly.

"The men took advantage of space as it became available. I suppose we'll have to…" Aulus turned to the men lounging by the coals, none of whom had moved. "Rufus, Julius, the rest of you, clear the barracks at the rear of this godless place, and move your men into the others."

Marcus, who was now painfully familiar with the standard layout of a Roman fort, quickly did the math. "We need two-thirds of the space. Clear two barracks at the front, as well. We can share."

Aulus opened his mouth, but Crispus cut him short. "I want my men moved inside as the buildings are cleared. They'll help." He moved angrily toward the door, waving for the men rising to their feet to follow. "Neither I nor they want them standing out in this shit."

The group clattered off into the darkness, leaving Marcus alone with Aulus and the women. There were five, all seemingly native. They edged closer to each other as the men departed, all but one staring at Marcus with undisguised hostility.

"What are the whores doing here?" he asked, deliberately using a word that cut.

"Fiona." Aulus nodded toward the cluster of women, and the one who sat expressionless simply inclined her head and continued to stare. "That is Fiona. My natural wife."

Marcus nodded, not believing the man for a moment. She was by far the more attractive, a small, brown-haired woman with hazel-green eyes and wide, inviting lips that held a natural pout. He stared in turn, deciding the woman was sensuous rather than pretty, with a carnality that could almost be touched. The other side of that blade, he realized with a grim smile, was that it was six months since he'd been with any sort of woman, other than the ones that haunted his mind. Even a hag might look good at this stage.

Out of vanity, he was about to acknowledge the woman in her own tongue: a stilted, accented version acquired six years before from Cartimandua and her people. But the woman spoke first.

"Who is this lump of dung, Aulus?" Her bland gaze did not betray the words.

"He's a tribune. Just some farty junior officer who arrived with the centurio," Aulus replied in the same language. "They're here to take command. There's an entire cohort with them."

"What does that mean? For you? For us?"

"I don't know yet, but I told him you're my woman. What they're going to do I don't know, but this one's an officious little prick."

Marcus held all expression from his face, hiding his pleasure and thankful that, for once, he'd kept his mouth shut. "What's she saying?"

"She asked who you are, and I told her you have come here with the centurio to assume command."

97

"The other women?"

Aulus hesitated and Marcus waited, his expression sardonic. *Right, you bastard, you can pass one off as yours, but what's your excuse for the others?*

"Women from the settlement," Aulus said finally. "Friends of Fiona. They're here because of the inclement weather."

Probably whores after all, Marcus decided. They had passed by the dark huddle of native huts on the road leading up to the fort, which was no surprise. Every outpost had such buildings outside the walls, housing traders, hostlers, craftsmen, taverns, tarts, and whores alike; the army drew them all like horse turds draw flies. The surrounding settlement had seemed rather large, even in the dark, but when he thought on it, that only made sense. They were now beyond the hills, and the land was supposedly low and fertile. It was likely swarming with barbarians. He wondered what, exactly, did lurk beyond the walls.

"The women don't belong in here, you know that," he snapped. "It's why we allow the settlements. They must leave."

Aulus nodded, but countered with, "I would remind you that the commander's family lives inside."

Urs chose that moment to arrive, carrying his master's kit. Aulus looked at the huge slave, decided on the man's status, and ignored him as he waited for a reply. Marcus motioned for the bear-like slave to wait. "But you are no longer commander."

"There are always exceptions, tribune. Your unit is regular legion. I imagine it's here as a reinforcement of convenience. This is a post for auxiliary cavalry and infantry. Once permanent replacements start to filter in from—"

Marcus lifted a hand to silence the man, one eye on the woman. Space would be crowded in the barracks, and other officers would likely be sleeping inside the residence. Eavesdropping on Aulus and his woman as they spoke could be useful, and if not, certainly entertaining. And besides—what was her name? Fiona? Fiona was not exactly a crone.

"Here's the way it will be," Marcus said briskly. "You will, of course, remain in command of your own auxiliary troops. Since none of us has, uh, family, you will maintain whatever room you now occupy with your woman. Urs…" He turned to the Briton. "Find me some decent quarters, the best that's left. And I'm hungry. I imagine the senior centurio is, too."

Urs plodded off. While Aulus spoke to the woman, Marcus shed his cloak and wandered over to the coals on the pretence of warming his hands, his ears on their words.

"The others will have to return to their homes. You may remain," Aulus finished, his voice low and apologetic.

So they're all living here. That sort of thing was near the top of the army's shit list. Yet it also meant the Eighth's arrival would thoroughly piss off a good number of senior rankers, particularly the cavalry, who fancied they were the gods' gift to the empire at the best of times. They'd be losing their quarters, their harlots, and who knew how much time idling about the fort, buggering the bull. Tomorrow would not find a happy band of barbarian auxiliaries.

"Shit," the woman said, in a sharp, loud voice that invited comment.

"Something wrong?" Marcus asked Aulus, assuming a look of innocence. "Isn't that their word for 'shit'?"

"She is naturally not happy with the new arrangements. Women do not like change. I'm explaining the facts."

"Fiona," Marcus said, curious. "Is she local, or from somewhere else?"

"She's Carveti. All the women are."

"He mentioned my name," the woman said. "What did he ask?"

"If you were from around here, or somewhere else."

"Listen to him!" she sneered, confident in her own language. "He throws the other women out, then asks about me. How long do you think it will be before he's sniffing around when you're not here?"

Aulus ignored the comment, though his jaw tightened. Marcus fought to keep his face a blank, and not shake his head. *Women! Troublemakers all. Just ask Father, curse him. Even now the man can't think straight...*

But this one, he realized soberly, would bear watching—in more ways than one.

99

Dawn came covered by a thick blanket of cloud that rolled ominously in from the north. The sleet had stopped, but an icy rain drummed steadily on the long rows of buildings crammed inside the fort, muddying the streets and the side lanes. Crispus had risen early, as had Aulus, and with nothing more than a measure of hot, watered wine in his belly, Marcus joined them both as they began their inspection.

The fort sat on a rise, well back from the estuary. It was apparent, from the surrounding countryside, that Luguvalium had seen little of Rome during the past fifteen years. The low, weed-covered remains of an abandoned marching camp gave evidence of former visits, as did one farther to the west, close by the shore. On a fair day, Crispus informed Marcus after hearing it from one of the garrison's decurios, Luguvalium could actually be pleasing to the eye. The fort was only six years old, and blessed with a magnificent view from the north gate that stretched almost to the *Hibernicus* Sea.

Marcus didn't give two *quadrans*. It was the northernmost outpost in Britannia, and no doubt farther from Rome than any other outpost in their entire empire. Why Cerialis had placed it there and left it manned was a mystery. It lay at the end of a road to nowhere that ran through endless hills teeming with barbarians before falling away to where it met the *Ituna* estuary. Which, Marcus grudgingly admitted, was likely the reason the place had been built: ready sea access to a site strategically placed at the northern tip of Carvetii and Brigante territory. And, he supposed, some godless fort, somewhere in the empire, had to be blessed with the dubious honour of being farthest from Rome. He just wished it wasn't the one to which he'd been posted.

Marcus quickly realized the job that lay ahead would likely prove worse than building one of Agricola's forts: repairing one of the fool things. With the exception of the granaries, a couple of storehouses, and the commander's residence, every building seemed to have sprung leaks. At least Aulus had some sense of priority in keeping the grain free of moisture, Marcus reasoned, but the men living in barracks could have been ordered to at least keep their own nests dry. The problem was the green lumber used to build the fort—a lot of it had warped even though nailed in place. Yet, except for a few major gaps, most of it was readily fixable.

The walls of the fort itself were not in bad shape either, but then, they were nearly new. The footings had been set hastily and without protection; perhaps a decent supply of tar had not been available. Even so, someone should see to it, for the first sign of rot was showing where the timbers met the wet soil. Treating it could still add years of use, but it would be a bitch to do. And while perhaps a few did need replacing, it was the slope of the ramparts that required immediate attention. They were eroding under repeated and heavy rains, and if they were not shored up and returfed, the palisades could well be undermined, particularly on the north side.

"How did it fall into such a state?" Crispus demanded as the three made their way back to the headquarters building.

"We're a cavalry unit, not engineers," Aulus mumbled.

"No soldier needs to live in a windblown barn," Crispus replied.

"What about the last commander?" Marcus prompted when there was no response.

Aulus sighed, as if resigned to the telling. "Gentlemen, Commander Secundus was not the problem. Maybe a small part of it, but not the real problem. It's Luguvalium itself. This place is the bum hole of the empire. We haven't been close to full strength since the fort was built, and this summer we were further depleted when Agricola skinned us for his campaign in the west. There's no spirit left, only fear."

"Spirit is found in leadership," Crispus growled.

"Fear! Ha!" Marcus echoed contemptuously, but he glanced backward at the *Praetorian Gate*, a shiver running up his spine. Sitting in this place for months on end, with only a few hundred men, would give anyone the shivers, he supposed. Why the governor continued to garrison the place was beyond him. Perhaps it was simply the usual bureaucracy of inertia: on the rolls, completely forgotten until a full status review was made; and no status review had been made, because there it sat, on the rolls, completely forgotten... Marcus shook his head.

"My men aren't afraid of a fight," Aulus protested. "There simply hasn't been one. Anyway, our job's just to keep a watch on what's happening out there, and we're doing that."

"What kind of trouble have you had?" Crispus asked. They had arrived at the headquarters building; each man stamped his feet as he passed through the open portal into the forecourt. "Casualties? What have you been sustaining?"

Aulus dropped his eyes, and sounded vague. "Not too many, so far. Sick, mostly."

"The casualties. How many?" Marcus persisted.

"Very few from the enemy, actually," Aulus finally answered, but seemed insistent on changing the subject. "What do you intend, then, other than renovating the fort?"

Marcus was not letting it go. "How much is very few? Or do we have to look up the reports?"

Aulus threw his hands up in surrender. "We've been quite lucky, really. Careful, I suppose. There haven't been any to speak of."

"Where have you been sending your people when you patrol?" Crispus asked, at the same time glancing at Marcus with one eyebrow raised.

"Mainly the hills to the south, but also east along the valley and up in the higher land to the east. There's not really been much activity."

"And the north?"

Aulus led the way into the huge cross hall and gave his cloak to a clerk who came running over to greet the three men. There seemed to be a good deal of bodies about the large hall, including more than a few decurios, all trying to look busy. Marcus cynically wondered how many had been there yesterday.

"We don't have the men to maintain patrols to the north," Aulus replied. "We spend most of our time in the hills. As I said, there isn't much barbarian activity, but that's where we find it."

No barbarian activity? Marcus brooded on the words as he rode out the next morning with a solemn Crispus, to gain an appreciation of the countryside. According to word from Deva, there was a growing number of barbarian hostiles, some in large bands, and all of them fermenting trouble throughout the north. They had seen part of it themselves at Galava, when a disciplined cavalry unit had crashed through the camp with infuriating impunity. While no actual battles had been fought before or since, raids and costly ambushes were on the rise. Yet Aulus Clemens had seen nothing!

"The man is malingering," Crispus remarked later, his voice firm.

"And that's the very least of it."

The two rode at the head of a small troop of their own cavalry, passing at a slow walk through the cluttered native settlement huddled outside the walls. There were scores of huts and hovels close by, and most of the inhabitants appeared to be women and children, poorly dressed but well fed, and clearly comfortable in the proximity of soldiers.

Farther out, where the terrain sloped down to the estuary, the land was farmed. Small holdings dotted the countryside, their round, conical roofs sitting like toadstools in the open spaces where the soil had been cleared. The trees were already on the turn, and Marcus realized it wouldn't be long before the leaf cover was completely gone. Winter was not far off.

"What do you mean, the least of it?" he asked as Crispus's words registered.

"I think he may have struck his own truce with the barbarians. You know the sort of thing: don't bother me and I won't bother you."

"Think so?" Marcus asked, and thoughtfully pursed his lips. Until something was really happening, such as Agricola moving north with a full army, such an arrangement did not seem totally unreasonable. Aulus was right in one thing: this place was the butt end of nowhere. But Crispus clearly expected him to say something different, and he did. "Do you think we can catch him at it?"

Crispus nodded. "Unless something arises in the meantime, I'd say give it a week or two for the man to get used to us, then we'll see. Until then, there's much to do. We need lumber. Aulus said there's a logging camp in the forest, a few miles to the south. We'll reactivate it, and keep the men occupied."

The two original cavalry squadrons attached to the Eighth Cohort were Vangiones from Germania, and these Crispus kept apart from the fort's regular cavalry. They were hard, violent-looking men who owed their loyalty to the troop's senior decurio, a man named Flavius, or simply "Bear." Both squadrons were under strength, but some minor shuffling following the losses at Galava left each with just over twenty men.

Marcus and Crispus, mutually it seemed, decided to accept Aulus's decision to patrol only southward, and dispatched their own riders to the northeast, following the course of a wide river that drained into the estuary. A kind of harmony fell over the fort, and as if to reinforce it, the weather turned fair. Patrols were sent out regularly, and a small fortified camp was set up about three miles away for the cutting and sawing of lumber. Not long after, renovations started on the fort.

In the frequent orders groups, Aulus soon made it apparent that all barbarian activity lay only to the northeast. It could only be there, Marcus snidely remarked to Crispus, because their own men were the only ones to encounter any. The pair stood on the south rampart watching another of Aulus's squadrons depart for the southern hills.

"It's only over there," Marcus pointed vaguely inland to the north, "that we find hostile barbarians on the move. Our men are being sniped at, Crispus. Two were wounded in the past week. The tribes are surly and sullen. They'd stab you in the back and rip out your liver, given half a chance. While over there," he pointed to where the patrol closed on the thick forest that marked the beginning of the great hills, "they might be patrolling the Pompeii docks."

"Patience, young tribune," Crispus muttered, "patience. If you look at the roster, you'll find Aulus has scheduled himself to lead a patrol two days from now. I think it's time to see what he's really doing, and I trust the Bear to find out."

The Vangione called Bear earned his name not from his size, but from the hair that covered his back, his shoulders, and his arms in a glossy pelt. A twenty-year veteran, he had no difficulty with the strange order; in fact, he seemed to have been expecting it. His patrol, which would consist of both squadrons, would proceed northeast, as normal. From there, he would double back and pick up the trail taken by Aulus. He and his men would follow a good half-day behind, which on the face of it sounded feasible. Aulus was expected to follow standard procedure: always return by a different path, to avoid ambush.

And as to the object of the patrol, Bear merely nodded. It was obvious.

A hand shook Marcus's shoulder not long after midnight and he awoke, his heart pounding. Urs's great, bearded head loomed over his cot, eerie and forbidding in the flickering light of an oil lamp. For a moment he desperately thought of grabbing his sword, then realized that if the big man meant him harm, there was no need to wake him.

"What's the matter?" he hissed.

"The woman," Urs whispered. "She left her room and went into the settlement."

"Damn." Marcus swung his legs onto the floor. He fumbled for his britches, found them, and began tugging them over his feet. "How long ago?"

"About half an hour."

Marcus rose to hike the britches to his waist, but stopped in surprise. "A half-hour? Why are you only telling me now?"

"I only just got back. Here."

One hand plunged downward and again Marcus jumped, but it reappeared with something that at first looked like a sack of onions. But as his eyes focused, he realized it was a man's bearded head, the tongue hanging obscenely over the lower lip.

Marcus shivered, and asked a question that sounded inane even as he voiced it. "Where did you get that?"

"It belonged to the man she met with," Urs said, looking pleased with himself. "A Carveti warrior."

"I see." Marcus was surprised, and suddenly doubtful. "Why would you kill one of your own people?"

Urs snorted his disgust. "I've told you more than once, they are not my people, any more than yours are. Besides, we have not been kind to each other in the past." Then he shrugged. "We also have an agreement, you and I."

Marcus finished tying his britches. "Did you have to kill him? It would have been useful to question him."

"The man was too big to take chances with, even for me," Urs muttered, his tone tinged with disappointment at the criticism. "I thought it important to stop him leaving with what the woman had told him. Anyway, you can ask her just as easily."

"You're right. And good work," Marcus said, resisting the urge to pat the big man on the back. "Where is she?"

"She returned to her quarters."

"Oh." Marcus was reaching for his tunic, and stopped. "Perhaps the poor bugger was meeting her to dip his wick."

"Then there would have been no need to remove him from his head," Urs said patiently. "The woman left before I killed him, and without any wick-dipping. Otherwise, she would not have returned to her quarters so soon, would she?"

The slave stared in such a manner that Marcus half expected the explanation to end with the word "stupid." He shook his head, trying to gather his wits. So why had the two met? The Bear's patrol had left that morning; did the woman have knowledge of its true direction? There was hardly anything else that was of importance. Though how would she know that the …

Urs interrupted Marcus's reasoning. "Would you like to hear what was said?"

The slave asked the question with such smug innocence that Marcus could have strangled him. Or at least died trying. "That would be very nice, Urs," he said, gritting his teeth.

"She has learned that the Bear's patrol will circle back and follow the trail taken by Aulus. So she told him." Urs glanced down at the head, jiggled it, and once more set it down by the cot. "He was to take the information to some other man, but they didn't say who. I took it to you instead."

"For which I am very grateful, Urs," Marcus acknowledged, and mulled over what needed to be done. The woman would have to be taken and questioned, obviously. Perhaps he should inform Crispus, and they could both do it. Yet it was the middle of the night, he rationalized, and the woman was by herself. She was also half his size. And alone. Marcus made up his mind. "I'm going to question her. Keep watch on the door, should I need you."

Urs raised his eyebrows slightly and his lips met in disapproval, but he said nothing more.

There were close on twenty rooms in the building, but Marcus had assigned himself the one next to that occupied by Aulus. He didn't knock, but simply burst inside. The woman sat at the foot of the bed, her hands raised in the act of pulling a pale linen shift over her head. She was completely nude, her ripe figure bathed by the soft glow of the flickering yellow lamps that rested on the side table. Startled, her hands moved the shift to cover her body, but she seemed unafraid.

"What do you want? Aulus will have your balls for—ahhh, shit!" Fiona's voice faded, and she glared as if unsure what to do next.

Marcus smiled grimly at her frustration: the woman thought he didn't understand. For a moment he toyed with the idea of keeping matters that way, but there was no more to be gained in doing so. Besides, he would enjoy her surprise. "What were you doing outside the fort?" he demanded.

The dialect was different, but the words were understood. Fiona's eyes widened with surprise, and her teeth bit down on her bottom lip as she tried to measure how much he knew.

"I visit my friends while Aulus is away, since you won't allow them inside."

"In the middle of the night?"

Marcus walked to the bottom of the bed and folded his arms, staring down at her as he waited on the answer. The woman's eyes showed her struggle as she weighed the options, which he decided were precisely nil. But a solution did occur, and with it a sensuous pout that made her intention so clear he could have laughed.

"I suppose it is the middle of the night," she whispered softly, and the pout grew more pronounced, "but it's lonely with Aulus gone. There was nobody to be found, so I returned." Fiona sighed and put a hand to her forehead, the shift falling as if by accident. She pretended to fumble for it, gazing upward with eyes that were nothing short of wanton.

Marcus found himself staring at the soft, dark nipples and the lush roundness of her breasts, his body responding with a vigour that astounded him. He couldn't remember how long it had been since he'd legitimately satisfied such a craving. Reaching out with one hand, he cupped her chin, his eyes moving to her face. Fiona stared back, smiled, and ran her tongue over her lips, leaving a moist trail that glistened in the lamplight.

Marcus groaned as his breeches threatened to tear. He bent over, his mouth finding hers, delving and probing with his tongue. He felt her hand at his waist, frantically untying the cord, her breath a whimper as she tugged hard, finally pulling his britches to his knees. He kicked them away, and Fiona fell back on the bed, tossing the shift to one side. She moaned, her head moving from side to side in a mist of sleek black hair, her knees bending as she eased herself upward on the bed.

Throbbing, unsure of even containing himself, Marcus fell groaning on top, one hand on her soft, dark mound, his teeth gnawing at her nipples. A finger probed inside to ease the way, and it was as if he'd been suddenly doused by a pail of cold water. The calculating bitch was as dry as a pail of desert sand! The woman's passion was a sham. But his own was not and he entered her anyway, rough and hard, both hands moving upward to clasp her wrists.

Rising on his elbows and gripping her arms, Marcus slowly and methodically eased himself in and out of the woman, his mouth taut and his eyes staring. For a few moments Fiona continued to play the game, groaning and moaning in mock passion, then, with one wild toss of the head, her eyes opened, caught his, and held. He almost laughed as the light dawned.

Each glared at the other, Marcus with an amused, contemptuous smile, she with features twisted by hate. The rhythm of his movement never stopped, and neither did her passion, only it was now fuelled by rage. Kicking, grunting, and spitting venom, Fiona twisted and bucked in a vain attempt to throw him off. Marcus grimaced and held firm, his weight the advantage. He tried delaying the perverse pleasure, but it proved impossible. His shoulders shuddered, and his hips thrust forward in endless, jerking spasms that left him weak and exhausted.

When it was over, both lay unmoving, their faces not a hand's breadth apart.

"Bastard!" Fiona hissed.

"Bitch!"

Marcus fought for breath, his grip still tight on her wrists. He knew the woman was merely biding her time, and had been from the very start—and there could be only one reason. He moved her arm and clutched both wrists with one hand, and with the other reached out and flipped the pillows aside. A small, wood-hilted dagger lay beneath one, the blade unsheathed. Grinning with triumph, Marcus heaved himself up and grasped it, intent on taunting her with its discovery.

The easing of his weight took but a moment, and Fiona seized it. With a vicious jerk of her elbow she pulled one hand free and slid it quickly below Marcus's belly. Her fingers found their mark and she squeezed hard, her teeth clenched tight with the effort. And for good measure, she squeezed again, and might have done so a third time, only everything quickly became a blur.

Marcus roared his pain, twisting away from Fiona and off the bed. Both hands snaked instinctively downward toward his groin, his mind oblivious to the dagger. He rolled on the floor as a scream sounded nearby, barely heard through the blistering roar of fire that raged between his legs. Something moved above him on the bed, but the pain commanded his attention. He looked to his groin and, through the tears, saw a small dagger stuck in his thigh, so close to his testes that the blade might have been intended to remove them.

The scream echoed again, fainter this time, followed by a loud curse. The shriek demanded its own attention despite the pain, as Marcus realized the danger he might be in. He forced his eyes upward to Fiona.

The woman stood naked, not two paces away. A long, thin wound stretched the length of her torso, leaking blood like a sliced throat. The cut started high on her left shoulder, crossed one breast, flared down her belly, and vanished into her pubic hair. The dark crimson fluid formed a glistening, shiny coating over her breasts and her belly, and trickled down over her thighs. Marcus, vaguely aware that the screaming had stopped, wondered how it had all got there. The woman reached down and cautiously touched her breast, bending her head to assess the damage. Then the door burst open.

Urs rushed into the room and stopped dead, his mouth gaping. He glanced first at the woman, her head bent low over her wound, then at Marcus, naked on the floor, his knees spread, hands clutching his scrotum, and a small dagger stuck high on his thigh.

The slave blinked, as if unsure. Fiona did not. Without raising her head, she swung one leg and delivered a bone crushing kick to his groin. Urs lurched forward with a cry of agony, one hand clutching his gonads. A second kick caught him on the nose, and he staggered sideways. Marcus watched through a haze as the woman dodged the slave's grasping hands and disappeared through the doorway. With a force of will he didn't realize was possible, he staggered to his feet and followed. The knife fell to the floor with a clatter.

"You are earning a reputation, young tribune," Crispus growled.

"Not one I particularly want," Marcus muttered gravely.

The pair stood atop one of the two towers built over the gate that faced south, each squinting, the better to see a troop of cavalry emerging from the forest perhaps two miles away. There were about a dozen horses, and none moving fast. Usually, if the horses were not hard used, they had to be reined in as they neared home, for each wanted to toss its head and gallop the last stretch to the stable. These animals were plodding in line, heads held low, their riders hunched over in the saddles.

"I can't remember the last time the Twentieth had a full alarm called by a naked tribune, let alone the cause a naked tart," Crispus continued absently, his eyes narrowing. "I do, however, think it's about ... "

The centurio's voice faded. What might have been amusement moments ago had grown serious. The distant riders were obviously in trouble. One swayed from side to side as if trying to remain in the saddle, and the lead trooper had a body slumped across his mount's rump. Crispus roared down to the gate, "Guard! Sound general alarm. Alert the *medici*. Get a squad here immediately. There are soldiers outside who need help."

"There's only thirteen of them," Marcus murmured as he limped forward and leaned on the parapet. Then the centurio's orders registered, and he turned with the question, "Sound general alarm? If the enemy is out there, those men would be dead by now. Perhaps they've become separated from the others."

"I think it's time to shut down the logging, too," Crispus said as he set his meaty hands alongside those of Marcus, fingers tapping against the wood. "That corpse says different, young tribune. And the general alarm is not for the enemy outside, it's for the enemy inside."

"Huh? Oh, shit … "

"That's right. I want the Eighth turned out in full fighting order before the rest of Aulus's men find they've been abandoned by their friends."

Aulus Licinius Clemens almost certainly knew he wasn't coming back. Only two under-strength squadrons of his cavalry remained inside the fort, along with the infantry detachment, which numbered less than fifty souls. The men were unaware they'd been abandoned, but Crispus, with brutal persuasion, quickly determined that every last one knew what had been going on. The remaining centurio and six decani were seized, along with the two troop decurios and their seconds in command. Each was stripped, whipped, and placed in leg irons until the next contingent arrived from Deva.

Crispus, in the mood he was in, dearly wanted to execute all eleven, but Marcus, with no little persuasion, prevailed. Not because of any personal reluctance, for the men were traitors, even if they were nothing more than pragmatic traitors. It was more a matter of weighing repercussions, for repercussions were matters with which Marcus was quite familiar. A great pile of shit *could* very well run downhill if the eleven were not killed off immediately, but a mighty avalanche could well thunder down if they were executed, and someone on high decided that Marcus Sabinius had overstepped his *nominal* command. Only one of the two choices was retrievable.

The final count of Aulus's remaining men came to just over seventy, and there seemed little choice what to do with them. There was ample space amongst the ranks of the Eighth cohort, and so they were assigned to the dubious mercy of the decani. They would *all* be treated as foot soldiers, cavalry or not; though nobody but the cavalrymen themselves seemed to care.

Before the day was over, they gleaned the full story of the patrol from Bear's surviving troopers, for the hairy decurio was no longer there to tell it. They had been betrayed, ambushed by Aulus himself, who was in turn backed by a disciplined column of barbarian cavalry—probably the same one that had attacked at Galava. The only salvation seemed to be that Aulus had been taken down by the Bear before he too was slain.

The logging site had been built like a small marching camp: a low rampart faced with a ditch, topped by a neat row of peeled and sharpened stakes. Marcus was amazed to see how many trees had been felled and trimmed in less than two weeks, all neatly stacked, bucked to length, and waiting to be sawn. But the attack on the patrol raised a question of security: should the sawing begin as scheduled, should it be postponed until more intelligence was gleaned on the enemy, or should matters rest until further orders were received, which was the soldier's usual answer to any given problem?

After watching Marcus vacillate for the best part of an evening, Crispus resolved the issue. "Tribune, we're here until Agricola marches north, or he finds an auxiliary cohort to replace us. That probably means all winter. We can't skulk around this fort like rabbits hiding in a warren. I would suggest, with all due respect, *sir*, that we bring in the damned logs, and saw them up under the protection of the walls. I don't want to start losing sawyers too."

And *that*, as Marcus knew by now, was what *nominal* command was all about: get it done, tribune. He rode out to the camp the following day with orders to halt the logging. Without a reliable screen of mounted pickets, the men felling the trees were far too vulnerable. The neat stacks would be hauled in, and the camp abandoned.

Nearly all the supply wagons had returned to Deva, so the logs would be skidded the three miles back to the fort. The camp centurio informed Marcus it was probably best anyway, for the skidding was simple. One log, or two if they were small, was hooked to chain traces and dragged in behind each horse. The work was slow, and to Marcus it seemed a huge waste of manpower when he saw the first convoy: a single line of sweating horses, each dragging its load, hemmed in by two full centuries of infantry. But it was, after all, the army, and if a winter-locked garrison had a limitless supply of anything, it was time.

The day was cloudless and Marcus chose to ride over to the camp with Urs, something he did regularly. The pile of logs had dwindled as November began, bringing with it a light fall of snow that made the skidding easier. The logging camp would be abandoned by the end of the week, when the last of the timber had been hauled in.

Though Crispus's civility seemed once more on the rise, the short journey offered a chance to get away from the man's natural irritability. The centurio seemed bent on returning to his old ways, though Marcus was no longer the target of his barbs. Crispus never left the men alone, not for a moment. Starting at dawn, he worked them to the point of exhaustion. If it wasn't the logging or the endless repairs on the fort, he was pushing them through field drills and battle tactics until every last man, himself included, was ready to drop in his tracks. Marcus shook his head as he thought on it; he couldn't understand the man.

The well-worn path to the camp was open for the first two miles, and he soon met up with a train of horses closing in on the fort. The long column now made greater speed with the snow, the heavy logs sliding easily over the icy cover. The men were in good spirits, their breath steamy in the nippy air, and each one ready with the banter as Marcus and Urs passed. Armed drivers drove each horse, and solid ranks of soldiers marched alongside, shields and spears ready. It was all very impressive, yet Marcus wondered, not for the first time, if it was necessary. There had been no sign of hostiles since the shattered patrol had limped back to the fort.

The trees began to close in a mile from the camp, and the final half-mile followed a winding path through dense forest. The trail had been cleared back for a good fifty paces on either side, which offered some protection from surprise. Marcus and Urs had ridden less than halfway when the slave reined in his horse, calling for caution.

"What's wrong?" Marcus turned in the saddle.

Urs held a hand cupped to one ear, his face puckered in a puzzled frown. "Do you hear that?"

"What?" Marcus listened carefully. The faint echo of voices drifted through the trees—and above it the thin, distant clash of metal.

"Someone is—"

"They're being attacked." Marcus quickly replaced his helmet. The forest seemed suddenly huge and forbidding—and very lonely. There were only two choices: push forward and see what was happening, or turn around and race back for help. The thought crossed his mind to split the difference: send Urs to find out what was going on, while he went for help. But no, that would likely get him in more trouble than he'd ever seen, especially if nothing was—

"Master!" Urs cried.

Marcus pulled back on the reins. "What now?"

"Someone is coming."

Marcus listened carefully, and at first heard nothing but the distant clash of arms through the eerie silence of the forest; then came the steady patter of a single set of feet and, a moment later, heavy panting. With a wave of his hand, he urged Urs toward the cover of the trees, and quickly followed.

They were barely hidden when a lone figure staggered down the trail, gasping for air. One hand clutched the side of his belly. The man belonged to the Eighth: a helmetless soldier, his *lorica* firmly strapped in place, but his shield gone and his only defence a short sword. It was in his right hand, moving steadily up and down like a runner's baton.

When he was sure the man wasn't being followed, Marcus urged his horse forward. The soldier whirled, fright on his face, which quickly faded when he saw who it was.

"Sir," the soldier gasped.

"Are you wounded, man?" Marcus asked, glancing at the hand that clasped the side of the man's lorica. There was no sign of blood.

The soldier's face showed surprise, and his eyes fell downward. His lips curled in a grimace. "No, sir. I'm winded. It's a stitch in my side."

Marcus shook his head in disbelief. "What's going on up there?"

"They hit the camp, sir. Hundreds of them. Mostly on foot."

"How did you escape?"

"I didn't, sir." The soldier glanced down at his feet, his face sheepish. "I was off by myself gathering nuts, sir."

"You were what?"

"Hazelnuts, sir."

"Then the gods must love you!" Marcus said, his eyes moving down the trail toward the camp, then back toward the fort. The soldier looked on, impatient.

"I was on my way for help, sir," he said, and gestured toward the camp. "No one man could be of use back there."

Marcus nodded agreement, and turned his horse toward the fort. "Want to double up, or stay here and hide until we get help?"

The man looked to the dense forest of scrub bush and raised his eyebrows. Then he looked back to the horses, and bit his lip. Urs seemed to understand the dilemma. "If we run into trouble, sir, carrying two could make a sad difference," he suggested.

"Right, then, let's move," Marcus said, and slapped his horse's rump. Without being told, Urs did the same. Behind them the soldier turned and trotted toward the safety of the forest, clearly content to wait things out.

The two horses broke from the forest at a full gallop, both men whipping feverishly to gain speed. Careless of the slush-covered ground, the pair raced toward the low outline of the fort more than two miles away. While in the distance, and off to their left, a column of barbarian cavalry slithered slowly across the silent landscape like a giant centipede.

Marcus drew in his breath, half his mind fighting panic, and the other half trying to gauge the distance of the new threat. It would be a close-run thing. Yet what choice was there, other than to cut and run east, or turn back into the forest? Neither option offered more hope. He drew his sword, and slapped the flat of it against his horse's rump.

The lead barbarians promptly urged their horses to a gallop, riding hard to cross the path back to the fort. The rest of the column stretched out behind as it picked up the pace. Marcus screamed for Urs to keep up, then realized the steady thump of hooves no longer pounded behind him. There was no time to turn and see what had happened to his slave. Marcus leaned low over his horse's neck and again urged the animal forward with the flat of his blade.

Perhaps the first two or three riders might stand a chance of stopping him, Marcus decided as the gap narrowed, and the barbarians spread out. He edged his horse eastward, which he quickly found was not the thing to do. The gap failed to widen, and the distance yet to ride simply grew greater. He pressured his horse back until it was again galloping straight for the fort. The lead barbarian, a good length ahead of the others, seemed more confident with his distance, and angled his horse to meet Marcus as they closed. The man's spear rose, poised ready to throw.

It was sickeningly clear that there was no avoiding the clash. Bracing himself, Marcus jerked the reins savagely to the left. His horse squealed in fright as its hooves slid over the slick ground. Hind legs flailing, seeking purchase, the beast skidded, then just as quickly found its footing and, with a lunge that almost cost Marcus his seat, galloped westward. The spear flew harmlessly past his shoulder.

Marcus found himself racing down the length of the column, the startled faces of a score or more barbarians flashing by on his sword side. Had there been but a squadron, it would have been magnificent. He might have passed them all, turned on the fort, and at least had a fair race to the gates. Instead, farther down the long line of cavalry, riders were breaking rank, preparing to meet him face on.

Marcus closed his eyes and yanked the reins hard to the right. The horse again squealed, and again he felt its haunches sink under his weight. Then the frightened animal lunged forward, and he opened his eyes wide to find a wild, startled face barely a yard away. He thrust blindly with his sword. The blade bit deep into the man's eye, and he was past.

For a wild, dizzy moment Marcus realized he'd crossed through the column and broken free. Elated, he slammed both heels hard against the animal's belly, and glanced over one shoulder. A jam of riders wheeled and swerved in the slick snow, all trying to break free and give chase. He turned forward with a grim smile, which promptly disappeared. A rush of noise and a dark, looming shadow thundered in from his right, and he lashed out blindly with his sword. The weapon jarred as it struck something solid, and the shaft of a spear flashed in front of his eyes. The dark, shapeless mass rammed the side of his horse and he found himself suddenly weightless, spinning helplessly through the air.

"Discipline, dammit, discipline."

The words echoed through Marcus's mind as he fought to regain his senses. Pain stabbed hard at one arm, then at his leg.

Again the voice roared. "Look at you. You snare one lousy Roman, and go wild. You know better than that. Show some order!"

The painful pricking stopped and Marcus lurched to his knees, staring blindly through an icy film of slush at a forest of dancing black shadows. He wiped a sleeve across his face and the shadows solidified into a jostling wall of barbarian cavalry. He was surrounded, ringed in by a circle of horses, each rider holding the sharp end of a spear dangerously close to his throat. A final command rang out, and one by one the spears were raised. The horses edged away, though other riders moved into the gaps left between, merely enlarging the circle. Trembling, Marcus remained kneeling in the centre.

A single barbarian rode forward. "You heard what he said. Order! And once you've done that, one of you will rid us of him. One, and only one. This is not a boar hunt, you blood-crazed pack of fools." The rider's voice was female, and Marcus knew instantly who it was: the woman with the copper-coloured hair.

Her horse wheeled to go, but the first voice countered, its tone clearly annoyed, "For the love of Dagda, he's a tribune. The man is coin to bargain with, a hostage to trade."

"The only good Roman is a dead one," the woman replied, turning back, her spear resting across the pommel of the saddle. She glared across at the man who had spoken: an older, fair-haired barbarian with sandy eyelashes and a heavy, drooping moustache threaded with grey.

"There's no point in killing the poor sod just for the sake of seeing him dead," the man argued.

"I think we know this one, if that's any help." A third rider edged his horse forward, a bearded man, his long hair tied back with a leather thong. He was dressed as if out for nothing more than a ride: wool tunic and pants, leather jerkin, and an ornately decorated pair of boots. When nobody said a word, he added, "I must say it: this has the grist for a fine story."

Chapter VIIII

Lavatris, A.D. 78

Rhun and Cian were posted to *Cataractonium*, the first outpost north of Isurium. The place held bitter memories. As a boy, Rhun had once lingered a full night and a day by the side of the river here, his heart empty inside his chest, waiting on the return of his father, mother, and sister. The battle itself had taken place in a meadow about ten miles to the south. A man called Bran had lived there, the proud owner of a clutter of pens, a mean hovel nestled in the trees, and a long stretch of grass that, in a good year, could graze a score of horses or twice as many cows. Only his da had returned that day, and only after Rhun had long abandoned hope.

The newly built fort stood close by the bank of a river that for much of the year was simply a broad stream, waist deep and crystal clear as it bubbled down to join the Abus. The east rampart sat on the site of the old village, not far upstream from where the river changed its course; a course that began in the rugged hills to the west, then angled south seeking the lowlands of the eastern plain. The village had been destroyed after the battle, the locations of the crude round huts marked by nothing more than dark circles of ash. What had once stood there was no more than a memory, best pushed aside.

The two squadrons ran their patrols exclusively in the hills and valleys to the northwest. Sometimes they paired up, and other times Rhun might ride one path and Cian another. The tasking set by the legate quickly formed its own boring pattern, with little satisfaction to be found except in the ride itself. Or, of course, those times when Criff came with them.

The bard often rode with the patrols that summer, and Rhun encouraged him. The official reason was that his presence helped break the barrier between Rome and the tribesmen, but that was just an excuse. When the weather was fair, riding the hills and dales was in itself enough to give pleasure; but when Criff rode along, every crag and cranny held a name, and for every tor and tarn there was a story. The lush, green vales were in many ways much the same, for every one was home to a sheltered, bubbling stream that tumbled along the valley floor in search of the Abus. Yet each, in its way, was unique, hiding roaring falls, sheltered ponds, granite crags, and scars. While off to the west, crowning it all, lay the treeless, wind-swept hills of the high country.

It was there, on many a warm day, with a steady breeze blowing hard against the skin, that Rhun's bittersweet memories of a former life ached deepest in his heart. Which was the oddest feeling of all. For as a child, other than the brief time his home was at Stannick, he'd never left the village at Ebor.

But Rhun found nothing of the bittersweet in the tribesmen who lived there. He was shocked, for once again they were not his people, not the people he thought he remembered. And when he spoke of it to Criff, the bard simply smiled, shrugged, and listened.

In July the two squadrons transferred to a fort at *Lavatris*, a small stronghold still under construction. It lay deeper in the hills than any other under the legate's command, forming one more link in the chain of outposts that would soon straddle Brigantia. The fort lay close to Stannick, but Rhun felt no desire to see the ruined fortress.

The patrols from Lavatris took them deeper through the high country, and into the tall hills and craggy slopes his own people called mountains. Here there were no forests, and few trees to be found, only wide, barren spaces that rolled across the roof of Brigantia under a windblown blanket of coarse grass and scraggly shrubs. This was where the tribe's land fell away to the northwest, and merged with that of its cousins, the Carvetii; and it was here that Rhun found his proud memories to be in the starkest contrast to what he saw.

In the sharp ravines and the small, hidden glens dwelt people who might well have resided in caves, their tiny round huts built of weed-caulked stone or mudded willow offering no better shelter. They wore clothes of poorly woven wool, or crudely tanned skins, and their dialects were, for the most part, beyond understanding. The revelation distressed him. Some of these people had sent warriors who, he proudly remembered, had marched south on Isurium with Venutius's army. Yet, if he dug deeper into his memory, they were the ones Cian and his da had casually called "head-hacking hill climbers."

Rhun had already found disappointment with his own people at Eboracum. Several of the kin had returned the past few years, and a small cluster of homes had risen on the south side of the river. In the fondest part of his memory, the people of the village had possessed a wit and wisdom that held him spellbound as he listened by the fire pit in his father's lodge. Essa, the house skivvy, had kept him in awe with her wit, or her way with the plants and herbs. Yet now … well, it seemed they had really known nothing; nothing beyond the small, backward world in which they lived.

In early August Rhun and Cian shifted tactics, mainly because the hills were proving too harsh for the horses. They agreed to run the two squadrons as one, patrolling both at two-thirds strength, which left about twenty men behind to rest. The change worked remarkably well. Rhun and Turren would alternate with Cian and Luga, which suited them all; and Criff, who seemed to have nothing better to do, often rode out with both.

There were two taskings: keep track of barbarian movement, and ferret out weapons and contraband. There was little of the latter, for the thatches had long since been cleared, and most of the freemen and warriors who were likely to be armed were nowhere to be found. But if they discovered a cache, neither Rhun nor Cian punished. They took the arms, confiscated all metal, and skimmed supplies by order of the *procurator*, but much of it they left in place, especially the food and the seed. And always, where possible, they avoided outright confrontation.

Cian was particularly quick with his tongue, which had always been a source of trouble; but in the hills, Rhun found it useful in softening the harshness of their orders. Even so, as the patrols moved farther north and east, the hostility grew. They were often forced to rein in their own men as they faced cursing, spitting, axe-swinging tribesmen; tribesmen who might later take aim from behind the nearest boulder. And in fairness, Rhun found times when he too could cheerfully have drawn his own sword, ready to kill and maim.

On the far side of the highest hills, where the grass grew coarse and the trees were scarce in the valleys, Rhun and Cian stumbled upon a familiar face. Turren had been nursing a high fever when they were ready to leave the fort, so Cian had ridden along, in the company of his shadow, Luga. A single trail led downward at a place where two wide, twisting ravines converged to form a single valley. Rhun was leading, and broke free of the sparse forest above a small farmstead, almost hidden where it nestled between the two streams that tumbled from the ravines. A large circular hut dominated the tiny cluster of buildings, its stone walls rising over half a man's height and its conical roof, a greyish-brown crust, rising perhaps twice as tall.

To keep whatever surprise there was, Rhun pushed his horse to a steady lope, following the nearest stream; Criff and Cian rode up alongside. As they drew level with the hut, they saw a flurry of movement on the other side. Rhun yelled for the rest of the squadron to close up and they burst past the farmstead and into a clearing. Off to one side, between the two streams, were twenty or thirty barbarian warriors and a gaggle of women and children.

"I think the poor buggers were eating," Rhun called out as he turned his horse to face the panicked barbarians, his three dozen disciplined troopers forming up behind.

"So what's the strategy here?" Cian asked, his face an enormous grin. "We give them a lecture on pickets, or sit back and watch them die of embarrassment?"

"Let's just go over and thump sense into them," Luga grunted.

The women and children had broken away, and were running across the farthest stream to the hoped-for safety of the trees beyond. Two warriors, one almost as wide as he was tall, stumbled toward a pair of chariots standing empty in the shade of a single tree. The dozen or so horsemen amongst them seemed to be having less luck. Their ponies

121

grazed loose a good hundred paces away, and the animals trotted off as their riders ran to catch them. Those men who were on foot simply looked flustered as they fumbled for whatever weapon they could lay hands on. Only one bolted, a tall, lithe fellow who followed the women, leaping over the rocks as nimbly as a deer.

"This is why I ride with you." Criff leaned back in his saddle, grinning from ear to ear. "This has the grist of *many* a good tale."

The chariot drivers gained their carts and wheeled about, each plucking a spear from the side rack. The would-be riders, except for two who had managed to claim their mounts, fell back to join the others waiting on foot. The small band shuffled back until they were bunched under the shade of the tree, then stood staring nervously at the forbidding ranks of cavalry.

"They don't seem keen to attack," Rhun said dryly.

The two chariot drivers manoeuvred their carts in front as if in protection, and gamely hefted their spears, pointing and jabbing at the two ranks of horsemen. Several others also waved weapons and jeered, but it was all half-hearted.

"What they need is a good, lusty druid to get their piss boiling," Cian suggested.

"What they should do is just piss off," Luga growled.

"I suppose, but *we* can't stand here all day," Rhun said, his voice almost a sigh. He set his spear crossways on his saddle and edged forward. "I want to talk to the fools, not kill them."

Even as he spoke, it struck Rhun that he was speaking of his own people. The narrow gap that kept them apart, sympathetic though it might be, was growing wider than he'd realized. Raising one hand as a caution, he urged his horse into the stream, its iron shoes clattering loud on the loose rocks. Cian and Criff kept pace.

Halfway across, his uncle grabbed Rhun's arm. "I'll be a swine's sister," Cian muttered, then roared at the top of his voice, "Hey, you—Dag!"

The broad, stocky man in the chariot stopped waving his spear and raised one hand as a shade against the sun. Dag was clearly puzzled, for he turned and spoke to the man next to him, who simply shrugged.

Cian kneed his horse forward until it was on the far bank of the stream, and removed his helmet. "Dag, you useless tit. I'll wager five *sestertii* to your one that those three lumps of dog meat can't haul your fat arse around that tree faster than your skinny friend." He pointed to a tall fir tree that stood at the end of a long stretch of pasture beyond the farmstead. The stout charioteer, clearly baffled, again turned to the man in the second cart. Soon the pair were arguing. "Or don't you have the nerve?" Cian taunted.

Rhun looked on, amused. He could imagine what the men were saying. Likely prominent were "Don't be a stupid idiot" and "What else do you suggest, arsehole?" The beefy one solved the problem by wheeling his cart to face the distant tree and gesturing wildly to the second driver, who finally moved his rig alongside. When they were neck and neck, each one looked over his shoulder toward Cian.

"Hey, it takes their mind off anything stupid," Cian muttered as he saw Rhun's questioning look, then raised his spear high, and just as quickly jerked it down again.

"And adds a certain glory to the story," Criff said, and grinned.

Whips cracked and the ponies, three to each cart, took off like rabbits, two dozen hooves churning the dust as they careened full tilt down the clearing. The carts bounced dangerously behind, slewing wildly sideways as the wheels struck hidden ruts or half-buried stones. The pair hurtled over the stubbled pasture in what seemed to be an all or nothing grudge race. But as the two chariots slowed to circle the tall fir, it was readily apparent that the outcome was not at all in doubt.

Dag, almost imperceptibly, held his team back as they neared the tree, reining his cart tight on the inside. The other man took the turn wide, his chariot edging out far more than warranted for the speed they travelled. Seizing the advantage, Dag steered his ponies close against the tree's trunk, so close that one wheel bounced over the roots. His team shot out the other side ahead of his opponent, and both men were soon whipping their way back to the farmstead. Dag kept glancing over one shoulder, and Rhun suspected it was to be sure the second chariot remained decently close.

The pair crossed the imaginary start line and Dag circled his ponies, drawing them to a halt in front of Cian. The other driver prudently rejoined the other warriors, which Rhun was glad to see, for

Dag would be less constrained in his speech.

"Nooo! Cian! It can't be. You got killed at Bran's..."

Rhun chuckled to himself as the heavyset chariot driver finally recognized the source of his torment. With Criff alongside, he kneed his horse across the stream, his face set in a deliberate scowl.

"You cheated," Cian replied, his tone amiable enough.

Dag shrugged. He was a heavily jowled man with great black moustaches and bushy eyebrows. A set of nose hairs hung from his nostrils like tusks, and his grin opened on a set of yellow, broken teeth. *A maiden's nightmare*, Rhun thought, and waited for a whining protest, but it was not forthcoming.

"I had to," Dag said. "I don't have any money."

"I don't either," Cian said and turned around, fumbling with the pack behind his saddle. "But I do have this."

He tossed a folding metal mess plate that was standard issue. It was something easily replaced, yet Dag would find use for it. It would be there long after any five sestertii, even if he could have paid it.

"It's been a long time, Dag," Rhun said, vaguely recalling the name. The man had filled a place behind him and his father in the long column that had clashed with the Romans at Bran's beck. The memory grew firmer: the big man had been driving a chariot, even then.

"Do I know you?" Dag asked.

Rhun ignored the question. "You know of Cethen, son of Corr, both of the Eburii. I need to know how he fares."

Dag's face became guarded, and he looked helplessly to Cian, hands spread in appeal, as if expecting help. Cian's gaze seemed to be absorbed by the small band of barbarians standing nervously on the far side of the clearing.

"I don't know any such man," Dag finally said.

"The woman called Morallta. I suppose you don't know her either?"

Dag smiled ingratiatingly and shook his head.

"Then if you don't know two of the greatest leaders of your own people, you must surely be a band of thieves, for there is no other reason to travel as you do," Rhun said, and turned to Cian. "You know this man. Will it offend you if I treat him as a thief?"

Cian's face assumed an expression of hurt. "Offend, no. Disappoint? Yes. Dag, how could you fall so low?"

"I'm not a thief! I'm a-a—aaaagh!" Dag fell silent, cornered by his conundrum.

Rhun smiled. "So, how does Cethen fare?"

Dag glanced over his shoulder, and Rhun's smile widened. It was as he suspected: as long as the others cannot hear …

"Cethen fares well." Dag scowled, waiting for the next question that must surely come.

"Tell me something, so I know you don't lie."

Dag's dark features pulled into a frown as he puzzled over the question, and he glanced again at Cian. Rhun could almost hear the man's reasoning, or perhaps it was his rationalizing: Cethen's brother is with them, it cannot be harmful.

"He's in the hills of Cumbria."

"And Morallta? Is she with him?"

"Of course."

"And how many warriors are with them?"

"I can't tell you that," Dag blurted, then quickly added, "because I don't know. Honest."

"Are you able to reach him? Talk to him?"

Dag glanced uncertainly at the two ranks of cavalry, and gulped. Both Rhun and Cian smiled, aware of the man's dilemma. He obviously knew of Cethen and where he was, but was it safer to admit it, or best to deny? His gaze turned reluctantly to Cian and Criff, both of whom nodded their approval, and Dag found himself doing the same. "Yes."

Rhun leaned back in his saddle, satisfied. He reached into his pack and withdrew a small leather-wrapped bundle. He'd been carrying the package for more than a month. "We have a message for him. Tell him his oldest son would meet with him."

Dag's shoulders slumped, the wind leaving him in a sigh of relief. He squinted into Rhun's face. "You! You're … "

"Rhun."

Dag gestured to the chain mail armour and the patterned shield. "Are you really … ?"

Rhun nodded. "Dag, do you know where the fort is at Lavatris?"

"Which one is that? The things are popping up like pig pens."

"It's the newest one. Past where the land slopes north to the river, a good day's ride toward the east. If Father wants to talk, tell him to send a message there."

Rhun leaned over to pass the bundle to Dag, but Criff suddenly spoke. "You should have told me. I'll take it."

"You?" Rhun and Cian spoke together.

"I've nothing better to do, and Cethen knows me. And there are a few others with him, I'm sure, that I'd like to see again. And I'm sure they'd be pleased to see me. It will all have the makings of—"

"A good story," Rhun finished.

"Hey, Dag," Cian spoke up, his eyes glinting with amusement. "I see you were getting down to a meal. Do you mind if we join you?"

Rhun chuckled. The look on Dag's face was beyond price. The man glanced wildly over one shoulder at the others, all waiting nervously by the edge of the stream. He mumbled that perhaps everyone was now finished eating.

Two months passed, and Samhain was over. As winter drew its first warning breath, Rhun and Cian began running their own squadrons again, alternating with each other as the tribesmen cut back on their raiding. There was snow on the high ridges of the central hills by mid November, but when Rhun's patrol returned to Lavatris, they did so in a driving rain. No sensible Briton, he decided, would be caught outside in such conditions; and as his horse plodded once more into the shelter of the fort, he wondered at the logic of his own troops being out there as well.

Once the horses had been stabled, groomed, and fed, he and Turren made their way to their respective quarters, Rhun's yet another set of small rooms at the end of a barracks block assigned to his squadron. Dry clothes, a fire, and something warm stood high on his list of needs; a jug of spiced wine, perhaps, or a scalding mug of mead. He opened the door expecting to find the usual cold, Spartan interior, and was surprised to be greeted by a glowing light and a rush of warm air.

"Saw you ride in," Cian said cheerfully. He was sprawled on a chair clutching a steaming mug of something that looked inviting. Rhun had no eye for it, though, for a young boy sat close by, on the only other chair. The lad stood as Rhun closed the door and shed his cloak, stamping his feet to get the warmth into them.

"His name is Bryn, and all he's willing to say is that he wants to talk to you," Cian offered.

"I see." Rhun took a closer look, and found the lad's face vaguely familiar. His tousled hair was fair, with a tinge of copper. He had blue eyes and his boyish features, which had an impishness about them, were sprinkled with a faint mask of freckles.

"Are you Rhun, son of Cethen Lamh-fada?" Bryn asked solemnly.

"Yes, I am," he replied, equally solemn.

"Then I'm supposed to give you this." A hand disappeared inside his tunic, and came out with a cloth-wrapped package similar to the one given Criff and Dag two months before. It didn't need opening for Rhun to know what it was.

"How did you get here?" Rhun asked.

The small features wrinkled in surprise, as if the answer was obvious. "On my horse."

"Yeah, they've got them too." Cian grinned. "Four legs, head one end, tail the other."

"I realize that," Rhun said impatiently, "but he didn't ride from wherever he came from all by himself, did he?"

Bryn supplied the answer. "Some of my father's men brought me until I could see the fort. I was told to ride in the gate and ask for you. If you weren't here, I was to give them the other package. Which I did. And then he came." He pointed to Cian.

"And he's been in safe hands ever since," Cian said. "For two days now."

Rhun squatted in front of the boy as he began unwrapping the soft, folded leather. "So," he began, his fingers fumbling with the tie, "do you know the man called Cethen, lad?"

Bryn giggled. "Of course I do!"

"Oh?" Rhun peered into the blue eyes, and the answer dawned even as he mouthed the question. "Why do you say of course, boy?"

"Because he's my da!" Bryn cried impatiently, his tone clearly conveying a low opinion of Rhun's intellect.

"He's—!" Rhun turned to Cian, his mouth open, speechless.

"Say hello to your brother, Rhun," Cian said.

"He had another son!" Rhun said. Then, a moment later, as the importance of the boy being there struck home: "He sent his son!"

"Your da's letting you know he trusts us," Cian murmured, "and that you can trust him."

Chapter X

Cumbria, A.D. 78

If it had been left to the bitch with the copper-coloured hair, the one who thought she was the gods' "great fury," he wouldn't have lived long enough to blink an eye. Though perhaps not, Marcus decided as he thought more on it; she'd have likely stretched his death over a week, and enjoyed every last moment. In the end, though, he still would have been just as dead.

During the two and a half days the barbarians journeyed into the hills, Marcus found that Criff and the man called Cethen seemed the only two interested in keeping him alive. Another man joined them the second day, a short, hard looking ape named Dermat, with dark, greying hair and a foul disposition. Yet the churl had a kernel of common sense. When his counsel was sought, he glared at Marcus, who sat tired and bleeding in the saddle, both hands tied to the pommel. With a hog-like grunt of disgust, the barbarian muttered, "Nowt to be gained by killing the sad-assed prick."

That seemed the end of it, and it was apparent to Marcus that the man's word carried more weight with the red-haired bitch than that of the man Cethen. But when they came to a barbarian hill fort, set high at the end of a lake where two narrow valleys offered paths of escape, the conflict was revived and redoubled.

By then, Marcus was literally at the end of his tether. He'd shivered two sleepless nights on the trail with no cloak or cover, and with both hands tied behind him with a rope that trailed like a tail. Everyone delighted in pulling on it, often yanking him off his feet. Only the man called Criff thought to feed him, though the one named Cethen watched and nodded approval the first time it was done. And as to other needs, he'd fouled himself the second day, and lost count of the times he'd been forced to piss himself, either in the saddle, or wherever he made his bed. There had been no choice, yet the barbarians blamed him anyway, jeering or baiting as the whim took them.

He was beaten, punched, pushed, and spat upon, at every hovel or farmstead where they halted. The women and their brats were the worst, their taunting deliberate and malicious. The barbarian cavalry were less vicious, doing no more than what was expected. Which, if Marcus was honest with himself, was the way it was, for he'd seen enough of it in Rome when prisoners were paraded, or criminals trudged their miserable way to the arena. None of which changed the fact that he was battered and bruised, and stank worse than a pig.

The largest structure in the hill fort was a lodge built of upright timbers closed in by mud and wattle, and topped by a barn-like roof of log beams. Inside, ox-hide partitions ran down one wall of the building and curtained one end, but the rest was a large, open room. A fire blazed in the centre, the smoke drifting upward through a crude hole cut high in the roof.

Marcus was flung face first on the dirt floor close by the flames, his hands still tied. He rolled over, shivering and grateful for the warmth after almost three days of bone-chilling cold. He gazed cautiously about the crowded lodge, anxious not to attract attention. Everyone stared at him with obvious contempt.

Then a screeching wail came out of nowhere, and something slammed hard into the small of his back. "He's mine," a voice screamed. "I want the weasel. He's mine."

Another blow struck the base of his spine, then his shoulder, and a loud babble of voices broke out. Marcus tried to roll clear, but that placed him dangerously close to the fire. Blinking tears of pain, he tried focusing on his attacker. When he finally saw her, his belly turned to ice. "Shit!"

"Don't shit me, you whining turd!" Fiona screamed. Now caught up between Criff and Cethen, she struggled to break free, her legs kicking the air and her body heaving. "I have a claim on him. He's mine. I have the right!"

"What gives you the right, woman?" A tall, slim figure moved into view, her features those of a malignant cat. She glanced down at Marcus, lips curled in triumph.

"Look, we went through this before we got here," Cethen cried angrily. "Where's Dermat?"

Marcus was relieved to see the short, stocky man who had settled the problem once before, push his way through the crowd. The feeling of relief didn't last long.

"Calm down, woman," Dermat muttered, and surprisingly, Fiona did exactly that. "What gives you the right?"

Fiona shook her arms free, and made a display of settling the sleeves of her loose woolen gown down along her arms. "He raped me!"

"That's a filthy lie. The bitch sedu—oof!" Another boot struck home.

"He tried to murder me, too. With a knife. Look." Fiona tugged at a tie on the shoulder of her gown, and allowed it to drop to the top of her thighs, revealing a livid scar running the full length of her torso.

An angry murmur rippled through the lodge. Marcus decided it looked a damn sight worse than it was. It was still livid from healing, though most of it would eventually be nothing more than a thin white line. Only in two areas, one upon her breast and the second above her pubic mound, had stitches been necessary. Glancing at the hostile faces, Marcus decided most of them weren't even looking at the woman's scar. They were ogling her tits and her pubes! It was too much to take silently.

"She tried to murder *me*! She—oof!" Marcus tried to wriggle round and face whoever was kicking him. "The bitch took the knife and she—oof!"

"I'd say that gives her the right!" Morallta said, turning to Cethen in triumph.

"He's valuable," Cethen insisted. "Criff says his father's now a legate. If he's killed, we'll regret it."

"We know who the man is, Cethen," Dermat replied sombrely.

"And that the youth could be worth something to us. But look at what he did. The woman has the right."

"But the bitch lies. She—aagh!"

"Let him speak," Cethen said.

"You'd take the words of a Roman over one of our own?" Morallta sneered. "The worm will say anything to save his miserable life."

"And the bitch will say anything to get me kill—aagh," Marcus gasped as yet another boot caught the small of his back.

Cethen sighed and looked at Dermat, who simply shrugged and rolled his eyes. "Maybe so," Cethen said, then turned to the crowd and changed his argument. "But I'm curious. Aren't you? If nothing else, it might be amusing to hear the tale he spins."

"Ah, the tale! The heart of everything," Criff chimed in, his voice eager. "Let's hear the story."

Several voices seemed to agree with the bard, and Marcus quickly spoke again. This time no boot interrupted his words. He talked as fast as he could, leaving nothing out, not even Fiona's mock passion as she writhed on the bed. A patter of laughter rose when he described grasping the knife and the blow to his balls, which died just as quickly as he told of the blur that followed. His words had the plaintive ring of truth as he described rolling on the floor, and his bafflement at Fiona's wounds.

"So, are you going to take the word of a Roman over that of our own?" Morallta demanded again, even before Marcus finished.

"I can vouch for part of his story."

The deep male voice came from the far side of the lodge. Dermat called the man forward, and Marcus was shocked to see Urs elbow his way through the crowd until he stood between Criff and Cethen. The slave was not tied, nor did he appear beaten. Marcus remembered the fading hoofbeats as they both raced toward the fort, and decided that the wretch had chosen to change sides. Or perhaps—and it was a forlorn hope—the man had seen their race was doomed from the start, and simply stayed out of it.

"I can vouch that she had him by the balls." Urs grinned, and Marcus cursed to himself, for the words did nothing to help. The man proved a sight more willing to talk than he'd ever been before. "I burst into the room because the woman screamed. She was standing by the bed as naked as a bairn, and covered with blood." The slave then pointed to Marcus, who groaned as the words spilled from the man's worthless lips. "But him—he was on his back, legs in the air, and both hands clinging to his apples as if they might drop off. She'd crunched him so hard there was water in eyes."

Even Cethen chuckled, joining in the laughter that followed.

"But," the slave continued, his words flowing clear and filled with emotion, as Criff might have spoken them, "but the oddest thing of all was, right here—" he touched Marcus's thigh with his foot, just below his groin "—was an itsy knife, sticking out of his leg like a second pecker! He'd stabbed himself, as well!"

Urs raised both hands, signalling for quiet as everyone again laughed; his face was a parody of seriousness as he finished. "It was not the manner in which my master normally greets me."

"What happened then, idiot?" Dermat asked, clearly annoyed by the slave's flippancy.

Urs placed a hand over his face, fingers spread, and bowed his head as if ashamed. "I'm loath to admit it, but she kicked me in the plums so hard I think they bounced off my backbone. I bent over, and she landed another one right on my nose. See?" He fingers slid down and gently jiggled a bump on the ridge of his nose. "It still hurts. Let me tell you, that woman," he pointed to Fiona, "should be handled carefully."

"Enough of the buffoon," Dermat grunted, clearly not amused. "Which leg did he stick with the knife?"

"The right one," Urs replied firmly, no longer acting the fool.

Dermat bent down. With his own knife, he sliced a long tear in Marcus's britches, his lips curling in distaste as his hands parted the damp cloth. A long, puckered scar was revealed, obviously an old wound; but above it, close by the groin, was a small slash closed by four stitches, the marks still angry with healing.

"He almost saved you the bother, Fiona," a voice called out.

"It bears the man's words out," Dermat said as he climbed to his feet and confronted Fiona, his dark eyes boring into hers. "I'm not saying your words are not true the way you remember, lass, but think hard. Is what he says true for the most of it?"

Fiona's eyes fell, and she licked her lips as if thinking on Dermat's words.

"He could be of value to us," the dark man added.

"Some of it may have been the way he tells it," she finally conceded.

Marcus was fed later that night, but he wasn't untied or given leave to clean up. Soon after, he was tossed into one of the small hide-curtained rooms that lined one side of the lodge, and simply abandoned. There was no cot, only a bundle of what looked to be dirty clothing piled against the wall. Marcus kicked and rolled across the dirt floor and flopped on top, squirming about until the odorous mound formed a snug, comfortable nest. He drifted off to sleep to the sound of loud voices, most of them arguing.

It was well into the night when he awoke, startled by the absolute silence inside the building. It was as if the gods had carried him to another world. Then he saw the dark figure crouched inside the hide curtain, almost hidden behind the tiny flame of a clay lamp. It knelt hardly more than a yard away, quietly staring.

"Who is it?" he asked.

"You stink." Marcus recognized Morallta's hard voice.

"Piss and shit will do that if you're left to wallow in it." Marcus wondered wildly why the woman was there, and his mind could provide only one answer. As if to confirm it, he heard the soft whisper of a dagger sliding from its sheath. A rush of panic filled his veins and he drew back, ready to kick and screech his helplessness. But another voice spoke quietly from the far side of the curtain.

"There's a matter of honour here, Morallta. I will kill to defend him." A second light floated eerily into the room, and Cethen silently crossed the short distance to Morallta, and crouched alongside. A second blade glinted in the wan light of the flames.

"Honour? What sort of honour warrants a single life taken from those who have no honour?" she sneered.

"Your problem is, *you* know nothing of honour," Cethen replied, anger in his voice. "And you show no respect for mine. I owe this man's father a debt, a huge one, even though in turn he owes me debts just as great. But if you want reasons you understand, take this one, for it's true: this youth is of far more value alive. One day, Morallta, young

Bryn's life could rest on it."

"I'd rather see my boy dead than live under Roman rule. He's a Carveti, not a slave," she hissed.

"The boy's Brigante, and I would rather see him live."

Marcus felt the woman stir, and saw Cethen raise his blade.

"You … "

"I have a limit," Cethen growled, "and it has been breached. Do anything to this man and I will strike, though it would wound me deep."

"It is you who goes too far," Morallta snarled.

"I go further," Cethen said, his voice taut, now almost a tremor. "If he is murdered by anyone, I will remove any of my people who would follow, and sue for peace with the Romans. After all these years of hardship, there are many who will follow."

"You saw what he did to Fiona! How can you let that go unavenged? And you speak of honour!"

"Come on," Cethen snapped impatiently, "you know what happened there as well as I. She as much as admitted his words were true. And I'll tell you this, right now if you squeezed my balls like that, the least you'd get is a face full of burning oil."

Morallta's features, barely visible in the glow of the flame, remained etched with anger. "But to be ready to take a blade to me! For your lousy honour!"

"Yes, for my honour. And that alone should be enough!" The tension gradually seemed to ease from his face and he sighed, shaking his head. "But, woman, since you want more, there is also this." One hand reached into the darkness about his belt, and reappeared with a package.

Morallta unwrapped it, staring in puzzlement. Marcus saw it was a bundle of wax writing tablets, the sort used in a headquarters building to save parchment. "What is this?" she demanded.

"Writing. Roman writing."

"I know that, fool. What does it say?"

"Criff tells me that my children, all three, are here in Brigantia." Cethen's voice grew soft. "This writing confirms it. It's from my oldest, Rhun. It appears the legate has taken care of them since Stannick."

"While he was humping your wife."

"And while I was humping you. Sometimes I think…" Cethen sighed and stopped, looking down at the floor.

"Finish it, prick," Morallta sneered. "You think he got the best of the bargain."

Marcus listened to the exchange in silent amazement. First at the depth of the anger between the two, which he'd sensed earlier. Second, and it dawned slowly, at who exactly the man was—the husband of his father's whore. And the fool seemed to have been unaware that his children even lived, let alone who cared for them.

A glimmer of hope filled Marcus's mind. Did this Cethen fellow mean to trade him, get his own children back? How old were they now? The decurio would be of no use. Only the Tuis brat was still young enough to be used as a bargaining…Shit, he'd been adopted! Marcus groaned as another thought crossed his mind. *Would Father's stupid sense of military honour even allow him to think on it?*

"How did you find out about this?" Morallta waved the tablets.

"Criff. After we met up with him and Dag. It was given to him by my oldest, Rhun." Cethen shook his head as if in disbelief. "He's some sort of officer in one of their cavalry units."

"Why didn't you tell me any of this?" Morallta demanded angrily.

"You didn't ask," Cethen replied, equally sharp. "And don't pretend you'd have been any different. Anyway," he shrugged, as if relenting, "I needed time to think."

Marcus could have kicked the man. The fool began by taking a firm stance with the woman, then backed off by offering his excuses. No wonder she had him by the plums. His eyes turned to Morallta, ready for the next outburst, but she seemed lost in thought.

"So that's why you want this pig turd to live," Morallta murmured, as if at last hearing something she could understand. The knife slid back into its sheath, and Marcus breathed easier. "You think he'll kill your own brats in revenge."

"Bollocks!" Cethen snapped, and appeared ready to continue; then he bit down on his lip, his eyes lidded, as if his mind was digesting her words. He sheathed his own blade, and held both hands outward as if helpless. "I can't take that chance, can I?"

Both stood and faced each other, Morallta's face still a reflection of indecision. Finally, she reached up and tugged not too gently on one of his moustaches. "It is sufficient. He won't be harmed. As to the rest, we'll speak on it tomorrow."

Morallta disappeared through the curtain of hides as silently as she had arrived. Cethen stared after her for a moment, shook his head in disgust, then turned his attention to Marcus. "Women!" he muttered, then once again crouched. "The children. Tell me of them."

Marcus couldn't believe it. Here they were, in a stinking hovel somewhere in the western hills of barbaria, and this oaf wanted to talk about his brats. It was incredible; yet what he said next could also mean his life. With a sigh, he turned his mind to what little he could remember of the man's miserable family.

The barbarian Rhun he'd barely met, so there was little to be told there... His mind leapt to the dockside in Gaul. The young cavalry decurio! Of course! The resemblance to Coira, while slight, would be noticeable if they were put side by side. And he had seen him once as a boy, in Rome, before the sullen simpleton was packed off for his schooling.

And as to Coira herself, well, that was as good a place as any to start, though he would have to watch his words. They certainly shared a passion for each other, only his was carnal, and hers was loathing. No, maybe the youngest, Tuis, would be a good place to begin, but without mentioning the adoption—though that likely rankled him more than it would this lout.

"That is good," Cethen murmured much later, when Marcus finished and Cethen's questions had been answered. For the longest time he sat silent, staring into the soft glow of the flickering lamp. Then he stood, murmured, "By the way, you stink," and left.

Marcus eased back against the comfort of his foul bed, mulling over the strange visit. His life seemed a little more secure, at least for the present, and there was always hope that one day he might be traded. Though there was still that copper-haired bitch! She might have the looks, but her mind was as vicious as a cobra's. He was amazed the half-witted fool Cethen could attract such a vixen, and even more amazed that the fool put up with her.

Such antagonism, when he thought on it, he'd seen equalled only by that of his parents, who at least had the sense to divorce and save themselves the agony of speech. These two were like a pair of jackals, tearing at each other.

Their antagonism that night was mild compared to the quarrel—no, Marcus decided, not quarrel; it was damn-near an all-out battle—that occurred a week later, when Morallta learned Cethen had sent their son, Bryn, with a small troop of warriors to arrange a meeting with his brats. By the bearded gods of Greece, the woman had a temper!

Chapter XI

Eboracum, A.D. 78

Rhun had more than once adopted the adage "It is far better to beg forgiveness than to ask permission." But the maxim had its limits. A man can push only so hard with his shield, particularly if he's a mere troop commander. And if that were doubled, and *two* troop commanders traipsed off to the wilds of Cumbria, one to find his father, the other his brother, there would be little hope of absolution. And there was more to it. Cian would also be seeking his daughters. How far did he dare test the legate's patience?

An official request was dispatched to Eboracum.

The reply took a surprisingly short time. It arrived in the form of a full troop of cavalry that rode through the gates of Lavatris less than a week later. The officer in charge was familiar, and at first Rhun simply wondered why the man was there. The primus had also served in Lower Germania and he'd seen him often, but always from a comfortable distance. Which was a good thing. Whatever your rank, it's best not to attract the attention of a primus pilus.

The cheek plates of the helmet did not hide its owner's age. The man was at the top end of his forties, perhaps even over fifty. And Titus Aurelius Urbicus had been glad to return to his old posting at Eboracum, for the transfer had been sought by the legate Sabinius. The request had been based not only on the man's ability, but also his familiarity and luck. Such was the army's way: both men had served at Ebor when Stannick was taken; each trusted the other's competency;

139

and, just as important, each trusted the other's luck. The legate had simply brought in his own man.

Rhun saw the troop ride in and took no further notice, but not a quarter-hour after its arrival, he was summoned to the headquarters building. Puzzled, he clomped into the great cross hall, unsure what waited there. A single figure stood leaning against the east wall, arms crossed. It wore a mail corselet with sleeves to the elbows, britches, a baldric from which hung a long cavalryman's sword, and a pair of finely tanned, fur-lined boots. The face below a mop of short, yellow-blond hair wore an impish grin.

"Before you start bitching, the primus says I'm going." Coira pushed herself away from the wall. "Now take me to see my new brother. I understand you have him here."

The fort commander, a man named Claudius Paulinus, hosted the meal that night, and it proved to be a full-fledged feast. The guests included the primus and almost a dozen senior officers from the fort. Cian was also invited, which pleased him no end; on the other side of that blade, Rhun looked trapped. Coira was there as well, completely at ease, and insisted that Bryn attend the table. The boy should learn, she said emphatically, that there was more to the world than the back hills of Cumbria. The commander's dining room was as good a place to start as any.

As was usual at any mess table, the senior officer controlled the conversation. Those of lesser rank, depending on how much less, contributed only to fill in the gaps. Coira quickly noticed that the single exception was Cian who, as usual, didn't seem to know what the word "rank" meant—at least in military terms.

She listened, satisfied, as the primus rambled on, not only because it was expected of him, but because his words were of interest. She had learned at Eboracum that, once Titus was free of the parade square and out of his uniform, he was as easy to speak to as Gaius. A forbidding, callous icon of Rome's power he might seem to others, but she saw him as a grizzled, grey-haired man with friendly eyes and a rough sense of humour—who happened to be a soldier. Coira smiled as the primus told the story of his first arrival at the Eburii village, his words and eyes directed mainly at Bryn.

"And our legate disappeared. Splash!" Titus chuckled as Coira whispered the translation in the boy's ear. "Nothing was left but a circle of bubbles. He'd fallen in, but we didn't know that. We thought he'd been pushed, for our eyes were on Venutius. We were angry! At his loss, of course, but also at ourselves, and Venutius's perfidy when he jumped from the ship. The man had not broken his own word, but he'd broken your father's word."

Titus leaned forward and plucked a honeyed apple pastry from the table. Munching on the flaky sweet, he continued. "Your father jumped in, fully clothed, and pulled him to the surface. Just like that!" Titus snapped his fingers, releasing a shower of crumbs. "There he was, one arm wrapped around the dock, and the other around Gaius. Then he—" Titus pointed to Cian "—dropped a rope, but your father refused. He beckoned instead to the ship, and we threw one of our own. We hauled Gaius on board, half dead and raving, and as cold as a slab of chilled beef; but of course he recovered, as we all know. I think it was the three gallons of wine we forced down his throat on the way back to Petuaria."

"Why do you think the barbarian did it?" Claudius asked, dutifully filling the brief silence that followed the expected chuckles.

Titus smiled. "I asked him that. I leaned over the ship's rail and called out, 'Why?' All he did was stare at me, then roll over and swim back to shore."

Bryn listened enraptured as Coira translated, but when he heard the question, he answered impatiently, "He did it because he gave his word to the bargain. Da would never go back on that, even with Romans, though they don't always keep theirs."

Coira translated, word for word, unable to keep the amusement from her voice. Titus shook his head and laughed, as did everyone but Rhun, who continued to look uncomfortable. Her twin, unlike her, was ill at ease. Of course, her brother hadn't the benefit of spending the past half-dozen years in a senatorial household. It wasn't that he was overawed—she'd learned that when they met at Camulodunum— he simply retreated into a shell of reserve. She saw a complete change when the primus launched into a matter dealing with yet another fort, this one sited farther into the hills. Now on familiar ground, Rhun suddenly became absorbed.

Coira bit her lip, remembering her first glimpse of her brother that year. His manner had been no different then. She'd been hunting with Vellocatus, a day that in itself had been an adventure. They had returned to Cartimandua's sprawling compound at dusk to learn of Rhun's arrival. It was not her brother who came bounding forward to greet her, though.

Cian had been wild, laughing and teasing, tears in his eyes as he whirled her around in a great circle, despite the fact she was now half a hand taller than him. Rhun had stood silently watching, and when Cian was done bussing her for the tenth time, he moved forward and took her stiffly in his arms. It was a quick, cool embrace, and when he stood back, she had looked into his grey-blue eyes and seen nothing in them but cool appraisal.

Cian had chided him for his aloofness, and her brother simply shrugged and claimed to be tired. Yet later that night, when she'd sought him out in a corner by the fire after the feasting, Rhun was far from tired. He'd had his share of the wine, and she was surprised at how it oiled his tongue. He was flirting with two of Cartimandua's serving girls, and the pair could hardly shut him up. But when *she* tried coaxing him to talk, it was like trying to smelt gold from a lead pig.

Her first comment, that she was pleased the legate had seen fit to send them both to Camulodunum, had been met by sarcasm: "So *you*, at least, don't call him father."

Coira sighed. "No, I don't, but Tuis was young. He needed a father."

"And where was Mother on this?" Rhun didn't sneer, but she decided he might as well have.

"Mother, even today, is technically a slave, Rhun. But neither she nor Gaius act as if she is. I do believe, if she were to ask for it, he would officially free her. In fact I know it, because she told me he offered to let her go at Stannick. But you know our Mam." Coira smiled, slowly shaking her head as if wishing things were different. "There's a stubborn streak in her that won't let her ask a man for anything. She was like that with Da, if you remember. The only difference is that Gaius's stubbornness matches hers."

"So what's that got to do with Tuis?"

"*You* asked where Mother was on this," Coira said patiently. "So I'm telling you. In Rome, Gaius and Tuis grew to be like father and son. Tuis was always underfoot, always around. He'd turn to Gaius when he needed things; and Gaius, in turn, seemed to enjoy having him there. I believe he genuinely loves the boy." Coira shrugged as if to say that was simply the way of it. "So, maybe a year ago, he decided to adopt him. It's commonly done in Rome. He did ask Mother, though he didn't have to." Another shrug. "She's a practical woman, Rhun. An adoption assures Tuis's future, and it makes Gaius happy. What's wrong with that?"

Rhun's expression seemed to imply that something was, but he'd said nothing. One of the house menials edged by with an armful of logs, and threw them on the fire. Neither of them spoke until the man was finished, then Rhun turned his brooding eyes back to his sister. "And you? What do you call him?"

"Gaius. That's his name, Rhun," Coira said, then she displayed a broad smile meant to charm. "Of course, sometimes it's 'arsehole' or 'stubborn bastard,' but only under my breath, and not very often."

"So…"

"I never call him father, which is what you really mean, and why should I? I don't need a new father. I still have the old one somewhere. There's never been a 'feel' that he was gone. But I can tell you this, Rhun. Gaius and our own father may be as different as salt and honey, but they do have one thing between them: when the tar's boiled off the sludge, they're both fair men."

"Fair!" Rhun snorted. "To you and Tuis, maybe!"

"And of course he did nothing for you!"

"Did *to* me, more like," Rhun complained, though Coira saw his eyes shift, and thought perhaps his words lacked conviction. "He might as well have sent me to prison!"

"Yes, I can see that," she snapped. "Look at you. A total mess! Not much of a brother to be proud of, are you: a cavalry officer on his way up if he keeps his bum clean, and a fine-looking one at that—though that's probably the only thing Gaius had nothing to do with. That last time I saw you at Ebor, your hatred was so deep, even Mother couldn't speak to you."

"She wasn't exactly being a—"

"Mother was doing what she had to do!" Coira cried, then glanced guiltily over her shoulder; Elena, sitting alongside Vellocatus, quickly averted her eyes as if she'd been watching. Coira lowered her voice. "You spent three months at Ebor, angry and snarling every day. Something needed to be done. Gaius was stuck there. He was only second in command, and you were a total embarrassment. It was either send you back to Da, or ship you to others who might succeed where he had failed. To be honest," she laughed nervously, trying to make light of it, "you'd been bashed hard on the head at Stannick, and I thought your brain was addled."

"So why didn't she send me back to Da?" Rhun hissed. "He had the right of it."

"I can think of a dozen reasons," Coira said, and began counting on her fingers. "She didn't want you dead; she wanted a better life for you; she couldn't bear to let you go? Or how about: she's your mother, she loves you! Take your choice. If you don't like any of those, I can come up with a few more."

"The place he sent me to—Coira, you have no idea what it was like! Spoiled Roman brats who equate 'barbarian' with 'ignorant pig.' Masters who beat the skin off you if you didn't jump on command. Try learning alongside arrogant, snotty kids who are half your age, and know twice as much. Try fighting every day of the week, just to keep a sense of pride!"

Coira leaned back in her seat and eyed him critically. "It seems they did what Gaius asked, if you ask me. And quite well, too, I would say."

"And where were you and Mother, all this time?" Rhun asked bitterly.

Coira released her pent breath in a long sigh; there was an undercurrent in her brother's words that tugged at her conscience. "We could have seen you when Gaius's brother died—what was it, two years ago? No, closer to three. Gaius was detached to Aquitania at the time. Mother and I did go to the school where you'd been sent, but you'd just been dispatched to another, that offered some sort of military training. You left with what the master called 'a problem of attitude.'"

Coira smiled as she spoke. "Gaius thought it best to wait until matters improved. In fact, he insisted on it."

"Then he could have sent word of some kind," Rhun grumbled, but not with any spirit. "He could have let me know what was taking place. What he was doing."

"He did," Coira said brightly, and with one hand gestured casually around the inside of the huge lodge. "You're here, aren't you? And Cian too. Mother was mostly responsible for that."

Before Rhun could reply, Aelia came by and placed a hand on Coira's shoulder, giving it a gentle squeeze. "Your mother and I will be with Catey, doubtless receiving a lengthy opinion on your relatives." She smiled at Rhun. "I think she likes your uncle in particular. I would guess he's a bit of a rogue." Aelia nodded to them both and left.

Rhun watched her go, his eyes following her every step as she made her way through the small crowd. When she reached the entrance to Cartimandua's quarters, Coira reached out with one foot and kicked him hard on the shin.

"Don't sit there with your mouth hanging open," she'd said. "I'm talking to you."

Coira sighed. Despite his mawkish gaping after Aelia, there was a stiff, unbending side to Rhun. It could be seen in the way he sat listening to Titus, rapt, but stoically keeping his own counsel. She noticed the primus's tone seemed to have changed, though, and forced her attention back to his words.

"So what do we do with the boy?" Titus asked. "Is he a hostage, to be kept here pending your return?"

Rhun shook his head emphatically, and his jaw clenched. "That was not mentioned. Da trusted us with Bryn to bring the message; we must trust him in return."

The primus frowned, then nodded. "I suppose it will serve as a sign of our own goodwill. Tell me, how are we to carry out this meeting?"

Coira saw Rhun's eyes open in surprise at the word "we." She smiled as she saw the trace of a curl at the corners of Titus's mouth.

"Er, I-I'm sorry, I should have brought his reply," Rhun stuttered. "Our numbers are to be no more than ten, other than Bryn, and each will be marked with a red cloth on his arm. We travel west along the trail that links the old marching camps. I know them. We then follow it down the other side of the hills until it meets the Roman road running north. We continue five miles farther, and from there will be led the rest of the way." He looked up at the primus, his eyes unable to hide either his surprise or his disappointment. "You're going too, sir? Isn't that sort of giving them—well, you are, after all, the primus."

"The legate and I discussed the wisdom of any sort of meeting with your father," Titus replied slowly, as if choosing the words carefully. "We decided at first that it might be of some use, then discarded the idea altogether. Then another matter came to light that has caused us to change our minds."

Coira was curious, but the primus said no more, which was fair enough. Like legates, primus piluses did not explain, they simply gave orders. Yet she'd never heard of any such matter, and wondered. She was more interested, however, in tossing her own small barb at her brother. "So who else will make up the ten?" she asked.

"I told you, you can't go. You're a—" Rhun quickly fell silent. He knew full well how much his sister was her mother's daughter.

"A woman," Coira finished for him, fighting back irritation. She decided to tease instead. "Are you now so Roman that you can't accept the fact that women are better than men?"

Cian raised a clay mug brimming with wine, his words a soft slur. "Hey, I've always thought they were."

Rhun was annoyed. He didn't know what had taken place at Eboracum between Coira, his mother, and the legate, but his sister should have remained there. Yet, thinking it through, he was damned sure his mother would have wanted to go too, if only out of simple curiosity, and to ride guard on her daughter. So the legate must have held her back, likely because he didn't trust her. All of which left Rhun wondering if he was simply thinking too much.

Cian managed to have Luga assigned, even though the great hulking cavalryman was his second-in-command. The primus had reluctantly accepted the argument that Cian's optio knew the hill country up north as well as he knew his own village. But after that, Titus cut the rope. The remaining five would be Tungri troopers drawn from the rest of the regiment, not Britons. "Sniffing at temptation is one thing," the primus muttered, "but I'm not going to ram it up their noses."

They started early, before daybreak on a morning when the first frosts lay light on the ground, and their breath blew misty in the air. Late afternoon found them on the west side of the barren hills, in a bone chilling wind that cut through cloak and clothing like a knife. But the high, craggy ridges grew less harsh as the trail angled off to the northwest. Dusk found them in a wide valley by an old marching camp set, as usual, close by a river. The trees had been cleared back from the weed-covered berms, offering an unobstructed view on all four sides. With the shadows lengthening, it seemed pointless to travel farther. They pitched two tents tight inside one of the river side corners.

One of the Tungri guards roused them all from their sleep before first light, his voice a harsh whisper: "Someone's out there." As if to confirm as much, the sound of shuffling feet drifted from the far side of the camp, along with a faint echo of voices.

Rhun scrambled from under his cloak and fumbled for his shield along with everyone else. Sword in hand, he climbed the low rampart to find Titus already there.

"Over on the far side. See?" The primus pointed across the broad camp to where black shapes flitted eerily in the darkness. The voices grew bolder as whoever it was realized they'd been discovered.

The two guards drifted in from the darkness leading four horses, and a moment later Cian and Coira followed with four more. The light was growing fast, the sun barely hidden beyond the rim of the valley's eastern slope. The shadows had now turned into vague grey shapes, at least fifty or more, stealing across the camp. Something whirred through the air and thumped harmlessly into the ground somewhere ahead of them.

"Bugger the saddles," Titus murmured as he saw Rhun and the others lifting their gear. "Put the bridles on and be done with it. Where are the other horses?"

"Wandered too far," Luga replied, setting a saddle down in exchange for his shield.

"We can double," Rhun said, and nodded across the encampment. "They're not mounted."

The rim of the sun began to edge above the horizon, slowly wiping the shadows from those approaching. The enemy was more an angry mob than a group of warriors, a rabble strong only in numbers, young and old armed with rusted swords, crude spears, wooden pitchforks, and cudgels. Screams blew across the enclosure as the bolder ones surged forward. At around thirty paces they stopped, none willing to lead the final onslaught.

"The moment we turn our backs to mount, they'll be on us like a horde of rats," Rhun muttered.

"Tighten the line," Titus called out. "Shields together. Climb on top of the rampart. We fight them off from there."

"Get back, lad." Coira motioned to Bryn, and then to the river on the far side of the mound. "Can you swim if you have to?"

"I can fight," he replied indignantly.

"Then you be our reserve," Cian said, and pushed the boy behind him.

The leader, a large, hairy creature with a felling axe, barked orders and began pointing. The mob spread out, moving ever wider in a circling movement. Some climbed over the embankment and down to the river, clearly intent on coming in from behind.

"Coira, take a horse and the boy," Rhun called. "We'll hold them off."

"I'll not leave," she shouted.

"It's not for you, it's for Bryn," Rhun said, then just as quickly groaned, "Ah, no!"

A number of barbarian horsemen had appeared farther up the valley, riding in column. The small band of riders galloped headlong down the slope, coming from beyond the farthest reach of the encampment. As the leaders drew near, the column fanned out in two lines, slowing only as the horses crossed the ditch. The first rank cleared the low embankment and charged on, the second close on its heels. Farther up the slope a second troop had appeared, hardly noticed, and formed up in the same manner, only its leader held it there, sitting his horse and watching.

"They're friends, or we're buggered," Titus muttered.

At the first sound of the pounding hooves the large, hairy barbarian turned, panic on his face. Screaming in anger, he shook his axe, then ran like a rabbit for the nearest rampart. The others fled as quickly, scattering in a dozen directions. The barbarian horses never broke stride, cantering through the fleeing, ragtag horde with casual ease, each rider wielding his spear as if at practice. It was over almost before it started, leaving a score of bodies scattered about the enclosure. The two ranks did a single sweep of the camp, then formed up again inside the far rampart. It was as neat a piece of action as any Rhun had seen.

Back on the slope, the leader of the second column broke away and galloped his horse toward the camp. When he drew level with the neatly formed ranks of the first troop, the lead rider fell in alongside, and they continued on together. At fifty paces, each twisted his spear until the point faced downward and, in unison, ostentatiously rammed the weapon into the dirt.

"Well, at least they don't intend to skewer us," Titus muttered.

"Nor will they," Rhun said, grinning.

"I'm seeing double," the pilus said as the pair drew closer.

Rhun's grin broadened. The two riders were twins like he and Coira, only identical, and perhaps ten years older. Each one was so much like the other, he recalled, that they could only be told apart by the bend in their broken noses. And the pair didn't help matters: they dressed the same, their weapons were the same, and even the horses they rode were nearly identical. The only difference, no doubt demanded by an irate commander, was that one wore a red ribbon attached to his shoulder, the other a blue. The pair reined in, their horses hardly breaking sweat, though both animals breathed steam in the cold air. Each rider's face was expressionless, and as serious as a belly wound.

"Cavalry to the rescue," the blue one finally said. "As usual."

"There is no cost for this service," the red one added, then, after a pause, "this time."

Blue scratched his chin. "Though if you have a jug of very good wine ... "

" ... we can be bribed."

The words were spoken in a dead monotone, which Rhun figured was a regular banter enjoyed among their kin. A wave of sadness passed through him, for he was no longer part of it.

Coira recognized the pair as well. "Which one of you is Luath, and which one is Borba?" she asked.

Each pointed to the other and said, "He is."

"Thanks a lot!" Coira threw up her hands and laughed.

Cian and Luga both found the back and forth patter hilarious, and even the pilus chuckled. Rhun suspected part of it, however, was nothing more than Titus's nervous relief. Thank the gods, though, that Bryn was safe.

"Your help was timely, Luath," Rhun said, remembering the way it was with the colours from his father's stories. "And you too, Borba the Blue."

"That's what we're here for," Borba said, lowering his head in acknowledgement.

"This time," Luath added pointedly.

"Of course, when *we* travel, *we* don't light fires at night," Borba said.

"They attract bandits, Romans, and other pests."

Rhun realized they had been careless, but the reprimand irked. "We had no idea bands like this roamed the area. Not in that kind of strength."

"Oh yes, it's terrible," Borba said, his voice deadly serious. "Never had them before the invasion, you know."

Luath leaned forward in the saddle and spoke directly to Bryn. "Do you want to come back with us now, lad, or stay with them?"

"Where are you going?" Bryn asked.

"We won't be far," Luath replied.

"Aye, we've been given care of a wandering flock of sheep for the next few days," Borba said.

"Your da wants us to make sure they don't get into trouble."

"And you know how silly sheep can be," Borba finished.

Bryn looked at Luath, then at Coira, and grinned. "Then I'll stay."

"Yell for help if you need it, then," Luath said, and nodded at the others. "Rhun, Coira, watch your backs."

"Cian, Luga, you do the same," Borba said, then finally broke into a smile and asked, "By the way, did you two stupid buggers ever finish that fight that Venutius stopped?"

"Yeah, last week," Cian quipped. "I got killed."

"But he's too brainless to realize it." Roaring his laughter, Luga thumped Cian on the back.

"That explains a lot." Borba smiled again, and offered a casual salute. Both brothers wheeled their horses in unison and, holding them to a walk, headed back toward their troops. The banter kept up as they moved out of earshot.

"I'd forgotten Cethen's twins were identical."

"Me too. I thought the girl looked better than the other one, though."

Rhun caught no sight of the twins again, though from time to time the crack of a breaking branch echoed through from the forest, or the occasional thud of hooves could be heard drifting through the trees. They crossed the road that led to Luguvalium after following a well-used track that angled off to the southwest. It was there that they came upon the first piece of cloth, this one red, tied to a bush alongside the trail.

"I thought we were going to be met," Titus grumbled when he saw it.

"I suppose we already have," Rhun said, and pointed to the cloth. "By Luath and his brother."

The primus grunted, clearly not happy, and urged his horse forward, brushing through the low branches. Rhun fell in behind. Strung out in a single line, they headed deeper into the dark Cumbrian hills. A weak but stubborn sun poked through the heavy cloud cover, but brought little warmth, and only the soft plod of hooves on the leaf-cushioned dirt broke the cool silence.

The trail seemed endless, the miles impossible to count. The little-used path wound through thick stands of trees that, for the most part, clung stubbornly to the sharp slopes of the hills. It twisted and turned as it traced the course of countless bubbling streams, crossing only where the land was level. It skirted a hundred hidden ponds and waterfalls until finally, as if by magic, it broke free of the forest at the head of a long, deep lake, made small only by the huge valley that formed it. A crimson ribbon—Rhun had lost count of them by now—lay off to the right, and the primus once more turned his horse to follow.

The trees crowded thick along the water's edge and the land alongside the lake, for the most part, was low and even, allowing the trail to follow close by the shore. Where the earth grew marshy, or where a hillside plunged steeply down to the water, the horses simply circled away, following the track until it once more found its way back to the shore. The balance of the day passed quickly and the weather, finally, brought a welcome warmth.

They came upon a large stream late in the afternoon, its waters tumbling from a ravine hidden farther back in the trees. A pasture-like spit of land had formed over the years where the stream emptied into the lake: a low, fat finger of green jutting out from the shore. A cluster of round, cone-roofed huts had grown up alongside, set well back in a thick, neatly ordered stand of trees. The dull roar of a distant waterfall rumbled from somewhere back in the hills.

Rhun found himself strangely saddened. The cluster of hovels likely belonged to some chieftain and his kin. Their life seemed so narrow, all eking an existence from the hidden lake and the land itself, with no knowledge of the world beyond this poor, yet beautiful piece of Britannia. They would live their lives unaware of their ignorance. And yet, as he gazed across the sparkling surface of the lake, an odd throught struck him: *So what does it matter?*

A small crowd, all of them poorly dressed though fairly clean, stood outside the largest of the huts as if waiting, and Rhun decided that Borba or his twin must have ridden in ahead of them. The hut, he noticed, was half the size of the one they'd had at Ebor, and he wondered if it was where his da now lived. If so, it did not speak well of his circumstances. Or was it simply that his old home at Ebor, like so many things, was greater in Rhun's memory than in fact?

The pilus reined in fifty paces short of the village, and the others did the same. Rhun recognized his father at once, as well as Bryn's mother with her dark, reddish hair; there were perhaps one or two other familiar faces, but the names would not come.

His da seemed older, greyer, more weathered than he remembered, the lines of age and hard living etched deep in his face. What would he be now, approaching forty years? Certainly close on it, if not past. His eyes were as pale and blue as ever, though he was thinner. His belly no longer showed the small edge of comfort gained when living peacefully beside the Abus.

Bryn was first to dismount, laughing as he ran toward his father. Cethen picked him up, lifted him high above his head, and hugged him tight before setting him down. Rhun was surprised to feel a twinge of what could only be jealousy. The boy ran next to his mother, who simply bent down, kissed his brow, and returned her attention to the small column of riders. Cethen straightened, took a couple of steps forward, then halted as if unsure what to do. Rhun smiled. That was another thing he'd forgotten—his da's familiar, limping gait.

Cethen's hands were at his sides. One moved slightly, beckoning to someone behind. A young, dark-haired girl stepped forward, pretty in an elfin sort of way. Rhun guessed she was about fifteen, and knew at once who she was. Cethen placed a hand on her shoulder and pointed toward Cian. Then, straightening his back, he walked toward his two children.

Rhun quickly determined that the woman Morallta and his father rarely aimed their spears at the same target. He also discovered, equally quickly, that his father might string the bow, but it was she who shot the arrows. Cethen seemed to fit the role of a senior centurio, with lots to say and some to command, but Morallta was the pilus. But a dark, hard man who rode in from the hills as darkness was falling—Dermat, Rhun vaguely remembered—was the one to whom they all deferred, most of the time.

Events moved quickly following Dermat's arrival, which was announced by a clatter of many hooves and a good deal of shouting. The noise had still to settle down when he strode into the large hut, tossing his cloak to one side as his glance took in the new faces.

"Cian," Dermat murmured, and they briefly clasped each other. "And Luga!" His face broke into a grim smile. "I'll be buggered by a bear! You two haven't killed each other yet?"

"Not this week," Luga said, grinning foolishly through his black beard as they embraced.

"Rhun—you've grown, lad," Dermat said, simply nodding at him; then, turning to Coira with his arms out, he looked her up and down. "So have you, Coira lass, and done a much better job of it than your brother, I'd say."

Coira embraced him too, and turned to the pilus. "Titus Aurelius, Dermat. I believe you know of each other."

"Never met. Not face to face, anyway," he replied, and clasped Titus's wrist in the Roman manner.

An awkward silence followed the greetings. Dermat broke it by briskly rubbing both hands together, looking about the circle of faces, and asking, "Everyone had something to eat?" A muttered affirmative and a nodding of heads followed. "And to drink?"

Not everyone seemed so sure. "Well, I've had neither. Cogan?" Dermat caught the eye of a small, harried looking man, whom Rhun had discovered was the true owner of the lodge, and the head of the small village. "Let's pillage your beer supply, and find something solid for me. I'll eat while we're talking."

Cogan nodded and glanced to the far side of the lodge, his eyebrows raised. A dowdy woman stood in the kitchen area, clearly his wife, for she sighed and rolled her eyes before turning to see what she could find.

"Good, then." Dermat rubbed his hands once more, then wasted no further time, motioning everyone to sit down. "So tell me: is this a family reunion or, since you're also here," he nodded toward the primus, "is there something else?"

"I agreed to this meeting only because your da wanted to see you," Morallta interrupted, her voice hard. "And so his brother Cian could see his daughter. Beyond that, I see no point. Not unless they want to join us."

The woman strikes straight to the heart of it, Rhun thought. He preferred forthrightness, but it was unusual for his people, who believed certain formalities should be followed before striking hard at the heart of a matter. It was not the Roman way either, not unless terms were being dictated. He puzzled over what served best: get straight to the matter at hand, or dance around first, with a pretence of politeness? The pilus seemed to prefer the latter, for his jaw tightened.

"Is there any chance of that happening, Rhun?" Cethen asked the question the moment they were settled, ignoring the others.

"Joining you?" Rhun was caught by surprise, and turned to his sister. Coira shook her head. He nodded agreement, his reply definite in his mind. "No. No, Father, not at all."

Both the pilus and Cian looked at him, as if surprised at his firmness. Cethen, however, simply looked downward, and said nothing more.

"It's true," Rhun continued, compelled to explain. "I can't go back. Da, if the Romans were going to be thrown back into the sea tomorrow, it might be different. Even then, I might go with them, just to see the world. But none of that's going to happen." He leaned forward, intent only on his father. "If you had seen what's to be seen out there, Da, you would understand. Huge cities, buildings, more people than you could ever imagine. There are oceans, and mountains—real mountains, not big hills. And ships—fleets of ships. I've seen only part of it, and it's, it's … " Rhun leaned back and sighed. The idea was ridiculous, but he was actually arguing Rome's side. "Father, let me say this. As long as they want to, the Romans are here to stay!"

There was a long, uncomfortable silence, broken finally by Morallta. "So you fight and kill your people for the Romans!"

Coira moved to respond, but Rhun placed a hand on her arm. "I haven't fought my people, nor will I. Not my *own* people," he said. "Those to the north, those who've always been our enemy, yes. But for the Brigantes, and the Carvetii too, Roman rule is inevitable. If it has to happen, I want to see it happen with as little killing as possible."

"Hah! You believe the cause is lost before the fight. You would have us throw our freedom away!"

"Freedom?" Rhun smiled at her, surprised at his own sudden insight. "Freedom is for kings and chiefs. Beyond that, it is nothing more than your allegiance to whoever stands on your shoulders. It's the way of the world."

The woman irked him. He stared at her flushed cheeks, the cold eyes, and her grim, thin lips, stretched tight with an anger that more than rivalled his, and he wondered what kept his father there. And yet—Rhun felt himself blush—this was also the same woman who, years past, when his voice was growing deep and his body changing, had more than once haunted his dreams at night.

"There is a trade-off," Titus said, his voice calm. "No loss of freedom. We simply strike a bargain."

Dermat raised his hand to silence Morallta before she could start. "I know how that works. We pay your taxes, and do as you say," he said. "What's left of freedom after that?"

"Freedom comes in many forms," Titus insisted. "And you get value for your taxes. We build roads. Towns, villages, and houses, they all improve, and greatly. Trade and crops increase. And above all, you no longer need fear your enemies. Rome will fight them as if they were her own. Which they would be." Titus gestured vaguely with one hand, as if unsure of the direction. "Look to the south of this province. The people grow wealthy there. And," he shrugged and grinned, "we fight their enemies. Who, at the moment, appear to be you."

Rhun wondered to what extent the primus believed his own words. The man knew, as surely as he did himself, that Rome's word was as good as the next governor—or the first procurator who proved dishonest, which they nearly all were. The governor Agricola was, from what he'd heard, strict, yet fair. But what would the next governor be like? The primus was persuasive, but there were always three sides to any argument, he thought cynically: yours, mine, and the truth that dangles somewhere in between. And truth, as everyone knew, lay only in its perception. Which Dermat proved with his answer.

"Ah, but there you have the wrong of it. We believe the enemy is you."

"So is that why you are here?" Morallta cut in again. "To offer us the chance to be your slaves, and in return protect us from anyone who tries to make us *their* slaves?"

Titus simply shrugged. "I think we both know that this coming year, your land will see our armies. There's been too much trouble to ignore. You've seen our forts creep to the limit of your territory. Luguvalium, for example." The primus paused, as if expecting comment; the three immediately across from him exchanged glances, but said nothing. "Since Rhun and his sister had passage here anyway, I came to let you know that Rome is still open to an agreement on how it will be done. If you have no interest, then so be it."

"And that was all?" Dermat asked, his tone implying he expected more.

"Why, should there more?" Titus asked, and raised his brows in question.

"Why can't you ball-bearing bastards say what's on your mind!" Morallta cried. "You're worse than a gossiping skivvy!"

"Of course there is." Dermat grinned, vainly trying to ignore the interruption. "There is really only one reason *you* are here. And I must say this, I'm impressed. You travelled from where, Ebor?"

Titus nodded. "They call it Eboracum now."

"Bad tidings travel faster than I would have thought. As I said, I'm impressed."

"And?"

"And nothing. We're keeping him safe. Should the day ever arrive when our backs are pressed hard against a stone wall, he might help find a door there for us."

"Then you must realize two things. The first is that Rome doesn't bargain. The second is that, should anything happen to him, the reprisals will be enormous."

"We're used to taking risks," Dermat said, then glanced pointedly at Morallta. "But we also guard what is of value. Who knows, perhaps the situation may one day forestall some other matter."

Rhun sat back, wondering what, by the two heads of Janus, the pair were talking about. A glance at Coira and Cian showed they were just as baffled.

Dermat had one more item to discuss, but left it until the meeting had broken up and he found himself alone with Titus. The dour chieftain bit down on his lower lip as if reluctant to say anything at all, but it quickly became apparent that he found his question too important not to ask.

"I'm certain we would have heard of it by now," Dermat began, casually waving his hand as if to show the matter was of no consequence, "but tell me: the spoils taken from Stannick when it fell—did they include among them a golden torque?"

"A gold torque?" Titus's voice revealed his surprise.

"Uh-huh, a torque. A neck ring. It's formed in the manner of a rope. A dragon's head on either end." Dermat seemed ready to shrug the matter off. "It's a bauble that's been with my *tuath* for many years. I would buy it back and pay well, if it were found."

Titus looked at the man's face, and wondered how much truth was in his words. He had certainly not heard of any such piece, but that meant nothing. "No," he said, and for emphasis added, "I can honestly say I've never heard of such a bauble being found. And something like that would surely not go unnoticed. However…" He narrowed his eyes. "Should it be found, is it worth the price of our man?"

Dermat's teeth again bit into his lip, this time hard enough to make Titus think he might draw blood. "It would likely have such value, if found," he finally murmured, then nodded as if certain. "In fact, I don't doubt that at all."

"Then you can be assured, if I learn of such a prize, one way or another you will hear from me," Titus said, his mind whirling. "In the meantime, I said Rome does not negotiate. We both know that's not true. Is there anything you can throw into the arena?"

Dermat slowly shook his head, though his face remained thoughtful. "Not at this time. And certainly not likely in the near future, after hearing threats of invasion in almost the same breath. Really, primus…"

"But the torque…?"

"Let me say this." Dermat stared hard into Titus's eyes before turning away. "Should you discover its whereabouts, pass word to me. Or to Cethen Lamh-fada."

Titus was left to brood upon the matter, eventually deciding that, while the information was no doubt of importance, it seemed of little value unless the piece was found. If the trinket had not surfaced by now, it would likely never be recovered. Some fat, sweaty trader had probably added it in his horde within a week of the battle, and no doubt melted the piece for its gold. On the other side of that blade, the legate would want to know everything that might be of use. Perhaps some enquiries might be made...

They had only one day before the party would have to return to Eboracum. Cethen took the twins aside on the excuse of viewing the hidden falls, which lay beyond where the stream disappeared into the forest. All three were soon clambering through a rock-cluttered ravine, drawn on by the rumble of tumbling waters. The chill dampness grew colder as the gorge narrowed and they climbed higher. A faint mist hung in the air as they neared the very top, to find a dark torrent of water gushing through two enormous, slab-sided walls of granite. Tall, leafless trees towered high above the ravine floor, made even taller by the steep sides of the ravine. The place always left Cethen feeling a greater sense of sanctity than any druid's oak grove.

A number of logs, washed over the falls by spring floods, had lodged partway down the steep slope, close by the foot of the falls. Cethen chose one and sat down, staring at the twins as they did the same. The change in the two had at first been far too much to absorb, and the previous night he'd found his eyes drawn to their faces as if pulled by hidden strings.

He hardly noticed the Roman clothing they wore; they were his children. Rhun had been only a sprout when he'd last seen him, and now he was a tall stranger, certainly no longer the scrawny boy. His hair was cut short, which looked odd, and he wore none of it on his face, which was alien. But it was the lad's eyes that struck him most. They were grey as much as anything, with perhaps a hint of his own blue; but much more important, good sense lay behind them, even though, in some manner, they remained veiled. His son seemed unsure—but then, that made sense, he supposed. The boy was caught in the middle, and had likely chosen the side he did for lack of alternative.

And Coira. By the gods, she had her mother in her. Which brought bittersweet memories that reminded Cethen that neither child had spoken a word of Elena. Even his brother Cian merely said she fared well, and then only when asked. After that, his mouth talked of nothing but his own daughter.

Coira casually swept the hair back from her eyes, and placed her chin on the knuckles of one hand. It was a gesture he'd seen Elena make a thousand times, and it brought a lump to his throat. The girl's hair was turning her mother's shade, a pale yet tawny honey, though Coira's would always be the lighter—more of a straw colour. Cethen bit his lip. She had Elena's stubborn chin, but they were his eyes. They were a deeper blue, perhaps, but that likely showed a will stronger than his own, which he knew lacked resolve—or, as Morallta constantly reminded him, something called iron.

"This place is timeless," he mused, his eyes moving to the falls where a limbless tree had caught on the lip, and dangled high above the roaring cascade. "Who will remember us?"

Coira and Rhun glanced at each, eyebrows raised. Cethen noticed, and smiled. "I'm feeling old, but I'm not there yet. Nothing tires more, though, than when things don't sit balanced inside. There's so much that I'd like to do, if…" He sighed. *"Ifs" are nothing more than wishes.* He turned to a safer subject. "You told me Tuis was doing well. Tell me more. How does he look? What is it he likes?"

So the two told him, but danced carefully around the boy's relationship with the legate. Cethen nodded, satisfied with the answer, though he felt certain there was more to it. The lad was healthy and growing well; he simply wasn't there to see it. Which was pig shit! Anger stirred briefly, then slowly faded. The gods had given him another boy, a lad almost the double of Tuis, and he'd arrived within months of the first one's disappearance. Which, in fairness, had a certain balance to it. It was just that the same Roman whose life he'd saved, dammit, was now the one who had the boy's care. That man had haunted his life ever since ramming his fool ship into—

"The soldier. Titus. He told you we have the legate's son?" Cethen asked, forcing his mind to another track. "You seemed confused."

"He kept word of it to himself," Rhun replied. "The legate received the dispatch from Deva the same day he received the one telling of Bryn's arrival."

"It makes you wonder, doesn't it?" Coira mused.

"And he sent Bryn back!" Cethen's heart lurched as it struck him what might have happened. "He could have—I never thought of that! No wonder Morallta was pissed."

"Bryn was a messenger, Father; you cannot hold a messenger hostage for a prisoner taken in battle," Coira pointed out, but her expression reflected her own sense of disbelief.

"Where is Marcus?" Rhun asked.

"He's at ... " Cethen gestured farther down the lake, then changed his mind. Damn! This was his own son, wearing a Roman uniform. Was the question honest, or was it leading? Why, oh why, was life not simple? "He's at one of the camps," he mumbled, his hand taking in the entire range of hills to the south. "He's healthy enough, though he's treated as a slave. If it were up to me ... well, I don't know." He shrugged, then looked up and grinned, remembering the day, standing on the dock, when Elena had ransomed the legate. "How about five gold pieces? I'd insist on full payment this time, because we wouldn't get Venutius in return."

The twins laughed, and Rhun asked, "Was Marcus hurt?"

"A small cut to his thigh." Cethen chuckled. "Inflicted in an earlier, er, skirmish, you might call it."

"You mean an earlier battle," Coira said, her voice cool. "I've seen it. He got it at Bran's Beck. As far as I'm concerned, it won't hurt Marcus Sabinius Trebonius one bit if he spends some time as a slave. It will do nothing but good."

"We're not talking about the same scar," Cethen said, and since it was such a good story, he pressed on with the telling of it.

"So what are you going to do with him?" Coira asked when he was finished.

"It's not my choice," Cethen said. "Morallta would have killed him, but I think Dermat's convinced her of the folly in it. As you likely figured, Criff was newly arrived when we took him. It was his recognizing the boy that saved him." He paused, thinking a moment on the bard's presence with them. "I really don't know where that man stands. I've met him in the strangest places. Did I ever tell you about the time in the hut at Ebor?"

The hut by the Abus! But the river Abus held more than one

memory, and Cethen suddenly no longer felt like spinning stories. He sighed again. "Never mind. Between the two of us, we kept the boy alive long enough for the woman to listen to reason. One day, I think we'll need him. In the meantime he'll be safe, unless the Romans do something to really set the tribes' piss boiling."

"The Romans will be here next year," Rhun said.

"Then we'll move farther north." Cethen shrugged at the idea. "The tribes up there will welcome more warriors, as long as Rome is the enemy."

"That's a matter the primus might have raised last night—the people being forced farther north," Rhun said.

"Which would have raised a further point for Dermat," Coira mused, and lowered her voice in imitation. "But Titus, you've already put a stop to our enemies fighting us. They all want to fight you, instead."

Cethen laughed. "That sounds more like your mother talking."

"Why don't you come back, Da?" Rhun asked suddenly. "Titus didn't say so, because he couldn't, but I'm sure Rome would support you as a chief. At Isurium, say. Nobody's ever replaced Maeldav."

"Ah, if there was only one choice." Cethen rose and turned to stare toward the falls. "There are too many people who count on me, son. You saw Borba and Luath—we go back a long way. And there are countless others. There's the woman, witch that she can be sometimes, and of course, Bryn. It's impossible, even if I took time to think on it."

"What about her?" Coira asked. "How does it stand between you?"

Cethen grinned ruefully, unsure how to answer. Just as he knew his two children had been doing the same thing, he chose to censor most of it. "Sometimes she's there, sometimes not. We take each day as we find it, other than the training and the cause. That's really her life. She's a fine warrior, though. And me? Silly as it sounds, I guess I'm sort of a legend too, you know."

"The parapet thing?" Rhun asked, clearly intrigued. "They think you'll slay Gaius on the burning parapets of Eboracum?"

"That's only a part of it. Though it's incredible, isn't it?" Cethen groaned his frustration. "The old druid—can't remember his name, now. He lost his credibility after Stannick was sacked, but since Gaius what's-his-name returned, the old bugger's become a seer again."

"Do you believe it?"

Cethen laughed, recalling the druid's lie. "Of course not. At least most the time," he added with a wink. "But in the end, it's just one more lousy, rotten commitment." He sighed and sat down again, turning to his children, his mind confused. "Tell me again, why are you so certain the Romans will prevail?"

Coira and Rhun stared at each for a moment, as if wondering where to begin. Then, each talking around the other, they told him of Rome, Germania, Aquitania, and all the places between; then they told him of the places that lay beyond. Coira spoke of the great city itself—the tall buildings, the aqueducts, the forum, the Circus, and a dozen other wonders. Rhun spoke of the spiderweb of roads that spanned half the world, and the massive fleets that sailed its seas. They described Rome's huge armies and cohorts, scores of them, stationed from Britannia to Judaea, a standing force paid to do the bidding of their masters.

They spoke more gently when describing how they had grown accustomed to living within Rome's embrace, and the knowledge they'd gleaned: reading and writing, the luxury of running water, heated floors, and sewers that rid the home of stench and human waste.

Cethen heard it all and believed less than half, for any more than that was too much; when the two were done, he sighed. He gave Rhun a long, hard look, and beckoned him to move over beside him. At the same time, he swept his eyes over every corner of the ravine, taking in each shadow, rock, and tree. Satisfied, he reached inside his tunic and withdrew a heavy, linen-wrapped package. "Here," he said, pushing it sideways into his son's ribs. "Hide that. Quickly."

Rhun took it and dropped it down the front of his own tunic, where it formed a heavy, circular lump above his belt. He tugged upward on the leather to make it loose, then let it go. The tunic and the mail draped outward, and the lump disappeared. "What is it?" he asked when he was satisfied with the result.

"Hang onto it, the both of you. Keep it hidden. If you never see a use for it, pass it down to hands that I trust as much as yours. It's the torque."

"*The* torque?" Coira squeaked.

"Venutius entrusted it to me before he died."

"He did?" both twins said together.

Cethen nodded, then couldn't help smiling. "Well, sort of. He really had no choice."

"But—but it's *the* torque," Coira said, her voice full of awe.

"I know. It's a great responsibility. To be honest, I've got no idea what to do with the fuc—the stupid thing!"

"Sort of?" Rhun asked. "How *did* you get it?"

Cethen scratched the top of his head, wondering what to say. More than a few parts of his life were painful to talk about, and this one stood high in the tally. But he couldn't tell the two of them only half the story, for it was too important; so he took a deep breath, let it go, and started.

"I made a bit of a mistake at Stannick," he said. "I might tell all of it one day, but it likely makes no difference to anyone except me. The end of it, though, was that I found myself outside the walls with a small part of Morallta's cavalry when the Romans stormed the place. In fact," Cethen held one hand to his forehead and sighed, feeling that perhaps a full confession might offer salve for his conscience, "some people say I actually led the first Roman assault. What happened, though, was that we ended up being left outside. Me and—I don't know, ten or twelve others. We hid in the woods, waiting to see what happened, and it happened fast. The Romans rolled over the largest part of the fortress as if the walls weren't even there! Then they ran through the second in much the same manner. And while the third took longer to breach, it was done soon after."

Cethen paused, remembering the sad debacle as if it were a fresh wound. He leaned forward, cradling his head in hands, elbows resting on his knees. When Coira prompted him, he spoke to the damp, moss-covered ground at his feet. "It's the same old story. Those with the horses get away. Which," he lifted his head long enough to look Rhun in the eye, "didn't include you, did it? Anyway, Venutius was one of those with a horse, naturally, but he'd taken a spear in the side when fleeing. Our small group was hanging about, hidden in the trees, useless but unable to leave. It was horrible."

Cethen found his eyes watering and he shook his head, ashamed. Coira waited, then prompted him once more.

"I was alone, close by the edge of the forest, and saw a group of them break free of the fort. I kept hidden, but rode through the trees to see where they were heading. The Roman cavalry outside the fort were mostly to the north, you see, and Venutius rode west, fighting his way through the ones on that side. Dermat was there, too—I saw him—and Venutius was in the middle, on my side. They and the Romans were all mixed up in a mad panic, stabbing, slashing, everyone killing each other.

"The old bugger seemed to have escaped, then he faltered and fell back. I watched him head off into the cover of the trees, farther up the hill. All by himself. He rode slumped over in the saddle. His horse was hurt, too. Its chest was covered with blood; I think it had bolted." Cethen sighed and leaned back, closing his eyes for a moment. "Remember those thick woods, on a small rise southwest of the old part of the fortress?"

Rhun nodded, though his face was a blank, and Cethen returned his gaze to the moss. "He'd fallen across a deadfall, and I think that broke his back, too. The torque wasn't wrapped like it is now. It was right there, out in the open, maybe an arm's length from where he lay. I think he had it hidden in his tunic, like I did, and it fell out. Anyway, I picked it up, then went to see how it stood with him."

"And?"

"He was dying, and knew it. He turned his head and saw me standing there with the torque. His eyes were, well, they were full of hate, but I don't think it was directed at me. I think it was because of what had happened. Anyway, he looked at the torque, and told me it belonged only to whoever had the balls to lead the people." Cethen felt sheepish as he spoke the rest of it. "I'm sure he didn't think that was me. And certainly not Morallta, because he said, 'And it's not that Carveti bitch, either.' Then, when he thought more on it, he said, 'Or the other bitch who once had it.'"

"Cartimandua?" Coira asked.

"Cartimandua." Cethen grinned. "He couldn't bring himself to say her name, even as he was dying. The two never did stand on the same side of a battlefield. Although ... "

"Although what, Da?"

Cethen chuckled. "Just before the end, he mumbled something about her not being that bad a bitch, deep down."

"Did he take a long time dying?"

Cethen stared at his son, pursed his lips, and slowly shook his head. He moved one hand to the dagger tucked in his belt and patted the hilt. "He lingered for awhile, but when the pain got bad ... well, he didn't want that.'

"Who else knows of it, Da?" Coira asked.

Cethen looked at his daughter, then his son, and felt a guilty relief as he gave the answer. "You and me. And I suppose Venutius too, so don't make his spirit angry. I'm sure the miserable bugger would come after you."

The three sat in silence for a long time, the steady roar of the falls unheard as they each chased their thoughts. Rhun finally made to rise, but Cethen gestured blindly for him to stay where he was. When he finally raised his head it was to look first at his son, then at his daughter, with a tear-stained face. "You know, the old bugger managed to blade my back, even when he was dying," he mumbled, his lips twisted in anger.

Haunted by the past, Cethen stared at Rhun. "While I was there putting Venutius out of his misery, your mam rode up to where I'd been hiding in the forest with the others. This time she had two horses. Cian's girls were on one, and she, you, and Tuis were on the other. She ... she ... " He broke off and bent his head forward, clasping it in both hands.

"She what, Da?" Coira asked gently, though curiosity added urgency to her voice.

"Ah, shit!" Cethen sobbed, then slapped both knees and sat upright, taking a deep breath. Both his daughter and her brother needed to hear it; and, hard as it was, the telling of it was important to him, too. "Borba and Luath, they were both still there, and she met them. They couldn't find me, so they took Cian's girls. It was Nuada's dying wish they be raised by their own. By me. They talked for awhile with your mam, but she said she had to go." He looked toward Rhun. "So she took you and Tuis, and left. If—if—oh son, if I'd been there, I might have been able to keep you!" He stared at each twin in turn, his frustration still raw, and the words gushed out. "Who knows, I might have convinced her to stay!"

They departed the next day, but not early, for there seemed no hurry to return. Rhun was mounting up outside Cogan's lodge when Cian's horse reared, sending him crashing to the ground. He lay writhing in the dirt, moaning in pain and yelling his anguish, both hands clutching his leg. Everyone ran over to help. Rhun knew his uncle well, and was surprised at the intensity of his outburst.

"I think it's broken," someone called out.

Rhun dismounted, as did Coira, and both rushed to their uncle. Cethen crouched beside him with his daughter Emla, who had hold of one hand. Cian's face was twisted in pain, his mouth clenched, though his complexion, other than being redder than usual, looked perfectly normal.

"Get him inside," someone else cried.

"Bind the leg first," another voice suggested.

Cian, after a flurry of help, was carried into the lodge and set down on a cot. They removed his britches and there was, indeed, a patchy red area on his thigh where he claimed it was broken. As if to add further proof to the injury, his foot was turned inward. Someone called for a woman who might do the splinting, and another called for a jug of beer. Titus stood by the door of the hut, watching from a distance and saying nothing.

When they departed not long after, leaving Cian in the lodge to recover from the break and make his own way back, Rhun returned quickly for a final goodbye. Emla sat by the cot holding her father's hand. "Is there anything I can do?" he asked. "Anything you need?"

"Naw," Cian said, and glanced at Emla, a warm smile on his face. "I'll be alright. I've got good care."

Rhun bit his lip doubtfully and turned to go, but Cian called him back as he started through the door: "Hey!"

"Yeah?"

Cian winked. "Keep an eye on Luga. The dumb bastard needs a lot of steering."

Chapter XII

Cumbria, A.D. 78/79

The snows came early to the hills and remained, deep and heavy, until spring. It made for little movement, but Marcus was certain the barbarian Cethen and his woman, along with their puffed up regiment of cavalry, were active throughout much of it. He hardly saw the pair at all, which made a balance: if the one who wanted him dead and the one who wanted him alive were at least together, then he might feel a degree of safety. Not that he had time to worry on it, for when he wasn't toiling like a slave, he brooded on the hard, degrading manner in which he was treated.

Marcus had been stripped of his body armour the moment the barbarians had him off the field and into the forest. He was stripped of the rest of his clothes the day after arriving at the hill fort, which was a relief in one way, for they were soiled and stank. Yet the coarse, poorly woven castoffs he was given in return were better only for their dryness. The stink of goats and cattle clung to the threads and took long in fading—or, he supposed, perhaps they simply took time to get used to.

They threw him out to work with the menials, but always inside the walls of the hill fort: slopping pigs, mucking pens, cutting wood, grinding grain, and tending to half-wild, half-starved, stinking four-legged creatures of every ilk, including half-savage hounds. The most humiliating were the goats, the stupid, stubborn animals he had to muck and milk, then form the reeking liquid into racks of fetid cheese.

168

At first he'd refused to do any of it, of course, including eating their slops, which brought about the first of two humiliating clashes, both on the very first day.

"I hear you're planning on starving yourself to death." Cethen's manner was genial as he poked his head into the tiny hut where Marcus slept. He wrinkled his nose and invited Marcus outside.

Marcus grunted and climbed from the pile of straw that served as a bed. He stepped into the open, a ragged blanket wrapped about his shoulders like a poor man's cloak, squinting as his eyes adjusted to the brightness of a wintery sun. "I'm a Praetorian tribune," he said angrily. "I should be treated with dignity until ransomed."

"Let's go over there and sit down, lad," Cethen said calmly, gesturing toward a community fire that burned in a ring of stone, not far from the hut. Several people sat by its edge, old men mostly, chatting and keeping warm.

"You'll be held to account for this," Marcus threatened, but found himself talking to Cethen's back. "Damn you!"

Cethen sat down on one of the logs scattered round the fire, and held both hands up to the flames. He peered over one shoulder with raised eyebrows, and a grin that left no doubt that the prisoner's behaviour was hurting nobody but the prisoner himself. With a curse, Marcus followed and took another log alongside. The warmth of the flames felt good.

"I'll be held to account for a lot more than this one day, boy," Cethen murmured, and sighed his pleasure as the heat got to his hands. "Personally, I find it rather stupid to starve to death in the meantime."

"You have no pride. No honour."

"Son, it's honour that got me in this fucking fix to begin with." Cethen chuckled, as if amused by the irony. "And I suppose it's pride that keeps me here. If you're trying to insult me, find something disagreeable."

"I will not be treated like a slave. I'd rather die first."

"Your choice. Certainly not mine," Cethen said easily. "Starving is your only option, though, for we're not going to end it all for you. You're a hostage. Though if you really do want to do it faster, I suppose you could probably, well, you know ... " He ran a finger across his throat and made a gurgling noise. "Of course, you'd have to find a knife. Perhaps hanging is a more readily—"

"My father will be furious at my treatment. The reprisals will be enormous."

"You forget, lad, that your father once did what you say you'll die before doing." Cethen paused as if thinking the words through to make sure he had the right of them; then he nodded his head in satisfaction, and continued. "Which was to be a prisoner, and toil as a slave. But I will make sure your father knows how you died. I know him well. He'll think you're as stupid as I do."

"And how are you going to let him know?" Marcus asked, though the moment the words were out he realized how childish they sounded.

"Shouldn't be too difficult." Cethen stood, turned his back to the flames, and rocked on his heels. "I expect to be meeting with my daughter Coira in the next little while; and the other twin, Rhun. Of course, it's early, so all they'll be able to do is relay your progress. It takes longer than that to starve to death."

"Bastard."

"That's much better. Far closer to the target." Cethen turned to go, but snapped his fingers as if suddenly remembering. "I did manage one thing in your favour."

"What's that?" Marcus sneered. "A better pile of filth for my bed?"

"No. You need to be guarded. Fiona figured she had the right of it, but Dermat wants you here under his nose, and she lives … well," Cethen gestured somewhere vaguely south, "elsewhere. I found you the most benign yet reliable guard possible."

"For that I'm to be thankful?" Marcus said in scorn. "One barbarian savage is supposed to be better than another?"

"Yes, since you ask, though you deserve far less than what I've arranged." Cethen's face grew tight, as if he were running out of patience. "For what it's worth, you only got the man because the choice appealed to Morallta's sense of irony."

"So who or what is—oh no!" Marcus cried, as the answer struck him.

"That's right. Your slave, Urs." Cethen grinned slyly. "Not that it matters, does it? You're going to die of starvation."

The second encounter took place that evening, when Urs appeared at the doorway of the small hut with a large bundle of straw. He edged through the door, tossed it to one side, then promptly disappeared. Not long after he returned with a second bundle, and heaped it on top of the first. Then, using both his feet and his hands, he moved the pile about until it formed an even pallet on the dirt floor.

"I suppose you're planning on sleeping there," Marcus growled.

Urs made a point of sniffing the air with obvious distaste. "I have no choice."

Marcus had been mulling over Cethen's words. The arrangement could have gone many ways, he realized, and the sandy-haired barbarian was likely correct: the slave would in all probability prove the more benign taskmaster. Urs still had an interest in keeping him alive, which none of the other ignorant plebs had, especially if matters grew awkward, such as a Roman attack on their pitiful hill fort.

"I see you are still a slave," Marcus ventured.

"A slave with a responsibility. You."

"I would have thought your own people would have done better by you."

"I told you before, they are not my people," Urs muttered, and stepped back, inspecting the straw pallet. "Not that it matters, but they did offer better."

"What? Milking cows instead of slopping pigs?"

"No. Not at all." Urs sat down on the straw, crossed his legs, and looked directly at Marcus. "I could have freedom if I fought for them. They want me to. I'm larger and smarter than nine of their ten."

"So why don't you?"

"I don't know how many times I must tell you. They are not my people." Urs shook his head, gazed at the dirt floor, and sighed. "The tall one, the one with the sandy hair and the pale blue eyes, he can't seem to understand either. All I want is to go home without looking over my shoulder for a Roman sword. I need the bronze wafer you promised."

"Your release?" Marcus breathed the words, only half willing to believe the man's motive. "You know, you were really better off in Rome."

"You might have been, but I was not," Urs snapped. "I may have been better fed, better dressed, and in better health, but I was not better off." He shook his head and stared at Marcus as if in despair. "You people just don't understand."

He sighed and flopped back on the straw. "Look, three years was the agreement, and more than six months have passed. My burden now is no different than it ever was: look after you, watch your back, and don't run. The only difference is, now I'm the one who decides how it's done."

Marcus studied the slave with narrowed eyes. Could the man's painful need for his freedom be used to his advantage? "No, I'll be the one who decides."

"You haven't decided well so far." Urs grinned and gestured expansively with both arms, taking in the crude interior of the hovel. "No, I'll be the one who decides. Not that there's a choice. It's those 'barbarians' outside who carry the cudgel."

Chapter XIII

Eboracum, A.D. 78/79

Rhun's squadron was ordered back to Eboracum not long before the winter solstice, leaving Cian's old troop at Lavatris under the temporary command of Luga. Rhun's men were housed inside the fortress in one of the many vacant barracks. The greater part of the Ninth was detached elsewhere, spread across the northern hills as they built the governor's string of forts and cut out the roads that linked them.

On the evening of his arrival, Elena appeared at the door of her son's quarters: two rooms and a small admin area at the end of the barracks block, large enough to offer modest privacy. She tapped on the door, then poked her head inside and withdrew it a moment later to announce, "He's here."

Coira and Tuis followed two steps behind as she stalked in, stamping her feet to shake off the snow. Rhun stood on a chair at the back of the spartan quarters, arranging a war axe, a long, rust-pocked sword, and a small painted shield in a cross pattern on top of a bear hide. *Trophies*, Elena guessed.

He glanced their way and, as an icy blast of wind trailed them inside, said, "Shut the door; there's little enough heat here."

"And a fine hello to you, too," Elena replied, but quickly closed the door on the small, windowless room. Her son had only a pair of oil lamps burning, one a huge object made of brass that emitted a large flame from its bowl-like base. Though a long way from keeping the room hot, it threw enough heat to make life bearable with a thick woolen tunic.

Rhun turned and embraced his mother, then his sister, and, much to the lad's annoyance, tousled his brother's hair. Rhun's grasp was firm but not warm, Elena noticed. Nor, after a quick glance into her eyes, did he seem to want to meet them. Which was no different from their first encounter at Camulodunum, or from any other meeting over the summer when duty brought him back to the fortress. She had thought that Rhun might show a greater warmth after meeting with his father but, if anything, his mood seemed to have grown more introspective. And, when she pondered on it, so had her daughter's.

"Can I get you anything?" Rhun asked, then shrugged as he looked around the room, barren but for a large wooden wine locker that doubled as a small table. "Wine, red wine, or more wine?"

"No, that's fine," Elena said, but Coira elbowed her in the side.

"Hey, the boy's home for winter. That deserves a drop of something."

Rhun seemed to hesitate at his sister's words, then nodded, opened the locker, and surveyed the contents. Inside were more than a score of pottery bottles, and an assortment of dried food that, like the bottles, had begun to gather dust. Selecting a wine, he turned to a shelf on which were arranged a colourful collection of drinking vessels in a precise line—one ornate brass cup and a half-dozen clay mugs. The mugs looked well worn, but he found three in moderate shape and set them on top of the locker alongside the brass cup. Producing a knife, he removed the bung, and silently poured the wine.

Elena broke the silence, her hand out. "I'll take the brass one, Rhun."

"I've seen that before," Tuis said, his expression curious.

"So have I." His mother smiled as she took it.

When all four had a drink in hand, Rhun raised his own and solemnly intoned, "Life's too short to drink cheap wine." Then he grinned wryly, as much to himself as to the others. "But it's a sight better than no wine at all!"

"I'm surprised you still have this." Elena held the brass cup high to inspect it.

When Rhun had been sent away, it had been with only a small

bundle of possessions: his clothing, a few items for personal hygiene, a small whittling knife, and the cup, a final gift from his mother. The ship had departed from the dock within walking distance of where they now sat. Her son had been dragged sullenly aboard, cursing his mother and damning all Romans in general, Gaius Sabinius Trebonius in particular. When she'd passed up the bundle, he'd promptly tossed it back onto the dock, where it might have remained, if a crewmember, at a nod from Gaius, had not quietly retrieved it and taken it aboard.

Rhun seemed surprised. "It was the only thing they let me keep. Even then, they …" His jaw set, and he shook his head as if ridding it of the memory. "The ba—they gave it to me when I was sent away for schooling. I never knew where it came from."

"It was a wedding gift. From Cian. There were two." Elena smiled sadly, gazing at the cup as she remembered. "I threw this one in with my things when I left Stannick in search of Coira. One of the Ninth's soldiers picked it up as loot at Bran's Beck. I saw it being used in the centurio's mess, and Gaius bought it for me."

"And the other?" Rhun asked, his expression curious.

"Probably in the ashes at Stannick."

"I see." Rhun sucked on his lower lip, then turned to Coira, his look taking in her clothing. Like Elena and Tuis, she was dressed in a warm woolen shirt and britches, a sleeved sheepskin tunic belted about the waist, and lined winter boots. "Are you going somewhere?"

"No, just trying to keep warm." Coira wrinkled her nose. "The tunics will be off soon, though. We're heading out to the practice field."

"All of you?" Rhun sounded surprised, and his eyes returned to his mother.

"I'm not old, boy," Elena growled and tossed her hair, one hand sweeping the tresses back by habit. At thirty-eight years, Elena was aware that she was not only fit, she was not hard on a man's eyes, either. You didn't live inside a Roman fortress without knowing it, even if half the soldiers inside were half depraved, and almost totally deprived. "I fought alongside your da, and would have fought at Stannick if given the chance."

"On which side?" Rhun shot back, then immediately had the

decency to look sorry. "I …"

"Never mind," Elena said, laughing and shaking her head, for it was the sort of remark she might have thrown at Cethen long before the "troubles" started. "Your sister and I keep ourselves fit, and we drag your brother along with us. We love it. And anyway, what else is there for us to do?"

"Don't you take care of the legate?" Rhun said, and his face coloured. "I mean, take care of his residence. Keep it clean. Cook. Do his clothes."

"She's not a slave," Tuis said, sounding annoyed.

Elena smiled at her youngest, then answered Rhun's question. "I do sometimes, but only when I want. There's staff for that. In fact, as far as keeping the place clean, a good deal of it's taken care of by soldiers on punishment detail. In many ways," Elena felt her cheeks flush, "it's almost as if I'm his wife."

'Who knows everything, long before others do," Rhun said, but his tone was not harsh.

"Such as?"

"That I'm to be here all winter."

"Well, you are. I assumed you knew."

"All I received was an order to report here with my squadron."

"I think Gaius—the legate—has you here for staff training," Coira said. "Headquarters stuff, that kind of thing."

"What?" Rhun cried, slopping wine over the lip of his cup. "There is no way …!"

"You can't stay where you are forever," Elena said firmly, not surprised by the outburst.

"Why not? I like what I'm doing."

"Well, I'm glad to hear that," Elena replied, which was true. She and Gaius had spoken more than a few words about her son the past few years, usually following one of Titus's reports from Vetera. "But you can't spend the next twenty-five years as a squadron commander."

"Why not?" Rhun cried, but his voice lacked conviction.

"Because you're not that thick. Not most of the time, anyway," Coira said.

"Rhun, you know as well I. There are many reasons why you can't,"

Elena said, ignoring her daughter. Her son's words vaguely reminded her of a hundred discussions she'd had with his father. "The system itself, boredom, your sanity? And you're going to need more than field experience to gain promotion. You need to know how the army works. You need lessons in tactics. In history. In staffing. You need to improve your reading. You need to—"

"There's nothing wrong with my reading," Rhun interrupted, though he frowned, as if pondering his mother's words. "Nor should there be. Those buggers at the prison camp he sent me to rammed it down my throat. I can read orders, and that's all I need."

"There's more to reading than orders," Coira said softly. "Ask Aelia. She has writings by Greeks and Romans that would surprise you. They certainly surprised me."

"Some of them are real interesting," Tuis offered.

"Aelia?" Rhun asked, his tone neutral. The frown disappeared.

"Uh-huh," his sister replied coyly. "I should have her speak to you."

Rhun shrugged as if indifferent. "Whatever."

"Leave him alone, girl, I'm sure the message hit its target," Elena said, for there were other things she wanted to learn. "I heard Cethen asked after Tuis, but made a point of never asking after me." *Nor would he,* she thought, *because he's a proud, stubborn fool.* "Have you heard from him since?"

Rhun shook his head, but nonetheless raised his eyebrows.

"It was Cian I was curious about," Elena explained, which was a half-truth. "Is he truly resting up with Cethen until he heals? Or have we lost him again?"

"He'll be coming back once his leg is set and mended," Rhun said stiffly, then drained his wine. "I've no reason to think otherwise."

"Well, I have," Elena said, though it was no more than a feeling. "I've listened to Titus tell the story. He didn't say so, but I had the impression that he doubted the leg was broken at all."

All three watched carefully as Rhun's lips tightened, and his features again fell into a frown. When he spoke, it was to dismiss the idea, but Elena saw it had not been banished from his mind.

Cian shifted on the straw pallet and cursed at the dull, throbbing ache in his leg; he was sure it had not been set right. The old crone who'd pulled on it, twisting it worse than a priest's prophecy, had told him it was healing well, but the limb ached worse than a rotten tooth each time he moved, and the board to which it was bound felt like a lame third leg. And the limb itself itched! It itched worse than anything he could remember, mainly because he couldn't scratch it, nor could he get rid of the fleas. The fleas! It was hard to tell which was worse: the fleas, the bugs, or the lice.

After the others had gone, he knew he'd likely fooled no one about the broken leg, especially the primus, for at the time the thing had been whole. The look on the man's face spoke a hundred words, but Cian didn't give a damn. After all those years he'd found his daughter, Emla, and he simply could not leave.

It was hard enough to learn that Murgen, his youngest, had passed on; a fever took her, the first year in the Cumbrian hills. That left only Emla, the one who looked like Nuada: the same dark hair, the pert, elfin looks, the tiny white teeth. At first it seemed a blessing from the gods, but Nuada's lively, impish ways and her outrageous nature had not been handed down to the lass along with the looks, which was a shame.

The girl was fifteen. She lived with a lumpish youth called Fergor on a farmstead several miles west of the settlement, somewhere beyond the falls. The farm was his father's, an equally lumpish farmer and warrior called Ferg, whose home and hog pens had little to choose between them. Cethen as good as apologized to his brother, saying Emla had taken a liking to the boy, and nothing could dissuade her.

All this, Cian had learned after the others left. Even so, the next day he accepted Fergor's offer to ride back to his father's farmstead, when the lad rode in to retrieve Emla. Cian enjoyed the journey immensely, most of it passing in a one-sided conversation with his daughter as they rode through the silent hills. Her sole contribution, delivered in a monotone, was lavish praise for Fergor and his father's farm, which came into view shortly before midday.

The cluster of huts and pens was sited well enough, when first seen from the crest of the hill that hid it. Set well back from a narrow stream on the floor of a small, lush valley, it looked pleasing from a distance. Tiny fields that had been cleared from the forest would be a rich green in the spring, and in many ways it was much like the dales that fed the Abus. Cian found the setting pleasantly familiar and, as they rode down the slope, he began to think that perhaps his daughter's choice was a good one.

Then his nose caught the first whiff of the farmstead, and he wondered if something had died and been left to rot. Hardly had the thought occurred when, with no warning, two enormous hounds leapt from amidst the trees, belatedly baying as if finally aware of intruders. Emla and Fergor's mounts simply flinched and plodded on, clearly familiar with the outburst. Cian's horse squealed in terror and plunged sideways, kicking with its heels. There was a satisfying thump of hooves on flesh, a brief yelp, and Cian found himself sprawled on the ground, with one leg bent backward.

"I think Wolf's jaw is broken," Fergor muttered after dismounting to crouch solemnly alongside the hound, which lay on its side, whimpering.

"Aye," a second voice growled, as a huge, round-shouldered figure lumbered from the trees, with eyes only for the dog.

"That fella's horse kicked him, Da." Fergor pointed accusingly to where Cian lay gritting his teeth. Cian grabbed at his thigh which was a mistake.

"He didn't mean to," Emla said defensively.

"We'll have to put him down," Ferg muttered, sadly shaking his head.

For a moment Cian, in his pain, wondered which they were talking about: him or the fool hound. "Hey," he cried, "I could use some help."

Both men turned from the mewling animal to stare balefully at Cian. Fergor looked particularly surprised. "Is something wrong?"

Cian told them, without paring his words, that there most definitely was—and they could both sodding-well do something about it, and forget their stupid, half-bred, ill-trained, idiot mongrel dog. It was not an auspicious beginning.

An old woman came from farther up the valley, hobbling into Ferg's hut as evening was falling, a bundle slung over one shoulder. Cian had been carried in on Fergor's back, both arms wrapped around the lad's neck in order to keep himself in place. The stink inside was intense, almost a fog, as if the night pots had not been tossed for a week, the washing not done for a month, and the rushes on the floor unchanged for a year. At least the straw was fresh, for it was from this year's crop. Emla brought several bundles inside and laid them along one wall.

Cian's britches were removed, as was his chain mail and leather undertunic, and later that evening the woman set the leg and lashed the limb to a board with strips of grimy cloth. Emla covered him with a wool blanket ripe with the odour of stale sweat and unwashed feet. Later, when he was up to eating and she fed him, he critically studied the food piled in the bowl, and reluctantly took a taste. It was good, quite good, but he couldn't help wondering what was in it.

Cian sighed in despair. He couldn't understand what had happened to the girl. Nuada had been fastidiously clean, with a fresh complexion and the delicious scent of fresh soap always part of her presence; and so had the two children—including Emla! The rest of his kin had been the same, for it was important. Huh—even the Romans were fanatics about it. When on patrol, he found himself itching, sometimes literally, to get back to the baths at Lavatris, and douse himself in the makeshift pools. Yet here he was with his only daughter, sprawled on a straw pallet in what was now her home, and it felt as if he was bedding down with the pigs. He belatedly wondered if the girl was actually married.

The crone would not allow him to move for several weeks, and then only to hobble among the shabby clutter of hovels with a crutch, the damaged leg dragging behind, like a bird with a broken wing. By then the fleas had migrated to the straw, and shortly after that the lice followed.

Brooding on his straw pallet one night, Cian, not for the first time in his life, seriously contemplated his future. He did so while scratching every part of his body that could be scratched, as the old, odorous crone hovered over his naked thigh probing the break with fingers that, in all fairness, seemed quite adept. Later that night, when the loud, rutting groans of Fergor and his daughter once again filled the inside of the hut, he still had no answer to his quandary.

"Ah, bugger it!" Cian mumbled, but when he tried to roll over and deaden his ears, the aching leg told him it was not a good idea.

Chapter XIV

Aquae Sulis, A.D. 79

The Ninth Hispana would take to the field early that spring, but it would not, as expected, campaign alongside the Twentieth Valeria Victrix. Nor would it be fielded in support. It would be tasked instead to police the greater part of Brigantia: the mountain-like central hills, and all lands to the east. The strategy was simple, and one agreed to at the joint staff conference held over the winter at *Aquae Sulis*. Agricola presided, of course, flanked by the two senior officers of each of the four legions stationed in Britannia. Much to his surprise, Rhun found himself detailed to attend, along with a scattering of others with an informed familiarity of the north country.

The legate stopped over in Camulodunum on the way south. It seemed that Cartimandua was expecting him, for a lavish meal had been prepared and was served Roman style, on couches that faced inward toward a long, low table. There were more than a dozen present, including Vellocatus and the commander of the fort. Rhun found himself off in one corner next to the man, who droned on about cavalry field tactics and the relative merit of Batavi troops versus Tungri. It was obvious he would rather be with his own mess, enjoying a relaxing ale and the usual banter.

Cartimandua lay beside the legate on the couch across from the centre of the table, and guided the table talk. Rhun quickly noted that the pair were completely at ease with each other. Vellocatus, her husband, had placed himself opposite, and seemed quite content to eat, listen, and speak only when he had something to say. The man was the same age as his wife and had an easy, pleasant face, with a ready smile that at times seemed to hold a trace of mockery.

As the evening wore on, the queen centred more of her attention on Gaius, leaving the others to their own devices. She would reach out and touch his hand, or perhaps set hers on his arm or shoulder to emphasize her words. Her eyes did not leave the legate's for longer than necessary, and her laughter was often more a giggle. Gaius did not appear uncomfortable, though, which was surprising, for Rhun usually found him to be stiff around others. He saw that her husband appraised the two more than once with narrowed eyes; but that mocking smile would cross his lips, and he seemed more amused that annoyed. Perhaps, Rhun decided, all three had at one time travelled the same path.

Rhun kept half an ear on the fort commander's droning and the other half on the table talk. The mention of Marcus caught his attention, when Gaius raised the matter of his son's captivity. It was well-known that the Carvetii held the youth, and the legate asked for help wherever it might be found. Rhun realized the man was employing the adage that, if a blind man shoots enough arrows, one will find its target. There was no help to be found here, though, and Gaius probably knew as much. Cartimandua merely offered the usual platitudes, as did Vellocatus, and the conversation might have moved on, but the visit to Rhun's father was mentioned.

The old queen's attention abruptly shifted, and she stared hard at Rhun. "Tell me of the meeting."

Rhun glanced at the legate, who nodded his approval. So he spoke of the trek into the Cumbrian hills, and the meeting with Dermat, Cethen, and his woman, naming them all. He'd been not long into the telling of it, though, when he saw Cartimandua had more on her mind. Her expression grew impatient, and she finally waved him to silence.

"My first husband, Venutius. Did your da say how it was, at the end?"

Rhun gulped and told the story, but stopped short of his father's final thrust with the knife. He simply finished by saying, truthfully, "It was a belly wound, from a spear. Those take a long time dying."

"A belly wound." Cartimandua seemed to savour the words, then

183

asked, "Did he die brave, or did he scream his guts out?"

"Father said he died well."

The answer didn't seem to please her. "Did your da say if he spoke of me?"

"I believe he mentioned you," Rhun said cautiously.

"Liar," Cartimandua snapped, her eyes two slits, as if she were gauging him.

Rhun shrugged helplessly and affirmed that, believe it or not, that's what happened.

"So what did he say?" she asked.

"It wasn't complimentary," Rhun replied, wishing he'd kept his mouth shut.

"So you speak the truth," Cartimandua crowed, then added, "Or you remember what your father said, anyway. So tell me, what was he wearing?" She leaned forward, her eyes once more intense.

Rhun knew where she was casting her net, and was deliberately obtuse, feigning puzzlement. "Venutius? Father didn't say. A wool tunic, perhaps? It was late summer, I think, or perhaps autumn, and—"

"You know what I mean, turd," Cartimandua rasped. "But if I have to chisel the words for you, did he have the torque of Brigantia on him?"

Rhun shook his head as he spoke, again telling the truth, though he chose the words carefully. "No, he didn't. Da said so. And *he* raised the matter, not I, because when he talks of Venutius's death, everyone asks if he was wearing it."

"Was the bitch that travels with your father there? She'd gladly wear it if she could."

"Morallta? I never saw her with it," Rhun said, then added, just to tantalize the woman, "But of course, that doesn't mean she hasn't got it."

"You think she has?" Cartimandua demanded.

"No," Rhun said. "She'd be flaunting it as her claim to lead the people. Besides, I'm sure Da would have said something if she had it. No, logic would have it hidden at Stannick, for surely if someone had it, there would have been word."

All of which was true, he told himself, at least in terms of logic. It was just that his father did not follow the logic of most chieftains.

And for that, Rhun thought with an insight that startled him, his father might just be the greater of them all.

Cartimandua seemed to lose interest, except for one last question that he found amusing. "So, turd, what *did* he say about me before he died?"

"His choice of words were not the best," Rhun said, trying to sound apologetic. "I believe he offered the opinion that you weren't a bad old bitch. Not deep down."

Rhun held his breath as Cartimandua pondered the words, and noticed that everyone else at the table did the same. Finally she nodded her acceptance, and smiled. "At least he thought of me before crossing over. I suppose he wasn't such a bad old bastard, either. Not deep down." She paused, then gave a deep, throaty chuckle. "About two paces down!"

"From here to here, and each one able to call upon the other within a matter of hours."

The huge model of northern Britannia sat in the reception hall at Aquae Sulis, the only practical room to hold it. Agricola paused, his eyes searching the score or more faces gathered there, as if to be certain everyone understood. From the gasp that had accompanied its unveiling, Rhun was sure they did, for the model was a simple one. Many of the forts had already been built; it was just that nobody had seen them all laid out in such detail. The enormous undertaking seemed suddenly daunting.

A great string of forts crept north on either side of Brigantia, then stretched across the hills at the top to meet each other. Lavatris, as far as Rhun could see, was the last to be built on the east side of the model, and only a few remained to be built to complete the link across the hills. Yet Agricola had not stopped there. The model showed other forts probing farther north through the lands of such tribes as the Selgovae and Votadini, and even on to the vast highlands of the Caledonii.

The strongholds, each marked by a small red dot, seemed endless, but Rhun smiled to himself at how typical of the Romans this undertaking was. Rome to Germania was a far greater distance, and if its model were set on the floor and marked with similar red dots, it would likely resemble a man with the pox. And the spacing would be no different: each outpost was within a good day's march of the other, or a few hours distant, for a rider dragging a spare horse.

"These will be completed this season." Agricola pointed to the string of forts uniting east and west; then his finger moved farther north. "And this one here, and this, and this."

Rhun remembered Morallta's sneering conviction that Rome was not invincible. Not for the first time did he sigh, and wish his people could see what he could see.

When the briefing was over, Agricola and his generals spent the balance of the afternoon inside the huge spa, which had been cleared for the governor's use. Greatly outranked, a rabbit in a den of foxes, Rhun accompanied them, as instructed. He would rather have been freezing his rear in the hills of Brigantia.

Aquae Sulis was not the pride of the Roman Empire, Rhun decided, for he'd seen better baths in the forts of Germania. But the engineers were working on it. They'd built an enormous, lead-lined reservoir to hold the hot water that surfaced each day, then channelled it to the bathhouse farther south, which housed a warm bathing room, cold water pools, a dry heat room, a large change room, and latrines. And if the structure was basic and crude, then in fairness to the builders, it was at this point only temporary.

Rhun found himself on a bench in the dry heat room with several other junior officers, each with a towel, and all patiently waiting for the governor to move on so they could do the same. He was certain that each one, like himself, would have rather been elsewhere. They had followed Agricola and the other senior officers into the warming room, then on to the hot pool, and finally a cold plunge, all of them trailing behind like the tail of a donkey. A scented oiling and massage were all that remained, and the ordeal would be over.

A voice called his name, and he saw the legate beckoning to him from a stone bench where he sat alongside the governor. Cursing under his breath, Rhun rose and padded over. What do you do when you're dripping like a sweating horse, there's a damp towel loose around your middle, and everyone is half naked: stand at attention, or casually at ease? He slumped into a stiff, awkward stance that was neither one nor the other and said, "Sir."

Agricola took care of the dilemma. "Relax, trooper. The enemy's outside, not in here." He gestured to a bench across from where the two were sitting. "Rest your rear."

"Sir." Rhun sat down, his eyes unwittingly appraising the general, who was a good deal less intimidating when naked. The man was not large in stature, but had the look of a soldier: cropped hair, weathered skin, stern, straight lips, and eyes that were flinty but intelligent. And, unlike those of some commanders he'd seen on the Rhenus, they held no hint of cruelty. Agricola had a reputation for fairness, both with the legions and the "barbarian" auxiliary troops.

"So what do you see, son?" Agricola asked with a grin.

Rhun gave an honest answer. "A general, sir."

The governor chuckled and turned to Gaius. "A diplomat, not an orator. Does he look like his father, or his mother?"

"I'd say more of his father. The nose. Maybe the jaw. Yes, a definite resemblance. Though as I recall, his father was a good deal more successful with the face hair.'

Rhun cringed and he felt his cheeks flush. The fair, wispy crop he'd started above his upper lip was not without a certain bushiness, he thought; though Coira had mentioned, not long ago, that the weed could use water.

"I understand your father is a man of his word, Rhun?" Agricola said.

Rhun nodded agreement. "Sir."

"Which isn't bad, considering he's a Brigante warrior." The barb was spoken with a smile, as if intended to spark a response.

Rhun did not disappoint. "He feels that Legate Sabinius is also a man of his word, which he says isn't bad, considering he's a Roman soldier." It was audacious, but Rhun spoke with a grin, telling himself that he didn't give a pail of pig swill whether the governor liked it or not.

"Good; very good, Rhun," Agricola said, ignoring Gaius's raised eyebrows. "And now that you've freed your tongue, tell me: the Cumbria hills—can you speak of them and not compromise your duty to your father?"

Rhun, taken aback by the candour of the question, hesitated before replying, "I haven't seen much of them—certainly not as much as your people have in the west. Tall, steep hills, many lakes, a web of streams, and heavy forests. Deep, wooded valleys and sharp fells, all wandering this way and that; it's easy to get lost. A rugged country in which to campaign. Yet I suppose it also breaks the people up, isolates them."

'Which says nothing I don't know." Agricola's eyes searched Rhun's. "A sweep through the lot, in force. Early spring, as soon as the snow goes. What will happen?"

"I'd guess it would scatter them, for the time being," Rhun said. "They would run before the army, or filter into the forests and return later. The 'die and be damned' warriors might clear out, though, and join with the northern tribes. But only if the forts are established, and you're seen as likely to stay."

"They won't remain and fight?"

"If you were to just do a sweep and leave, then yes, they would. But you're not going to do that." Rhun's breath left him, and he felt oddly sad. "Already many of them, in their hearts, believe Rome will prevail. With the forts going up, those who do stay are, naturally, less likely to continue fighting than those who migrate north. And there would be little pressure on them to do so."

"And Marcus Sabinius, what of him? If we strike fast, what would you guess the odds are of getting him back?"

Rhun's eyes widened at the question, and he paused, thinking it through. Agricola, and the legate too, had probably gone through this a hundred times. And his thoughts on the prospects, he realized, were likely no different than theirs. Perhaps they were looking for more…

"I doubt I can tell you anything you don't know. If you have them trapped, I suppose they'd use him as their way out. In fact, they've told us as much," Rhun said. "If not, they'll keep him to bargain with, when the time comes. I'll say this, though—if the copper-haired woman has him, toss reason to the winds. I wouldn't lean on her shield, for Marcus's sake."

"That's much the way we see it." Agricola paused, thoughtfully stroking his chin. "And why would you, with your father a warrior chief in Cumbria, tell me this?"

Rhun raised his bare shoulders in a shrug. "It's nothing you don't know already, sir. And even if not, it's still only a prediction. But my answer: if Rome's advance is going to happen anyway, and the diehards do flee north, those who remain will live. Which solves my own dilemma. And as to reprisals, you are Agricola, sir, not Suetonius. I see no conflict in my words."

"You think with your mind, not your heart."

The words were more of a question than a statement, and Rhun smiled ruefully. "Much of my heart was left at Stannick, and more of it," he bowed his head to Gaius, "was pummelled flat in Italia. It still beats, but the mind seems to work the better of the two."

"Tell me." Agricola again smiled as he turned the subject. "What of this legend that your father will one day slay the legate on the parapets of Eboracum, while the fortress burns. Did he really see a vision?"

Rhun was momentarily thrown by the question, then he laughed as it struck him how his father would answer. He would make light of Agricola's curiosity and enjoy telling the truth of the prophecy, how it was invented by Venutius's old druid Trencoss, and the reason why. Rhun set out to do exactly that, and soon found himself at ease with the story, even when the new legate of the Second Adiutrix joined them, a man called Demetrius Catus. When he finished the tale, however, and the laughter died, Rhun grew suddenly aware that he was in the presence of an imperial governor and two legates. He quickly made his excuses.

There seemed to be no sign that the room was about to clear, so he made his way to the nearest empty bench and sprawled on top, face down. His mind drifted to the governor's briefing, and his orders on the timing of the campaign itself. The start was still a few months away, but he knew his life at Eboracum would be disrupted. Which was a shame, because while the staff work was irksome, the time spent refining his written Latin had proved surprisingly enjoyable.

The lessons on grammar were a light enough penalty for the time spent in Aelia's company, though of late she'd begun prattling on about the writings of Greek philosophers and Roman poets. There might be no way out of reading them, if he was to keep seeing her. And—Rhun shuddered at the thought—she was the legate's daughter! What would the man do if he ever discovered the real reason he visited—

" …at the time you buried my brother."

The harsh voice intruded on his musings, and Rhun opened one eye and saw that the two legates had left the bench they'd shared with the governor. Catus stood several paces away, his back to Rhun as he spoke to Gaius. The man's voice was not loud, but it had a penetrating, nasal quality that carried.

"As I recall, Demetrius, it was you who tended to the burial of Lucius," Gaius said.

Rhun wondered if he should move, but if he did, it would show he'd heard. How long had they been there? His eye again closed, this time feigning sleep.

"There is more than one meaning to the phrase," Catus said.

There was a long pause, then, "And what meaning am I to deduce?"

"I have since learned Helvia was helpful in settling Lucius into his new command before he died," Catus replied.

Gaius snorted his disgust. "Over the years, my wife appears to have helped more than one contemptible officer settle into his post. Which is reason enough why she is no longer my wife. And I trust you heard my words, Demetrius: contemptible officer! Deduce what *you* wish from that."

"But none of the others died the day you found the woman playing you for a fool."

Rhun opened his eye and saw Gaius flinch. Would he attack the man? But while the legate paused, tight jawed, he held his temper. "There you go, then. Why would it be so with your porcine brother?" He laughed bitterly. "Because, you see, long before I returned to Lindum, I was fully aware of the facts."

"Then I stand corrected. I should have said that none of the others died the day you returned to deal with the matter."

"Demetrius, listen to yourself," Gaius said, his voice strained, yet surprisingly even. "Your words lack substance. Let me put things clearly. Your brother may have deserved killing for reasons of which I am unaware, but I fail to see why they'd include dallying with my wife."

"There was a child that also died," Catus sneered. "My brother's. All that was left of him."

"By the shores of Elysium, am I suspect in that, too?" Gaius cried angrily, his voice genuinely incredulous—Rhun thought the legate might lose control of himself. "You are an ass. A blind and stupid ass. That birth was the pivot point of my patience! I divorced the woman because of a child that was obviously not mine. That is all. I was a long way from there when the poor creature died. Shit! Now I've heard it all."

"I spoke to her in Rome recently," Catus interrupted.

"Aah! So that's it!" Gaius paused long enough to snort his disgust. "So tell me, what *is* on your mind, Catus? Or am I supposed to ask how she fares?"

"She told me that you killed Lucius."

Rhun ceased breathing, bracing for the response. At that moment, he could have been roped to an elephant and not dragged away. When Gaius responded, his voice was taut and stretched, his words slow, as if carefully chosen.

"Catus, you go too far. If you have a complaint, bring charges. But I warn you, do not slander me, or I'll slice you open from gullet to groin. And above all, you will not spread lies to further your fantasy."

"But your wife—"

"You lie. I am not a fool, Catus. For Helvia to say as much, she would implicate herself."

"She implied the deed. And when I put it clearly, she didn't deny it."

"Hah!" Gaius laughed out loud. "My entire marriage was spent playing such games with the woman. Think about this: what better way to spite the husband who threw her out?"

Rhun, his eyes again closed, began breathing again. There was another pause, followed by one final, barely controlled comment from Catus: "I am not satisfied."

Rhun listened to the flip-flop of bare feet crossing the floor and relaxed, his mind turning over what had been said. It appeared the legate had an enemy, and an implacable one. Obviously the death of the man's brother, however it occurred, stood unresolved. Rhun's mind wandered back, trying to recall what he'd heard in the past, for there had been rumours.

An ice-cold trickle of water struck the pit of his back. Rhun whirled on one elbow to find the legate standing alongside the bench with one eyebrow raised, a dripping ewer in his hand, and a sardonic look on his face.

"So, young Rhun, what do you think of the new legate Catus?"

There was no point in denying what he'd heard. It was also not the time to point out that decurios had no business offering opinions on senior officers. Rhun swung his legs to the floor and sat up. "He's a man I would watch closely if he were at my back, sir."

"I agree," Gaius murmured. "And since no one I know is blessed with eyes in the back of their skull, you might do that for me. Should the occasion arise."

Rhun fumbled for an answer, but the legate was already wandering toward the exit. It was time to leave. The room was becoming terribly hot.

At the end of January, with two months before he returned to the field, Rhun lost Turren as his squadron optio. Huge, ugly, and seemingly slow in both motion and wit, Luga had proved himself time and again as Cian's right-hand man; but without Cian, leading and administering a full squadron exceeded the poor man's limits. When Turren was transferred to take over as decurio, Luga was relieved in more ways than one.

The gods, however, always perverse in working their ways, brought Cian back from the hills shortly thereafter. He rode into the fort at Lavatris in mid-February on the same horse he'd ridden out, both looking the worse for wear. The chain mail bore signs of rust, the horse was gaunt, and so was Cian. He remained there for two days, confined to the fort while Luga helped clean him up. The moustaches went, and every hair on his body was cut back to the roots as the hospital orderlies powdered and salved him from head to foot. After that it was to the baths, in a separate copper tub, where it took another half-day to scrub him pink enough to satisfy the *medicus*.

Once he was presentable, with his armour oiled and weapons shining, Cian was dispatched to Eboracum. The fort commander at Lavatris had no idea what else to do with him.

"You're more than a month late, trooper," Titus growled.

The primus glared at Cian, then at Rhun, then swung his gaze back to Cian, eyes raking him with obvious distaste. The three men stood in the headquarters building at one end of the huge cross hall, where anyone who cared to do so might listen.

"You were given six weeks to heal to the point of being able to ride. Your brother told me there should be no worry on that account," Titus continued, his voice icy. "Allowing an extra two weeks for buggering around, that's two months. You've taken more than three. Making your mind up, were you, or just malingering?"

"It took time to heal, sir," Cian replied, deliberately favouring the leg. "And the hills were drifted in. They still are. It was difficult to move."

"It never stopped the patrols, soldier," Titus hissed. "I saw you limping. Did it not set correctly? Perhaps the surgeon needs to rebreak it. Perhaps I should help!"

"No, no, sir. The leg's quite alright," Cian said quickly and, with a sideways glance at Rhun, patted his thigh; his nephew had warned him not to exaggerate the injury. "Probably the ride down from Lavatris. It's still sore. A break takes a while to get back to normal."

The primus frowned as if puzzled. "Drop your britches."

"Sir?"

"You heard me. Drop 'em!"

Another sidelong glance then Cian, clearly puzzled, began working at the drawstring. A moment later they were below his knees, revealing a clean, white linen binding around his left thigh, and an equally white, hairless body.

Again the primus frowned. "Was it not the right leg that was broken, trooper?"

Cian licked his lips. "No sir, it was the left. Never was nothing wrong with the right."

"Take the bandage off."

Cian, sweating, bent and unwrapped the tight linen. He knew the limb looked normal, as might be expected, for it had been a simple fracture; but the thing *had* been broken.

Titus bit his lip and wandered to one side of Cian, as if circling him. When he was out of sight, he turned and sharply rapped the offending thigh with his baton. Cian's leg jerked involuntarily, and he cried out in pain.

"Still a bit tender, then?" Titus asked, nodding as if satisfied. He returned to stand in front of Cian, leaving him with his britches about his knees. Cian nodded confirmation, his eyes misty.

"Your daughter, is she doing well?"

"Seems happy enough, sir."

"Pleased to hear that, trooper." The primus turned and addressed Rhun as if Cian no longer existed. "This man's been away for three months. His edge will be blunted. Place him in the ranks of your squadron, Rhun, and see that edge is honed. I'll not see Turren replaced simply because the leader of his squadron decides to piss off and take Gallic leave. Is that understood?"

"Yes, sir."

"And see that your uncle's pay is stopped for another three months."

"Yes, sir."

Titus turned back to Cian and gave him a final once-over, his eyes coming to rest on the fresh stubble that topped his head. "At least you got yourself a decent haircut. You will keep it that way until you're back in the field," he said, then looked hard at Cian's face. "The shave didn't improve your looks any."

Instead of dismissing the pair, the primus stalked off as if he had business elsewhere, his hobnailed boots clumping across the wooden floor. Halfway to the headquarters' door he stopped and turned. In a voice that could be he heard throughout the whole building, he roared, "And don't just stand there with your prick hanging out, trooper, hoist your britches! This isn't a fucking whorehouse."

Feeling the heat rush to his face, Cian bent over and pulled up his pants, wondering if that was the extent of it. If so … His breath left him in a sigh of relief.

Rhun, glancing down, edged one foot back as if resisting the urge to give his uncle a good, swift kick in the rear. Instead he murmured, "I think you got off light."

"I suppose," Cian muttered half-heartedly, and simply because it was expected, added, "But he took my squadron away."

"What did you expect? You could have been flogged. Or worse. He knows damned well it was the other leg, he just never took you to task on it." Cian said nothing as he knotted his britches. Rhun placed a hand on his shoulder and said, "You'll get it back. Or another one. Within a year, I'd wager."

"There." Cian looked up from his britches and displayed the same *who gives a pig turd* grin he'd worn when he'd first seen Rhun at Vetera. "That's a good wager, and I'll not take it. I'm too good not to get it back," he said cheerfully. "But I had to find out, Rhun, and you have the right of it. You can't go back."

"What about Emla?"

"Ah, that's the sad part, Rhun. And it is truly sad, for the lass is someone I just don't know anymore." Cian sighed his torment and looked at his nephew. "I can't go back, and the lass isn't willing to go forward. I tried. In a small way, I wish I'd never found her again."

Chapter XV

Cumbria, A.D. 79

The winter was hard, and two great storms struck in February, threatening to drive spring onward into summer. Drifts blew in deep from the fells, plugging the valleys, blocking the trails, and isolating villages and farmsteads alike. It wasn't until mid-March that the icy blanket began to thaw, and people once more began to stir.

Marcus found the endless, snowbound landscape made little difference to life inside the hill fort. One month of drudgery blended with the next, as his body thinned and his mind grew numb. The dull, daily, back-breaking tasks were as endless as those of the lowest skivvy. Urs seemed to work no less, though he enjoyed a singular place among the tribesmen, possibly because he was large, but also due to his good nature. He was neither master nor slave, nor warrior or freeman; his status was more that of a camp follower who, as long as he toiled for his keep, was welcome to remain.

Marcus was never beyond the big Silure's watchful eye, yet he found the slave had the sense to keep his manners and his place. In the beginning it had been a touchy thing. When Urs threatened to ram food down his throat if that was what it took, the man had definitely overstepped his position. Which was ironic, for at the time Marcus had grudgingly decided the oaf Cethen had the right of one thing: there was no point in starving to death. Which produced the second irony: living on their dull, tepid, tasteless, short-rationed winter diet, a man could die of starvation anyway.

By the time the long winter passed and the first warm winds of spring began clearing the frozen hills, Marcus's mind had dulled liked a rusted sword. Each day blended with the next in its monotony, and the sharp longing for freedom, blunted over a brutal winter, seemed to fade with the melting snow. The promise was there, tucked in the recesses of his mind, but a sparse diet and an endless, boring routine had sapped the desire to realize it. Life was merely passing, and Marcus Sabinius found he could do no more than live it.

Reinforcing the fading hope was the fact that he had no idea where he was. The ride from Luguvalium had taken nearly three days, but that was all he knew. There was neither sight nor scent of the sea, only thickly wooded hills wherever he cared to look. A lake, anywhere from a half-mile to five miles long (it was hard to judge from the top of the log walls), lay not far from the small hill fort. Yet even if someone had told him what it was called, it would have provided no clue to his whereabouts. Marcus couldn't name a single lake in the entire province of Britannia.

The snows disappeared as March was dying, leaving only the odd drift clinging to the peaks of the mountain-like hills. The land began to green and buds swelled on the trees as the days marched forward into spring. On a day in early April, Marcus found himself alone splitting logs, a chore he found less bitter than most. The wood didn't stink, it didn't bite or kick, and it didn't require milking, mucking, or slopping; the constant swing of the axe did tighten the muscles, raise a healthy sweat, and, if properly paced, was not overly tiring.

It was while standing still, honing the axe, that Marcus noticed movement at the far end of the lake. A glint of light on metal, nothing more; most likely a weapon or someone's helmet catching the sun. Since nobody else remarked on it, he assumed it was a Carvetii war party, which meant the barbarians were on the move again. The man Cethen and his woman had been back and forth over the past month, staying over only twice: once to cadge provisions, and the second time to drop off several wounded. Marcus noted that no captives were brought in, either time.

A few hours later, as he was stacking the split logs, a large band of the barbarians came thundering into camp, men who were both mounted and on foot. There had obviously been a fight. Some had wounds, some were short on equipment, and most wore that hurried, harried look that spoke of things gone wrong. It was the same look he'd seen on the faces of his own people, that first day at Bran's Beck. Marcus quietly laid down the axe and tried to make himself as inconspicuous as possible.

Without any apparent command, the barbarians who lived at the fort began moving out. The animals inside were forced into the open, while those at pasture were gathered and driven deeper into the hills. Some, such as the milk cows, were herded along the track that led northwest. Carts and oxen followed, along with more of the bewildered farm animals, and a long, straggling column of bundle-laden tribesmen. Marcus bit his lip. The exodus could mean only one thing. If the barbarian was abandoning his hill fort, then a Roman army was surely on its way.

A figure stepped silently up beside him and he whirled, startled, then relaxed when he saw Urs.

"Your friends are coming," the slave murmured.

"I think you have the right of it," Marcus whispered, hardly daring to believe.

"You may smell the chicken, but it's not yet on your plate."

"Smell it? I can taste it, feathers and all," Marcus said, then glanced at the slave. "So, are you staying, or running?"

"One year has passed; there are two to go." Urs smiled. "I can taste that, too."

"But your chicken is not yet on the—" Marcus broke off with a curse as a troop of barbarian cavalry galloped through the gate, followed by a riderless horse and a single chariot. Two of the barbarians veered straight toward Marcus.

"No one has taken you from here?" Dermat shouted, as if surprised. "Stupid fools..."

Cethen's horse had its blood up, circling as if out of control. Pulling at the reins and cursing, Cethen caught the eye of the man on the chariot. "Dag, get rid of that useless pair of wheels. I want one of your ponies."

"But—"

"Look, you great fat fool, the middle one's leaking blood like a chopped chicken. It's going to drop at any moment, and you'll be stuck anyway."

"What'll I do?" Dag wailed.

"Ebric," Dermat yelled impatiently. "Catch that loose stray and bring it here for Dag."

Dag hurried down from the chariot, unhitched the offside pony, and passed the reins up to Ebric in exchange for the riderless horse.

"What do I do with these?" Ebric demanded, staring in disgust at the long leather reins and the scrawny pony standing at the other end.

"Just hold them," Cethen yelled, then pointed to Marcus. "Get on that. Now!"

"And you." Dermat tossed a knife into the dirt at Urs's feet, and pointed to where the bleeding pony sagged in its harness. "Cut the reins off the crow fodder, and tie the Roman to this one. Feet under the belly, and tight. Tie his hands, too."

"To what?" Urs asked, glancing at the animal's bare back.

"To each other, idiot," Dermat growled, and turned to Marcus. "Are you deaf? Get on!"

Marcus took one look and decided this was no time to argue. He mounted the pony. Great tufts of the animal's winter coat clung to its back and belly, falling away in handfuls as he steadied himself. The pony's rib cage felt like brittle sticks between his knees. Urs crouched down alongside, and Marcus felt a length of rein loop around his ankles, pulling them together.

"Tight. The knots will be tested, and you're a dead man if they're not tight," Dermat growled.

Marcus winced as both ankles ground painfully together, and the leather bit deep into his flesh. Urs wound the second piece quickly around both wrists, and Marcus found himself helpless on the pony's back as Cethen took the long reins.

"You." Dermat pointed once more to Urs. "Keep up with him, or it's at your own peril."

Marcus glanced around. The hill fort was almost empty. Cethen started toward the open gate, but paused when the pounding of more hooves sounded beyond. The barbarians tensed and readied their weapons. Marcus felt a flame of hope touch his heart, but it waned when a second troop of barbarians rode through the entrance. Several were hurt.

One of them, a man who looked hardly older than Marcus, rode his lathered horse alongside Cethen. He wore a sword at his belt, but both his shield and spear were gone. A wide patch of blood glistened around a dark hole in the shoulder of his leather tunic. "They must have seen the fort," he said, gamely fighting the reins with only one hand. "They've sent a large force of cavalry forward."

"I thought we had more time." Cethen looked anxiously at the gate, then down at the pony's reins as if seeing them for the first time. "Here, Ligan, take these and tie them to your saddle."

"Hang onto him; we have to go back," Dermat called as he urged his horse through the gate. "In the long run, he may prove of more value than a small army."

"I have to go back too," Ligan protested, and tried to turn his horse with his good hand.

"You're not fit to fight a rabid rabbit," Cethen said, edging his own animal alongside; he leaned over and tied the long leather reins to Ligan's saddle. "You know who this is. If things go wrong, his life's worth more than yours." That said, he lashed at his horse and galloped off through the gate after the others.

Only one other rider, badly wounded and slumped forward in the saddle, remained inside the hill fort. Ligan cursed and looked back at Marcus with the glare of a man told to muck out the pigs. His eyes fell on Urs. "You, get up behind that man and follow me." He pointed to the other wounded trooper. "Hold him in the saddle as long as he still lives."

Marcus watched as Urs climbed onto the horse and settled behind the saddle, one arm around the wounded barbarian's belly. The pony jerked forward and followed Ligan down the slope that led to the gate. Mind whirling, Marcus tried unsuccessfully to repress a rising sense of elation. The Twentieth—it had to be the Twentieth—were already in the hills. Which was early. And it was classic Agricola: do the unexpected. The barbarians had not yet concentrated, and he wasn't going to allow them time. Again, for he knew too well how the gods played their games, Marcus tried to fight back a rising flicker of hope.

Ligan kept them moving all that day, pausing only to allow the horses to drink. Time passed slowly, the animals plodding along in the midst of countless others fleeing northward. It was all the wounded barbarian seemed capable of. They spent the night in a makeshift camp: a small clearing ringed by enormous, thick-rooted trees that could readily serve as a temple fit for the gods. The flickering glow of countless fires showed through the trees; thousands appeared to be gathered there. Food was scarce, but there was enough to kill the cramp of hunger.

The badly wounded trooper died there, despite the care of the women who fussed over him half the night. The same women closed the wound in Ligan's shoulder left by a spear thrust; it was not deep, but it had leaked a good deal of blood. It pained the man dearly, for his face was ashen when he climbed on his horse at daybreak, and he sat unsteady in the saddle. But his mind was sharp enough; he ordered Urs to load the dead man's horse with an aged and crippled woman and a gaggle of small children barely old enough to walk.

The following afternoon found them tramping down from the hills onto a sparsely wooded plain that stretched as far as the sea. Perhaps the Ituna estuary itself, Marcus hoped, which should bring them closer to Luguvalium. And not for the first time, as the fresh, tart, kelp-ridden scent of the sea touched the air, he wondered what had happened there at the fort, after he'd been taken.

Ligan led them close by the shore as evening fell. The tide was out on a quiet sea, leaving a broad expanse of glistening sand. Seeing the low, dark blur of another coastline far to the north, Marcus reasoned it was the other shoulder of the estuary, which meant that Luguvalium lay inland, somewhere in between. How far, he had no idea, nor had he time to care before something closer drew his eye.

As the pony plodded free of the trees, Marcus saw scattered on every side the largest and most disorganized mass of humanity he had seen anywhere, including the city of Rome itself. He wondered if there was some sort of magic by which the barbarians communicated. It was as if they had all fled the hills in answer to a call borne on the wind. Thousands were gathered there: old men, women, children, and menials; warriors on foot, warriors with chariots, and warriors with horses. More than a few were wounded, but most by far were whole. The vast, makeshift camp seemed to cover all the open land that lay between the shore and the forest. He turned his head and saw others trickling in behind him, and even more farther down the coast.

His head bowed over the saddle as if in relief, Ligan towed Marcus through the chaos, clearly searching for something. Urs followed, leading the dead man's horse with its tired riders, and a tail of perhaps thirty or forty others trudging wearily behind. The ragged file had not gone far when someone called Ligan's name. Without looking up, he pulled the reins to one side, and the tired horse simply plodded off in that direction.

"Help him," someone cried, and a figure rushed forward to grasp the animal's bridle.

Ligan tried to dismount, but instead slumped forward, then slid from the saddle. Willing arms caught him before he struck the ground. Marcus watched dispassionately as the young barbarian was laid on the grass and quickly surrounded by women, all pulling at his bloody tunic. He blinked, struck by the oddness of the scene in the fading light; it was like spying on a band of ghouls robbing the dead.

He continued to watch vacantly from the back of the pony, the animal too tired to tug at the lush spring grass. He could do nothing even if he wanted to; he was tied, and his wrists, ankles, and butt were in agony. Even so, it was not long before his head drooped forward, and his eyes closed with a will of their own. He wasn't sure whether he was dozing or not when a hard slap caught him high on the thigh, close by where he'd stabbed himself with the knife.

"You're alive!"

Startled, Marcus turned to find Fiona staring up at him, and groaned. He glanced wildly about, hoping for once to see Cethen, or even Dermat. But other than Urs, there was not a familiar face in sight—and the slave's attention was elsewhere. The fool was more than a hundred paces away, knee deep in the incoming tide, playing with the brats he'd been leading all day!

Licking his lips, Marcus turned back to the woman and spoke the first lie that came to his lips. "I'm glad to see you are, too." His eyes fell to her belly, which was as round as a barbarian shield. The next words were out before he could stop them. "I see your whoring has finally caught up with you."

Fiona's eyes flashed and Marcus shied, expecting a blow. Instead she hissed, "Yes, you bastard."

Marcus blinked as the meaning penetrated. "Are you saying it's mine?"

Fiona ignored him, other than to spit and walk away.

"Hey!"

Marcus wrestled with the leather bonds on his wrists, and when they didn't give, he kicked his feet in an effort to loosen the ankle ties. The pony, which had finally lowered its head to crop the grass, lunged forward; but just as quickly, the creature's head was jerked back by the reins tied to Ligan's horse, and it lurched sideways. With a cry of panic, Marcus slid from the animal's back. A moment later he was suspended upside down beneath the pony's belly, his head resting on the ground. He heard a roar of laughter as he struggled angrily to free himself, but the beast lashed out with a hind leg, grazing his skull. Marcus fell still, afraid to move.

"You truly look like the stupid, idiot, useless turd that you are," a voice murmured nearby.

Marcus shifted his eyes sideways, unwilling to move his head. He saw first the pregnant belly, then above it Fiona's dark hair and angry face. "I asked if you're saying it's mine."

The green glinted in her eyes. "What word did you not understand? It can't be *bastard*, for you've been one so long, you must know the meaning by heart. It has to be the word 'yes'! In fact, I'm sure of it, for you don't know the meaning of the word 'no,' either."

"And *you* don't know the meaning of the word 'whore,'" Marcus snapped back, and flinched as the pony's hoof whipped past his ear. "I certainly didn't hear the word 'no' when you spread your legs."

Fiona laughed, but there was no humour in it. "I was trying to kill you, fool. Or has that slipped your memory?"

"Ah-hah! There you are, then! You got balled instead. So who got the best of it?" Marcus lifted his head as he shouted, then quickly set it back again; but the pony was now tugging at the grass, its hooves still. "And how you can say I fathered your brat is beyond me. What did you do, roll the dice and pick me?"

"I know whose it is, pig, I know." Fiona leaned down and thrust her face close to his. "I'd rather it be Aulus. He was a warrior, not a useless Roman fop. But a woman knows, dammit, she knows."

"A roll of the dice."

"I was careful with Aulus." Tears formed in her eyes and she turned away, mumbling. "Then you come along! You're nothing but a stinking, grunting Roman boar."

"Hey, I didn't stink then," Marcus called after her, a smirk on his face.

"That's what you think."

※

Cethen rode in the following day. Dermat rode with him, as did Criff and almost fifty other riders, many of them wounded. All three men were appalled at the chaos on the crowded shore, and the vast sea of manpower that sat doing nothing, other than idly wait.

"If Venutius was here, his brain would burst," Dermat cried. "Is no one in charge?"

"I think you have the grasp of it," Criff pointed out reasonably, and turned to face Dermat, his expression sincere. "Dermat, nobody's stepped forward to replace Venutius. You know that. The chiefs keep fighting the Romans, but they keep fighting each other too, depending on the day. All you do is ride about trying to pry the stupid buggers apart."

"This is—such a waste," Dermat muttered, staring hopelessly along the coastline.

Cethen shook his head. Criff's words sounded all too familiar, and he knew why. It was as if Dermat were being reproached by Elena. Someone had to do something, though. "Dermat, they all know you. Can't you get them moving?"

"Where?" Dermat murmured as if to himself. He continued to look about the ramshackle camp.

"If the Romans reach here in force, this will be a disaster," Criff said.

Dermat braced himself and finally spoke, as if by force of will alone. "Cethen, start with your kin. I'll find my people and what's left of Venutius's. Something like this should be big enough to stop the stupid buggers' squabbling."

"Where...? Cethen began, but Dermat interrupted.

"Over there." He pointed to the northern end of the cluttered shoreline, where the beach was open. "We'll assemble all those fit to fight down there, and start getting them organized."

"And the others? The people themselves, and those who're hurt?" Cethen asked.

"Yes. Yes, get them moving too, even if you have to push every last one." Dermat's voice grew louder, surer. "They have to get out of here. Get them away from the shoreline. After that they make their own choice: back into the hills and hide until it's over; or move north with us, because I don't think it will be over. There's no other choice." When he spoke again, Dermat rolled his eyes. "The Selgovae will no doubt welcome us."

Cethen picked out the injured riders who had ridden in with him and told them to follow. The others, the healthy ones, trailed after Dermat as he threaded his way along the beach in search of his kin.

Not for the first time in his life, Cethen wondered at the manner in which the gods had abandoned him. Dermat, all of them, had thought there would be more warning. And when the Romans appeared only three days ago, they had all thought the hills, their hills, would offer the sharper edge. But Rome had marched on, brushing aside all that stood in her path, shrugging off the spears and arrows of a hundred sorties, hurled from the forest as much in frustration as anger.

It seemed nobody was perfect, though, for the Romans were making a mistake, a large one—the costly error of time ill spent and failed chances: the enemy continued to scour the hills, and not the shores. Cethen wondered how long it would last.

His eyes fell on Ligan, who sat back against his saddle, hungrily wolfing a bowl of grey porridge. "Still on the right side of the weeds, I see."

"So far." Ligan pointed to where Marcus and Urs sat eating the same gruel. "So is your baggage. Are you here to take him back?"

"No, I'm here to leave him in your charge. Along with these men." Cethen motioned to the injured riders sitting their horses, fifteen in all. "They're hurt too bad to fight, but not too bad to ride. Take them north with your 'baggage.' And these people—" he waved one arm to encompass the entire camp "—some will want to go too. They need a shepherd."

"You want us to look after all of them?" Ligan asked, his face incredulous.

"No, dolt," Cethen snapped in irritation, then realized it might easily be a question he'd ask, tired as he was, and relented. "There'll eventually be other warriors, most of them unhurt. Dermat figures on us all moving north for the time being. The Romans are hemming us in too tightly here. We've just got to get organized ... "

Ligan lurched to his feet and scanned the faces of the wounded men. He smiled and waved to one, then turned back to Cethen. "So where are they now? The Romans?"

"Still back in the hills, but that doesn't mean we can stay here." He turned and pointed to Marcus. "That man is the main task in your life, Ligan, until Dermat tells you otherwise. And if Morallta says different, she can lick the sweat off your bum, or any other part you feel like."

"You're getting brave," Ligan said.

Cethen grinned. "I didn't say to tell her I said so. Anyway, I don't want to lose the Roman."

"I don't either!"

Cethen turned and saw Fiona looking up at him, her arms folded and a determined scowl on her face. "We've talked that over, lass, and Dermat says you don't have a claim."

Fiona said nothing, but for answer patted her enlarged belly. For a moment Cethen stared, then his face split into a huge grin. "Are you sure?"

"Certain of it. Absolutely certain. And as such, I have a claim on him."

"How would you know—" Cethen saw a sudden, fierce glint in the woman's eyes, and decided not to follow that path. "Then he's part yours, for the time being. But these men go along with the bargain." He pointed to Ligan and the ragged, bloody collection of riders behind him. "Between all of you, I'm sure he'll be well guarded."

"They feed themselves," Fiona muttered, then pointed to the small pony grazing alongside Marcus and Urs. "And the pony is mine."

Cethen nodded then, unable to contain himself, laughed out loud. "I feel doubly assured of his care, Fiona."

The ragtag army fumbled its way north for several weeks, gradually edging eastward as if in search of direction. It was a long, battered column of warriors, mounted and on foot, many bearing wounds or sign of illness. And scattered throughout, like a rabble, were the women, children, old men, slaves, and menials. Marcus numbly wondered how many similar columns were fleeing the Cumbrian hills. But then, he spent a lot of time wondering those first days. Trudging ahead of Dag's bone-thin pony, with Fiona perched on top like an overfed queen, he had ample time to do so.

His heart had almost cracked the day they left the crowded shoreline. Agricola's entire fleet had appeared, but all it served to do was speed the barbarian departure. The governor could have landed and destroyed them all. And the cowardly fool should have, Marcus thought, watching helplessly as scores of galleys edged farther up the coast.

The woman Morallta had been there by then, leading orderly columns of riders up and down the sand. Every warrior able to walk had ambled forward to mass on the shoreline, along with thousands of barbarian menials who simply grabbed any weapon handy. It was a huge army puffed up with numbers, but without fangs. Marcus seethed as Agricola's fleet held back, doubtless awed by the sight of so many, and awaiting help from the soldiers it supplied.

A week into the trek Cethen caught up, and two days later Morallta arrived. Almost a hundred well-mounted cavalry rode with each. Dermat followed soon after with a small army of foot warriors, and the march north gradually grew more orderly. That was about the time Marcus first noticed new faces whenever they made camp: scruffy men on stocky horses, carrying small round shields, wearing little armour and, for the most part, poorly clothed. Many wore woad.

The column began to break up soon after, settling down in small camps wherever space could be found. Marcus found himself in one of the many small valleys that coursed through the countryside like the deep wrinkles in an elephant's hide. The site was thickly wooded, but the land had been cleared back along a broad, bubbling stream that ended in a small lake a mile distant. Marcus judged the few barbarians who lived there to be more backward than any encountered so far. Each one looked grimy, ragged, suspicious, and as dense as a donkey.

This was Selgovae land. Urs had found that out and passed it on, along with his opinion that some sort of compromise had been reached. The terms had likely been founded on need, Marcus reasoned, because where they stood had likely just become Rome's northern frontier. Neither the Carvetii, the Brigantes, or the Selgovae appeared delighted with the new arrangement, but the parameters seemed to be simple: we leave you alone, you leave us alone, and maybe later we unite and fight together.

They cleared the land farther back from the river over summer, but only upstream, so they wouldn't crowd those who already lived there. They built small huts, fenced in livestock pens, and planted crops, though much later than usual. The tiny cluster of rude buildings soon looked similar to a thousand other small, forlorn barbarian villages.

Marcus, much to his disgust and despair, promptly reverted to his normal status: somewhere below the first rung of a scaling ladder. He spent most of his dawn to dusk existence building, cutting lumber, or tending the sparse field crops. The work did not wear on a man as it had in the close quarters of the hill fort. It seemed less tiring, for it was a step up from mucking hogs, and his own stink, which was bad enough, no longer kept him awake at night.

Urs toiled alongside, shouldering his full share. Marcus remained in the slave's charge, an overt fact that was never mentioned. There seemed no point. Should he try to rebel and escape, Marcus had no idea where to go. The area crawled with barbarians who knew him to be the legate's son—and if they didn't, his fate would likely prove far worse. They would kill him, or simply enslave him all over again. Better the master you know …

Fiona came down with her pains in late June. Marcus trudged in from weeding the fields to learn that her labour had started that morning. The birthing proved hard, for the child had not turned in the womb. Fiona's cries still echoed down the valley as evening came and passed, and nobody found sleep as the night dragged on. When the first grey of dawn finally slipped over the hills, there was still no child and the woman was exhausted.

As the sun finally climbed above the trees, it brought with it a barbarian beldam from farther down the valley, obviously drawn by Fiona's distant cries of pain. Marcus watched dispassionately from where he sat across from the hut, stuffing lumpy porridge into his mouth with his fingers. The witch was old and grimy looking, with dark features, tangled hair, and threadbare clothes. Yet oddly enough, she paused by the stream, set the large leather pouch she carried on a rock, and washed her hands and arms with a soft, greyish soap. Then, after a quick, knowing glance in his direction and a shake of her head, the old woman disappeared into Fiona's hut.

Curiosity drew Marcus to his feet as a low babble of bickering erupted inside. The woman reappeared at the door of the hut as if ready to leave, her face angry. Something was said inside, though; probably by Fiona herself, he decided. A hand appeared and dropped to the hag's shoulder, holding her back. More words were exchanged. The woman's eyes fell on Marcus who, fingers in his mouth, could only shrug. She shook her head once more, turned, and went back inside.

Soon after came a long, agonized scream, followed by a silence that was almost a sound in itself. Marcus sat down again and waited. Nobody seemed to care where he was and what he was doing, and it dawned on him that the barbarians were allowing him time for the child's delivery. For the longest while there was no noise at all. Time dragged slowly by, perhaps due to his growing curiosity. He wondered if Fiona had died. Then a faint wailing drifted from the hut, and he realized that, however it was with the mother, the bairn had survived.

By then the sun had climbed halfway into the sky. One by one, the women of the tribe began leaving the hut. Each looked sombre, and all avoided eye contact with Marcus. He grew certain Fiona had died. When one passed near him, his curiosity got the best of him and he asked after the child.

The woman glanced up, no joy in her face, and said, "It's a girl."

She hurried away.

Marcus might have gone too, but the open door held his attention. It hung twisted on its leather hinges, the inside dark and silent. He stood, then looked about, suddenly uncertain. The women who were still nearby were staring at him, like jackals watching a lion at its kill. With a grunt of disdain, he walked over and entered the hut.

The air hung heavy with the smell of smoke, dried sweat, and fresh blood. Fiona lay on the pallet that served as a bed, her skin chalk white and her eyes circled dark as if bruised. Beside her lay a small, silent bundle. The hag was down on her knees, intent on cramming the tools of her magic back into the floppy leather pouch.

Marcus, muttering to himself, decided that as long as he was inside, he might as well look at the brat. It lay on its back, eyes closed, and one small fist free of the cloth that swaddled it. He saw a mass of black curls, damp and bloody. The nose, the lips, the tiny ears, well, they were all there too—along with that clenched fist. He hadn't realized they could be so small. The child had a certain amount of ... what, softness? Helplessness? He could see where some men might warm to the gnome-like creatures.

The bairn opened its eyes and stared, a dark, wise, knowing look, but Marcus knew that was impossible. They quickly closed again and he chuckled, deciding it didn't like what it saw.

"She's still lovely."

Marcus turned, surprised at the sound of the faint voice. He'd thought Fiona was dead. She was watching him carefully through half-lidded eyes. It took a moment for the odd phrasing to register. "What do you mean, still lovely?" he asked.

A tear formed in the corner of Fiona's eye, and trickled down her cheek. Marcus felt a tug at his sleeve. He turned to see the Selgovae witch jabbering at him, and realized she was no witch at all. The woman was likely younger than his mother, and with more care might have been attractive. Her face expressed frustration as she spoke, though, and her words seemed incoherent. But when she finally slowed the pace he realized that, along with the hand gestures, they might translate into "Are you the da?"

Marcus supposed there was a remote possibility, and nodded.

What did it matter anyway? All it did, though, was release another torrent of words that forced him to shake his head and hold up both hands in despair.

Tutting impatiently, the woman went to the tiny bundle and unwrapped it, exposing the bairn's small, pink body. Damp, naked, and flat on its back, it flailed its tiny arms and screamed, its wrinkled face crimson. Marcus's first impression was that it was certainly a girl, and what was the woman's problem? But she was insistent, demanding he listen as she slowly repeated two words over and over again. This time he understood. It seemed to translate as "little people."

Puzzled, Marcus looked again, focusing on the tiny pink body itself. There did, indeed, seem to be something odd, something that did not sit as it should. It took a moment to realize what it was. The short torso, was it not in proportion to the arms and legs? And the tiny body itself, was it smaller than it should be for the head? It suddenly dawned on Marcus: the child was a dwarf. His eyes jerked upward to meet those of Fiona, who stared back with an expression that mingled sadness and contentment.

"Her name is Jessa," she murmured softly, "and she *is* lovely."

Chapter XVI

Eboracum, A.D. 79

The Ninth Hispana did not move as an army that summer, though the Twentieth had been campaigning since the beginning of spring. Agricola's objective for the Ninth was to consolidate its control of Brigantia, and extend its building program farther north. The string of forts Rhun had seen laid out at Aquae Sulis gradually took form as the legion, along with a small army of slaves and native workers, worked its way slowly from one site to the next.

Rhun found himself once more posted to Lavatris, then to *Verteris*, back to *Vinovia*, and then to the last fort built that summer at *Vindomora*. When autumn fell, the west side of the huge territory was permanently connected to the east, and Rome had established outposts as far as eighty miles north of Eboracum.

The day the squadron received orders to report back to Lavatris, Rhun had hurried over to the commander's residence on a visit timed to find Aelia alone. He was not disappointed. It was a warm spring morning, and she was in the atrium. She seemed amused by the visit, for he had dined there the night before and said his goodbyes, not only to Aelia, but to his mother, his sister, and his younger brother.

Rhun was out of breath, for he'd run into the building knowing the troop should already be on the road. "I forgot to give you this," he mumbled, feeling he should offer some sort of excuse for being there. He held out a small silver brooch bearing inside its finely wrought frame a jet carving of a woman's head. The piece had taken a good slice of a decurio's pay.

"It's very beautiful," Aelia said. "Thank you."

"It's supposed to be Helen of Troy," Rhun mumbled, his tongue suddenly wool in his mouth. "It's for all the help you've given me—you know, reading, the stories and stuff."

"There's no need for that." Aelia took his wrist gently in one hand and closed his fingers over the gift with the other. "I don't want payment. You've been a keen student and I found teaching … well," she hesitated, her large brown eyes thoughtful, "quite stimulating."

Stimulating! That was only the half of it, as far as Rhun was concerned. His sister had, as promised, spoken to Aelia about "elevating his mind." According to Coira, Aelia had reluctantly accepted the idea as a major challenge to educate the ignorant. Rhun knew that was a lie, but even so, he was surprised that Aelia had not declined. He suggested that it was more likely just a chore she'd taken on to break the tiresome fortress routine. Coira had shrugged, but smiled.

Rhun began his lessons cautiously, knowing that learning was a very small part of his reason for being there, but he had to show some interest. The woman's scent as he sat close to her, and the occasional, inadvertent touch carried into his dreams at night. Yet while Aelia appeared to like him, if anything more hovered behind those large brown eyes, it remained well hidden.

Winter progressed and along with it Rhun's reading skills. With a patience ample enough for both of them, Aelia started him on Plato. But when he remarked that the man's ideas were those of an impractical, misguided ass, she appeared amused and suggested Homer. As Rhun read through *The Iliad*, his interest began to grow—though it did occur to him that she might simply be catering to his barbarian, warrior instincts.

After *The Odyssey*, Aelia asked him if he was ready to return to the philosophers. When he hesitated, she thumbed through the racks in her father's quarters and, with a thoughtful gleam in her eye, came up with Hesiod. But Rhun's gaze had fallen on other works that intrigued him, two in particular, both by Ovid. One was *The Amores,* and the other *Ars Amatoria.* Yet when he slyly suggested that perhaps it was time to advance to the Roman poets, Ovid for example, Aelia simply smiled and returned to the shelves. With a pensive look on her face she handed him the poet's *Tristia*, and said they would begin discussing Ovid the following week.

All of which was now in the past, and there was little hope of being with Aelia until the following winter, if at all. Rhun bit his tongue at her use of the word "stimulating" and focused on her refusal to accept the gift. He gently removed her hand, set the brooch in it, and fumbled for something wise or witty to say. "Then think of it as something to remember me by," was all he could come up with.

"Why, are you not coming back?" Aelia asked coyly.

Rhun gulped, suddenly aware of the game she was playing, but it was a game made for two. "Well, if you don't want it..."

Aelia offered the brooch to Rhun, who stared at it, both surprised and deeply disappointed by the gesture. She laughed and took a step closer. "I told you, it's beautiful. Pin it on, please."

Rhun was elated as he took hold of the delicate silver frame and fumbled with the clasp. The damned thing suddenly had a mind of its own. His fingers turned to thumbs, and he bit his lip to hold back a curse. The pin finally came undone, and he moved to do as she asked. The back of his hand brushed against the gentle swell of her breast, and he felt his face grow warm. Aelia didn't move, but he could feel her eyes studying his face. The scent of blossoms filled his nose, and he grew acutely aware of the gentle rise and fall of her breathing. Unlike his own, he realized, which was growing ragged, and his face flushed even warmer. Finally the pin found its place and he stepped back, his breath rushing out in a sigh of relief.

"You know, Rhun," Aelia touched the brooch to make sure it was secure, then let her hand move gently to his cheek, "you would find your life far more rewarding if you speak what is on your mind."

And with that she leaned forward and, rising up on her toes, kissed him. It was not a wild kiss filled with passion, but a soft, tender kiss, with gently parted lips that lingered on his own. Her hand slid to the back of his neck to hold the moment, then she released him and stepped away with a small, scented sigh of contentment. "Thank you," she said.

Rhun was vaguely unsure whether her words were for the brooch, or the kiss. Vaguely, because he barely heard. His response had shocked him beyond belief. His chest heaved as if struck by a cudgel and he backed away, thanking the gods for the heavy drape of chain mail below his waist. Even so, he was acutely aware that something should be done, for he could no longer stand there. Murmuring a few words that were totally incomprehensible, Rhun backed away, then edged quickly toward the nearest exit.

At first Aelia looked puzzled. Then, to his embarrassment, she lifted one hand to her mouth to stifle her amusement. His back smacked into one of the wood posts and he turned, tripped over the step to the walkway, and finally stumbled from the building cursing his own ineptness. He couldn't recall speaking a word to anyone in the squadron until it reached Isurium, where his mind was finally able to free itself and think of other matters. And the incident both tortured and sustained him for the rest of the season.

"Want to go home for winter?" Gaius asked late that summer, deliberately casual as he let the question drop. His small family sat for a rare evening meal together in the private section of the residence, and all chatter died in an instant. Even Metellus, in the act of pouring the legate's wine, stopped what he was doing and waited expectantly.

Elena broke the silence, but her expression was not serious. "I'm already home."

"You know what I mean," Gaius said, then, deciding to play the same game, added, "Of course, *you* don't have to go. You can winter here with the rest of the troops. Anyone else want to go to Rome?"

It seemed that Aelia, Coira, and Tuis definitely did, and even Metellus nodded.

"Well then, that settles most of that." Gaius felt quite pleased with himself, though he knew there would be resistance when he discussed the rest of it. Elena likely knew it would come at some time, but Tuis and she were close; the mother would have more difficulty with the weaning than the boy.

"When would we leave, father?" the lad asked.

"In less than a month. I want to be back in Rome before the end of November."

"Will it be just us?" Aelia asked.

Gaius frowned, at first puzzled by the question. Then it occurred to him that perhaps his daughter harboured hope of Marcus's return, despite the fact that he'd slipped through the Twentieth's net on its sweep through Cumbria. There'd been no trace of the boy at all, in fact, and there was some doubt that he remained alive. That was a matter he pushed to the back of his mind, while still aware he had to deal with the possibility. Agricola, bless the man, had been trying to find some intelligence on his son's whereabouts, but interrogations had turned up nothing.

"I'm afraid so," he said, his voice gentle. "There's been no sign of Marcus so far, and I doubt he'll be found before next spring. And really," he added, for his own conscience as much as his daughter's, "I don't think our being in Rome will make any difference."

Aelia nodded and fell silent, but she looked troubled, as if her father's reply was not satisfactory. Coira noticed and grinned. She opened her mouth to speak, at the same time punching Aelia lightly on the shoulder as if ready to tease. Then she caught Elena's warning glare. Her mouth promptly closed again, and her cheeks turned red.

Gaius was preoccupied with tasting the wine. The ruby liquid was properly aged, and tasted well. He looked up and said as much, gesturing for Metellus to fill the other wine glasses. An odd silence had fallen on the table, and he noticed that Coira seemed to be comforting his daughter, for she'd placed a hand on Aelia's forearm. He smiled. It was a pleasure to see that the barbarian girl, whose nature was as far removed from Aelia's as the moon, could please his daughter so much. Perhaps that was why he indulged the young woman, though at times he wondered if perhaps—

"Father."

Gaius turned his attention to Tuis, who seemed concerned for Aelia as well, for he also touched her lightly on the other arm as he spoke.

"Yes?"

"I don't suppose Rhun is going to Rome too, is he?"

Gaius blinked in surprise. It was an odd question to ask, but then, the decurio was the lad's brother. It wasn't feasible, of course. There was no reason to send a young barbarian troop commander, even one who showed promise, traipsing off to Rome for the winter simply because his family was going there. Aelia seemed to agree, for she seemed to be wondering about the question too.

"No, he's not, Tuis," Gaius said gravely, then drained the wine glass in one long swallow, his eyes fixed on the boy. Perhaps, since the mood at the table seemed to have grown sombre anyway, now was a good time to raise the matter of the lad's future. Elena would not be happy, which annoyed him, for he often circled such issues because of her contentiousness; well, she would simply have to accept it.

"You like Rome, don't you, Tuis?" Gaius asked, and cursed silently as he realized he was again vacillating.

"Of course. It's a big place. Exciting."

"That's good, that's good," Gaius said, nodding. Then, annoyed with his dithering, he spoke more bluntly than he intended. "Because when we return next spring, you'll remain there. A tutor is all well and good, but you're ready for a more formal education."

"Whoo-eee!" Tuis looked about the table, decidedly pleased.

Well, that part, at least, went as expected, Gaius decided, feeling just as pleased, but he kept his face expressionless as he glanced involuntarily at Elena. He was surprised to see the woman seemed neither happy nor annoyed; in fact, her mind seemed to be elsewhere. He wondered if she'd even heard.

Elena could have kicked her daughter; if she'd been close enough, she would have. The fool girl had been about to tease Aelia about Rhun, something Gaius would not find amusing. She knew how it stood with the pair, and Coira would even have pushed the matter if she could—a surprising role for her daughter. For herself, she simply wished it would all go away. So far she was fairly sure there'd been nothing but harmless flirtation, but the last thing any of them needed was for the matter to grow serious. Gaius, to put it mildly, would not be pleased.

Her son had more than once arranged escort duty to Eboracum during the summer and into autumn, always contriving to further his "lessons" on each visit. She could have shaken him! And Gaius, too; for a man who was so practical and sharp in matters military, he could be as obtuse as an ox where his daughter was concerned.

Aelia was Gaius's pride and pleasure, and his mainstay in keeping his personal affairs in order. Perhaps because of this, the man seemed to hide behind his shield when it came to his daughter's other needs in life. Elena often suspected Aelia's large, placid brown eyes masked a bright and very determined young mind. Nothing, it seemed, had happened to date to give Gaius's daughter reason to remove that mask. Elena certainly didn't want her oldest son to be the cause.

She glanced at Tuis, grateful for his question. Unlike his da, the boy possessed a good deal of insight. Though she wondered where it was now. Tuis was staring at her as if expecting something more. Glancing at Coira, she was surprised to find the same expression there; even Gaius wore it. Only Aelia seemed preoccupied, staring into her wine as if her mind was somewhere else. Had she missed something?

Chapter XVII

Bremenium, A.D. 80

The garrison was no different from a dozen others where Rhun had been stationed; it was, at the moment, simply the farthest north in Britannia. Built quickly that spring, the fort lay between the Selgovae peoples to the west and the Votadini to the east, and barely within the southern reaches of either tribe. The ramparts, palisades, and gates had naturally been constructed first; the buildings inside, especially the granaries, followed soon after. There had seemed no great urgency for the rest, particularly the barracks, but the tents would see far too much service before the last troops found shelter in the crowded buildings late that summer.

Rhun had returned to regular duty with the Fourth Gallorum when it pushed north beyond Brigantia. Once the regiment crossed the *Tinea* river, the unit was split in two; half remained behind at *Habitancum,* a good twenty miles farther south, and Rhun's squadron pressed on to *Bremenium* with the rest, his role reverting to that carried out in Germania. It was a tasking for which he and his troopers were grateful. The Ninth Legion, its auxiliary infantry attachments, and the conscripted labour carried on with the sweat work of construction; the cavalry patrolled and, as they liked to tell it, kept them all safe.

Turren, after a bad fall during a training exercise, was attached to the headquarters unit, where he would likely wait out retirement. Cian assumed command of his old squadron just before spring, but it was with a certain reluctance. The new arrangement was like old times, certainly, with the great hulking figure of Luga riding alongside, and the comfort of again being his own man. Yet he and Rhun had developed an easy manner of running their troop, for his nephew had never been pushy about who was in charge. Theirs was the best squadron in the entire regiment, and Cian knew that with absolute certainty—but then, fifteen other optios felt the same way.

The Fourth's praefectus, the same Cornelius Griphus who had crossed Marcus's path at Gesoriacum, remained at Habitancum. There were rumours he would soon be relieved and sent on to better things. Cornelius's second-in-command, a man called Priscus, took charge of Bremenium, and Rhun found himself with a certain flexibility in running the patrols. The roads between the forts were well travelled and, except for the dispatch riders who rode them hard and fast, were normally travelled in force. The two squadrons once more began riding the hills together, for the most part keeping within striking distance of the fort. It was little different from when they rode the hills of Brigantia, only the natives were cruder, far more difficult to talk to, and certainly more hostile.

Gaius had returned to Britannia at winter's end, and chose early summer for a full tour of his jurisdiction, including all detachments. The schedule was circulated ahead of time, which let each commander know exactly how long he had to whip his people into shape. For Rhun, who thought his troop always ran at peak efficiency, the main concern was who would accompany the legate on his northern inspection. It had been a long winter, and he'd spent as much time daydreaming as he'd spent running his squadron. The constant tedium of patrolling had, in fact, seemed to encourage as much.

Gaius's inspection party would no doubt include a good part of the Ninth's headquarters staff, but would that be all? After a good deal of prying, all he could determine was that only two women travelled with the legate. Which two, he had a pretty good idea—but he could always hope…

Cian didn't seem to care who rode with the legate, only telling Rhun he was fairly sure it wasn't a pair of camp *cunnies*, so what did it matter anyway? But as the date of the inspection drew near, he seemed to draw into himself, as if preoccupied. Then, about a week before the governor's arrival, he took his troop on patrol by himself, offering Rhun no reason other than that was what he wanted.

The path Cian took led toward the endless hills that darkened the horizon to the west. It was a long ride, made in haste—a loop that edged into land not yet patrolled, land that had, for the present, been more or less ceded to the tribes. Six times he called a halt as they rode the farthest reach of the patrol, each time edging off by himself as the men rested the horses. Wherever he found a tree that stood out from those around it, he pulled a length of red ribbon and a length of blue ribbon from inside his tunic and tied them to one of the lower limbs.

Branaught and one of the scouts waited under a clump of tall pines that sat, much like a watchtower, atop a sharp granite crag. Bran pointed upward as Rhun reined in alongside, indicating a single blue, unweathered ribbon tied to one of the branches.

"Hmph," Priscus muttered, dismissing the piece of cloth. "Some sort of boneheaded curse."

The regiment's second-in-command had chosen to ride with the patrol, which Rhun realized was because of the two women. The man's request, which was really an order, had seemed reasonable enough, and he'd been surprised at Cian's hostility. His uncle seemed annoyed beyond reason and, when he irritably suggested that Rhun tell Priscus to bugger off, the two had words. With Cian cursing under his breath about the off chance of running into enemy cavalry—*"And then what would we do?"* To which Rhun had retorted, *"We've got more than fifty men here, so sodding what?"*—the patrol had started out with neither talking, and Priscus riding between the two, oblivious to any conflict.

"It could be a curse," Rhun muttered, and turned to look pointedly at his uncle; Cian scowled back, and slowly shook his head as if to say "I told you."

Coira, who rode behind with her mother, spoke only one word:

"Shit!"

"See any more, Bran?" Rhun asked his new optio.

Branaught gestured toward the west. "I sent the other two out again. Ostor found a red one off in that direction. I told them to be careful, but to go see if they could find any more."

Cian stared gravely at his nephew. "So … what do you say, Rhun? Think we should follow them?"

"I don't know, Cian." Rhun spoke deliberately, spacing the words. What in the name of Nemesis was going on? "Do *you* think we should?"

"What are you apes playing at?" Coira hissed.

"I heard the story of those Cumbrian ribbons," Elena said, her voice taut with anger as she kneed her horse forward until it was alongside Rhun, "and I know what they mean. Did you two arrange this? Without telling me? Have you any idea … ?"

"Hey, I didn't do a thing. Honest." Rhun glared at Cian, which was enough for Elena.

"So what did you do, you brainless bugger? Gaius is going to—"

"What are you talking about?" Priscus interrupted, staring at them all in turn. "What are those things?"

"They're a sign," Cian said solemnly.

"Yeah? From who?"

Ignoring Priscus's question, Rhun turned to Elena. "Do we follow them, or ignore them? I don't care; it's up to you."

"I didn't talk to anyone, really," Cian added, his face red. "I just put a few lousy—"

"Shut your gob, Cian," Coira hissed, and looked at her mother. "What do you think?"

Elena sighed, and instead of answering turned her face westward, her eyes staring blankly.

"I asked, from who?" Priscus repeated. "*What* is going on?"

Rhun saw his mother's slow nod, as if she were making up her mind. He decided the truth was best; besides, he could think of no self-serving lie that would pass muster. "Brigante cavalry. It's their sign. You must have heard of them: a disciplined unit, led by a woman with dark red hair, and an Eburi chieftain."

"There are rumours."

"No rumours, sir." Cian shrugged. "The man is Cethen Lamh-fada. He's my brother."

"He's also my father." Rhun sighed. Priscus glanced nervously over one shoulder, as if to make certain of the two troops of cavalry waiting patiently behind. Rhun wondered if the man remembered that most were Brigante tribesmen. "He likely wants to talk to me."

"Us," Cian corrected.

"And I'm sure he wants to talk to me, too," Elena said, and glared at Cian. "Cethen is my husband."

"What?" Priscus gasped, and turned to Coira as if seeking confirmation.

She shrugged. "Don't look at me. He's my father too."

"*Shit!*"

Rhun raised himself in the saddle and removed the ribbon, passing it to Cian, who tied it below the tip of his spear. It dangled prettily down the staff for about the length of a man's forearm.

"I don't like this," Priscus muttered, tightening his grip on his horse's reins.

"No worries." Rhun slapped him on the shoulder. "Trust me. It's likely just a visit, but we'll no doubt learn much. Let's go find out."

Priscus again looked over his shoulder and seemed to decide that two troops from his own regiment were enough assurance. Either that, Rhun decided, or he was hoping he hadn't fallen into a nest of barbarian deserters.

The blue and red ribbons led them farther west, for the most part following neither trail nor track. Rhun led the troop deeper and deeper into the forested hills, while Priscus grumbled about the terrible risk, and how the way back stretched with every hoofbeat. But he gave no order to turn back, and Rhun smiled to himself, wondering if it was because Priscus was afraid it might not be obeyed.

Branaught was waiting for them in a place where the forest had thinned. As they rode up, Rhun caught the distant yapping of dogs. He raised one hand, the troop reined in, and they all sat listening. All but one hound soon fell silent, its lone barking echoing eerily through the stillness of the trees.

Cian rode up alongside and glanced sideways, eyebrows raised. "You and I?" he murmured.

"And me," Priscus added, his voice determined.

"And me too," Elena and Coira said in unison.

"That's going to leave a headless snake sitting back here," Rhun said, nodding toward the rest of the column.

Priscus shrugged, as if indifferent. "One of *you* stay here, then."

Rhun grinned. "Bran, can you and Luga keep them all out of trouble?"

Branaught also shrugged his indifference. "They'll remain alert, even if I have to slap Luga awake to do it."

Rhun nodded and kicked his animal forward, the others falling in behind. They cantered the horses downward through widely spaced pines to the edge of a natural meadow. The usual stream meandered through its centre, with a well-worn track following its course. The far side of the natural clearing rose upward, and Rhun realized they had ridden into a valley. A small farmstead sat on the far side of the stream, well back from the burbling water.

A figure emerged from the hut, his movements cautious. He was a big man with too much weight on him, and one arm that ended above the elbow. He peered intently at the intruders, then his eyes fell on the ribbon-bedecked spears. With a pronounced limp, he ambled toward the stream. The dogs, a good half-dozen hunting hounds, led the way, once more howling and yapping as they bounded through the water.

"I'll bet the old fox got his wounds fighting us," Priscus muttered.

"I'd say we got the best of it," Rhun said quietly. He studied the man as he approached, sensing something familiar about him. His clothes were coarsely woven, and he had long, greying hair on both his face and his head.

The man growled something that caused the dogs to hold back, then squinted upward, even though he was less than ten steps away. "Rhun?"

Balor! Rhun remembered the name, even as his uncle called it.

"Balor! Balor, you old goat!" Cian cried, and urged his horse across the stream first, sliding to the ground in front of the older man. "You're still alive, you bug-ridden old bugger!"

Balor's features split with pleasure and the two fell into a bear hug, whirling and laughing and pounding each other on the back. Rhun smiled as he watched, the memories flooding back. Balor had been a freeman, a warrior of the kin; his small farmstead had been downriver, close by Cian. His smile broadened as both men pranced about on the grass, pounding each other as if locked in combat.

Elena, with a cry of joy, slid from her horse and joined them, and soon all three were united in a huge embrace.

"I take it they know each other," Priscus said dryly.

"I think they may," Rhun said, and kicked his own horse forward.

When the pounding finally stopped, Balor squinted up at the twins. "You grew up."

"And you've shrunk." Rhun grinned. "Last time I saw you, you were a giant."

He and Coira dropped from their saddles as Balor roared with laughter, and the three were soon doing the same wild dance. When they finally settled down and everyone stood looking at each other, Rhun belatedly introduced Priscus. Both men simply nodded, and an awkward silence followed. Cian broke it by asking the old warrior what he'd done since Stannick, which led to the inevitable question.

"The arm went at Bran's Beck, as you know," Balor muttered, and couldn't help a sideways glance at Priscus. "The limp was at Stannick. I, er, I … " He looked sheepish, then raised his arm in a gesture of embarrassment. "I broke an ankle jumping off the wall when I got away. It never did heal right. It doesn't hurt, though, unless I walk too far."

Rhun broke a second awkward silence by asking after his father.

"I'm to fetch him, and you're to stay here," Balor replied, and scratched at his neck as if trying to recall the instructions. "There's more. Your men, they have to remain beyond the valley. Your da vouchsafes they won't be attacked. I'll have young Morg fetch him."

Balor turned and yelled the name, and a lad in his teens appeared. He dawdled over, taking his time.

"Go tell Cethen his kin's here," Balor ordered.

The youth glanced farther down the valley, a pained look on his face. "Da … "

"Here." Cian thrust the reins of his horse at the boy. "Don't bring her back lathered up, or I'll have your hide."

Morg's face lit with pleasure, and in no time at all he was on the animal's back, thundering off through the trees. Cian shook his head.

Cethen rode in on another path, one that dropped from higher in the valley to join a track that ended in front of Balor's hut. He'd chosen to ride the chestnut, the one stolen from the legate Gaius Sabinius ten years before. Gadearg was at least fifteen years old, but his coat glistened; though the flesh had begun to hollow around his eyes, the animal was alert and fit. Fiona and the twin Borba rode behind.

Borba nodded to them all as he dismounted, then took hold of the chestnut's bridle while Fiona moved to help Cethen dismount. He ignored her and instead sat transfixed, his eyes on Elena.

"Come on, Da, I'll help."

Rhun stepped forward and Cethen forced himself to move, swinging his good leg over the pommel. He slid from the saddle, careful to keep the foot wrapped in a tight linen bandage free of the ground. With one arm on his son's shoulder, Cethen found his balance, carefully avoiding Elena's concerned gaze. He looked up to find them all staring, and grunted at their doubtful expressions.

"Get over here, you daft buggers," he shouted, an edge to his voice, and held out both arms, balancing clumsily on one foot. "It's been a hard winter, but I'm not dead yet."

Coira and Cian came over and clasped him tight, but it was far from the dancing bear hug with Balor. It had indeed been a hard winter. Cethen knew he'd lost more weight, his face was pale, and his moustaches and hair now had more of the grey than the fair. The pale blue eyes were lively enough, though, despite a tear or two as he studied his daughter's face before letting go.

"Damned leg," he muttered, then turned and hopped over to sit down on a log bench, careful to keep the bandaged foot extended. "Old age isn't creeping up, it's galloping."

"What happened?" Rhun asked.

"Stepped on a stupid piece of pottery, and it festered. They had to cut it again, to free the poison," Cethen lied, unwilling to admit to a gash from an auxiliary spear—certainly not here, with a strange Roman looking on. The man was clearly an officer of some kind. "Who's the primped-up horse faerie? I thought you'd come by yourselves."

Cethen's eyes went to the Roman as he spoke the words, but they first rested briefly on Elena as if with a mind of their own. He felt his cheeks flush. His wife stood off to the side of Balor's hut, her arms folded, her expression unreadable.

"I'm the man in charge," Priscus said smugly, using the same language as Cethen. "Your son had no choice in the matter. Priscus—Priscus Bolanus. I'm also the faerie who decides whether or not to call in two troops of cavalry, if I think you're worth the taking."

"Take me, in your mind's eye!" Cethen snorted derisively and shifted on the bench to gain more comfort. "Not unless I want to go, and I don't." He nodded to the path he'd ridden in on, again giving a lie as fact. "I have five times as many men to put a stop to it. It would be a shame to lose a single one, just to satisfy your vanity. Besides, you're assuming your troopies would do it. If I recall, most are Britons."

"I ... " Priscus began, his expression suddenly uncertain.

"Anyway, this is a truce, and you don't break truces. We don't, anyway. And I know the Ninth's legate doesn't, either. He'd have your head. Fiona, give the bugger some beer and shut him up," Cethen finished, hoping his bluff would hold. Cian and the twins wouldn't have it, of course, but they were only three against many. Maybe four, if you threw in Elena. What, in this godless land, was the woman doing here?

Balor produced a large clay crock and an array of mugs. Fiona pulled out a ladle with a good measure of its contents, then held it up to ask if anyone wanted some. It seemed that everyone but Elena did. When she'd passed the drinks and set the crock where everyone could pour their own, Fiona sat cross-legged on the grass, her own beer cradled in her lap. Cian, likely from habit more than anything else, lifted his drink and winked. She sneered, made a circle with her thumb and index finger, then stabbed upward with the finger.

"Haven't changed a bit, little brother." Cethen finally allowed a smile, but it went only as far as his lips, for his mind was in turmoil.

227

Elena remained over by the hut, unmoving, and that bothered him. To his relief, he saw Rhun and Coira turn toward her. They would get going with her whatever it was they were going to get going. It wasn't up to him to get things started. After all, she was the one who had come here. In fact, she was the one who had left in the first place.

Cethen closed his eyes at the unfairness of that. Elena had not had much choice in the matter, not the first time, anyway. Yet, dammit, she should have abandoned Bran's farm when she promised, and she hadn't! He'd blame her forever for that. If only the woman had done as she'd said, none of this would have happened. Cethen sighed, Coira's words barely heard.

"Mam, come and join us. You can't stay there all day."

Elena's mind was awhirl. Cian was the cause of this, and sod the scheming clod, for he'd given no warning. Gaius would be livid, and sod that too, for the man was so inflexible. He would inevitably learn of this, and she knew the path his mind would follow: *you arranged to meet your husband, and never uttered a word!* Yet she could hardly blame him.

She would get the truth from Rhun, that was certain. Yet…when the first of those ribbons had appeared, he'd been as surprised as she. Damn, damn, damn! Gaius had been edgy about coming north to begin with, claiming it was dangerous. She'd brushed that off, of course, and now this! Supposedly a short day patrol, in force, to show the "girls" the country while he did his inspection. Why hadn't she listened to her brain instead of her belly, when the first of those ribbons appeared?

She looked at Cethen as he edged over to the log and sat down. By the gods, he'd aged. Of course, he was hurt, he was thin, and they were both ten years older. Yet that brief, familiar, lopsided grin hadn't changed a jot over the years, and it had dug at her heart. That look would spread across his face like sunshine when he was pleased; though it had quickly faded when he pretended not to see her sitting there. That nervous tug on his moustache had followed, which meant inside he was as taut as a strung bow. He was certainly as shocked as she had been, and she knew exactly what was now going through his mind.

Elena sighed as Coira spoke. She decided that since they were here anyway, she'd break the barrier and, as usual, speak first. Her pride in such matters had never been as great as Cethen's. Taking Coira's hand, she climbed to her feet and edged closer. Rhun handed her a mug of ale and she sat down across from her husband and tipped her head slightly to acknowledge him. "Cethen."

"Elena."

"Good to see you."

"Me too."

"Oh, for the love of Lug," Cian interrupted. "No one's expecting you two to hug each other and start kissing. Just relax, have a drink, and have a good old family catch-up." Then, as if realizing the words were not quite appropriate, he lamely finished, "Well, we could at least tell each other what's been going on."

Elena sighed. Cian could be as erratic as an arrow shot wildly in the air, but in the next breath he could aim straight for the target.

Coira stepped into the arena with a suggestion of her own, clearly hoping it would ease the tension. "So, Da, tell us how young Bryn is doing."

His response was unexpected. Cethen scowled and muttered, "As well as expected. I haven't seen the boy in weeks. Morallta has most of his care."

"I see." Coira blinked, and moved on to what seemed to be a safer topic. "And your foot. What were you doing? Walking around with no boots? How did it get infected?"

"An accident. Shit happens." Her father scowled as if uncomfortable, clearly ending any discussion in that area.

Her mouth moving in a silent curse, Coira turned to Borba, who sat by himself at the end of the log, assessing the contents of his clay mug. "So how's Luath, Borba? It is Borba, isn't it?" she asked, her eyes on the blue ribbon dangling from his shoulder.

Borba drained his mug and stared at the ground, shaking his head. "Poor bugger. Lost a hand over winter, clear up to his elbow. Went back to the farm. Oh well, one of us should be looking after it. All for the best, I suppose."

"I'm sorry," Coira said, and Elena could almost have laughed at her daughter's foundering. What else might she turn to that was not someone's tragedy? But Borba wasn't finished.

"Aye," he moped on, "the bugger's likely plowing my wife as well as his. Even as we speak."

"Shit!" Coira cried, rolling her eyes.

"Hey, don't worry, girl." Borba seemed to perk up, and grinned. "Neither woman ever knew the difference. Or at least," he suddenly frowned, as if giving the words more thought, "they claimed they never did."

"Give it up, Coira, before this turns into a wake," Cian called out, and raised his mug. "Let's talk of old times. Hey, Priscus—sir."

Priscus, who was staring into his empty mug as if pondering his own execution, glanced up. "What, trooper?"

"Did I ever tell you about the fight Luga and I got into?" Cian asked, leaning forward and slopping his ale on the grass. "And for no good reason other than I was playing with his wife's tits, the jealous bugger." He turned to his brother. "We've still got to settle that, you know, or one day Venutius will come back to haunt us. It was at *Samhain* ... "

The talk quickly drifted to friends, family, and old times, which in turn, inevitably, led to what had happened after Stannick, and to who—even though much of it had been plowed over when they met nigh on two years ago. They talked about Balor when he was younger, and old Sencab and his nets, and just about everyone who had lived at the village. Borba, Balor, and Cian traded lies, while the women sat back and, for the most part, said little. Priscus, who was clearly unsettled by the whole thing, tossed back several mugs of ale, and eventually sprawled on the grass looking uncomfortably bored.

It wasn't until Rhun finished describing how Tuis seemed full-grown at fifteen, tactfully ignoring the adoption and the fact that he was now back in Rome at school, that Cethen seemed to decide he'd had his fill.

"Ah, damn it all," he muttered, "none of it's as much fun or as easy as it used to be." He smiled ruefully and pointed at his foot. "Even a wound don't heal like it should anymore."

"A wound?" Cian picked up on the words. "I thought you—"

"A gash is a wound no matter how it's caused," Cethen said quickly, glancing at Priscus, whose eyes seemed to have trouble staying open.

"Where is Morallta?" Rhun asked suddenly.

Cethen glanced sharply at his son as if startled by the question, then down at Priscus, who seemed to have fallen asleep. "Why?"

"Da, I'm not trying to pry secrets." Rhun sounded exasperated. "I was just curious. If she's got Bryn ... "

"Oh." Cethen glanced furtively at Elena, as if reluctant to say more; then he gave that lopsided grin that had always appealed, shrugged, and spoke anyway. "I guess she goes her way a lot of the time, and I go mine. She's always been her own woman. I tend to pick 'em that way."

"Aren't they all?" Cian muttered, and Elena smiled for the first time.

"Do you both ardently chase the same cause?" Coira asked.

Cethen again glanced down at the Roman. Priscus's eyes were closed, but not quite. "Her ardour for causes always was greater than mine," he muttered, then, with an embarrassed glance at Elena, "And anything else, for that matter. Though I'm a sight more consistent."

"Does that mean she—"

Cethen interrupted his daughter, again glancing down at the sleeping Roman. "Borba, give me a hand. I gotta take a piss." He climbed awkwardly to his feet and, with a wink toward Coira, Rhun, and Elena, added in a lower voice, "I'm sure that all of you do, too."

"Do I need to go too?" Cian asked, making as if to get up.

"Please yourself," Cethen said as he hobbled off, one arm on Borba's shoulder. "Fiona is far better company, though, and a lot better looking."

Cian started to rise, then belatedly took the hint. He glanced down at his empty mug, then across at Fiona. He knelt forward so she could refill his beer then, with a good deal of effort, sat back again. By the time he was finished, he was sitting a good two paces closer. Elena simply rolled her eyes.

"That fellow Titus," Cethen said as soon as they were out of Priscus's hearing. "The primus. Is he still with the legion?"

"Saw him less than a month ago. He was inspecting progress on the forts," Rhun said, then smiled. "I think he wanted to make sure everything was in order before the legate made his inspection."

"He's well?"

"Yes," Rhun replied cautiously, obviously puzzled.

"That's good, that's good," Cethen said, and glanced sideways at Borba, as if reluctant to speak. "I wonder. There were thoughts he hinted at when we met. Does he still hold them? They begin to show merit, though I don't see them bearing fruit this year."

Coira and Rhun seemed to know exactly what their da was talking about, and both looked pleased. It took a moment before Elena understood Cethen's veiled words. Her mind jumped ahead by a Roman mile, and saw exactly what would happen. There was no doubt in her mind: he would receive full amnesty if he could bring the legate's useless son back with him. But, and the thought struck her like an arrow, what else would that mean?

"To tell the truth, nothing has been mentioned since," Rhun said, a large smile spreading across his face. "It's possible, though."

"Well, you do get the idea, I suppose," Cethen said vaguely. "I just wanted to know if he held the same thoughts."

"Would you two stop that shit?" Borba burst in. "For the love of Lug, speak what's on your mind. I'm getting fed up living this way, too. What's it been, now? Two, three years? I often think fondly of the farm. The valley." He snorted and kicked the dirt. "Luath humping my wife."

"Well, you at least get the idea," Cethen said lamely. "The time just isn't ripe."

"When will it be?"

"Who knows? Sometimes, I think never," Cethen admitted.

Coira snapped her fingers, as if the thought had just occurred. "What's happening with the legate's son? Perhaps you might arrange ..."

"No. Not possible," Cethen said, though he did pause to weigh the idea.

Elena could see his brain turning over, examining the chance of freeing Marcus. Or was he mulling over whether he even wanted to try? Her husband had many ties with this land, not the least of them Bryn. Who, she realized with a shock, was the only family left to him out here! He couldn't leave the boy, that was certain. Nor would anyone expect him to.

Cethen sighed and gave his answer. "No. Dermat has his fist firm on that one. The boy's too great an asset to give up, even for gold. One day we may bargain our lives for him."

"If you return without the legate's son, then there's no point in coming back," Elena said, surprised that anyone thought he could get away with returning empty-handed.

"I suppose." Cethen frowned, then his face suddenly brightened; he snapped his fingers and grinned. "Though it does remind me, the lad's a father."

"He's what?" Rhun said, then burst out laughing. "Then the mother has to be one of our own women. That's pure Plautus!"

"Who?"

Everyone stared at Rhun, who turned scarlet. Only Elena vaguely knew the name, and realized that while her son might be missing Aelia, the girl's lessons had certainly stuck. She casually waved a hand in dismissal. "Never mind; is the boy married?"

Cethen seemed to find that amusing. "Definitely not. It's a long story."

"What did he have?"

"A wee girl," Borba offered.

"And the bairn's mother?"

Cethen and Borba both jerked their thumbs to where Cian sat with Fiona. Everyone turned for a closer look, just in time to see the girl leap up and kick at Cian's beer mug. Ale flew across his face, and the mug spiralled off toward the stream. She stalked off toward Balor's hut, eyes flashing and hips swaying.

"Quite a woman, huh?" Cethen grinned. "Though her temper's not near as bad as Morallta's."

Rhun led them from the small clearing late that afternoon, satisfied with the meeting. It was later, much later, that he learned Cethen had wintered there while his wound healed. His tiny village lay hidden in the trees, hardly more than a mile distant. The cluster of huts was much like the one that had once been home to the Eburii, only it was set close by a small loch rather than a river. A score of other wounded lived there, along with Borba, just a few of his men, and almost as many women.

Marcus Sabinius was also held there, living in the middle of it all, virtually unguarded. The two squadrons of cavalry could have ridden through the encampment at any time and destroyed it, rescued the legate's son, and returned him to Eboracum covered in glory. Rhun was thankful that neither he nor Priscus had known as much.

Chapter XVIII

Caledonii Territory, A.D. 81/82

The Caledoni chieftain was not a large man, and had no more the look of a great warrior than any of the hundred others who travelled with him from the north. His hair was dark and long, as was his full beard, and he wore the same wool clothing and leather jerkin as those worn by his men. Bluish-black tattoos swirled around his eyes, across his forehead, and spiralled down his cheeks. He called himself Galgar and claimed to have more Caledonii tribesmen at his call than there were stars in the sky. He also claimed that, despite all past differences, it was a common interest of every tribe north of Brigantia to clan together and fight the Romans, while there was still time. And he, Galgar, would be their leader.

Cethen watched him speak and say as much, in the great hall of a lodge that belonged to a Selgovae chieftain called Crim. Crim and his kin lived less than half a day's journey below a great firth that marked the northern limit of his tribe's territory; a firth that matched yet another on the west coast, and together almost cut the land in two. Along with Morallta, Dermat, and others of their tribes, Cethen had travelled over fifty miles to get there, leaving the small valley where he'd passed the last two winters. Many other chieftains had also gathered, trickling in from what must have been every tribe between Brigantia and the lands of the Caledonii. And with every mile travelled and every new face met, Cethen found himself more disillusioned.

Crim's hall was not impressive, nor was his puny stronghold.

Certainly not by the standards of the one Venutius had built at Stannick, which made Cethen wonder: if the Romans could march through Venutius's huge fortress as if it were nothing more than a barnyard, what would they do to these people?

The hill forts and wooden strongholds had grown sparser and cruder, the farther north they travelled. The chieftains and those who followed them showed little order, and as much discipline as a cage full of weasels. Which did not speak well for the Caledonii, whose territory was farther still. Or perhaps—the thought had struck Cethen more than once—these people were simply more quarrelsome than his own.

Morallta was no more impressed with Galgar than he was; Cethen could see it in the slope of her shoulders and that downward twist of her mouth that he knew all too well. She sat alongside Dermat and others of their tribes, off to one side near the front of the hall. The older warrior wore a grim, brooding look that Cethen had seen many times before, and never when the man was pleased.

He eased himself farther up on the bench and tried to gain comfort by leaning against the wall, but the rough bark dug into his back. With a deep sigh, he shifted his rear instead. It was sore from long sitting, and the old wound in his leg was aching; in fact, the foot was throbbing too, because he'd stubbed the fool thing on the way in. Forcing his eyes back to the Caledoni chieftain, he tried his best to concentrate.

"The man thinks numbers are going to solve his problem," Morallta sneered later, when the haggling and posturing had ended, and everyone milled about the hall, helping themselves to Crim's beer. "Are we the only ones who see it? We need an army, not a mob!"

"He's likely our last chance," Dermat muttered, staring morosely into his beer mug.

"Our last chance?" Cethen thought that over, and reluctantly nodded agreement. "I suppose it is. After that, what?"

"You've the right of it. If we unite with Galgar and his people and don't defeat the Romans, it's the end." Dermat gestured vaguely northward. "After them, there's nothing left but naked sheep thieves."

"Unkind words is it, for our friends far to the north?"

The heavily accented voice came from behind as a hand fell heavily on Cethen's shoulder, and another on Dermat's. Both turned to find

Galgar standing there, a huge grin on his face. "Yet as our friend here says," he patted Dermat's shoulder, "you do have the right of it. The Caledonii tribes are the last chance of ending it in our lifetime. That's why we have to unite. My people can't do it by themselves."

Galgar glanced sideways at both men, brows raised as if seeking agreement. Cethen, with a start, saw that the Caledoni's eyes above the friendly grin were as black and sharp as jet. He realized, with an insight that would have made Elena proud, that Galgar was going out of his way to charm them. The Caledoni turned and looked directly at Morallta, briefly bowing his head as if in deference to her presence—and winked! Cethen saw her body stiffen and her mouth grow taut. He waited for the outburst, and was not disappointed.

"Perhaps you might bribe a half-dozen cohorts of Batavi infantry," she snapped at him. "Add a couple more regiments of Tungri cavalry, and you'll increase your effectiveness by, what?" Morallta's brow furrowed as if calculating the answer. "At least a hundredfold?"

"I don't know about a hundredfold, but I couldn't agree more." Galgar simply broadened his smile, and shook Cethen and Dermat's shoulders as if for emphasis. "A disciplined force like the Batavi would be beyond value. But if we do unite, I think I can muster fifty thousand warriors without them."

"Boudicca had eighty, and look where it got her!" Morallta's voice dripped disdain.

Cethen wondered how far the Caledoni's patience would stretch, and was surprised to see that his smile didn't even flicker. The man must be desperate. The hand fell from his shoulder, and Galgar shrugged as he edged a step closer to Morallta. His eyes fixed hers with a twinkle of amusement, and his lower jaw moved slightly sideways, which gave him a deliberate, roguish charm. Cethen realized he was playing Morallta too, to the point of flirting with her. And was the fool woman bending?

Cethen's eyes narrowed and stared at the man's profile. The Caledoni was a fair-looking man beneath those whirls and spirals, and not nearly as old as the thick, glistening beard made him appear. Both the man and his clothes were well-kept and clean, and he washed, for the faint fragrance of fresh soap caught Cethen's nostrils. In fact, it was scented! His glance caught that of Dermat, and the older man merely raised his eyebrows.

"From what I hear, the cavalry you lead would be equal to a regiment of Tungri cavalry." Galgar's eyes didn't so much as blink.

"No, not at all," Morallta said, her lip curling in a sneer. "We've been well bloodied, and we're far better."

Again Galgar's head bowed, as if acknowledging the truth of her words. "I figure we have, what, another two years? The Roman forts are already creeping across our friend's lands." He gestured toward Crim. "It won't be long, and they'll control the entire firth, plus the one that lies to the west. You'd know that, of course, for by then you'll be trapped below and between, if you remain where you are." He stepped back and again placed his hand on Cethen's shoulder "If we were to unite, two years gives all three of you time to raise a dozen 'Batavi' cohorts drawn from my fifty thousand."

Morallta pursed her lips, plainly struck by Galgar's words. Cethen, after quickly trying to calculate how many men it would take to form a dozen cohorts, gave up and glanced at Dermat to seek his reaction. The old warrior's face was as absorbed as Morallta's.

Marcus watched the first snow of the year from the uncertain warmth of yet another stick-walled, mud-coated, pine-raftered, reed-thatched hut. The doorway itself was nothing more than an opening. When the weather howled, it was closed over with a hide-covered rectangle of branches, bound together with leather thongs and hung by a pair of straps made of the same material. He wasn't sure which was worse: leave it open and freeze, or close the stupid thing and choke on the smoke that fought its way through the crude opening in the conical roof.

The solution, Marcus decided, like so many things in his miserable, misbegotten life, was a matter of compromise: leave the door partway open, but keep a large fire burning in the middle of the hut. The only trouble was, he had to keep it stoked and cut the wood to keep it burning. Which, on short rations, was telling on a body as thin and as lean as it had ever been in his entire life, and the year had not yet reached the winter solstice.

He'd long-since lost track of how many gullies, glades, glens, and ravines they'd halted in during the past three years, always moving north, always on the run, each move worse than the last. And the frustration and disappointment had been heartbreaking. Less than two months past he'd lain face down, his mouth buried in the mud, with a large, hairy, stinking barbarian sprawled on his back and an equally large knife at his throat. From the corner of his eye he'd seen, actually seen, the legs and hooves of a hundred auxiliary cavalry pass through the windblown sway of gorse and bracken not fifty paces from where he lay. And not one of them had turned to look.

Marcus sighed, for the hundredth time forcing the memory from his mind. It was too painful to leave there and brood upon. With his thoughts once more a weight in his chest, he forced himself back inside the hut. At least it was warm there, though, not for the first time, he wondered why he even bothered. Fiona sat on the edge of the cross-lashed frame that served as a bed, the brat on her knee and annoyance scribed on her face.

Besides the rude cot with its lumpy, hay-stuffed mattress, there was little else inside the hut. It could all have been strapped on the back of a pony, and indeed, that was exactly where it had been, carried from hill to glen on each leg of the long trek north. The last one, a hair-raising nighttime journey across the broad river that wound inland from the *Bodotria estuary*, had brought them finally to the southern hills of the Caledonii. Marcus's despair had deepened with every step, and only one thought kept hope alive: his own people had kept pace all the way.

"You think we're here for the winter?" he asked, knowing full well Fiona had no more idea than he had.

"Of course we are, so get used to it," she muttered. "And close the door, so we might survive it."

"Then don't throw so much wood on the fire. It's like living inside a *hypocaust*," Marcus complained, deliberately using a word Fiona wouldn't understand; yet a moment later he grew irked when she didn't ask its meaning. He closed the door anyway, which left the crude hut lit only by the flames. "The brat doesn't like it either."

He watched the dwarf edge onto the bed and move closer to the mud wall for its coolness. The whelp! The brat! The bairn! The woman still claimed it was his, but he was certain that was a lie. There'd been nothing like that in *his* family, so how could there be now? Yet the woman insisted! Why? She despised him, he knew that, so surely she would have selected a father from the others who'd had her. There were no doubt many who qualified, though the likeliest was Aulus, who'd been killed—when? It seemed like a decade ago. Marcus sighed and squatted on the floor, after first pulling the deerskin mat back from the fire. At least he had the satisfaction of knowing the man was dead; there was something in that.

"Da."

Marcus gritted his teeth. The woman had the brat calling him *Da*, which he was sure she did only to annoy. He turned and looked as the child slid from the bed and tottered toward him. It was slow. Very slow—though in body only, not in wit. The whelp had taken almost two years to learn how to walk, unable to keep its balance, rolling wherever it wanted to go, and often using all four limbs as arms and hands. Yet when he'd been bored, which was nearly all the time once darkness fell, it had amused him to watch it at play. It would lie on its back, perhaps feeding with one hand, while using the other to dress a doll held securely between its two bare feet. Or sometimes it would balance a piece of wood, and—

"Watch it," Marcus muttered, raising both hands to catch the bairn as it fell giggling forward.

The brat was how old now? Certainly more than two years. Yet it still couldn't walk properly! With feet splayed sideways, it waddled wherever it went, falling more often than not. As it tumbled gleefully into his lap, the small, awkward child reminded him of a puppy scurrying over to get its back scratched. If the gods had given the whelp a tail, it would have wagged like the wind when its owner was pleased. At least, at the end of a miserable day, which was every last one of them, there was always one living creature pleased to see him.

In fact, the brat was the only friendly face to be found, for even Urs was gone. The slave had approached him shortly after what the barbarians called *Beltane*, bringing with him a small, thin sheet of copper. Only the gods knew where he'd got it, though it was likely from the barbarian Dermat; or perhaps the bard Criff, for he'd shown up again, briefly, around the same time. Urs had thrust the sheet into his hand, along with a pointed piece of iron that was obviously meant to serve as a stylus.

"Here," the slave had said, "I want you to make your mark on it."

"What is it?" Marcus asked, though he knew even as he took it. The piece of copper was a certificate of emancipation, etched in a surprisingly neat hand, and written in grammatically correct Latin. All it seemed to lack was the name of the slave's owner.

"The three years have come and gone," Urs went on, a trace of defiance in his voice.

"This is no good, you know," Marcus said, his own voice surprisingly calm, for it struck him that three years had, after all, come and gone, and as far as the slave was concerned, he hardly cared. "I'm not your owner, as you once were quick to point out. It also doesn't meet the prescribed form."

"Yes it does," Urs insisted stubbornly. "It's a copy of a real one."

"Where did you ... " Marcus started to ask, but stopped. The huge slave would never tell, and Marcus had no idea what one really looked like anyway. Instead he shrugged and hedged. "What are you going to do? Join their lost cause? It is lost, you know."

Urs, surprisingly, sat down and looked Marcus candidly in the eye. It struck him that such direct contact with the slave had been rare, and as always, he was startled to see the depth of intelligence in the man's iron-grey eyes.

"It's a price I must pay," Urs said slowly, adding, almost as an afterthought, "for the time being. Otherwise, I must look to remain here as your keeper, and there seems no end to that task. I have honoured my side of the bargain. Three years."

"But they will lose, you know," Marcus said, pushing aside the doubt in his mind, for his own continued captivity was a sign that Rome was not doing as well as she might. He knew that Agricola—surely it still had to be Agricola—was pushing the forts northward, for that was all the stupid barbarian warriors ever talked about. Yet what was the man doing beyond building his idiotic forts? That wasn't doing Marcus Sabinius a speck of good.

Urs's answer surprised him: "I know it's a lost cause, but I'll be gone before they lose it." Urs shrugged. "As I've told you before, my home is in the south. And with this," he pointed to the copper plate, "and when the gods give me a clear break…"

Marcus had shrugged in turn, and bent to scratch his name on the copper. When he handed the sheet back to the slave, though, he did something that was so odd, he later doubted he'd even done it. On impulse, he stuck out one hand. "Let's wish each other luck, then."

Urs's features showed his surprise, but he reached out and clasped Marcus's wrist. "Aye, I'll do that. With pleasure. Good luck to you, young Sabinius."

"Good luck to you too, Urs," Marcus replied, but before releasing the beefy forearm, he added, "and should our paths cross, let's do our best to help each other."

Urs hesitated, then his face split in a grin and he nodded his huge bearded head. "Let's do that. Though the gods know, you're more likely to need help than me."

Marcus often reflected on the slave's words as the months passed. They crossed his mind now as he hefted the brat and set it on its feet, watching sombrely as it smiled. It was waiting for him to play with it. He had to, of course, because that was what its infernal mother wanted him to do. His puckered his lips in thought. Perhaps there was a way to make at least one chore less boring, and at the same time keep his mind from turning to mud. He stared hard at the tiny creature, wondering if it could learn how to scribe letters and figures.

Marcus saw Urs several times over that summer, then yet another winter set in, and that seemed to be the end of the man as both of them moved on. The latest hut he shared with the woman and her child had been hastily thrown together, along with a score of others, in a glen nestled in the hills even farther north of the Bodotria. That he knew, but little else. The days turned into their usual endless drudgery, each one ordered by either Fiona or one of the convalescing barbarians who came and went through the tiny village.

The small camp seemed to serve as a hospice for those who ran afoul of a Roman sword, and Marcus found a certain gratification in seeing the wounded arrive, often unable to walk. That meant his own people were meeting with success on some small level. And as yet another summer vanished and the days again grew shorter, Marcus found himself obsessed with a further form of gratification, one that grew humiliatingly addictive.

It had started not long after spring, following a week of biting weather. Bitter winds forced everyone early to their hovels, keen for the warm comfort of whatever blanket could be found. Marcus was washing his body as usual by the dim light of the fire, when he noticed Fiona staring from the bed. She lay next to her sleeping bairn, peeping through half-lidded eyes, her lips parted in that wanton pout that had been so pronounced his first day at Luguvalium.

"Come here," she murmured huskily, and set the sleeping brat in its cot. She beckoned with one hand as if calling for a skivvy.

Marcus padded over to the cot, strangely self-conscious, the towel dangling in front of his body as if by accident. The woman simply ignored it, and reached beneath to grasp his scrotum. Instinctively he backed away, but she held on, growling at him to stay put; then she slid her hand upward and slowly fondled his penis. With a mind of its own, the thing snapped to attention, though in truth, it had been halfway there anyway.

Without a word, Fiona's hand disappeared beneath the blanket. With her eyes gazing steadily into his face, she moved her hand gently back and forth beneath the covers, her breathing heavier with every twist of her arm. When her laboured gasps reached a ragged peak, matched by the wild thrashing of her hips, Fiona frantically kicked the blanket aside, offering Marcus a brief glimpse of pale thighs, a soft, plump belly, and the glistening dark triangle of her sex.

"Get on," she gasped, and when he hesitated, she snapped, "Now!"

Strangely reluctant, Marcus had obliged. At first he moved steadily back and forth, feeling almost detached from the woman; but the years of frustration suddenly burst inside him, and his body began thrusting and humping like a rutting stud. A rush of pressure pounded through his groin as part of his mind vaguely heard a loud, wailing groan erupt from Fiona.

Without warning, she threw him from the bed onto the dirt floor, where he lay panting, his throbbing organ convulsively spilling its seed. "N-n-not a second t-time," Fiona gasped, shuddering as her own spasms faded.

"Bitch!" Marcus muttered, and staggered to his feet. He moved angrily toward the bed, but stopped short as Fiona rolled onto her knees, a dagger waving in the same hand that moments before had grasped his groin.

"Try it, and I'll scream," she sneered, then nodded toward the door. "If I don't get you, they will. And you'll be just as dead."

Many times since, Marcus wished he'd ignored the threat, but he knew it would have been no use. Even if he'd wrested the blade from her grip, what would he do next? He'd simply spat on the dirt floor, returned to his bed of hides, and gone to sleep. At least in the arms of Morpheus, he found something resembling peace of mind.

Fiona had used him often since, and oddly enough, she no longer pulled away in the final throes of passion. The act itself, always at her command, assumed a regularity that took place, he eventually realized, a few days before her monthly bleeding. Once that registered, his anticipation had grown both shameful and galling. As part of his mind waited out the month with the eagerness of a fourteen-year-old, another part became filled with degradation and shame. It was debasing, unmanning! The woman used him as if he were no more than a female slave!

Marcus's eagerly awaited humiliation might have gone on forever for, despite his self-pity, he was never less than a willing partner. But not long after the winter solstice had passed, Fiona fell ill.

The sickness began with a sore throat, soon followed by a hacking cough: a sickening wheeze that settled deep inside her chest. A vile, greyish-green phlegm came up that never did clear, and her body glowed like a bed of burning coals as the fever took its grip. Marcus found himself watching the woman's ravings with mixed feelings. While his mind was mostly cool and dispassionate, at other times he found himself curiously concerned with her recovery. Probably, he convinced himself, it was because the bitch he'd grown used to was likely better than the one he hadn't...

In spite of help from other women in the makeshift village, with their endless dosing and stinking balms, Fiona's sickness worsened. Her fever never did break, and in the middle hours of the night, she simply stopped gasping for breath and died.

Yet something peculiar happened earlier that evening, as one of the crones was tending the woman. A brief spell came when Fiona's eyes grew less glassy, and her voice, so long senseless and raving, was suddenly soft and clear. "Marcus," she whispered.

He looked up, startled; the woman never called him by his name. At best, she used "Roman"; at worst, well, there were a dozen others always ready on her tongue. The hag, who'd been fussing with some of her useless potions, raised her head and caught his eye. She nodded as if to say *"Ah-hah, I was expecting as much."* Marcus sat puzzled, wondering if the crone's odd gesture meant the moment was a good sign or a bad one.

"Marcus..."

He heaved himself reluctantly to his feet, crossed the hut, and sat down by the bed. One hand went to the woman's forehead to find out if the fever had lessened. It was hotter than ever, and Marcus was suddenly struck by despair, for he'd thought perhaps the tide had turned. He suddenly realized that, bitch that she might be, he didn't want her to die.

"Sleep, girl," he mumbled.

"You—you know, you're not such a bad bastard, when you're not working at it." Fiona managed a weak smile.

"And you're not such a miserable bi—" Marcus began, then stopped. "Just rest. Get better."

"I—we need to talk."

A tear rolled down Fiona's cheek, and he found himself strangely uncomfortable. "Go ahead. I'm listening."

"Jessa. Someone will have to look after her. She's..." One hand reached out and touched the edge of the child's cot. "She's special. So very special."

"Don't worry. I'll see to it. Cethen whatever-his-name will take care of her," Marcus said, adding, "Or the Morallta woman. She'd do it. After all, she's Carveti, like you."

"Marcus, *you* must take care of her. She can't live like this." One hand waved weakly toward the crude mud walls of the hut. "She deserves better."

"Hey, *I'm* living like this," Marcus protested, but found the words strangely hollow, for he knew that one way or another, he'd be rid of it all one day.

As if reading his mind, Fiona said, "One day you'll be free of all this. You can surely do better by your own daughter."

"But she's ... " Marcus fell silent.

"But she's what?" Fiona cried fiercely, her voice suddenly stronger. "A dwarf? A barbarian? Or what else—she's not yours?" She glared into his face, vainly trying to rise on one elbow. "I can tell you one thing, you weasel, and swear to it by every god that cares to listen. And with my last breath, you will have it: *you* are her father! And if those eyes of hers don't tell you as much, then you're a bigger fool than even I credit you for."

Marcus watched, strangely moved, as she fell back on the bed, her eyes closed. He shrugged, choosing his words carefully. "Fiona, I promise I'll see she's taken care of."

Tears welled up and trickled down both burning cheeks. "On the other hand, Roman," she whispered, "you can be a real bastard."

Marcus hung his head, not knowing what to say. The old woman edged over to the bed so she could wipe Fiona's face, and in doing so knocked something clattering to the floor. The noise was enough to wake the brat and it rolled over, staring at him with bleary eyes. A single chubby hand moved up to its neck, and a small, rasping cough followed.

"Da, froat hurts."

"Ah, shit!" Marcus muttered, much louder than intended. He felt unbearably trapped, far beyond his imprisonment; he was a bitter, caged animal treed by a hundred hunters, cornered not only by the barbarians, but by this woman, her child, the gods—and by life itself!

"Marcus, what did she say?" Fiona's voice revealed alarm, despite her weakness.

Marcus sighed and climbed to his feet. "She wants some water," he lied.

He made a pretence of getting some, and leaned over the brat's cot. Its forehead was warm, very warm. He returned to the bed, where Fiona appeared once more to have fallen into delirium; yet as he settled his weight alongside, her eyes opened. They stared, unblinking, two dark, hazel orbs full of accusation. Marcus stared back and, taking both her hands in his own, made his promise. It wasn't one that would need keeping for any length of time.

"Fiona, I swear I'll personally look after Jessa."

But she wasn't to be put off, and Marcus almost could have laughed at her canniness. "For how long, Roman? For how long?"

"There's no need for that," he said and, giving in to an inexplicable impulse, he leaned over and kissed Fiona on her forehead. "There's no trick here, girl. For as long as I'm alive, and she needs looking after, I'll do so."

Once more tears trickled down Fiona's cheeks as she lifted her hands, pulling his to her lips. They were hot against his fingers as she kissed them. "Thank you, Marcus," she whispered, "thank you."

She was smiling as she closed her eyes, and before morning came, she was gone.

And Jessa's throat had almost closed.

And his own was hurting so bad that he hated to swallow.

For almost two more days Marcus managed to remain on his feet, listlessly helping the crone tend to her helpless charge, pushed on by a strange, forceful feeling of responsibility. He found he didn't want the creature to die, which was odd, because he really didn't feel for it, one way or another. It was Fiona's brat, and now she was gone it belonged to the tribes. Perhaps he just felt sorry for the—the child.

Then the racking, hacking cough started burning its way into his chest, and his entire body seemed on fire, bathed in a slick coating of sweat. As the fever closed its grip, Marcus vaguely remembered staring down at the child in its cot: a small, damp, burning being that inspired an awed respect. The tiny girl was coping with hardly more than a whimper.

After that, there was little to be remembered.

Marcus awoke to daylight and a rancid smell of sweat and muck that he slowly realized was his own—as was nearly every other foul odour that filled his nose. The inside of the hut was a haze of smoke from the fire that blazed in the centre, even though the door was partly open. A pale, wintery sunlight slanted in through the skewed frame, along with a draft that felt pleasant and cool.

He lay still as a log on the bed that had once been Fiona's, feeling weak and exhausted as he slowly gathered his thoughts. After a while he tried to stir, but found something pressed gently against his left shoulder. Marcus thought that over for what seemed a very long time, and finally decided that whatever it was needed attention. The weight was not unduly heavy, and he tried to turn sideways to find the source.

Eyes fighting to focus, he saw the top of a small, dark head resting not a handsbreadth beneath his chin. The sight startled him for a moment, then he felt the steady rise and fall of breathing against his chest, and he smiled, oddly relieved. One hand slid downward and settled gently on the child's back.

The small head lifted. Marcus found himself staring into a pair of deep, doe-like eyes. The thought flitted through his mind that barbarians scarcely ever had dark brown eyes, at least not with the frequency of his own people.

"You feeling better, Da?" she asked in a small voice.

Marcus simply nodded, numbly sorting through a curious rush of emotion surging through his mind.

The child was quiet for a moment, then, a catch in her throat, spoke again. "Mam's gone, Da."

His hand tightened against the small back as tears inexplicably filled his eyes. Jessa wriggled her way upward until her head lay alongside his, and kissed his damp cheek; then she snuggled once more into his shoulder, after a long, hard hug. Marcus couldn't stop it: his chest heaved in a long, silent spasm of sobs.

Chapter XVJJJJ

Eboracum, A.D. 82

"That was nice," Elena said, half because it was true, and half because she knew Gaius liked to hear her say as much. And perhaps, she decided on reflection, half because there was something she wanted.

Gaius grunted and sprawled over on his back, flinging one arm sideways. The gesture had grown instinctive over the past few years, and Elena rolled sideways until her head rested on his chest. He crooked one leg comfortably over hers, and she nestled in with a sigh as he fumbled with the blanket, pulling it up to cover them both against the cool of the morning. She resisted an overwhelming urge to doze and instead pondered how to begin. Directness seemed the only way.

"I was thinking..." she began.

"Yes, you can," Gaius growled. Before continuing he raised his back off the bed to rid the sheet of an irritating ridge thrown up by their lovemaking. "And Coira too, I suppose. You'll be picking at me until I say yes, so we may as well settle it now, before we both grow miserable. You'll remain attached to the headquarters unit, though. Agreed?"

"How did you—"

"Because you've been acting like a caged wolf. Only you don't pace back and forth and snarl like wolf, you just pace and grow moody." Gaius yawned before repeating, "So, agreed?"

"Of course. Though both of us will carry weapons?" Elena asked, remembering the time at Stannick when she'd followed Gaius into a full-scale battle totally unarmed, and with her horse led by its halter. It seemed a lifetime ago.

"That depends. Who are you going to use them on? Me, or the barbarians?"

"That depends on who presents the greater danger," Elena replied and relaxed, deciding his mood was good, and there was no better time to hint at the reason for Rhun's scheduled visit later that day. She cringed at the thought of how the meeting would go. Gaius had no idea what was on her son's mind, she was sure of it, and again wondered how a man could be so aware in so many ways, yet so obtuse in others. It had been no different with Cethen, she supposed, yet he could often be prompted into thinking that what *she* wanted was actually what *he* ...

"And what if your path should cross that of your husband again?" he asked, his tone suddenly careful, perhaps even tentative.

Elena groaned under her breath. It was not the first time Gaius had raised the so-called *clandestine* meeting with Cethen, and she knew it wouldn't be the last. Yet the encounter had hardly been one to offer concern; her children were there, his brother, and several others. And so what? Gaius and she were not married, and Cethen, after all, was her husband!

She quickly shook that particular thought from her mind. Gaius, deep inside, knew that what she'd told him was true, it just didn't stop the occasional picking. The chance meeting had been at Cethen's call, and everyone knew it, including Gaius. Priscus, as much as anyone, had attested to stumbling across the ribbons. Thank the gods that for once Cian had managed to keep his gob shut about setting the bait.

But it was more than the encounter that irritated Gaius. Cethen's small army of cavalry, or at least that of his woman—her husband, surely, was not leading them—had been seen numerous times over the past years. The small force had been in Cumbria when Gaius's son was taken, and it had helped cover the retreat into the north country, often at severe cost to Rome. Now it was known to be active north of the Bodotria. Cethen Lamh-fada was an increasingly sensitive issue for Gaius, and she knew full well the cause lay in more than one direction.

"Then I suppose," she replied carefully, "that would depend on the danger that he, and whoever he is with, might present."

"So if there was no danger ... ?"

"Then I wouldn't rush in with a sword and remove his head," Elena said practically. "And why would I? He's the father of my children."

"So you still think of him as your husband. Cethen of the *long arms!*"

Elena could have reached out and shaken the man, especially for his choice of words! All she wanted to speak about was Rhun, yet she could sense Gaius's pleasant mood slipping away as his thoughts played over her past. The next question would undoubtedly be why she considered herself still married to Cethen—a notion about which she herself was unsure.

Technically she was Gaius's slave, though he treated her as a freeborn woman. He had, in fact, offered her emancipation more than once, and had actually given it to Coira. Yet for some perverse reason, she herself had refused. There was a clause for her freedom in his will, he'd told her, and that had seemed enough. Yet was there another reason for refusal? As a slave, there was a certainty in her life; as a free but penniless woman, it left her nowhere.

That wasn't really true, and she knew it. If she was to be treated like a chattel, which she was, then it might as well be official. On the other hand, was she simply avoiding a final betrayal of Cethen? Maybe Cethen had already divorced her. Yet if so, how, in this bog-bottomed world, would she know anyway? She never thought to ask him ...

"No!" Elena cried and sat up, frustrated. Was every man's pride as fragile as a raw egg? For the longest while she'd thought Gaius, with his stubborn, distant, disciplined ways, was above such concerns. Yet the more intimate they had grown, the more he seemed to pick at her former life. Elena rose from the bed and slipped a shift over her head, staring down at Gaius as she did so.

"How can I think of him as my husband?" she asked, shaking her body to settle the garment. "I don't even know who *I* am!"

Gaius glanced up from the clutter of documents on his desk, wincing as the hobnailed boots crashed down on the wooden floor. Rhun! No matter how many times the youth entered the residence, it was always the same: a precise slam of a booted foot against the floor, and a pained expression that clearly indicated he'd rather be anywhere else in the empire but here. Which was turning into a nuisance, considering half the boy's family was housed inside the same structure. He just wished the lad would relax. When he'd first entered the legions, Gaius mused, things had been different.

Back then, there had been little desk work for a junior tribune, and great delight in sneaking up on senior officers and crashing those iron cleats on the floor until your foot hurt. And here—well, Rhun's expression contained no delight, only rigid control. The boy did it because he thought it was required.

It was the lad's lack of background, of course, coupled with that barbaric school he'd been sent to. They'd no doubt drilled the boy until his tail was dragging or wagging. A fear of authority was hammered in so hard at those places that, unless a person was born to it, he wore it like a slave's chain. No, there was nothing like a good start in life, Gaius grunted to himself.

"So what is it?" he asked. "You look like your bowels are bunged. Feeling well?"

"Er…I was wondering, sir…" Rhun's eyes focused on the wall behind the legate's head. "It's about…"

"Stand at ease, dammit," Gaius muttered, then gestured to one side of the desk. "In fact, sit down. You're making me uncomfortable. Your squadron preparing to move out, is it?"

"Yes, sir." Rhun edged backward and placed his rear on the edge of the nearest chair, looking relieved by the question. "We hope to join up with the rest of the regiment at, er…*Trimontium*?"

Gaius noted the query in his voice. "The entire army is assembling there. Ninth is to seize firm control of the territory on both sides of the Bodotria. Agricola will be leading most of the Twentieth up in the west, securing the lands north of Luguvalium. It will stretch our forces pretty thin."

"That's the Novantae," Rhun said drily. "There'll be lots to keep the men busy."

"Very. It also seems the governor is set on launching an expedition to *Hibernia*." Gaius wished he'd kept his mouth shut. It was not the province of legates to discuss strategy with auxiliary decurios, especially when that strategy lacked sense. The governor had grown intrigued with the great, green island that lay to the west, ever since the fleet had landed there while supporting the campaign against the Carvetii. Agricola's new expedition seemed based on nothing but a whim.

Gaius coughed and changed the subject. "Your mother and sister will be travelling north with my headquarters unit. I think they're bored." He smiled. "They might change their minds, though, after a summer campaigning."

"I doubt that," Rhun said, then asked, "Is Aelia going too?"

Gaius laughed, amused at the idea of his daughter travelling north on campaign; yet at the same time he felt a surge of warmth, just thinking on it. "No, she'll remain here. As you're well aware, the girl spends most of her time reading anyway, or taking care of what's necessary to run the estate. I don't know what I'd do without her." He paused and cocked his head to one side as he stared at Rhun. "Why do you ask?"

"I, er ... " Rhun unconsciously rose to stand awkwardly in front of the chair, his chest suddenly heaving as if he were gasping for breath. "I, well, I suppose t-that's the reason I'm here, sir."

Gaius felt his face tighten as his mind froze. "It is?"

"I—we—that is ... we want to get married, sir. I'd like to ask your—"

"You *what?*" Gaius rose to his feet, stunned.

"We've been t-talking about it f-for s-some time," Rhun stuttered, something he never did, and wet his lips to stop it. "Over the past winter, we've been ... "

"You've been what!" Gaius demanded, his mind racing to his daughter and her behaviour, which seemed to be the same as ever; to Elena, who hadn't said a word about anything and who no doubt knew; to Coira, who'd likely put the pair up to it to begin with; and finally to Rhun himself, a barbarian upstart who had been ... been—exactly what *had* the ingrate been doing with his daughter over the past winter? He didn't want to know.

"I—we've been talking, and ... " Rhun spluttered, shifting

awkwardly from one foot to the other. "Well, Aelia has—"

"Stand straight when you're talking to me, boy," Gaius roared, then turned grimly toward the door. "Orderly! Metellus! Anyone! Get your miserable carcass in here."

Rhun's squadron was on its way north the following morning, an hour before the sun edged over the horizon. None of the men asked what was wrong, though something obviously was, and he saw no reason to enlighten them. The small column of riders rode out of the fortress through the Praetorian Gate two abreast, as neatly as if on parade. Branaught, his optio, soon found it best to keep his distance, falling back and riding with the troop, leaving Rhun to take the lead and brood by himself.

And brood he did: on the injustice of life, and on that of the legate Gaius Sabinius in particular; on the Roman army, its command structure, and the ruling officer class; on his mother and the gods, who between them had made him who he was; and on Aelia, the quiet, beautiful, sweetly scented Aelia, who...

Rhun shook his head, refusing to let his mind go there. It was the barbarian thing that was the problem, of course; that, and the fact that he hadn't been born Roman, hadn't been born rich, and hadn't been born into the same class as the legate. It hadn't meant a thing to Aelia, though, for she loved him for the man he was. She'd certainly told him often enough, as he had told her. Yet, by the time the squadron overnighted in Cataractonium, his mind was casting doubt on that, too.

Was he simply a source of amusement, someone or something to help pass the time in what must, for her, be nothing more than a dull, boring outpost of the empire? Certainly she was lively enough in his company. And certainly she was eager for them to spend time together. There was her ready patience as she taught the finer points of her language, and what appeared to be a sincere enjoyment in sharing the writings of the Greek philosophers and the Roman poets. In fact, he was finally beginning to enjoy reading some of the scrolls himself—a few, anyway.

Which raised another question. Was Aelia simply patronizing? Plato was, after all, an ass whose theories were great if you ignored human nature. But when he'd told her as much, all she did was laugh and seem to agree. As she did when he expressed the opinion that while Homer wrote entertaining stories, unbelievable as they might be, they were no less believable than those spun by the bards and priests...

The woman *did* have feelings for him, he was sure of it.

When the troop idled its way up to Vinovia on the second night, Rhun was at least talking to everyone, though only in monosyllables. He was seriously considering his career, and looking to other possibilities, but there were not many. His life had become totally dependent on the Roman Gaius Sabinius, he realized with dismay, and even if he stayed with the army, it would still remain dependent. What else was there?

There was his da, of course, who would be overjoyed, and— And there was the torque!

Which, when he thought on it, would solve any and all of his pecuniary lack. Its value would bring him to Aelia with a degree of independence. Yet how could he possibly betray his people by misusing the torque? And it wasn't only that, Rhun realized when his mind probed deeper. The problem was far more than simply money. It was about a race of prejudiced, biased, class-structured, primped-up Roman arse nuzzlers who didn't give a frog's fart for anyone but their own kind!

If it weren't for the fact that his da was on the losing side, and the gathering of the tribes stood no more chance than a one-armed gladiator with his feet tied, that direction might have been something to consider. Mind you, with the torque in hand, perhaps he and his father...

Though that red-haired woman he was with would never...

Yet there was the man Dermat—he seemed competent enough...

Rhun shook his head, his mind a muddle of thoughts going nowhere.

The squadron ambled into Vindomora late the third night with Branaught, as ordered, setting a deliberately slow pace. By then the optio had a fair idea of what was preying on his commander's mind, and tried several times to break his mood. But Rhun would have none of it, preferring to enjoy the perverse solace of his misery.

He managed to maintain the mood all the way to Habitancum for the fourth night, and finally on to Trimontium where, by then, his mind had settled on Aelia herself. What would she do when he was no longer part of her life? Thinking over the woman's options offered a perversely gratifying sense of pain. She would doubtless find some Roman clotheshorse to bed with, probably inflicted on her by Gaius Sabinius himself, and spend the rest of her life raising his brats. She would regret it, of course, but then, so would he, for the rest of *his* life! There had to be something that could be done.

"Want me to report in for you?" Branaught asked as the rest of the troop dismounted outside the fort's main gate. "Doesn't look like we'll be in barracks. Probably in one of the camps."

A huge bivouac had sprung up outside the newly built fort. A marching camp had been dug and staked farther east, and another was being marked out for digging off to the south. Several cavalry regiments were already housed there from the looks of the horse lines, and both men hoped that some of them belonged to their own regiment. There were also probably half a dozen infantry cohorts in camp too, and Rhun knew that at least one was from the Ninth.

"Just what we need, out in the open." Rhun ignored the question, glancing at the sky, where dark banks of cloud were building to the north. "It'll probably rain tonight. Maybe even a late snow. I'm getting fed up with this shit."

"I think maybe I should go and report in," Branaught said, and grinned. "You're as likely to tell the camp praefectus to shove his shield up his backside."

"No, I won't," Rhun muttered, then forced a smile. "I'd tell him to use his sword." He kicked his horse in the belly, sending it toward the gate. "Come on, we'll both do it. If I cause any trouble, drag me out by the ears."

The headquarters building was busy, even though the shadows of evening had crossed the wood palisades and darkened the main street. An orderly was busy lighting lamps, while another fired one of the braziers to take the chill from the air. Rhun and his optio entered the cross hall and headed for the likeliest looking table, which was manned by two clerks doing their best to look harried.

"Reporting in from Eboracum with one troop. Fourth Augusta Gallorum. I think most of the regiment's already here," Rhun said. "Any idea where?"

One of the clerks frowned and ran his finger down a large wax tablet scrawled with rough notes. "You just got in from Eboracum?"

"That's right."

"A single squadron?"

"Yeah."

"Fourth Gallorum?"

"I just fucking-well said—" Rhun started to growl, then felt Branaught's hand fall on his shoulder. He sighed. "Yeah."

The man turned instead of answering, and called out to a group of men chatting by the steps to the pay office. "Hey, Pervicus, I think the lost are found."

An older man broke away and walked over, ignoring the two travel-stained troopers as he spoke to the clerk. "This the Eboracum squadron?" When the man nodded he said, "Give me the new orders."

"Somewhere here…" The man fumbled through a pile of half-curled scrolls, all held down by a bronze weight in the lewd shape of a naked woman. "Yeah, here it is."

"We've had this thing for what, two days now? What did you do? Walk here?" The centurio snorted in disgust. Dangling the scroll in one hand, he began reading the words half aloud, while sipping from a clay mug clasped in the other. "Upon arrival … return to … post haste …" He looked up and stared at them both. "Which one of you is called Rhun?"

Rhun sighed, wondering what swinish tasking the legate had dreamed up, for the orders had certainly been issued by the man. "That's me."

"You're to return to Eboracum immediately. And from the looks of the wording," the centurio tossed the scroll to Rhun, "you'd better haul your carcass back there a lot faster than you did on the way up here."

Rhun and Aelia were married less than a week after his return to Eboracum, a journey that took less than three days. Had he known what waited for him, he would have made it in two.

The interview that took place with Gaius Sabinius on his arrival had not been pleasant. Rhun had the sense not to utter a word, though, truth be known, it hardly mattered, for he hadn't the slightest idea what the legate was talking about. When it was over, and it didn't take long, Gaius stalked out of the room, his face grim.

Rhun found himself briefly alone, his mind a fog as he tried to understand what he'd been told. The legate's speech had been totally convoluted, but it appeared he'd approved Rhun's marriage to Aelia, albeit reluctantly, and that for some odd reason, he was being promoted to regimental optio, once a vacancy opened.

He was puzzling this through when Aelia herself entered the room and stood by the door, an odd smile on her lips. "Well, aren't you going to kiss me or something?" she asked when he didn't move.

"What is going on?" Rhun asked, looking over one shoulder, unsure whether or not the legate was watching.

"We discussed getting married, did we not? Now we're going to do it," Aelia said, and decided that since Rhun wasn't going to move, she had better; the poor man looked like a trapped deer, frozen in midstride. She walked over and kissed him, hard, then stood back to study his face. It was pale, drawn, and worried. One hand rose and caressed his cheek, vainly trying to ease the strain.

"But..."

"It was *you* who wished to seek father's permission, my dear. I warned you. You should have let me do it."

"But how...?"

Aelia smiled to herself before replying. She had no idea which way Rhun was going to leap, but there was no choice other than to be direct. As for herself, she found the circumstances almost amusing, for her words might have been found in a Greek comedy. "Among quite a few other things, I told him I was pregnant."

Rhun looked stunned, and for a moment was speechless. The only words he could finally muster were, "But we've never even..."

"I know that far better than you, my dear. In fact, I know it all too well." She patted his cheek, and none too lightly. "It's nothing that can't be corrected, though. The first child will be just a little later than father expects. By then I imagine he'll be quite used to the idea."

Chapter XX

Caledonii Territory, A.D. 83

Winter had gone, and just as spring follows, so did the endless trek from one makeshift shelter to another. Sometimes it was a mattress of dry leaves, spread under a lean-to of prickly spruce; other times a crude hut, like as not one that had been abandoned; and just as often it was only a stinking hide blanket, with no other canopy than the clouds. Food was always short, but not the ever-present wind that howled through the hills and bit clear to the bone; so much so that the warmth of a decent fire was prized as much as food itself.

And as never before, Marcus found the hills crawling with barbarians. Most were poorly disciplined and as terrifying as wild animals, if for no other reason than their ignorance. Great bands of warriors travelled in gang-like columns, each night bedding down in makeshift camps like herds of cattle. Most were barely articulate, and as erratic as rabid dogs—the more so when full of drink. Even their own kind grew fearful as tempers flared over fancied slights, men taking offence at as little as a sideways glance. Marcus learned to hold his eyes low, keep his head bowed, and above all, ensure Jessa remained hidden from their ill humour.

Those who now held him captive were little more than the camp followers of the Carvetii and Brigante warriors who had fled north and still clung loosely together as a tribe. They all considered themselves far superior to the Caledonii, and Marcus, if asked, would have agreed, for it was a familiar pecking order. A similar gap had always existed between the Romans and the barbarians, though much wider; but here, it had no effect on his status, and the lowest tasks remained exclusively his own. If there was any change at all, it was in the manner he was watched.

Marcus and Jessa had become a fixture of the camps, which produced a paradox, but not one that he gave much thought. Those who watched him had grown lax over the years, for many of the original warriors were no longer there. Yet his urge to escape, once a flame that burned hot, had cooled to nothing more than a bed of ashes, the past two winters. It was not entirely dead, though, and the gusty spring weather blew upon a small spark that once again fought to rekindle the coals.

As evening drew near on a day that Marcus judged to be around the onset of May, a stir of excitement spread through the barbarian camps like a wind-driven fire. The reason was not long in learning, for there were many who still loved to taunt him with the least hint of Rome's misfortune. And when Cethen rode through the small cluster of huts with several of his own people, he confirmed the rumour as fact.

"One of the Roman armies looks like it's been left on its own. Galgar's going to attack it, I'm sure," he told Marcus as he dismounted, stretching his arms and back as if to relieve the ache.

Marcus stood close by a smokeless fire of split logs over which hung a black iron cauldron. An unappetizing mix of greens and grains bubbled inside, beneath a surface scum of herbs and dust. Marcus, as was his job, idly sliced a dark haunch of salted venison into small cubes and tossed the stringy meat into the pot. The odour, to a hungry man, was not that bad. Jessa certainly seemed to agree, for she stood next to her da staring wide-eyed into the pot, one thumb in her mouth.

"I sort of knew something like that," Marcus mumbled, and threw another chunk of meat into the pot, causing the boiling liquid to slosh over the rim onto the flames. "So what does it mean to me?"

"Easy, that stuff's hot," Cethen muttered, and backed away from the fire. "It means you'll stay here for now, because they're confident. But if things do go wrong, you'll be on the move again, and fast. I'm to see that two of our own men are left to look after you."

"And to make sure I don't run." Marcus flung another chunk at the pot, and this time it was Jessa who stepped hurriedly back as the water slopped. Quickly reaching out to steady her, he murmured, "Easy, Jess.

Da didn't mean it. Are you alright?"

"Uh-huh," she said, and moved forward again, setting one hand against his leg.

Cethen's expression turned sheepish. "If thing's don't go well for us, watch your back. There are those whose piss will be boiling, and they'll take it out on anything Roman." He tugged at his moustaches for a moment, apparently lost in thought, then shrugged as if he'd reached a decision. "There's a large warrior whom you know. He's travelled with us this past winter, I think because he doesn't know what else to do. His heart really isn't in it, though." Cethen snorted as if in sympathy, then nodded toward the edge of the dense forest, hardly a hundred paces from where they stood. "I might leave him behind too."

"Urs? Why?"

Cethen didn't answer. Instead he walked over to his horse and grabbed its reins from the red-haired man called Borba, who sat a large bay. Both animals, Marcus saw, had once seen the inside of a Roman stable. The tall Briton grunted as he heaved himself into the saddle, then finally turned to answer the question. "Sometimes the watchers need to be watched."

Marcus nodded his understanding, but said, "That's not the 'why' I meant."

"Yeah, I figured that." Cethen sighed. "Let's say I'm just getting tired of this. Or maybe I've learned from Vellocatus: it never hurts to have both sides grateful in time of need."

"So where do you go now?"

"Galgar's called a meeting to make sure everyone's game to go down and slaughter a legion," Cethen replied, and nodded down the valley. "Not that it matters; he's made up his fool mind anyway." He flicked the reins with a grunt of annoyance, and the chestnut started up the track. "Reminds me of old times at Stannick."

Marcus watched as Cethen and the other three riders moved off into the trees. Just before they disappeared a question occurred, and he shouted it. "Do you know which legion it is?"

Cethen turned, his head shaking as if in sympathy. "The Ninth."

"Shit!"

Marcus watched the trees long after the four had vanished, then turned back to the fire. He picked up Jessa and held her in one arm, cursed again, and tossed what was left of the haunch into the stew, bone and all. He stared into the flames, brooding. Once more a Roman army was close enough to almost touch, and once more he might well have been a thousand miles away. Life had become an endless cycle of hopelessness.

There had been times, especially over winter, when he wondered if the gods meant to keep him chained to the barbarians until he died—not from illness or slaughter, but from nothing more than old age. That he might die young Marcus no longer considered, not since the fever. It was as if he'd been cursed to be forever dragged from one hill to another, one camp to the next; prodded and beaten by ignorant barbarians, not one of them able to read or write; doomed to an endless, mindless existence that did nothing but dull the brain and satisfy the random whim of some half-witted, backward, hairy, unkempt, clod of a…

Marcus sighed and slumped down next to the fire, Jessa on his knee. To look busy, he stirred the pot and poked at the flames. Another group of barbarians trooped by, all on foot, all armed, and as savage as a pack of hyenas. They sounded like a pack of hyenas too, he decided, but kept his head down and hugged the small girl to reassure her.

The child, may the gods bless her, was the only constant in his life. He had packed her across what seemed the length and breadth of the entire province of Britannia, slung on his back in a makeshift carrier along with a load of baggage the equal of any packed by a Roman infantryman. A load that he figured came close to half his weight; though he didn't begrudge carrying the girl. Yet even she, in her own small way, was becoming a source of worry. If anything actually did happen to him, who would look after her?

"Can we do some more words, Da?"

Marcus looked up and smiled. Jessa smiled back, a small stick ready in one hand, her brown eyes large and eager.

"Only if you do it right," he warned, and scraped a smooth, even patch in the dirt with his foot. "Let's start with numbers first, though. How do you say seven?"

"Oh, Da!" Jessa shook her head, as if to show the question was too easy. "It's septem."

"So put it down, oh smart one."

The child giggled and made a "V" in the dirt, followed by two vertical lines.

"I don't know about the evenness of those lines," Marcus teased, then said, "Now spell it."

Both of them ignored the two armed tribesmen who ambled over not long after. The pair settled down on the other side of the fire without a word, and stared hungrily at the contents of the iron cauldron. Marcus recognized neither one; even if he had, he suspected it would have made little difference.

"I tell you, the commander is making a mistake!" Galgar said emphatically.

"Or setting a trap." Dermat's face, as usual of late, looked grim and doubtful, more so when shadowed in the flickering flames of the campfire.

"Then it's not a very clever one," Morallta snapped, and set one hand on Galgar's shoulder as if to show her agreement. "I think they're more likely to realize their mistake and close the distance between each legion before it's fully dark. If they don't, I think—"

"If they stay where they are and dig in, they'll not be able to reach each other very fast," a man Cethen knew simply as Rib interrupted. "Especially when it gets dark."

Rib was one of Galgar's people, and the Caledoni king picked up on the words. "See how it is? The Romans grow too confident. They've no idea of our numbers, and in their hurry to join with their ships, they out-march themselves."

"The smallest force *has* been left temptingly close to the hills," Dermat said cautiously. "Yet it has the stink of a trap."

"Then we strike them from those same hills, and disappear again if one of the other armies comes to help," Morallta said, and again clapped her hand down hard on Galgar's shoulder. "If not, we destroy them."

"Perhaps all of them. One at a time," Galgar added, and the hand on his shoulder squeezed, as if in encouragement.

Cethen, who sat farther back from the fire, wedged between Borba and Ligan, didn't miss the gesture, and grunted his annoyance. His eyes slid sideways to see if anyone else had noticed, and he saw the twin looking his way, eyebrows raised. Cethen sighed and returned his gaze to Morallta, for the moment ignoring Borba's questioning look.

The attack that Galgar wanted was inevitable. Nothing would stop it, short of the three Roman armies suddenly marching together to make one, and that wasn't going to happen. He just wished everyone would finish their bickering and get on with it. There wasn't much time left. Perhaps a hundred chieftains had come together for the hasty assembly and most, for once, were listening. The king could call for the attack at once, of course, but Galgar wanted everyone behind him. And perhaps, just perhaps, he wanted to make certain where the Romans *would* finally settle for the night, before deciding.

The hills teemed with warriors: not only the Caledonii, but many from as far south as Brigantia, and others as far north as the *Vacomagii*. Cethen was sure the Romans had no firm grip on the number that shadowed their armies, any more than he did. He suspected Galgar couldn't put a figure to it either. What was certain, however, was that there were more than enough to attack one under-strength legion. And as to Morallta, he realized as his eyes fell on the hand resting on Galgar's shoulder, he wasn't sure he even cared about that anymore. It was just that a man had his pride and his position to tend to, and it wasn't so much how it was as how it looked.

Borba elbowed him in the ribs. "I'd watch that little bugger if I were you."

Cethen sighed. "Yeah, I know. The strange thing, old friend, is that I really don't give a faerie's fart about what she does. It does seem, however, that everyone else does."

The tribes began filtering in from the hills as darkness fell. The single legion that trailed the other two had built its camp on the flat, fertile plain that stretched below. Morallta's scouts had followed the three armies throughout the day, and reported as much. The largest legion, the one leading the Roman force, had camped close on five miles to the east; the one that marched at the centre seemed to have wandered off course. It had angled toward the southeast, where it had finally dug in just as far away, but down toward the *Tava*.

GRAHAM CLEWS

The Romans had left no soldiers hidden in ambush, and their cavalry, which had been riding all day, was for the most part settling down inside the temporary camps. It was enough, even for Dermat.

"Galgar wants some of your people to circle east, and keep watch between this legion and the rest of their army," he said, when he and Cethen left the clearing. Each rode to join his own people waiting in the dark forests that cloaked the hills to the south and the west. On every side, the night was a blur of shapeless shadows, each moving to the subtle creak of leather and the soft clink of weapons and armour.

"He doesn't want us in on the attack?" Cethen asked in surprise.

"Probably does," Dermat muttered, "but he's more interested in knowing when help is on its way from the rest of their army. And once the shit starts flying, it surely will be on its way, and he needs to know at once. That's far more important."

"How many do you think I should send?" Cethen tried to recall how many riders he still controlled. His people were now almost entirely Brigante, a change which had been gradual. As the small force of trained cavalry had grown, he and Morallta had formally divided them, for the most part in accordance with their tribe. It was a natural process, fuelled by growing differences between the two leaders themselves: those who were Carvetii were keeping more to themselves, and those from Brigantia were doing the same.

"I'd say at least a couple dozen," Dermat said. "Maybe twice that."

"Shit, that's ... " Cethen started counting.

"How many you got altogether?" Dermat asked.

Cethen knew that one, for Borba had given the figure before the gathering; to his relief, it popped into his mind. "There's a hundred and fourteen."

"Then it's either one in four, or one in two," Dermat said, and grinned at Cethen's fumbling. "I'd say split it down the middle, and send half."

"Yeah," Cethen murmured, and set his mind on wondering who he should put in charge. It would be Ligan or Borba, of course, but he hated to part with either. "Maybe Borba could ... "

"Actually, if I were you, I'd go myself. Save pissing around."

"Maybe. What are you doing?"

"I'll be with the rest, doing the usual," Dermat grunted, as if in disgust. "Charge the buggers head on, and hope for the best. Maybe this time we'll have enough of a surprise to make it work."

"You sound like Elena," Cethen said, and instantly drove the notion from his mind without dwelling on why it was even there.

Dermat smiled. "I did suggest to Galgar that his people don't start yelling and screaming until they're actually fighting the bastards. In fact, I suggested we might even try sneaking up on them."

"Think he'll do it?" Cethen asked, taking the words at face value. "What did he say?"

"Well, I didn't actually speak to *him*." Dermat reined his horse off to one side, where a small, shadowy army of foot warriors waited. He gave Cethen a friendly punch on the shoulder and nudged the animal with his knees to send it forward. "I spoke to Morallta."

"Because he's more likely to listen to her than even you," Cethen muttered under his breath as Dermat rode off through the trees. He stared upward at the black sky, where no stars glinted through the invisible clouds, and plaintively called out to the gods, "Why me?"

A few moments later he caught up with Borba and Ligan, who were trying to muster their people in column. It was not an easy task in the dark.

"Where we going?" Borba asked.

"It's a mistake doing this at night," Cethen muttered as he fumbled for an answer, wondering how all the other, less disciplined, thousands were forming up for the attack. He gestured loosely across the plain, hidden somewhere in the darkness below. "Half of us will circle the Roman camp and patrol between it and the other two armies. We're to give warning if—no, not if, *when* they start charging out to help."

"Half?" Ligan said. "Which half?"

"I dunno," Cethen said vaguely, "the first half."

"So what happens to the second half?" Borba asked.

"It stays, and goes in with Morallta's people, I suppose." Cethen found himself growing irritated, mostly because Dermat hadn't mentioned anything on that. Maybe he should have asked.

"So who looks after the last half in the meantime?" Ligan asked.

"You can, if you want; I'm going with the first," Cethen said, then sighed. "I really don't give a shit who looks after it. Sort it out between yourself and Borba."

"I'd rather go with you," Borba said. "That's a lot better than riding around in the dark with a horde of Caladonii hill climbers. They'd as soon stab us as the Romans."

"Me too," Ligan said. "Maybe you could get—"

"Bugger it!" Cethen cried. "Both of you come. In fact, why don't we take the whole fucking lot with us! There's not that many of us. Another, er ..."

"Fifty or so," Borba offered.

"Another fifty or so aren't going to make any difference to Galgar," Cethen finished, then fell silent, as if that were the end of it.

He sat brooding in the saddle as the column started down the dark, rustling slopes of the hills, dimly aware of a thousand others, hidden by the night on either side. His mind flitted back and forth across a nagging range of possibilities, until it finally settled on the fact that he was not doing exactly what he'd been told to do. With yet another sigh he added, "If I can find Morallta or Dermat, I'd better let them know."

A dark copse straggled along a small rise, less than a mile from the Roman camp. Galgar peered through the cover of its stunted trees, though it was hardly necessary to hide. Scores of flickering fires marked the inside of the camp, and from time to time tiny black figures crossed the orange glow, marking the Roman guards walking the makeshift rampart. The night had grown cool, and quick gusts of wind blew inland, helping mask the whispering advance of his gathering army.

On either side of the copse a rustling mass of shadows began to move forward, and one by one the chieftains on the rise drifted away to join their people. Soon only a half-dozen remained, and those too began to make ready.

"Time to go," Morallta breathed, her chest tight with excitement. Beneath the chain tunic, her heart pumped like a drum; she could feel the blood pulsing through every last strip of vein. Her limbs, her feet, even her hands were alive to the beat of it.

"I want you and your riders to remain close by me," Galgar murmured, staying her as she turned to leave. "The foot warriors will go first, but cavalry will be needed once a gap is torn through the stake wall. There'll be panic inside, and cavalry riding through will add weight."

"Yes, yes," Morallta said impatiently, and pushed on by, towing her horse by its reins.

"You'll be in front of my own cavalry," Galgar continued, falling in behind. "You're the best we have, and I need you there. Are you good with that?"

"That we're the best? Of course I'm good with that," Morallta snapped at him, though her body was trembling with excitement. To steady herself, she stopped the horse, intent on loosening the spear tied to the saddle. It was about time anyway. The weapon would be needed, and she wanted it ready; readiness was everything.

Morallta smiled as the shaft came free, and she hefted the weight in one hand. The raw fever of danger was building inside and, as usual, its strange, tingling thrill coursed through her body, rushing through her belly and down to her groin. It was a feeling like no other.

"That's not what I meant, and you know it," Galgar growled, pulling his own horse to one side as the last two men filed past.

"You coming?" the man called Rib asked as he edged by them.

"Yeah, right behind," Galgar muttered, then turned to Morallta. "Are you trying to be clever? All I'm asking, is—"

"Yes, dammit, yes," she said, scratching at her breasts, which itched under the mail as if ants were crawling over them. She was unable to hold back her sarcasm. "I'll be there protecting your skinny tail, ten strides ahead of your own cavalry. I won't accept being anywhere else."

"Then why not say so," Galgar snapped back, then stared at her through the darkness, doubt on his face. "Are you alright?"

Morallta took a deep breath, for she was taking far too many small ones. She licked her lips and stared back. "Of course I'm alright."

"Are you losing your nerve, woman?"

"I have never lost my nerve in my life, you little prick," Morallta snarled, and thrust her face into his. "And it's not lost now."

"Then why are you panting like a broken horse?" Galgar demanded, his breath close enough to be hot on her face. His features suddenly registered surprise. "You *are* afraid!"

"The only thing I'm afraid of, arsehole, is missing this fight."

"Then why—" Galgar stopped, and his eyes suddenly fastened on hers, no more than a handsbreadth away.

Morallta stared glassily back, her chest heaving with the wild, demonic excitement that churned inside, as it always did, when battle loomed. Galgar's eyes, black as coals, widened in understanding, and her mouth twisted in a grim smile. The man's face was close, too damned close, and his mouth was open, and she could see the wet on his tongue...

"Aw, shit!" Morallta moaned as she dropped her spear and reached out.

"Back there," Rib muttered, and gestured over one shoulder.

Cethen told Borba and Ligan to remain as they were, and followed a narrow trail that wound through the dark scraggle of trees that capped the rise. When he first heard the grunt of heavy breathing, it came from a good twenty paces away, yet he knew it at once for what it was. The sound was all too familiar. Dropping the reins to stay his horse, he quietly drew his sword and crept forward.

The buggers hadn't even left the track, Cethen realized when he saw the two shadowy forms on the ground alongside the horses. Morallta—it had to be Morallta—knelt with her head down and her bum up; Galgar was behind, hands on her shoulders, thrusting like a mad dog. Cethen stifled the urge to roar and leap forward, something he would have done in an instant a mere year ago. Instead, for the moment, he stood still and watched in bafflement. Then, realizing that something had to be done, he crept forward and placed the tip of his sword at the centre of Galgar's anus, just as the man shuddered to a final, quivering halt.

"Don't even twitch," Cethen growled. Then, as both stiffened, he abruptly changed his mind; with pressure on the sword, he lifted one boot and set it on Galgar's pale, naked butt. "Sprawl on the ground. Together. Or I'll spit you both on one blade."

Morallta hesitated, then eased forward onto her belly. Cethen pushed down with his boot and Galgar followed, sprawling on top of her. The tip of the blade vanished between the naked cheeks as the man's legs straightened out. Cethen could have laughed, if he weren't so pissed.

"W-who is it?" Galgar asked.

"It's the 'slow-witted fool' you told to keep watch on the Roman camps," Morallta said angrily, and tried to free herself.

"I said don't move," Cethen growled, placing more pressure on the sword.

"Do as he says!" Galgar screeched, then, calming himself, he tried turning his head. "There are Romans out there. I've got a whole fucking army waiting to attack. Can we deal with this later?"

"Yeah...the Romans," Cethen mumbled, aware the words sounded foolishly vague, but nothing else came to mind; in fact, he had no idea at all what to do next. "That's why I came here. To let Morallta know I'm taking all of my people out with me. In case she's looking for them. Which," he added in disgust, finally pulling his thoughts together, "she doesn't seem to be."

"For the love of Lug, either spit us or let me up," Morallta snarled, then added, "I doubt you could get both of us at once, anyway."

"I'd at least get this arsehole," Cethen replied.

"And in the true meaning of the word," a voice said tersely from behind; it belonged to Galgar's man, Rib. "Though if you use that sword, I'll use mine."

"Doubt it. Before you use yours, you'll feel the end of mine," Borba spoke up a moment later, sounding slightly out of breath. "Drop it."

"No, you put yours down," a third voice cried from farther back in the darkness, only to exclaim almost at once, "What the...ooph!"

"Don't worry, it's just me," Ligan called out. "This one's not getting up. I think that's all of them. What's going on up there?"

"Get over here, both of you. You won't believe this," Cethen called, and again put pressure on the sword as Galgar tried to move.

"You too," Borba ordered, pushing Rib forward until both stood alongside Cethen.

A moment later Ligan appeared from the shadows, carrying two swords. The four men stared dumbly down at Galgar, still sprawled atop Morallta, who lay with her arms stretched forward and her head raised off the ground. Both had their britches around their knees, and both wore expressions that threatened to kill.

"Personally, I prefer to stick mine in the other side," Borba murmured.

"Shit, Galgar," was all Rib could find to say.

Ligan, always the most pragmatic of Cethen's people, asked, "So, what now, Cethen?"

He shrugged. "I don't know. I just stumbled on them. They were going at it like a pair of rutting rabbits."

"Let me up, you prick, or I'll have your balls roasted," Galgar growled as he fought to gain a semblance of dignity. "And I won't cut them off first. I'll spread you over a fire and—"

"To do that, you first have to get out of this," Ligan observed. "And with respect, talking like that don't help. You were, after all, stuffing his woman."

"I'm not his woman, damn you," Morallta hissed. "I'm not anyone's woman."

"And that's the fucking truth," Cethen murmured.

"If he says he's going to have your balls, then you may as well kill him now," Borba suggested. "No point in letting him live to do it. There's only his man Rib here."

"There's another one back there," Ligan put in, jerking a thumb back along the trail.

"Fine, so that's three. Oh, and Morallta." Borba glanced down, his eyes resting wistfully on the pale buttock that peeped out from beneath Galgar. "Though she'll not weasel on us if we spit all three. I mean, how's it going to look if everybody hears she was being humped when Cethen comes along and—"

"Let's talk this over," Galgar interrupted, his tone terse, as if fighting to hold his temper. "I admit I started this, but don't forget who I am, and where you—"

"No, you didn't," Cethen interrupted in turn, and pointed to Morallta. "She likely started it. That woman gets hornier than a ten-peckered stag hound at the first *sniff* of danger. I'd wager she near ripped your britches off."

"She really like that?" Borba asked, clearly intrigued.

"Would you just piss off!" Morallta lowered her head and pounded her fists hard on the dirt.

"It wasn't quite like that," Galgar said, "though I have to admit—"

"Look." Cethen eased the pressure on the sword. "I really don't give a pinch of pig plop about you plowing her. Honest. The woman's yours, if you want her. In fact, I insist on it. But there is one thing I want."

"What's that?" Galgar, for the first time, managed to fully turn his head and look upward, but the sword remained firm where it was. "Money? There's not exactly a potful to be had, but maybe..."

"My son. Our son." Cethen nodded toward Morallta. "Find him, and see she returns him to me. And he stays in my camp. That's presuming you still want me and my people in yours. Is that agreed?"

Galgar considered, nodding. "And all this?" He shifted his eyes back and forth, then down to Morallta.

Cethen smiled grimly to himself. If only Criff was here to tell the story! He shook his head, dismissing the thought. "If anything is told of this, it comes only from your people, not mine."

"Then agreed," Galgar muttered, and sighed as the pressure eased between his buttocks.

The Caledoni chieftain quickly sat back on his knees, hitched his britches, and began frantically tying the waist string. Morallta remained prone on the dirt, her buttocks bare to the night. In a terse, muffled voice she said, "Would you useless pricks all just leave!"

Cethen reached down and hauled Galgar to his feet. As both men turned toward their horses, Cethen placed one arm on his shoulder and grinned. "I'll tell you, though," he said, his voice low, "when she does get that sniff of battle, there's nothing quite like it. It's just that a man needs to live the rest of the year, too."

"Aye, you have the right of that," Galgar murmured, then both men turned their heads toward a loud roar that rose from the direction of the Roman camp. Galgar cursed and swung into the saddle. "Shit, they're starting without me."

Chapter XXI

Caledonii Territory, A.D. 83

Gaius rode over to where the headquarters unit marched, his face mottled and his temper flaring. The moment he dismounted, he began picking at the straps on his chest armour, which for some reason refused to come loose. The edge of a buckle stabbed his finger and he cursed. Growling his annoyance, he looked up and caught the eye of Elena, who stood next to the wagon where his personal effects were stowed. The woman's eyebrows were raised and her lips pursed as if amused, which only added to his irritation.

"Help me take this off," he muttered, and simply raised his arms so she could do it. "It's nothing but a nuisance anyway. Where's the leather one?"

"Catus?" Elena asked, her fingers picking at the straps, which came undone as easily as bowed-tied laces. The molded armour fell away in two pieces, and she helped set both on top of the wagon.

"Curse the man," Gaius said. "He's like a wolf on a bare bone. Too stupid to know there's no meat, and too hungry to stop gnawing."

"Maybe he'll choke on the splinters." Elena offered him a mug of undiluted wine. "Here. I saw your foul mood ride in a mile ahead of your horse."

"And there's good reason. Those same splinters are picking at my craw," Gaius muttered, then nodded his thanks and drained half the smooth liquid in a single gulp. He exhaled, then looked up and down the long stationary column, again growing angry. "How long has this lot been sitting on their rears?"

"Calm down," Elena said. "No more than a usual rest period. In fact, look." She nodded to the front of the column. "The head's starting; the tail will follow."

"It's about time. Titus is turning soft," Gaius grumbled. Then, remembering the cause of his temper, he turned his mind back to Catus. The man had marched north with half his legion, joining with the Ninth and the Twentieth at Trimontium for what promised to be a final push north. And ever since, with every mile, the one-sided quarrel (for that's what it was), had grown like an open, festering sore. He drained the mug and handed it back to Elena. "Would you believe it? The man is now talking of revenge, or at least as good as saying so. The fool's posting is up at the end of the season, and he's on about 'having satisfaction' before he leaves."

"Satisfaction? Then find him a good woman." Elena smiled, and took a sip from her own mug.

"An ape would make a better match. The man's worse than his brother."

"So, what next?"

Gaius shrugged. "Wait until he does something rash, I suppose. It's as if he wants me to challenge him. He's mad!"

The driver coughed discreetly, and Gaius glanced toward the head of the column. The infantry was on the march, and the next wagons in line were already creaking forward.

"Don't wait for me. Get them moving," Gaius ordered and mounted his horse. Turning the animal toward Elena, he asked, "You riding, or walking?"

"How long before we camp?"

Gaius glanced westward, where the sun dipped toward a horizon made jagged by a sea of hills. "I'd guess a couple of hours."

She unhitched her own horse from the wagon as it lurched into motion. "Then I'm riding."

Gnaeus Livius Numideus was a steady, reliable, plodding sort of praefectus, with none of the headstrong, ostentatious flair that Rhun usually found in cavalry commanders. Certainly he was a different man than his predecessor, Cornelius. Perhaps it was age, Rhun mused, for Gnaeus Livius was well past forty; or perhaps it was simply that a dull mind lurked behind the man's dour features. Whatever the reason, he ran the regiment with a methodical hand that would have warmed the heart of a peacetime drill instructor.

In some ways, Rhun found it a blessing. As Livius's second-in-command, he realized the rigid, well-ordered pace had helped his transition to optio—a promotion that still left him feeling somewhat of a fraud. It also left him feeling that in some manner he'd betrayed the men of his squadron who, with the exception of Cian and his merciless hazing, wished him nothing but luck. Most of them, in fact, seemed to find his sudden fortune natural. Certainly his mother did and said as much, though Coira was often as bad as his uncle.

Livius's firm, steady approach, however, when translated to the field, was as frustrating as riding a horse with no reins: you were merely along for the ride. Which was how it was as darkness closed in, and Rhun found himself riding alongside the praefectus as the larger part of the regiment made its way back to the Ninth's camp. He had a bad feeling about it that ran deeper than the eerie chill of the tar-black night.

Over half the regiment, nine squadrons, had been acting as screen for Agricola's advance. Rhun had ridden with Cian's and Branaught's troops ahead of the vanguard, and had been fortunate enough to glimpse part of the fleet where the Tava estuary narrowed to almost a river. The next day would likely see the army camped on its shore, mingling with the men of the fleet, and everyone looking for a few days' rest.

But as night fell, Rhun found himself wandering the hills with Livius, as hopelessly lost as Odysseus and his crew. Agricola had ordered the reduced regiment to return and reinforce the Ninth; but he'd also charged its methodical praefectus with delivering two messages: one for Gaius Sabinius; the other for Demetrius Catus, legate of the Second. And there was neither sight nor sound of Demetrius Catus, his legion, or his camp.

"I could take a squadron and deliver it myself, sir," Rhun ventured for perhaps the third time.

"You're beginning to sound like a nagging wife," Livius growled, then, probably because Rhun's suggestion was not unreasonable, added, "They can't be far."

Rhun bit his tongue. Catus's camp should have straddled the path taken that day by Agricola and the Twentieth Valeria Victrix, as the governor marched his combined army toward the Tava estuary. Catus's temporary camp should not have been difficult to find: two to two and a half miles back from Agricola, and halfway to where the Ninth was camped. Yet the tracks left by Catus's force wandered east and south.

Livius plodded on, stubbornly convinced, as he had been more than a mile back, that the elusive camp lay no more than a hundred yards farther. His outriders doggedly followed the trail of dirt churned up by the passage of Catus's legion, and Rhun seethed, growing uneasier by the moment. The man was infuriating, yet it was hardly a surprise. He'd seen it before, both with Livius and other senior officers, all of them damned patricians. Once they'd set their minds on something, pride kept them in the same rutted track, unless someone a few links up the chain of command directed otherwise. Either that, Rhun thought cynically, or the gods took a hand and sent disaster instead.

There were no campfires burning when they finally stumbled on the encampment, which was odd, for a flicker of light would have made it easy to find. And there was no use trying to hide it from the barbarians, for they'd been following the three armies all day. As if to prove his point, torches were lit the moment they stopped at the entrance and hailed those within. What was doubly odd, Rhun decided, was that they were kept waiting in the dark while the praefectus and his orderly entered—and kept waiting, and waiting.

When Livius did reappear, he was in a vile mood. Viler, in fact, than the mood of Rhun and the two hundred waiting cavalrymen, all of them tired, hungry, and short on temper.

"Let's get out of here," the praefectus muttered as his orderly boosted him into the saddle. He jerked hard on the reins, turning his horse back the way they had come.

The men were already mounted, and in less time than it took for an arrow to fall, the column was on the move. Rhun edged alongside as Livius kicked his horse to a slow canter. He judged that silence was the best form of communication, and for a few minutes neither man said a word.

Then Livius spoke: "That man Catus is a useless tit!"

"Sir?" Rhun said cautiously. It was the first the time he'd heard the praefectus criticize anything other than his field rations.

"He can't be that stupid. He's up to something."

"What happened?" Rhun ventured.

Livius waited for a half-dozen riders to thunder by and assume station ahead of the regiment. When the sound of their hooves had faded into the blackness, he replied, "First he said he was sorry to keep me waiting, but I'd woken him up—which was horse shit. There was a half-eaten meal on the table, with wine freshly poured."

"Oh … ?"

"So I delivered Agricola's words, gave him the dispatch pouch, and he tells me to wait!"

"Wait?"

"Yes, wait! Left me standing there like a sodding trooper while he read the dispatches, 'lest he needs to send a reply.' Pompous ass. And a clerk and his orderly standing there watching! Never even offered me a drink."

"But, what—" Rhun began, puzzled by the comment, but Livius cut him off.

"I know. What's the point of sending a reply? We are heading to where the Ninth is camped, so Catus will likely see Agricola before we do."

"Did he know that?"

"Even if he didn't, I told him. Yet he insisted I stand there like a slave while he read the dispatches, 'should I need to send anything further to our friend Sabinius.'"

Rhun thought that over, and could find no explanation. "That explains the 'pompous ass,' but why do you say he's stupid?"

"I wanted to ask why he was this far off the line of march, only I hadn't figured out how to do it without getting my ears torn off— when he turned around and told me! Said he couldn't understand why Agricola wanted him there."

"Agricola wanted him there? Impossible!" Rhun said, though it crossed his mind that Agricola's army would have been stretched more than was wise, even if Catus was where they expected.

"He claimed his orders were to follow standard operating procedures, *and* march an hour to the east. Stupid bugger."

"So he..."

"So he adds an extra hour's march eastward while Agricola is still edging north, and sets his fat rump down in the middle of nowhere." Livius paused and turned to Rhun as if he'd thought of a possible reason. "I hear he and the legate of the Ninth don't get on that well."

"That's like saying Nero was slightly upset with his mother."

"Yeah," Livius muttered and flicked his reins, urging his horse to a faster gait. "The man's even got it rationalized. Said Agricola must have wanted part of his army closer to the fleet."

"Sounds like he's putting excuses on parade ahead of failure," Rhun said as he too urged his horse forward.

The orange glow of flames marked the Ninth's camp, though at first there was no cause for alarm; the fires appeared to be spread evenly, as a hundred campfires would be. Then the dull roar of battle drifted faintly through the night air, barely heard above the steady pounding of hooves. Livius called a halt, the better to listen. Now they heard shouts above the clash of metal, and even as they watched, the flames spread and grew.

"Riders to Agricola's camp!" Livius snapped, turning to Rhun. "And more back to the legate Catus, may he rot. The Ninth is in trouble."

"Sir..." Rhun began, then just as quickly fell silent. A trooper thundered in from the darkness, one of the outriders who had earlier ridden ahead of the column. The man savagely reined to a halt, gesturing wildly behind him.

"Barbarian cavalry," he cried, raising his spear. White specks of foam flew sideways as he wheeled his lathered horse.

"Stand to arms!" Livius and Rhun screamed, though the order was hardly necessary. Every man held a spear ready since first catching sight of the flames.

Behind them, Cian added to the cry. "Deploy in line, you slovenly sods. Luga..."

A barbarian rider charged out of the darkness, then another, and two more. Rhun would have laughed at their shocked expressions if he hadn't been intent on fighting for his life. The first horse skewed sideways, slamming into Livius even as the praefectus took the man in the chest with a spear. Both tumbled over in a rolling mass of limbs, horseflesh, and dirt. Rhun threw a spear at the second horseman—no, it was a woman—who deflected it and spun away to vanish into the night. The next two thudded into Cian's men, who were still trying to form line.

"There's more!" Rhun yelled, fumbling for a second spear.

Hooves pounded from the darkness, but whoever was in charge must have sensed trouble. A voice rang out, and the rhythmic thumping slowed as the invisible riders reined back. A dozen or more barbarian cavalry emerged from the darkness riding at a trot, and more shadowed riders followed—how many, it was impossible to tell. The leader raised one hand, which had to be an instinctive gesture, for nobody beyond ten paces could see, and screamed for a halt.

The man's eyes quickly took in Rhun and the dim lines of cavalry massing behind him. He uttered a single word; a word almost lost in the eerie confusion. Then, with a hard pull on the reins, he yanked his horse to one side, roaring over his shoulder to those who followed. The man waved to Rhun, called out once more, and dug both heels into the animal's belly.

Rhun waved back as the beast leapt forward, horse and rider quickly vanishing into the night. Other riders trailed behind, perhaps a hundred or more, wallowing indecisively as they glimpsed the dark silhouettes of the Fourth's massed cavalry.

Cian edged his horse alongside Rhun. "Was that...?"

"Uh-huh."

"I'll be damned."

Both listened in silence as the pounding of hooves faded into silence.

"Never doubted you would be," Rhun finally muttered, and turned his eyes to the camp, where the shouting was now louder, the flames spreading. "Mother and Coira are in there, Cian. Take your whole troop, and get that prick Catus to send help. But first speak to Branaught. Tell him to take his men and find Agricola." He glanced about, puzzled. "Where's Livius?"

"Over here," Luga called. "Give me a hand." The big man was on his knees, vainly trying to free the praefectus from under the barbarian's horse. Livius himself seemed in no better shape than the dead animal.

"Is he breathing?" Rhun asked.

"Yeah, sort of, but his leg's twisted. It's badly broke."

"Shit!"

"Looks like you've got command, young nephew." Cian grinned. "Any further orders?"

"Yeah," Rhun said, "keep a rein on your tongue. Catus is a right sod."

Rhun turned his attention to the camp. The main attack appeared to have launched from the southwest, where a large, domed hill sat close by the camp. The fighting now raged inside the ramparts: a seething mass of figures, lit up by the glowing flames. A dull, dawn-like orange, where tents blazed at one end of the compound, marked the area taken by the enemy. Everything they could touch seemed to be aflame, Rhun realized, which was foolish. It lit up their side of the battlefield for all to see, while leaving the Romans hidden in the blackness of night. But the dark line that marked the difference, Rhun realized with a silent curse, was almost halfway across the inside of the camp.

"They're still massing outside the main gate." Rhun squinted hard into the darkness, trying to pick out the faces of his decurios. Between them, they'd be lucky to muster two hundred men, and there were thousands attacking the camp. "We'll circle around, place ourselves behind, then strike."

"All together?" one man asked.

That probably means he doesn't think we should be, Rhun decided. And, when he thought on it, the trooper was correct. "We'll see when we get there, but unless I say different, it'll be in three waves; hit them on an angle, then slope off to the right. The second and third will each follow on a count of fifty. Standard drill: get rid of javelins as you see fit, then slope away in the same direction, shields up, spear ready. We'll reform to south, and decide where to hit next. Any questions?" There were none, which was as it should be. Similar attacks had been practised many times and put to use more than once, though never at night.

Rhun managed to lead the small force to the west side of the camp in good order, and placed himself at the centre of the first wave. And at first, the charge went well. The front rank held steady as far as he could see on either side, and thundered down on the enemy rear, which was far more disorganized than expected.

Away from the main line of battle, the barbarians seemed to have mustered no large, organized force at all. Many tribesmen were still trudging in to join the fight, plodding on haphazardly in groups both large and small toward the Roman camp, as casually as if strolling to a fair. Some talked, others walked in silence.

The first part of the regiment's advance struck Rhun as almost ghostlike: dark figures emerged magically from the night, bent low against the flickering light from the flames. Most had their heads bent toward the ground, watching where they placed their feet. Others, startled by the pounding hooves, turned with wide eyes and weapons raised and tried to fight. Rhun never did throw his javelins, but used his remaining spear to poke and stab as his horse loped almost casually toward the fiery glow.

The enemy was thickest near the earth rampart, which loomed suddenly from the darkness as if formed from a mist. The protective stakes were all but gone, and a steady stream of tribesmen poured over the low berm. Rhun shouted an order and sensed rather than saw the entire line of horses break into a gallop. Each man hurled a javelin in a final, tearing rush, seizing another as the line broke to the right. Rhun would have done the same with his spear, but a barbarian off to his right swung around, gamely trying to block his path. The man whirled an axe above his head and stumbled forward.

Rhun lowered the spear and thrust out as far as he could. The point took the tribesman in the throat, and the axe glanced harmlessly off the shaft; but the head jammed and snapped as he rode past, the barbarian tumbling to the ground. Rhun checked the reins and drew his sword, eyes searching for the trooper who should have turned ahead of him. The man was nowhere to be seen, but the dark shape of another rider loomed farther off to the right. That was more or less where his men should be, he reckoned, so he broke away and followed.

He came upon a score of the Fourth's troopers, regrouped around a small rise off to the south. Only two things were clear: he was a good way from the camp, and most of his men seemed to have vanished. He held those men who were left there for perhaps ten minutes, as other figures flitted by in the darkness. One by one, a dozen more troopers joined the tiny band, which in total, Rhun realized in dismay, was a fraction of the number he'd started with. It was, in fact, a mere tenth of the original force. A chill ran down his spine.

"I don't think anymore are coming, sir."

Rhun turned to find one of the troopers staring at him; he had no idea of the man's name. "Are there any decurios here?" he called out.

Only silence greeted the question, and Rhun groaned. His blood ran cold as his mind tumbled over the brief action. One moment the regiment's optio, the next its praefectus, and now he was effectively back to decurio. He'd lost his first major command. Not killed in battle, for surely nigh on two hundred men could not have been slaughtered; they had to be lost. He just didn't know where, in the dark pits of Hades, they were! Gaius Sabinius was going to rip his head off—if Gaius Sabinius was alive. And if he was dead, that would mean...

Rhun's heart pounded. If the legate was dead, then his mother and sister were too, and he wasn't prepared to think about that. Feeling sick inside, he began issuing orders, each one sounding hollow. "We'll ride back the way we came. See if we can meet up with anyone. If not, we'll go to the far side of the camp and find out if they need help. There seems to be less going on over there..."

"Hail the wall!" Rhun called, nervously eyeing the darkness on either side of the earthen berm as the small band of cavalry neared the camp's east rampart.

There had been fighting here, for a barbarian lay sprawled on the grass, a spear dragging from his back. Not far ahead a shadow rose eerily from the ground, staggered to his feet, stumbled a few steps, and fell down again. The trooper on Rhun's left casually speared the exhausted figure as it tried to crawl away.

"I said, hail the wall."

"Hail. Who goes?"

Rhun peered at the outline of the rampart, dark against a spread of flames that in some magical manner seemed both distant and close enough to touch. The silent black void that lay in between seemed at odds with the clamour of shouting voices and the steady clang of weapons. "Fourth Gallorum," he yelled, feeling foolish with barely a single troop behind him.

"Advance, be recognized. And do it slowly."

Rhun held his horse to a walk and guided it to the edge of the ditch, which was sprinkled with dead tribesmen. A sparse rank of auxiliary foot stood to arms on top of the low rampart, half-hidden behind a palisade of wooden stakes. Many were wounded—far more than might be expected from the number of warriors in the ditch. A centurio jostled his way through, nursing a right arm that was bound in a cloth that glistened even in the dark.

"Things seem in hand at this end," Rhun ventured cautiously.

"It's a bloodbath," the centurio said, gesturing over his shoulder to the far end of the camp. A great roar echoed through the darkness, and he whirled about, staring edgily toward the flames. When it appeared nothing more was going to happen, the man turned back. "There's thousands of them. Thousands. Did you bring reinforcements?"

"We've sent for them," Rhun hedged, his eyes trying to focus on the fighting. The far wall, he knew, was almost a quarter-mile away, but the battle line was much, much closer. The flanking walls of the camp still seemed to hold their integrity, which meant the fighting was on only one front, ragged though that front may be. He wondered if it had overtaken the command tent, and if so, what was happening to those who had been...

"So have we, I imagine," the centurio said dryly.

"Yes, but we know ours will get through," Rhun replied, feeling suddenly irritated. "You might pass that on."

The centurio stared at the small cluster of riders gathered behind Rhun. "I thought you said you were the Fourth Gallorum?"

"That's right. This is all I've got left," Rhun said, knowing the words would carry a message of death that was not there—or at least, he hoped it was not there. It was simply too embarrassing to admit the truth: where, in the blackest corner of this barbarian wasteland, *had* his men got to?

"Too bad," the centurio murmured, then shrugged. "So what are you going to do?"

That was a question Rhun was asking himself, but there was one other ahead of it. "Have you any idea if the legate is still alive? He had two women with him. Did you see if—"

"The women were safe, last time I saw them," the centurio interrupted, and gestured with the damaged arm. "The primus sent me back here with the walking wounded, so some of those not hurt could go back and fight. Both women were ordered to return with me, but as soon as old Titus was out of sight, the pair buggered off." A grim smile crossed his face. "He was pretty badly hurt himself. If he's still alive, he's gonna use my prick for a wick if anything happens to those women."

"Shit," Rhun muttered, his mind racing. That sounded typical of the two, especially Coira; yet what could he do for them? They likely couldn't even be found …

"You want inside?" the centurio asked, and nodded to the stake barrier. "We can make a gap."

"No," Rhun said, still hoping to find the rest of his command. As he wavered, a low chatter of voices drifted from the darkness behind him. It could be another swarm of warriors forming for an attack, or some of his own people looking for him. He turned his horse away from the rampart, the others doing the same without being told. "We can do more good out here."

"I suppose you won't be trapped inside, either," the centurio called back.

"Up yours, too," Rhun muttered under his breath and, deciding the foot soldiers were far better off behind the safety of their barrier, added, "Typical effing infantry." Rhun kneed his horse to a slow canter, and the night soon filled with the jangle of harness and the thud of hooves.

The chatter of voices proved to be tribesmen. They might have been a small raiding party or the vanguard of an army; it was impossible to judge. Not that it mattered. With only a few dozen men, Rhun decided it was more prudent to veer off into the darkness, shields facing the enemy. "Wheel to the right," he yelled as a grim wall of figures loomed out of the darkness, with the gods knew how many behind.

Rhun slammed his heels into his horse's belly and it leapt to a gallop, but the man to his right was slow to react, and their animals collided. Rhun's mount lost its balance as its off shoulder slammed into the other beast's chest, and he was almost knocked from the saddle. The animal stumbled on as Rhun fell sideways, fighting to remain on its back. Tossing aside his shield, he gripped the pommel as the horse whinnied in fright and staggered on its feet. Then, bunching its hind legs, it leapt forward. When he finally gained control and reined the animal in, Rhun found himself with sword in hand, no shield, and completely alone. The horse bent its head, snorting steamy clouds from both nostrils.

Then, much to his relief, a disembodied "Sir?" echoed from the darkness.

"Over here!" he yelled, and a moment later a single rider appeared. It was a trooper Rhun vaguely remembered as Edred, though he couldn't recall the squadron to which the man belonged. Edred seemed equally relieved to see him, and more so when he called him by name.

"Did you see the others?" Rhun asked.

"No, sir."

"Shit!"

Rhun spent what was left of the night trying to find his regiment while avoiding hordes of roving Britons, all of them seemingly as lost as him. He heard the crash of arms when the first of Agricola's army hit the camp in force, just after the first traces of dawn showed above the eastern hills. Several cohorts of Catus's infantry arrived a few hours later, but by then the fighting was as good as over. And for Rhun, it was time to find out what, exactly, had happened to his men.

When dawn finally came in all its sunlit glory, Rhun had gathered together less than a hundred troopers of the Fourth Augusta Gallorum Regiment. With no other choice, and feeling as conspicuous as a fox with a mouth full of chicken feathers, he quietly led them back through one of the side entrances.

Chapter XXII

Caledonii Territory, A.D. 83

A trickle of the wounded and the faint-hearted started long before dawn, their plodding feet and loud grunts of pain rousing Marcus from a fitful sleep. The night before, he and Jessa had finally settled around midnight in a roofless hovel in an abandoned cluster of huts made of flaking wattle and torn, weathered thatch. He pushed against the dilapidated door and peered outside at the shadowy figures stumbling up through the valley and farther into the hills. Some were so badly hurt, they kept their footing only with the help of others.

"It's a sad, bloody mess," one called as he spotted Marcus's bleary-eyed face framed in the doorway. "Everyone's running."

"Aye, and the Romans won't be far behind," another man cried.

Marcus said nothing, and peered farther down the track. After the initial spate, there seemed to be no more following. He remembered his father's comment that the first to flee the battlefield always spoke that way, for the words justified their flight. At that point, it meant nothing. Even so, he retreated inside and began stuffing their meagre belongings into the frayed sack that had served him the past few years. Jessa stirred, but he hummed softly, and she soon went back to sleep.

By daybreak, the trickle had increased to a small but steady stream. Tribesmen of every ilk flitted past, most unhurt, but with faces marked by fear, frustration, and defeat. The two men left by Cethen to guard him stared anxiously down the valley, as they saw more and more wounded mixed in with those who fled. And when the rabble of camp followers outside the hut began to pick up and leave, the pair became downright agitated.

Marcus set the sack down by the doorway with a sense of finality. It seemed obvious the barbarians had not succeeded—or perhaps even better, they had been badly mauled. Though only hundreds were passing through the cluster of huts, thousands were no doubt fleeing all around. Fleeing to the safety of the forests, and the haven of the hills; fleeing anywhere, as long as it was away from the plain that remained hidden somewhere below.

Which was where the Roman army, his father's army, was still encamped—likely within walking distance. Marcus found himself trembling. After so many years, did he possess even the will to try to break free, let alone the courage? Yet whether he tried or not, there would never be a better chance.

As the surge of fleeing barbarians began to subside, his numb mind realized it was important that, at the very least, he stay where he was for as long as he could. But suggesting as much to the two stubborn churls over by the ashes of the fire would push them to do the opposite.

"We'd better get moving," Marcus heard himself say, a cautious slyness in the words. "There's no point waiting for orders."

Both men glanced at him, their faces showing doubt. One muttered, "He said to keep you here until he got back."

"He might not be coming back, Corun," the second said, glancing nervously toward another half-dozen barbarians limping past the hut.

"What's happening down there?" Corun called out.

"It's slaughter. Plain slaughter. First we had 'em, then we didn't."

"They got help." A small, pathetic barbarian with the stump of an arm wrapped in a glistening, bloody cloth shouted by way of explanation. He didn't pause or slow his pace, but simply added, "Bastids!"

"I dunno, Eb," the man called Corun mumbled, time obviously wearing on his courage.

"We should go," Marcus urged, his mind willing them not to.

"I dunno either," Eb replied and stood wavering, which was exactly what Marcus wanted him to do.

And the pair still wavered a quarter-hour later, when the ragged flow of barbarians had dried up, and nothing was left but the cluster of empty huts and an uneasy silence. Then shouts echoed faintly from farther down the valley—shouts that held a sharp, angry edge that spoke of men not on the run.

"Bugger it," Eb muttered. "Let's get out of here. On your feet, Roman."

Marcus picked up the pack, then just as quickly set it down again. He pointed to the hut and said, "My daughter."

He stumbled back inside to where he'd left Jessa on the ruin of a wood-bough cot, with instructions not to move. She was chewing contentedly on a rare treat of a licorice root, but her expression was reproachful. "Da?"

"Shush," Marcus whispered, whisking her into his arms.

He stumbled to the back of the hut. Much of the crude mud plaster had crumbled off the wattle wall, and the thin lattice of branches had, in places, rotted and parted, leaving jagged holes. Marcus had earlier torn away at the largest, when the stream of fleeing barbarians was at its height. He squeezed through the newly widened gap, the sharp twigs tearing at his clothes and his skin. Once on the other side, he quickly pulled Jessa after him, one finger on his lips to keep her silent. Then, after once more scooping her into his arms, he loped toward the forest, using the hut as a screen against Eb and Corun.

He'd covered only half the distance to the woods when the angry shouts started. Risking a glance over one shoulder, Marcus saw Eb's head poking through the side of the hut. It promptly disappeared amidst a chorus of curses. Desperate, Marcus tried to run faster, the child jouncing in his arms. Her face, more anxious even than his own, peered over his shoulder at the two men running behind. A sick feeling of hopelessness filled his belly as the shouting grew, and their pounding feet grew closer.

"Da...the mens are coming," Jessa cried, her voice full of tears. Her chubby fingers dug into Marcus's neck, and he could have wept for her anguish. They would gain the forest, he realized, but it would be of no use; the two guards were so close they'd catch him before he was fifty paces inside.

Then, to make matters worse, the tall figure of yet another

barbarian broke from the trees and blocked his path.

"Shit!" Marcus sobbed, and his heart almost stopped as the figure slowly raised a bow, the arrow pointing straight at him. He whirled, instinctively placing his body between Jessa and the dart, stumbling backward as he lost his footing. Yet even as he fell, the bearded features of the barbarian registered in his mind, and hope surged in his chest. It was Urs.

"Bugger off!"

The deep voice rang loud from somewhere above, and Marcus craned his neck backward to see. Urs moved forward until he towered over them both, the bow pointing menacingly toward the abandoned hut. Marcus's eyes followed it toward Eb and Corun, who stood with their weapons drawn, hardly twenty yards away.

"Are you deaf?" Urs growled. "I said bugger off!"

"He's ours," Eb growled back.

"Then step forward and claim him. There's two of you."

"And ... ?"

"And one of you dies. Quick. The other, he maybe has a chance," Urs muttered, and his beard split with a grin. "As much chance as a tick on a toad's tongue."

"We gotta have him," Corun whined, a look of terror on his face as he turned to Eb. "If we lose him, the Carveti woman will flay us alive."

"So come and get him," Urs taunted, then, to encourage them not to, added, "Who knows, maybe the bitch is dead, and you'll die for nothing."

Eb threw up his hands. "Sod it!"

Urs kept the bow nocked until the pair disappeared beyond the ruined hut. Marcus staggered to his feet, Jessa clinging tightly to his chest, and watched as the two disappeared from sight. The trail leading down to the valley was now empty, but the sharp voices, once a distant echo, were drawing near.

"Good to see you," Marcus said, turning to his former slave.

"Yeah, and you're welcome, too," Urs muttered sarcastically, then pointed to a fir tree that stood taller than any other, close on the edge of the forest. "On the far side of that fir there's an empty burrow. If your father's still alive, you can place the proper proof of my freedom inside.

It's owed me, and you know it."

"But—"

"And if he has any loose coin, it won't hurt either. Place both in a pouch, and bury it in the mouth of the burrow. Leave a stone on top. I'll be watching for it."

"He might not be alive."

"You're his son. Get one made up. This time a proper one."

"What about the one that I—"

"The useless thing was stolen," Urs muttered, then shrugged, and relented long enough to look chastened. "Or I lost it. I don't know. I think one of the women may have taken it, but I can't truly say. Anyway," again he shrugged, "it wasn't a proper one. I need a proper one."

"Why don't you come with me?" Marcus asked, one eye watching the trail as the voices drew closer. "Perhaps my father will reward you."

"And perhaps I'll get killed first," Urs replied, edging toward the cover of the trees. His glance fell on Jessa, who stared solemnly back, then her grubby face broke into a smile, and he smiled back. "And take good care of the bairn. She's special."

"But…" Marcus was suddenly confused, and again looked down the empty trail.

"Take the bairn inside the hut, quick, and hide before they get here," Urs urged, his voice edged with impatience. "Set her out of sight, then call out in your own tongue from where they can't see you. Yell out loud who you are. Give them time to realize who it is before you come out, or they'll kill you first."

"But—"

Urs raised a hand, his eyes taking in Marcus's dirty, baggy tunic, his grubby pants, the patched boots and the knife stuck in his belt that had cut nothing other than raw meat, bread, and roots. "I'd strip down, too, if I were you. Quick-like. Get rid of all that rubbish that makes you look like one of us, and give them a faceful of your skinny bones. Show yourself as the prisoner you are."

"But…" Marcus shook his head and tried to make sense of it all; the slave's words penetrated the fog in his mind slowly, and he struggled to digest them.

"Do it now, lad," Urs murmured, and gestured down the trail with his free hand. "You've not much time."

Marcus turned to look, but as yet there was nothing to be seen, though the voices sounded as if they were just beyond the first cover of trees. When he glanced back, the slave had disappeared into the forest.

"Da …" Jessa murmured uncertainly, her voice trembling.

"Yeah, yeah rabbit," Marcus muttered. Taking a deep breath, he sprinted toward the empty hut.

A column of cavalry passed through the cluster of huts without stopping, the pounding of hooves quickly drawing near, then thundering on without pause. Marcus, peering from the dark recesses of the hut, watched nervously and did nothing. An odd silence followed their passing and seemed to last forever. Then the rhythmic plod of boots on hard-packed dirt drifted up from the valley like a dull roll of thunder. Jessa looked at her father in alarm, and her lower lip began to quiver.

"Don't worry, rabbit," Marcus urged softly, and laid a dirt-grimed finger on her lips. "They're friends." Which he fervently hoped they were. The child took a deep breath and shuddered. Marcus edged closer to the door and peered down the trail.

A voice barked a single curt order that rang through the trees, and the thump of leather boots eased as the soldiers slowed their pace. Two soldiers broke from the trees, appearing as if by magic, and a moment later a centurio, moving cautiously. A loose column of auxiliary infantry followed, in four ranks. The centurio barked an order, and a dozen soldiers loped forward with swords drawn, advancing on the small cluster of huts.

Now or never, Marcus thought, and shouted as loud as he could, "Centurio. Stop. Please. I need help. Help me." The Latin words came to his lips with surprising difficulty, and Marcus realized abruptly how long it had been since he'd actually spoken to a stranger in his own language.

The lead soldiers paused and the centurio, after a moment's hesitation, called out and halted his men. Time stopped for a moment, everything frozen in silence.

"Tribune Marcus Sabinius Trebonius," Marcus yelled from inside the hovel, his voice threatening to crack. "Twentieth legion. Out of Deva."

Marcus carefully set Jessa on the floor and told her, at all costs, to be very quiet. Then he pushed the battered door to one side and stepped into the open, hands raised and wide apart. He was acutely aware of the sight he presented: naked but for a grimy cloth about his loins; bare, filthy feet; a thin, chalk-white body; a black barbarian beard, and a tangled mop of hair that would have shamed a madman. "I've been held prisoner by these—"

The centurio interrupted. "Tribune?" The man eyed him with obvious doubt.

Marcus nodded vigorously, fighting the urge to laugh hysterically as he babbled on. "Yes, a tribune. Tribune Sabinius. Marcus Sabinius. Son of Legate Gaius Sabinius Trebonius, Ninth Hispana. A prisoner in these hills for four fucking years."

The centurio's face slowly split into a grin; perhaps his mind was already conjuring visions of bonus money. The man hesitated but a moment, then stepped forward and clasped Marcus's wrist. The men behind broke ranks and quickly gathered around, slapping his back, eagerly asking questions. Marcus tried talking to them all as best he could, torn between a mindless babble and a crazed laughter that left him feeling an idiot. Then the faint creak of the leather door hinge cut through his delirium and he whirled in panic. The child!

"No!" he cried, and tried to elbow his way back to the hut.

Several soldiers had already entered, one with a drawn sword. Curse them all, and damn himself! He'd left the child on the dirt floor for her own safety, and they... With a terrible, half-strangled cry of anguish, Marcus pushed his way blindly through the press of troops. They seemed to block his path at every step. He hurled himself forward, terrified in his anger, ready to kill in his rage.

The door opened. A burly, chain-clad soldier ducked from the hut with Jessa in his arms, the child's face solemn as she stared into his unshaven face. His grimy, ugly features smiled back as he chucked her chin with his finger, but Marcus hardly noticed. He wrenched his daughter free of the man's grip and clutched her tightly to his chest, silently vowing he'd never let her go again. A torrent of tears streamed uncontrollably down his cheeks.

Chapter XXIII

The Tava Estuary, A.D. 83

Rhun rode into the camp on the heels of Agricola's auxiliary infantry, appalled at the devastation inside the battered ramparts. Yet there were, surprisingly, fewer Roman corpses strewn amongst the charred wreckage than he'd expected. Many, of course, were on the north side of the camp, closer by the entrance where the barbarians had first surged through, but huddled bodies were scattered all over the camp. Hundreds of soldiers, perhaps thousands, moved among the still forms, gathering the wounded if Roman, killing them off, if not.

Oddly enough, the fighting appeared to have been lighter closer by the gate, and it was apparent that the men at that end of the camp, taken unaware, had quickly retreated farther inside—almost certainly on the run and totally panicked, Rhun decided. His eyes took in a growing number of corpses, most Britons, as he rode onward. The hardest of the fighting seemed to have taken place well inside, more toward the centre of the camp, where the ashes of the headquarters tent lay: a black, stinking rectangle of smouldering debris, tiny flames still licking at the charred leather where the walls had fallen in on themselves. That was where the carnage had been halted, Rhun decided, for not far away the commander's quarters sat untouched. Here the bodies lay deepest on the ground; and it was here, by a good count, that those wearing Roman uniforms were fewer. It was here that the lines had finally formed and held, and the battle turned.

With a cold feeling of failure, Rhun turned those of his troopers he'd managed to find in the confusion of the night over to one of the decurios, with orders to locate where the rest of the regiment had settled. If there was a single consolation to be found, it lay in the fact that every last one of his troopers looked as hangdog as he felt. Sighing, he pointed his horse toward the command tent.

The camp crawled with soldiers from all three legions and, as Rhun drew near, he saw the area in front of the legate's quarters was no different. A glimpse of a pale, short-cropped mop of yellow hair told him his sister had survived, and a moment later he saw another fair-haired woman who could only be his mother. She stood behind a man sitting on a stool, her hands gripping his shoulders. A man knelt beside him, doing something to the fellow's arm. A half-dozen others stood watching, and one of them, Rhun saw as he reined in his horse, was Agricola himself. With a groan that bordered on self-pity Rhun slid from the saddle, deciding that since he'd tumbled into a cesspit of his own digging, the governor himself might just as well share the stink.

His mother glanced up and saw him, and her face lit with relief. Coira simply waved. Gaius, the man on the stool, didn't even turn his way. A medicus bent low over the legate's sword arm, his brow furrowed in concentration as he closed a deep gash just above the wrist. Next to him stood the slave Metellus, his eyes half closed and a tray balanced unsteadily in his hands, its surface glistening with bloodied instruments.

Agricola glanced up and gazed at Rhun for a moment, then recognition came. "Ah! The barbarian fellow's boy—" He snapped his fingers several times, trying to remember. "Cethen something or other is his name, no?" Rhun nodded. "Do you think he was with this lot?"

"Not as far as I know, sir."

Agricola shrugged. "Well, I'd guess more than a thousand of them aren't going home. You might want to look among their dead, before they're burnt."

Rhun was not overly worried. He'd seen his father just hours ago riding in the opposite direction, and it was unlikely that he'd got himself into any more trouble. It didn't seem politic to say so, especially after losing most of his own command, so he held this tongue. And as for the governor's words, the suggestion was likely as close to sympathy as he'd ever get. Governors were, after all, practical people; he supposed that was why there were governors.

When a centurio marched over and snapped to a halt, catching Agricola's attention, Rhun turned to Gaius, who stared grimly forward, a small leather strap between his teeth and his eyes unfocused. "Reporting back, sir," he said sheepishly and, unwilling to admit to anything more until the figures were in, added more or less truthfully, "the decurios are taking the roster."

Gaius nodded, then twitched as the surgeon stabbed his arm with the needle and pulled a length of thread through the lip of the wound. Metellus simply closed his eyes. Elena massaged the legate's shoulders and glanced at Rhun with a grimace, her mouth tight with sympathy.

Rhun mumbled on, deliberately vague. "We were late getting in. It took a while to find where the Second had camped, sir. The attack was well underway when we got here, so we did the best we could from the outside."

Again Gaius simply nodded, and again he twitched as the needle dug in, his chest heaving. Rhun winced and, awkward with the silence that followed, said, "Glad to see you're alive, sir. I imagine that hurts."

Gaius's eyes widened and for a moment he looked flummoxed; then he spat the leather from his mouth and growled, "Not at all, fool. I'm having a fucking orgasm."

"No he's not, dear." Elena broke into a smile, and dug her fingers harder into the flesh of Gaius's shoulders. "He's far too steady."

Agricola finished with the centurio in time to catch the exchange, and roared with laughter. Rhun flushed. The governor bent and retrieved the leather, brushed it clean, then held it in front of Gaius. The legate clamped down on it with his teeth, and shook his head in disgust.

"It takes a while to come down after a battle," Agricola observed, then asked mildly, "You did find where the Second was camped, then?"

"Yes, sir," Rhun replied. "It wasn't where we expected: between here and where you were dug in. It was off to one side, angled down toward the Tava where the fleet's anchored. About as far from the Ninth as you were. We waited for quite a—"

Rhun was interrupted by yet another explosive spitting of leather, followed by Gaius's angry bark. "So where was the stoat, when I needed him?"

"You were not aware the Ninth was being attacked at that time, I suppose?" Agricola asked casually, his voice calm, ignoring the outburst. But then, Rhun reflected, the governor was not being stabbed by a needle. Even so...

"No, sir."

"And when did you become aware?"

"When we returned here, sometime around midnight, sir," Rhun replied, feeling a cold sweat on his back as the questioning drew near to the time when he'd lost contact with most of a cavalry regiment. "We could see the attack had started, and—"

"What did you do? Your first orders, I mean?"

"Oh." Rhun wet his lips, remembering the initial dispatch of Cian and Branaught. He'd forgotten all about them! This was going from bad to worse. "I sent two troops to get help, one to each camp. I sent that many because there was no telling how many enemy were—"

"No, no, that was good." Agricola thoughtfully pursed his lips, and bent down once again to retrieve the short piece of leather. He absently held it out for Gaius to bite, and said, "The one got through to us with no problem. We'd been alerted already, mind you, but it served as useful confirmation. And the other troop?"

With a belated plea to the gods to take care of Cian, Rhun was about to confess that he hadn't heard a thing, when he spotted Luga over the governor's shoulder. The huge man was shambling toward the command tent like a bearded bear, towing his horse by the reins. The animal's saddle held a shield, a spear, and his shorter javelins, all unused. "Er, the decurio's second-in-command is coming in now, sir," Rhun said cautiously, then added as he saw Luga stop short and motion him over, "Perhaps I'd better go and find out what he wants."

Agricola looked toward Luga, still gesturing vigorously to Rhun. The big man promptly dropped his hand and stood awkwardly in front of his horse. The governor crooked a finger, beckoning him over.

"What is it, trooper?" Agricola asked as Luga again dragged himself to a halt. The horse, a large, hammer-headed beast, promptly dropped its head and began tearing at the grass.

"I, er, I have a message for the optio, sir," he said, nodding toward Rhun.

The governor scowled. "Is it an imperial secret?"

Luga grew flustered. "N-no, sir."

"Then what is it?" Rhun hissed.

"Uh, it's, it's—well…" He turned to Rhun, anguish written on his face. "It's Cian, Rhun. They got him under arrest. For insolence. He's been flogged!"

A guttural sound accompanied the spitting of leather. "Cian? One of my men has been flogged? By who?" Gaius demanded.

"The legate Catus, sir."

"Catus!" Gaius roared. "What, in the name of evil, has that bast—" The legate caught himself and glanced guiltily at Luga, then at the governor. "Why has the legate of the Second Adiutrix arrested one of my men and had him flogged, trooper?"

Luga, nervous and stuttering, told them what he knew.

Elena calmed down as the morning wore on, relieved that her world was once more returning to normal. Life, she mused, had been so much easier when the children were small. All she had to worry about were scuffed knees, the odd fever, or a rough-and-tumble scrap with the other village youngsters. Though there *had* been the river. She smiled wanly, recalling the gut-wrenching anxiety of wondering if the little beggars had drowned when they weren't back at the lodge by dark. Even so, a full-fledged battle with two of her brood fighting for their lives—well, that did tend to gnaw hard on the nerves!

As always, it was the *not knowing*. Elena had been right there alongside Coira when the attack started, and they'd remained together for the most part, often fighting side by side to defend themselves. There had been no time to rationalize the dilemma of fighting for Rome. Besides, this time Rome's enemy was nothing more than a crazed rabble of wild, savage, half-naked hill men who, from what she had seen, had pretty well all been Caledonii anyway.

Yet when it was over, her motherly anguish hadn't eased until Rhun rode into the camp with the first light of morning, looking as if he'd lost his last friend. Her life had been more or less free of worry when he was posted to Vetera, which had been so far away it was another world. The frontier had also been in a state of relative peace; whatever danger he'd faced there, the knowledge was blunted by the old adage: only what you know is cause for woe. Her relief upon seeing him after this battle was overwhelming.

That relief had blinded her to what might be on *his* mind, and there was clearly something. When she'd thought on it, she feared that he carried word that Cian—or perhaps even his da—had been killed or hurt. Then, when the big oaf Luga showed up with his tale of Catus and the flogging, she decided her son was brooding over his uncle, and finally felt at ease.

She helped Gaius to his feet once the surgeon was finished, for Cian's arrest seemed of more concern to him than his wound. Half a jug of wine also helped, she noted, but Agricola also seemed interested in the flogging, which was a puzzle. At a time like this, why would his mind be occupied with the troubles of a single decurio, especially one whose tongue wasn't hitched to his brain?

She watched as the three men gathered around Luga, Gaius seemingly oblivious to his wound. *And why not?* she thought wryly; the man had suffered enough of them during his service with the army. His battered body was the source of much banter, especially in the bathhouse; from the jagged scar that crossed his skull to the long, puckered stitch-marks that traced the length of his spine, it was a route map of his military career. This livid gash, almost half a foot long, was just one more, one that would be no more than a pale, ragged line by year's end.

A hand fell on her shoulder from behind, and she heard Coira speak. "Turning out to be a lovely day, don't you think?"

Elena glanced up at the sky, which was partly overcast, then to the land sloping away to the east. A stiff, steady sea breeze blew inland, chilling the early morning air. "I'd hardly call it lovely."

"You're alive, and a stiff wind tells you that's a good thing. And," Coira playfully pushed her mother's shoulder, "the old she-bear's cubs are safe home again."

"Don't call me old, or you'll feel the flat of my blade." Elena dug a sharp elbow in her daughter's ribs, and grunted as it struck chain mail. Then she called out to Metellus, who'd come from the command tent with a tray bearing a jug and a half-dozen mugs, "I could make fair game of one of those."

The slave poured both women a measure of watered red wine, then carried on to where Gaius and the others were still wrapped in the heat of discussion.

"The man's brain will be floating by midday," Coira observed.

"It'll dull the pain," Elena said, then frowned as her eye caught movement across the camp.

A strange procession was nearing the legate's tent, picking its way through the night's carnage. It wasn't large, only a half-dozen soldiers trailing behind a single centurio from the look of his helmet. Alongside the centurio walked what looked to be a prisoner of sorts, though if so, he was a poor prize. The scrawny fellow looked almost starved. Sparsely clad in rough woolen pants and a thin undershirt, he had a wild tangle of black hair and an unruly beard that covered his face and fell a good way down his chest. Someone had draped an army blanket over his shoulders like a cloak. Strangest of all, the man had a small child cradled in one arm.

The decurio strode straight toward Gaius and Agricola, both now alone; the two appeared to be arguing. Rhun and Luga had edged well back, staring anywhere but at the two senior officers. The centurio slammed to attention alongside the legate, a broad, foolish grin splitting his face as if he'd suddenly turned simple. Oddly enough, the wild-looking hill man beside him wore the same expression.

Gaius finally turned and glared at them. "What do you want?"

The centurio, still simpering, simply gestured sideways. The grimy barbarian tipped his head to one side as if expecting something, and deftly hefted the child in the crook of his arm. "Shit!" Elena felt Coira's hand tighten hard on her arm.

"Don't talk to your mother like that, dear," Elena murmured, consumed by curiosity. Then she asked absently, "Shit what?"

"That's Marcus."

"*No!*" Elena cried and squinted at the apparition. "What, in the name of Dagda, makes you say that? It looks nothing—"

"It damned-well is," Coira muttered tersely. "I'd know the little bastard anywhere."

His father had changed little, Marcus thought as he hefted Jessa on one arm and steadied himself. And from the manner of his greeting, neither had his attitude. The angry tone sounded all too familiar. And as for the man on his right, someone of rank by the look of his molded chest armour and the purple ribbon, he looked to be downright hostile. It was as if he'd walked in on two jackals growling over a bone, neither one caring for distraction.

Marcus stepped a pace forward and said, "Father."

"Huh?" Gaius stared hard, his face slowly growing slack as the single word filled his mind. For a moment it was if he didn't understand. Then his jaw dropped and his eyes, at first blank, widened, and swept up and down Marcus's gaunt, ragged figure before resting once more on his son's bearded face. Then, head craned slightly back as if the better see, he finally found his voice. "Marcus?"

Marcus could only nod, for he suddenly feared that if he said anything at all, his voice would crack and those idiot tears would come pouring down his cheeks, and his father would be pissed. Then, just as quickly, he knew it made no difference, for the fool things were coming anyway; and, to his surprise, his father's own face was also wet as he stepped forward with open arms and clasped his son firmly to his chest.

Someone took Jessa and for a moment Marcus was afraid, then in the same instant he understood she was safe, and father and son stood there, each holding onto the other. The purple-beribboned officer coughed and found something else to do, but the trooper who had taken Jessa just stepped back and waited, looking down at the odd little girl in his arms, who stared curiously back with enormous brown eyes.

"Hello," she said primly, in a lilting, accented Latin. "My name is Jessa." And when he said nothing she asked, "What's yours?"

"Er, Rhun."

"Are you my grandfather?"

"Er, no," Rhun mumbled, then nodded to where Marcus and Gaius still clung to each other, though they now stood at arm's length, gazing at one another. "That's your grandfather."

"Oh."

Marcus glanced sideways at the tall auxiliary trooper holding his daughter, who didn't seem concerned in the slightest. Even so, he felt the need to have her near, and the trooper seemed to sense it, for he moved forward and handed Jessa back to her da.

"She's quite the young lady, Marcus," Rhun murmured as he passed her over. "Lovely eyes. She seems quite bright."

"Yeah, thanks," Marcus said, then paused as he realized the trooper had called him by name. It suddenly struck him who the man was, and he said the first thing that came to mind. "I saw your father last evening. In the hills. There was ... " He hesitated, aware of the carnage both inside and outside the camp. "He was well."

"And probably remains so. He's a survivor," Rhun said, and gestured toward where the fighting had been thickest. "I saw no sign of him."

"That's good," Marcus said, unsure what else to say.

"What's her name, son?"

Marcus turned to find Gaius carefully eyeing Jessa, who was in turn staring carefully back over his shoulder. He told him and his father nodded, eyeing her critically.

"How old is she?"

Marcus puzzled over the question, for in truth he didn't exactly know. "I suppose she'll be four this year. Sometime soon, I guess."

He found himself growing irritated at the questions, and also protective. There was a stool close by, surrounded by bloody snips of bandage. He stood Jessa on the seat and deliberately removed the threadbare blanket that wrapped her small body, leaving her standing in a plain woolen dress. If anyone had a problem with his daughter's appearance, then he wanted to know. Now. He glared at his father, who continued to gaze at Jessa with scepticism scribed on his face.

"Is her mind normal?" Gaius asked.

Jessa clearly understood the words, and Marcus was angry. He was about to retort when his father's woman edged past, and he was surprised to see that she, too, was annoyed.

"Of course her mind's normal," Elena said curtly, and knelt down beside the little girl. "You just have to look at her. And she's lovely, aren't you, my pet? Why, she has Aelia's big brown eyes, and they're just as alert and lively."

"Actually, her mind's not normal," Marcus snapped, glaring at his father. "Personally, I think it's marvelous!" He switched to his daughter's tongue. "This is your grandfather, Jessa. He wonders if you can think."

She eyed Gaius solemnly for a moment, then giggled. "He's funny."

"Uh-huh. And his name is Gaius," Marcus continued, switching back to Latin. "It has five letters in it. So why don't you say it with me? *Gaius*..." He repeated the name again, slowly, along with his daughter, then in a much softer voice he said, "Now, try and spell it for your grandfather."

Jessa looked around at the curious faces, and for a moment appeared shy. Then, when she saw a nod of encouragement from her father, she slowly tried the letters: "G-i-u-s." But as she finished, she looked puzzled. "That's only four letters, Da."

Marcus smiled through his thick beard. "That's right, rabbit. It's sort of like a trick. You see, there's an 'a' in there, too. So where do you think that goes?"

Jessa sucked on her lower lip, and her large brown eyes moved upward beneath a frown as she pondered the puzzle. Then, with the tip of her tongue peeping from one corner of her mouth, she nodded to herself. "It goes after the 'G'?"

"Ha!" Marcus crowed.

"Isn't that something?" Elena cried, and glanced up at Gaius with a smirk on her face. "Could you do that before you were four?"

Gaius said nothing. Elena scooped Jessa from the stool and, with a questioning glance at Marcus to make sure he didn't mind, wandered over to where Coira stood, watching the brief but telling exchange. "Want to hold her?" she asked.

"I—er..." Coira demurred.

Elena grinned and nodded toward Marcus. "I think the *little bastard* may have changed a sma' bit, my dear."

Chapter XXIV

The Tava Estuary, A.D. 83

That day and the next were spent burning the barbarians and formally cremating their own dead. Once that was done, Agricola decided the makeshift compound held the stink of death and the taste of a near defeat. Nothing would be gained by remaining, and tempting the gods to send more. The wounded would be treated, then transported down to the Tava where the fleet was moored, a day's march to the east.

And where, ironically, Agricola's own camp could be found partway in between. The soldiers of the Twentieth made much of their timely arrival, insisting it had prevented the Ninth's destruction. On the other edge of that blade, the soldiers of the Ninth claimed the enemy had already been fought to a standstill, and were actually being driven back with heavy losses when Agricola *finally* attacked. The glory of it all was theirs, not that of the latecomers.

Titus, from his cot in the hospital tent, agreed wholeheartedly with his men; whereas the primus from the Twentieth loudly supported his own. What started as friendly banter between troops working side by side quickly turned to hard argument as to which deserved the glory. Fights broke out and more than one man was badly hurt. Agricola and Gaius stormed in before a full-scale battle started, their tempers already raw. Despite a natural bias, each was angry with both armies, and the conduct of the two primuses. Yet they had also been quarrelling, which had not gone unnoticed, and had likely helped spark matters in the first place.

Gaius insisted that Catus had deliberately abandoned the Ninth, intent on wreaking revenge. A revenge that was pure folly, he pointed out, because it was not based on fact. Agricola had rejected the idea, insisting that not even Catus would jeopardize an entire legion to get even with one man. Then Gaius had shifted his target, pointing out that the Ninth wasn't an entire legion, because a quarter of it had been robbed by Domitian for service in Germania, and the remaining cohorts were under strength. Had the Ninth been even close to full strength, he argued, as they were *supposed* to be, then *any* battle would never have hung in the balance.

Agricola, whose own force was also short on numbers, hinted that the Ninth's legate was whining over a problem that any *competent* commander could overcome. He then peevishly inferred that Catus might have *some* reason to believe Gaius had dispatched his brother, Lucius. Gaius, who well knew that such a rumour persisted among the legions, and not without a certain admiration for its perpetrator, grew angrier still.

More bitter words tumbled from both, Agricola finally launching into a tirade that reminded Gaius to whom he spoke. Gaius, seething, had been about to tell the governor where he could march the entire Ninth legion—if it fit, which he had no doubt it would—when the first fights erupted. They abandoned their disagreement, and when order was finally restored, both men went their own way as if by unspoken agreement.

Rhun woke to find the sun warm on the roof of the tent and the leather walls flapping in a pleasant breeze. He rose from his blanket, stiff but cheerful, and intent on finding where Cian had been hospitalized. It had been too dark to find anyone the previous night, let alone a whipped trooper amongst tent after tent full of groaning wounded.

He was dressing when he received an order that sent shivers down his spine. In two hours, his presence was required at Agricola's headquarters, a modular tent that could be seen about a mile away. It stood in the second of two marching camps, both freshly dug by the fleet's marines, and waiting for all three understrength legions as they marched down to the neck of the Tava estuary. The governor was taking no more chances on distancing the elements of his army.

Rhun took his time, holding his horse to a walk as he brooded over the order. When he'd finally fallen asleep last night, it had been in the naive belief that the inept loss of his regiment might pass unnoticed. He should have known better. The fact that the rest of the regiment, with the exception of a dozen troopers, had floundered into camp during the course of the night, counted no more than a fart in the forum. His first assumption of command had been a complete failure, and now it was time to pay.

He eyed the headquarters tent, a dreary modular consisting of three sections, with little hope. The guards outside wore parade regalia on their weathered uniforms, including helmet crests. That didn't bode well.

Rhun stepped inside the outer module and stood awkwardly at the entrance, wondering what to do and who to ask. A couple of tribunes and two centurios warmed the benches lining the walls; he recognized one as the primus of the Second. A small army of clerks sat behind folding tables in the centre, though they were likely going about their regular duties, for they ignored him. The silence was overpowering.

A decanus peered through the flaps that divided this unit from the second. His eyes lit up when they fell on Rhun. "You the optio that went looking for the Second?"

That settled it, Rhun decided, the sick feeling growing as he nodded.

The man's head briefly disappeared, and a moment later he returned and pulled the flap farther back. "Come this way, sir." He beckoned with one hand; as Rhun passed by, he whispered, "Helmet, sir."

Rhun quickly tucked the offending headgear under one arm, hardly aware of his surroundings as he snapped to attention and saluted. A voice told him to step forward, and as he walked the few steps across the grassy floor, his eyes finally focused. A long table stood directly ahead, flanked on either side by two more to form a horseshoe. Agricola sat at the centre between the Twentieth's senior tribune and its primus. The legate Catus sat alone at the table on the right, slumped in his seat and looking bored. Off to the left, two orderlies who appeared to be scribes sat taking notes. As Rhun once more snapped to attention, he grew vaguely aware of several figures seated farther off to the side.

"Sir!"

"At ease, son," Agricola murmured, though his expression was anything but mild. "This shouldn't take long. We're about finished, but we find there are a few questions we need to ask regarding the night the barbarians attacked the Ninth's camp."

"Sir," Rhun mumbled. Now there was no doubt, and it was so damned typical! The sun had risen bright that morning on a land forsaken by every god he knew, but it had brought with it the promise of a glorious day. There had been a bounce in his step and that certain euphoria on waking that, ever so rarely, brought with it a surge of well-being and a heart-bursting joy at just being alive. He should have known—*whenever* a day began so well, before it was over, he'd inevitably be shat upon! Rhun took a deep breath and wet his lips.

"Optio, you were with Livius when he delivered dispatches to the Legate Catus, were you not?" Agricola asked.

"Yes, sir."

"Did you accompany him?"

"No, sir. I remained outside the camp with my regiment."

"Livius took the entire regiment to deliver dispatches?" The question came from the senior tribune next to Agricola, and the governor scowled.

"Er, no, sir. It was most of the regiment, but nearly half the squadrons were detached. We'd been riding advance, and were returning to camp." Rhun turned, wondering if perhaps Livius was one of those seated off to the side of the tent. Gaius was there, along with several others, but the praefectus was not among them.

"We questioned Livius earlier," Agricola said, as if by explanation. "He's understandably unable to be here. But go on ... "

"We expected to find the Second's camp on the way back, which is why we remained together," Rhun explained, holding his tongue on the several times he'd suggested that Livius send only one troop. "But it wasn't where we expected. We just kept on going, thinking we'd find it at any moment. Then later, the praefectus didn't want to break his force up in the dark."

The next question surprised Rhun, and for the first time he began to wonder if he'd been ordered there for something other than his own indiscretion.

"What did the praefectus say concerning his discussions with Legate Catus?" Agricola asked.

Rhun paused, and decided it was best to cull his words. "He said the legate was unhappy with the dispatches being so late, and that he'd suggested that the location of the camp was odd."

"That is specifically what he said?"

"In so many words, sir."

"That's not what I asked, trooper." For the first time the governor showed irritation. "Tell me specifically what he said."

Rhun glanced toward Catus, who glared back with a look of pure malevolence. "The words were not complimentary, sir," he equivocated.

"I won't say it again, trooper," Agricola growled.

"Yes, sir!" Rhun gulped and thrust out his chest, barking his words as if on parade. "He said the man Catus was a useless tit. He suggested the legate was stupid, and up to something. He mentioned that the legate kept him waiting, saying he'd been awakened, which Livius said was horse shit because there was a meal on the table, and wine waiting to be drunk. And ... " Rhun paused. "Should I go on, sir?"

"If you don't, I'll have your balls served up to the mess."

"Sir! The praefectus then said he was ordered to wait while the dispatches were read, should a reply be needed. Which he said was pointless, because we were going on to where the Ninth was camped, and not back to your own command. Sir!" Rhun finished. Then he recalled one other comment by Livius. "Oh, and he also mentioned that the legate said he couldn't understand why you wanted him to camp where he did."

"Oh?" Agricola raised his eyebrows and, drumming his fingers on the table, glanced briefly at Catus. "Did he tell Livius that I specifically ordered him to camp miles off the track?"

"Not in so many words, sir," Rhun said, and hurried on, for that was the second time he'd used that expression, and on the first he'd not fared too well. "Livius said the legate told him his orders were to follow standing operating procedure, *and* march an hour to the east. Which the legate apparently understood to mean a further hour to the east." He paused, then, with the image of Cian in his mind, he plunged on. "Livius expressed the opinion that the legate was being a stupid bugger."

"And what did you say to that?" Agricola asked, and stared at Rhun with a bland look that revealed nothing.

"Huh?"

"You heard me."

This is insubordination, Rhun thought, but decided that if you *are* in it up to your ears, then the only choice is to try swimming. "I believe I expressed the opinion that it sounded as if the legate was putting his excuses on parade ahead of his failure."

Catus abruptly banged one fist on the table and roared, "That's enough. I will not stand for this drivel from a snivelling junior ranker. He's Sabinius's man anyway—dammit, his son-in-law! It's a pack of lies."

"It tallies with the little Livius was able to tell us," Agricola said mildly. "Much of it also agrees with what you told us. Are you saying that was a lie too?"

Catus clenched his jaw. "We'll see about this in Rome."

"What happened after that?" Agricola asked Rhun, ignoring the comment.

Rhun sighed. This was the part he'd been dreading. "We rode on toward the Ninth's camp, and when we came close we heard the sound of fighting. We halted, dispatched riders to both your camp and that of Legate Catus to give warning, then continued on." He paused as Cian's whereabouts came to mind. "Question, sir?"

"Go ahead."

"I've had word that one of my riders sent to the Second was placed under arrest and flogged. Is there any word where he is?"

Agricola drew a deep breath and exhaled in a manner that said he was rapidly losing patience. One of the clerks off to the left coughed, then spoke up. "The man is in the Second's field hospital."

"Thank you," Agricola said, adding in a heavy voice, "and the man deserved to be flogged. Decurios, no matter how strongly they feel," he turned to look directly at Catus, "do not tell legates they are *nothing but stinking, cowardly pricks.* Those *were* the words the trooper used, were they not?"

"There was more," Catus growled, missing the irony of Agricola's emphasis.

"And what were they?"

"He said I had the backbone of a sna—" Catus noticed the amused expressions on other faces in the tent. "Never mind."

Rhun stood silent, his mind still on his uncle. Poor, dumb, idiot Cian! He never could keep his big gob shut. He wondered how badly he'd been beaten. From the malice written on Catus's face, Rhun guessed he was lucky not to have been stoned to death.

Agricola turned back to Rhun. "And after that, your regiment rode to assist in the defence of the Ninth? Is that correct?"

So now it finally comes, Rhun thought, his voice subdued as he answered, "Yes, sir."

"Very well." Agricola stared down at the table as if lost in thought, then turned to those on either side of him. "Any more questions?" There appeared to be none, so he nodded to Rhun and said, "Then you're dismissed. Wait outside, though, just in case."

"Sir!" For a moment Rhun stood in front of the table in disbelief, then he quickly pulled himself together, saluted, turned on his heel, and fled into the front module, his heart pounding like a ship's drum.

He slumped down on the nearest bench and breathed a sigh of relief. A hostile horde of frenzied barbarians were nowhere near as hard on the mind! And even now, as his mind flew back over the proceedings, he still wondered: was he clear? The governor had said to wait outside. Was the negligent loss of his men, for that was what Rhun considered it to be, still an issue? Or had it passed unnoticed in the greater scheme of things compared, for example, to the infighting going on inside the second module? Which, he realized as his mind relaxed, was still in progress; he could hear it through the cloth divider.

Rhun looked guiltily about the tent and started to rise, but nobody seemed to have noticed him, or the advantage of where he sat. If they had, they did not seem to care. He eased back onto the bench, deciding to do what he'd been ordered: wait. And in the meantime, the talk drifting through from the far side of the divider was interesting.

Others had been speaking before Rhun, and their words appeared to fit his own like a sword in a scabbard—though there were a few more tassels dangling. One of the junior tribunes had told of a loud disagreement between Catus and the Second's primus as to where the camp should have been located. And there was a further detail that Livius hadn't told Rhun, probably because his piss was on the boil: the legate had suggested the praefectus remain in camp with his regiment and return home at first light!

Catus himself said little as Agricola summed up, and when he did, it was not to deny anything said. He angrily justified every action while threatening repercussions from Rome. Which, Rhun decided, only made Agricola's blood boil; which was foolish, considering the governor's status here in Britannia.

It eventually became clear that Catus faced two issues: negligence or traitorous intent in the deployment of his command, and cowardice in the face of the enemy. In the end, Agricola rendered an opinion that stepped between both, without dropping either.

"Legate Catus," Rhun heard him say solemnly, "you overruled your primus pilus in the placing of your forces, and you did so in harsh terms. Further, you did not conform to clear, standard orders that had been issued for your deployment. I have difficulty believing these errors were honest ones. A tribune fresh to service would not have done as much. I cannot, however, prove that your decision, drastic as it proved to be, was done with intent. As a minimum, however, I have concluded it was negligent."

"That's pig shit. The orders clearly said an hour's—"

Agricola's voice cut into Catus's roar. "You will be quiet, or I will have you gagged!"

Rhun imagined the legate's swarthy face turning livid. A pause followed the outburst, then the governor continued, his voice slow and deliberate.

"Several appeals were sent, one borne by the trooper whose impatience overcame discretion. That man is a veteran with a distinguished record. While that does not excuse his behaviour, it clearly shows his frustration. As to other messengers, they were unable to locate your camp, for it was not where it was supposed to be!" Agricola stopped for a moment, as if catching his temper. "Which clearly shows negligence in its placement.

"Your delinquency in sending help, however, is the most serious issue. It arrived long after the Twentieth relieved the Ninth, when it was no longer needed." Agricola's eyes shifted briefly to Gaius, but without expression. "I find this not dissimilar to Seutonius's situation when he requested support from the Second Augusta. It was stationed at Gleva, I believe, when the Iceni woman went on her rampage. What was the name of the fellow in command?"

Rhun heard the snapping of fingers, and another voice muttered, "Postumus."

There was a murmur of agreement, and Agricola continued. "Postumus! Yes, Poenius Postumus. The name's appropriate in a way. And I suppose there's a further irony: his command was also numbered 'The Second.' Not that it matters. The man Postumus did not respond to Seutonius's appeal, did he?" There was silence, which Agricola must have taken as agreement, for he pressed on. "As I recall, the man did, however, have the decency to fall on his sword."

A pause once more followed the words, and Rhun pictured the governor peering owlishly at Catus, eyebrows raised in question. When there was no response, Agricola put it into words. "I don't suppose you're contemplating falling on your sword, are you, Catus?"

The weight of what was happening seemed to have settled on the legate's mind, for his reply lacked its earlier aggression. "That's ridiculous. Of course not. I was doing my duty."

"Yes, I thought as much." Rhun heard Agricola sigh. "Then it's my decision you be relieved of command. You'll be sent home at once. The details of what has transpired will be referred to Domitian, along with a recommendation that you be charged with dereliction of duty. I'm also suggesting the facts be reviewed to determine if cowardice was a factor. Do you have anything to say?"

Rhun didn't wait for the reply. The proceedings were over, and it didn't look as if he was going to be recalled. He rose from the bench, ready to go looking for his uncle. Then Agricola's words rang in his mind: *wait outside, just in case.* It probably *was* all over, even his getting lost in the dark, but he couldn't be sure. The last thing he wanted to do was bugger things up by buggering off. It was typical army, Rhun decided as he again sat down.

Cian lay face down on a cot, his long brown hair dark with sweat. His back, bare to the buttocks, was a bloodied purple where the thin willow rods had sliced through the skin, which was just about everywhere. A glistening coat of grease—Rhun thought it was likely goose fat laced with henbane—coated the entire mess, and rose and fell in pace with his uncle's quick, gasping breaths.

Rhun stood at the head of the cot, his eyes quickly taking in the rest of the huge tent. It was one of at least a dozen, all filled with rows of similar cots, all in turn full of wounded; and where there were not enough cots, men lay on blankets, bandaged and in pain. The fetid odour of dried blood, sweat-slick bodies, pungent medicine, and human waste blended with a hospital stink that was far too familiar. At least the slime on Cian's back seemed to keep the flies off, Rhun thought as he slapped a good half-dozen of the damned things away from his face.

He squatted by Cian's head, wondering if it was worth the hurt of waking him. Then a distinct whiff of mandrake twitched his nose, and he wondered if his uncle could be awakened. He stared down at the pained, lined features, and felt a surge of anger at the legate's pettiness; yet it was also aimed at his uncle's stupidity. Cian had served Rome long enough to know when to rein in his tongue, yet he had let it run loose. Shaking his head at the foolishness of it all, Rhun started to rise, but Cian, without opening his eyes, mumbled, "Hey, Rhun."

"That should be *hey, optio,* arsehole," Rhun murmured, knowing full well what the reply would be.

"Sorry, *sir.*" Cian smiled weakly. "Hey, *optio arsehole.* That better?"

"Just as long as you show the proper respect. How you feeling?"

A single eye opened and stared balefully at Rhun. Though there was no other movement, the gesture was eloquent. "Is that a serious question?"

Rhun smiled. "The last victim I asked, just the other day, said he was having an orgasm. Are you getting close?"

"I can't even spell it," Cian murmured, and groaned his disgust. "And the boy asks *How am I feeling*! Shiii-it!"

"Commanding officers are supposed to ask things like that," Rhun continued, keeping the talk light. "We don't really give a pig turd about the answer, but it lets the troopies know we care. Is there anything I can get you?"

"Yeah, a mug of honeyed hemlock," Cian muttered.

"I don't think there's need for that, yet," Rhun said.

"It's not for me, it's for that prick Catus."

"Then I bear glad tidings." Rhun grinned, relishing the message. "The commander of the Second Adiutrix is no longer the commander. The man's been charged with dereliction of duty and possible cowardice. He's off to Rome for trial. At best, he'll be thrown out in disgrace. And while Agricola thinks you deserve every last stroke of the willow for insolence, your thrashing didn't do a thing for the man's cause."

"Glad to be of help," Cian mumbled.

"And hear this—Agricola suggested that the honourable thing would be for him to fall on his sword."

"If they need someone to hold it, tell them I'm willing," Cian whispered, his eyes closing.

The silence stretched, and Rhun sat back on his heels, watching his uncle fade in and out of sleep. Despite the savage beating, he seemed well enough; at least, well enough when all was considered. Still, he sat waiting awhile, should Cian speak. Finally, when it looked as if there was no further point, he rose and prepared to leave.

His uncle seemed to sense the movement, and stirred. "I suppose you'll be off to Rome, then?"

"What makes you say that?" Rhun asked.

"If there's a trial, you'll be needed as a witness."

He probably would, Rhun realized and, strangely enough, he found the idea had appeal. Lots of appeal; in fact, he was surprised at how much. Not the opportunity to act as a witness, but of once more seeing the wonders of the enormous city. Aelia would come too, of course, and their son, though the child was too young to understand. "I suppose..."

"Don't dwell on it," Cian muttered, once more drifting toward a hazy sleep. "It might not happen. I like the idea of the man falling on his sword."

"Me too," Rhun said, and placed a hand on Cian's head to reassure him; it was about the only part he could touch without prodding an open sore.

His uncle nodded a sleepy acknowledgement. "Thanks..."

"I think Agricola will be staying here for awhile until the legions recover, so I'll be back," Rhun murmured and turned to leave, but Cian spoke again; this time his voice was oddly strong and clear.

"I should have thought of that."

Rhun stopped in mid-stride. "Of what?"

Cian lay with both eyes open, his tired features surprisingly alert. "Just remembered something. If you see Luga, tell him I need to see him before he and—" He broke off with a frown and tried to shake his head as if to clear it, which wasn't wise. "No, no! Just tell him I have to see him. He needs to..." Again Cian paused, as if his mind were elsewhere. "Look, just—just send him, will you?" he finally said.

"Sure. I'll try to find him."

"No, no," Cian insisted, "I have to see the big oaf now. Today."

"Sure." Rhun shrugged. "I'll get him."

The camp settled into a routine, one of the first signs being an orders group called by Gaius for the next morning. Rhun was roused much earlier than expected, though, summoned to the Ninth's headquarters tent by a bleary-eyed runner who'd likely been transferred there due to his wounded arm, wrapped in a fresh bandage.

Dawn was still less than a grey hint on the horizon as Rhun trudged across the huge camp, stifling a yawn. It was far too early to be about, even for the troops. The night guard was still on duty, two soldiers who creaked rather than snapped to attention; and only a single clerk sat inside.

"In the back, sir," the man called out, briefly lifting his eyes from a litter of documents piled on the field table. "He's not long in from his own quarters."

"Yeah," Rhun muttered, and strode through to the next module, his mind once more churning over possibilities. It inevitably came to rest on his own carelessness the night the barbarians struck the Ninth.

Surely the legate wasn't now dredging up that!

Only two people were inside, Gaius and the slave Metellus. A glowing brazier warmed the tent, and the slave was removing a steaming kettle from over the coals. The legate sat in a folding chair, holding a plate of fried oysters. A low table stood before him bearing two empty mugs, a platter of food, and two bowls of what appeared to be hot puls. A second chair sat on the other side.

"Mmmm." Gaius popped one of the garum-dipped mollusks in his mouth, and nodded to the empty seat. "Sit down, Rhun."

Puzzled, Rhun obeyed. The slave leaned over his shoulder and poured a thin, steaming brown liquid into the two mugs. A familiar aroma filled his nostrils, and Rhun smiled. It was a concoction his mother used to make, herb-laced barley water sweetened with honey. It had been a long while…

"Grab something to eat." Gaius set the oysters on the table and picked up one of the mugs.

"Thank you," Rhun said, but decided the drink would do for the time being. As he picked it up, though, he noticed a familiar-looking slab of honey cake, and took a slice. "Did Mother bake this?" he asked, frowning as he took a bite.

"You joke," Gaius said.

Metellus smiled. "Elena stays out of the kitchen, but she does keep the commander's staff on a tight rein. She often 'suggests' what should be served."

"I see," Rhun mumbled through the crumbs, his mind returning to why he was there. The answer was not long in coming.

"Livius's leg was amputated, did you know that?" Gaius asked suddenly.

"I saw him in the hospital tent yesterday, but we didn't speak. He was off with the faerie. I'd guess the medicus helped get him there, from the stink of his breath. I heard they sawed it off on the march here."

"Had to," Gaius murmured over the top of the mug, his lip testing the hot liquid inside. "They were trying to save it, but they hadn't gone five miles when it started bleeding like a fountain. They stopped the wagon and took it off in the back."

Rhun asked the natural question: "Will he live?"

"Toss the dice and pick a number. The surgeon says the odds are even."

"I see..." Rhun fell silent.

"I talked it over with Agricola, and he agrees you should stay in nominal command until a replacement is found," Gaius continued. "Any problem with that?"

Rhun felt his eyes widen in surprise, and for a moment he was lost for words. "Er, no, I..."

"Another five or ten years, and you might have been considered yourself. Especially after a hard action." Gaius seemed to find the drink had cooled enough, and took a long sip, his eyes fixed on Rhun. "You lack the experience for it now, and you're far too young."

"I...I totally agree, sir." Rhun almost choked as it dawned on him that Gaius was thinking he might want the command permanently; that he might actually have been expecting it. When, in fact, he was more concerned about losing the lesser rank he already had. He could have laughed, both in relief and at the absurdity. "Honestly, I hadn't thought there would even be a question."

"Ah, that's good, then." Gaius sat back, his gaze still on Rhun, where it remained to the point of discomfort. His next words seemed to come from nowhere. "So, what do you think about our man Catus?"

At first the bluntness of the question left Rhun feeling awkward; then he supposed that, since Catus was in disgrace anyway, the legate reasoned the man was a fair target. "I...er, I think the governor made the correct decision. There's a concern in the mess, though, that Catus's influence in Rome will pull him free of his own poisonous barb. I understand his family is quite influential."

"Very," Gaius murmured thoughtfully, his gaze unmoving. "What did you think of Agricola's hint about falling on his sword?"

Rhun allowed himself a smile. "It would be convenient, I suppose, but Catus is not the type to do it. He's more likely to dress the lie as truth, and eventually convince himself it is. I should think he'll deny the matter to the bitter end. I imagine we'll then see who has the more powerful friends: Catus or the governor. I don't think Agricola should lose sight of the fact that he will be here, and Catus will be there."

"Actually, he won't." Gaius spoke with a sardonic snort of derision, and finally lowered his gaze as if satisfied. "He appears to have taken the governor's advice, sometime last night."

For a moment the words did not penetrate, then Rhun almost dropped the steaming mug. "Catus? He bellied his blade?"

"Uh-huh," Gaius said. "Though it was peculiar, the way he chose to do it."

"Peculiar?"

"Yes. Quite odd. The sword he used wasn't his own. It was a standard issue weapon. Every soldier has one, of course. You'd have thought he'd do it with his own blade, wouldn't you?"

The question seemed drawn out, and Rhun found the legate's eyes once more staring as if awaiting an answer. There was none, of course, though the back of his neck suddenly prickled with heat. Cian! Though it would have to have been Luga, because last night his uncle couldn't have thrust his sword through a slice of cheese. All he could do was raise his head, and ... shit! That explained Cian's insistence on seeing Luga—which he'd done shortly after Rhun had mentioned Agricola suggesting Catus fall on his sword, which ...

Rhun hoped his faced showed less emotion than his heart. He cleared his throat. "I don't suppose too many people will be sorry. Who found him?"

"There's the irony." Gaius seemed to have difficulty keeping a stern face. "Before he went to bed, Catus gave his own weapon to his orderly for honing. The man slipped in about an hour or two ago to place it back in the scabbard, and found him alongside his bed. Our 'honourable' legate had his knees in the dirt, and a sword's hilt growing from his belly."

"Shit," Rhun whispered, then stared innocently into the legate's eyes. "You just never know, do you?"

"There was another odd thing." Gaius bit down on his lip and continued to stare. "Even though Catus's legs remained as if kneeling, the body seems to have fallen on its back."

"I doubt that's unusual." Rhun shrugged after pondering the point, his mind spinning. "I imagine there's a good deal of pain. It would be natural to pull away from it."

"I suppose," Gaius murmured. "Though what Agricola will make of him using a common sword, I have no idea."

"It sounds to me as if Catus finally made a noble gesture after all: he died by the weapon that built the empire," Rhun said, his expression unreadable.

"I'll suggest that to the governor," Gaius said dryly. "In the meantime, if you hear anything different, let me know."

"Of course, sir."

Chapter XXV

Caledonii Territory, A.D. 83

"To tell the truth, I've about had enough too." Borba belched and rubbed a hand across his eyes in a vain attempt to wipe them free of smoke. "More than enough. If the real truth be known, I'd had it up to my lugs three years ago. It just took one more kick in the teeth to make up my mind."

A low growl of agreement rumbled around the campfire with only one dissenting voice, and it served only to emphasize the words. "Make that four years—no, four and a half."

"Why is it," Borba continued, angrily batting at the air, "no matter what side of the fire I sit on, the smoke always follows?"

A further growl of agreement, much louder than the first; but Cethen had to admit that the twin's first words summed up the feelings of them all. All of the warriors huddled around the fire had been together since the start; they were a tight core of battle-hardened survivors who had started out with Morallta and Cethen more than a decade back, when Venutius had still been king. That was a lifetime ago. And now, of the originals who had ridden north, there had to be ... how many left?

Cethen turned, his eyes scanning the circle of faces around the fire, nowhere more than two deep. Most sat cross-legged on the ground, others perched on makeshift log seats, and a few more simply stood, some with arms crossed, others lounging against the trunks of trees. His mind began to tally, his lips moving silently with the numbers:

five, ten, twelve, thirteen or fourteen, and ... He finally gave up and tried naming them. There was Borba, of course. Luath, his twin, had long since returned to Brigantia to work their farm, though it would prove more difficult now with only one hand. Ligan was still there, a full-grown man now, and much wiser than the cocky youth reluctantly recruited by Morallta.

There was also stolid Ebric, who a year ago had grown tired of following Dermat's tracks and thrown his lot in with them. And of course there were the women. There were—what?—five left, and they often seemed the most resilient. Or at least for the most part of any given month, he thought, and grinned. There sat Innsa, who'd spied on the fortress at Ebor with him and at the same time baited Borba, who now often shared her blanket at night. Which was fair enough, Cethen reasoned with a smile, for his identical twin was back at the farm with both wives, and there was a good deal of ribbing about that.

And of course little Ficra: as tough and hard as an iron blade, and equally sharp. Cethen shook his head as his gaze fell on her small, fine-featured face. In many ways the woman reminded him of Nuada, and he chuckled again. What a pair the two of them had been while it lasted! And now there was Ficra glancing his way, more than once, too, with a look that said she might ...

"Forty-two!"

"Huh?" Cethen's eyes dropped back to the glow of the fire, where the ring of faces stared back, each wearing a look of amusement.

Borba rose with a flask in hand, staring at him with a broad grin on his face. "There's forty-two of us. That's ten ... twenty ... thirty ... forty," Borba sang as he counted them off, finishing with four fingers raised on the hand he held in the air. "And Innsa and Ficra make ... "

Everyone roared the final total, including Cethen. *"Forty-two!"*

"Idiots," he muttered as the laughter died and the small clearing gradually fell silent, but for the crackle of burning wood.

He'd never been good with the numbers, but he could remember them. Forty-two was what he figured his age was, more or less, and he wondered if that was some sort of omen. The question was a puzzle in itself, because there was nobody really left of his own people to tell him if it was an omen or not. Which was just as well, he decided, because he'd had enough problems with omens when the druids had still been around. Though the lack of them, he supposed, was a sign they'd all been in this land of unfamiliar gods for far too long.

"So?"

Cethen had no idea who asked the question, but he knew its meaning and chose to avoid it for a moment. "How many aren't here, Borba?"

"Of our own cavalry?" The twin shrugged, then paused to subtract the difference in his head. "Sixty-four, nearly all our own tribesmen, with about twenty of 'em fairly green."

"So that makes about what, ninety … six?"

"A hundred and six, but you're improving," Borba said. "So what do we tell them? Are we staying or going?"

"And Morallta's riders?"

"That many, and near as much again. Almost two hundred. And, for what it's worth," Borba continued, "Galgar considers one of our people to be worth five of his against the Romans, though Morallta places it at ten. It's a significant number, Cethen, but only when you look at it that way."

"And Morallta would," he murmured, and fell quiet.

"So … ?" Ligan asked the question this time, then added another. "You going to call a vote?"

Cethen nodded, deciding to call it in a manner that offered the way of least resistance, one that best matched his own feelings. There would have to be another vote with the rest of them, he supposed, but those who sat here would really guide the fall of the arrow.

He sighed and put the question. "Is there anyone here who is *not* ready to call it off, and go back home?"

There were many sideways glances, but nobody spoke or raised a hand. Which, in a small way, was a surprise, for most had nobody or no place left in Brigantia to return to—certainly he had not. Which was ironic, for his wife and at least part of his family were nearer now than they'd ever been: inside the Roman camp!

He felt the familiar anger, but it no longer boiled his blood. It was more a hard, dragging irritation. One day there would be a reckoning, he was sure of it.

Borba interrupted his dreaming. "So what happens now?"

"I suppose we'll put it to the others. Though I doubt the result will be different," Cethen murmured thoughtfully. "There's Galgar, of course. I don't know what he's doing after the thrashing he got, but I don't imagine it'll be much more than licking his wounds. When you think on it, there's probably not much choice but to go home. I don't want to die of old age up here."

"It sounds like you're already dying of old age," a woman's voice sneered from the depths of the trees, and Cethen groaned.

The man called Rib walked out first, his shield slung casually across his back and a sword dangling safely from his belt. Morallta followed a few moments later, appearing like a ghost from the dark wall of the forest. She held a spear in one hand and the reins of two horses in the other. Ligan squeezed sideways on his log to make room, and Cethen gestured to the space that remained. Rib offered a curt nod of thanks and sat down. Morallta chose instead to butt her spear in the dirt and lean on it. Cethen, who knew her all too well, decided the woman simply preferred to stand where she could look down on them.

Rib wasted few words. His eyes wandered briefly across the sea of faces, his head bending toward any he recognized before he spoke. "Galgar has called a gathering of the tribes. He wants chieftains of all rank, with no more than a score of their people for company. He doesn't want to feed an army, nor can he."

"Or break up a pitched battle when they all start fighting each other," somebody muttered behind Cethen.

"Why?" someone else called from the far side of the fire. "Why's he calling a gathering?"

"What's the point?" called another.

"So, he's trying to start it all over again?" Cethen said wearily.

"With what?" Borba asked.

Rib picked up on the last question, his voice edged with scorn. "You have no idea of the army Galgar can raise when the tribes are angry. What you saw the past few months is the least of it. The Romans may have fought off a wolf two days ago, but what they also did was inflame the rest of the pack."

"The Romans may have made the wolf pack's piss boil," Cethen suggested calmly, "but they also scared the shit out of it."

"Which I'll concede," Rib said, "but that's why they'll all come together. There's a common enemy howling at the door."

"He needs five times their number to even think of beating them." Borba snorted in disgust. "Especially the way the hill men fight: all balls and no brains."

Again Rib nodded agreement, this time with a wry smile. "That would mean about fifty thousand. Which is exactly how many Galgar intends to raise."

Laughter and disbelief greeted him.

"The man's been talking to the faerie."

"The number doesn't exist."

"If the Romans have time to stand their soldiers in lines, Galgar could have a hundred thousand and he wouldn't beat them," Cethen said, recalling too many times when, admittedly on a lesser scale, that was precisely what had happened.

"We almost had them a few days ago, with far less than five against one." Morallta finally spoke, her weight on the spear and her head bent, as if talking to the ground.

"And we almost had them at my own village, and at Bran's Beck, and a dozen fights in between. I've lost count of the times we *almost* had them," Cethen growled, his eyes on the flames, refusing to look at her. "Anyway, why should we trust Galgar?"

"Why shouldn't you? You both have a common cause," Morallta retorted.

"Aye," a jeering female voice called out from the darkest side of the fire. "You!"

A ripple of laughter followed the words and Cethen, who decided they likely came from Ficra, opened his mouth to deny it. But Morallta spoke first, and though clearly annoyed, managed to remain calm. "He'll have them gathered before the end of summer."

The words were greeted with more hoots of laughter, but most eyes remained fixed on the ground. The woman was, after all, Morallta.

"As I said, why should we trust him?" Cethen continued doggedly. "The man does not keep his word."

"When has he never kept his word?" Morallta sneered, finally raising her head to glare at Cethen. "Galgar bears you no grudge."

Which seemed true, Cethen silently acknowledged. And that had been a real concern, considering that less than a week ago he'd stood with a sword point prodding the man's bum hole. He smiled, though, noting that Morallta was deliberately vague as to why Galgar bore no grudge. Well, he certainly wasn't going to elaborate. Besides, there was another target he needed to aim at. "Where's Bryn?"

"Ah, so that's it."

"I was promised he'd be here. I'm to have the boy's custody."

"And you will."

"Morallta, Galgar agreed. Which shows just how reliable he is. But I'll tell you this, woman: I will have him back before we go."

Morallta tilted her head to one side, her eyes narrowing as if to gauge how far she should push the matter. "Galgar did agree, but did not say when."

"You know damned well when it was supposed to be. Now!"

"At the end of summer, it will be all over. The Romans will be gone. I know you don't believe it, but hear this." Morallta pushed herself upward on the spear until she stood straight, and lifted her head to speak to them all. "He will have his army. I believe it; I know it! In fact, the only reason I'm keeping my people in this godless land is because there will be a reckoning. And along with that reckoning will come plunder and glory. Galgar is preparing to move north, and the Romans will too. The difference is this: as Galgar marches, his army will multiply. As Rome marches, its army will weaken."

"Ha!"

"Think on it!" Morallta cried angrily. "Wherever they build, they must leave soldiers behind to guard. See the numbers they have now!" She waved a hand toward the east. "Then remember the numbers they had at the end of last year, when crossing the Bodotria! The main difference is in the men who now do nothing but guard the forts built along the way."

She was getting their attention, Cethen realized bitterly, as several of his people turned to one another and nodded. What she said was likely true. What would happen by the end of summer? Which, despite what she said, would turn out to be autumn, for summer would pass with incredible speed. Autumn was just a few months away. And there was still Bryn…

"I want the boy first."

"I want him for the summer."

Cethen bit his tongue as he thought that over. The boy was with the woman in the midst of thousands of Galgar's people. There seemed little choice. Would it do any good to talk to Galgar himself? Remind him of his word? No. Not as long as she had him by the balls, literally, and he knew too well how that worked. Grudgingly, he said, "And then what?"

"At the end of it, you might not be alive to worry," Morallta jeered, but before Cethen could voice his anger she added, "and I might not, either."

"I want a pledge," Cethen said, and gestured to the others, "in front of everyone."

"Oh, for the love of Lug!" she snorted, and spat. "If you must. Galgar will have his battle when summer ends. If I'm alive at the end of it, I promise I'll bring Bryn to you. And I swear to it on what I hold most dear," Morallta said. Placing her free hand across one breast, she lowered her voice to finish. "On the life of the boy himself."

"And if you're not alive?" Cethen asked, ignoring the depth of her oath, for he knew how the woman's mind worked.

"Then I swear I'll arrange to see it's done."

As he pondered the words, the barest of whispers came from Borba. Cethen grunted his understanding. "You never actually said when."

Morallta paused and bit her lip, then bowed her head. "The day after the battle is done."

Again the whisper, and Cethen thought Borba was being picky; but when he saw the woman's face, he decided that perhaps not. "You said you'd bring Bryn to me. Now tell me you'll leave him with me."

"*Shit!*" Morallta cried, and shook her head. "What do I have to do, bury my nose between your skinny arse cheeks? Of course I'll leave him with you. He's your son."

"Fine," Cethen said, stalling, for he was unsure of both the promise and what the others thought of staying on with Galgar. "We'll talk it over. And we'll first want to see what happens at the gathering. We'll let you know then."

Chapter XXVI

Pinnatis Castra, A.D. 83

"Agricola is going to build a permanent, full-sized fortress, about twenty miles north of here," Gaius said, then added, almost as an afterthought, "It will be built of stone."

He leaned across the table and took a handful of mixed nuts from a wooden bowl. Tossing a few in his mouth, he reached for his wine cup, and instead knocked it sideways with the back of his hand. The red liquid dripped through the narrow planks onto his tunic. "Damn!" he muttered, and called out, "Metellus!"

"Of stone!" Elena said, surprised. "They haven't even done than at Eboracum."

"We don't build them of stone unless we intend to stay," Gaius said, then appeared to ponder the comment, and grinned. "Who knows, maybe that means you'll get your old village back yet."

Anger at what might have been a barb heated Elena's face, and she glanced sideways at Coira. Her daughter seemed merely curious as she commented, "I wouldn't have thought they'd build anything permanent here. It's so … well, it's hardly worth the bother."

"No gold, no tin, poor wool, and teeming with half-naked savages." Gaius chuckled. "Makes you wonder, doesn't it?"

"So why is he building a fortress?" Elena asked. Having seen the awesome, sunlit sprawl of Rome, she was unable to understand why its citizens wanted to build even a hovel in Britannia, let alone another stronghold. "This land is full of nothing, at the far end of nowhere."

"That sounds very much like, oh, what's the name of that place?" Gaius snapped his fingers as if trying to remember. "Ah, yes. Eboracum!"

"That's different," Elena said indignantly. "We had the two rivers. And there were the traders. The land is rich and fertile there, and the trees, they're ... well, they're big and green."

"There'll also be a nice little river here, too, and the land's not at all bad," Gaius said, leaning back as Metellus returned and placed several platters of food on the table. "As to the fortress being built of stone, there's lots of it close by. It's not bad stuff, either. And there's lots of good lumber for finishing the buildings."

"What goes up first?" Elena asked.

"The walls," Gaius said, and laughed to himself.

"I know that, dammit; I meant inside."

"The granaries, and a few workshops to start with, I suppose." Gaius sat back while Metellus cleaned the worst of the wine from his tunic with a damp cloth, then he motioned the slave to refill the cup. "If time permits, perhaps the HQ and the commander's residence."

"Will we be able to ... ?"

"Yes. Agricola is by himself, and doesn't require much room. Besides, it'll only be for a couple of months at the most."

"He can build a stone fortress in a few months?" Coira asked incredulously.

"Unfortunately not. It'll take far longer than that, but the walls should be finished." Gaius offered an indulgent smile. "The army needs rest and a refit before it marches north again. Which will be in a couple of months. Most of the fleet went south for supplies, and won't return until midsummer. A building program will keep the men out of trouble, which is just—ah!" As Metellus moved away, Gaius caught sight of his son's gaunt figure walking through the open tent flap.

"Did I hear you say the governor is moving farther north?" Marcus asked, setting Jessa on the ground and motioning her to the table. The child walked clumsily over to the nearest seat and held her arms up to Coira, who for a moment looked perplexed. Then, as if lifting a load of soiled laundry, she picked the youngster up and set her gingerly alongside.

"She's house trained, and doesn't bite." Marcus grinned, nodding to Elena as he sat down across from his father.

Elena still didn't know what to make of the youth, and tried to bury her prejudice. The boy's beard was gone and his hair trimmed to just above the shoulders, but he retained a dark, bushy moustache that drooped over the sides of his mouth. It was not unattractive, but it would likely soon be shaved. His face was burnt to a leathered tan that suggested health, despite his hollowed cheeks. A finely woven tunic the colour of ox blood hung loose from his shoulders and was drawn tight about his waist by a thick, braided cord that served only to stress his leanness. There was no doubt he'd changed, both outside and in, but to what degree of permanence?

Metellus brought yet another platter from the rear of the tent and Marcus glanced hungrily around the table. "So, has this place got any garum? I'd kill for the taste."

Gaius eyed his son carefully, assessing his gaunt appearance as he would a stranger's. The last time he'd seen the boy he'd been barely into his twenties, and now, what was he? Twenty-five, twenty-six? The lad looked strong enough, once you got past the lean, stringy-muscled arms and the thin features. His memory was of a boyish face shaded with baby fat, and an ever-present scowl of discontent. Well, if nothing else, the scowl was gone; and, were it not for a nagging doubt that perhaps it had merely retreated, Gaius would have been far less cautious with his thoughts.

"So what now, son?" he asked.

Metellus cleared the table and replaced the food with a jug of heavy, sweet wine. The two women made to leave, but Gaius motioned them to stay, with the excuse that the child needed tending. The reason was transparent, for the little girl was quite content scratching on a wax tablet, oblivious to her surroundings.

"Well, the wine looks good. Perhaps some of that," Marcus said, his eyes moving over the table. "A bit thick, perhaps; it looks rich. Fig? Date? Is it good?"

329

"Fig, and yes, it's good." Gaius curbed a familiar twinge of irritation, for his son was being deliberately obtuse. "I imagine you'll be wanting to go home. Both of you." He nodded toward the child.

"I think I'll try it, then." Marcus poured himself a measure of wine and sipped at it with infuriating slowness. "Ah, now that *is* good. Nectar!" He smiled and looked toward Jessa, peering thoughtfully over the lip of his mug. "Home! Where is that, I wonder?"

"Yours is in ... " Gaius began, then stopped, wishing the boy's mind would remain focused for more than a moment. But it didn't seem to want to.

"Rome? Perhaps. But what about her? I wonder where her home is. I wonder where it should be."

"I suppose, if it must be, it will be the same as yours."

"If it must be?" Marcus turned, eyebrows raised as if in surprise. Gaius wondered if he was being baited. "She's my daughter."

"Of course," he said testily. It was just that the girl was so—well, so different; he hadn't been certain the boy was going to keep her. And the child's mother was, after all, a barbarian, and a not too civilized one, at that.

Marcus's mind, however, seemed to have once more flitted off. "I'm still a junior tribune in the Twentieth. Never did finish my tour, you know. I wonder what Agricola wants to do about that?"

"Not an issue," Gaius said, waving a hand in dismissal. He was surprised the boy had even raised the matter. "I doubt you're even listed on strength; but if you are, then it's not a—"

"I suppose I'm owed back pay," Marcus interrupted, his face suddenly brightening. "There's four—no, almost five years! They have to give it to me, surely, wouldn't you say?"

"Perhaps, but money's really not an issue. The amount is change in the bottom of the purse, all things considered. What you should be doing, is—"

"Ah, but it's *my* money. Hard-earned money, too. Every last denarius. And all in the cause of mother Rome!" Marcus leaned back with an odd smile on his face. "I need it."

"You don't need money!" Gaius burst out, irritated that the talk he'd planned was not heading in the direction he'd charted. "I can let you have—"

"I need to buy a slave. And quite urgently, actually," Marcus murmured. "Tell me, how much would a field trained Briton be worth? From the south, say. Strong. Intelligent. Well-proportioned, and sound."

"You don't need to buy a slave! There are lots at home, and—"

"I want one in particular. He belongs to you, though I suppose that's open to debate, since he's been wandering the hills for as long as I have." Marcus gestured westward with the mug of wine. "A great lug of a man with the body of a bear, and the brains of a fox. I need to buy him from you."

"What's the point, if he's a runaway? If we catch him, the man will be taken and—"

"I know, and I don't want that to happen," Marcus interrupted again, much to Gaius's annoyance. "I want to buy him so I can officially free him. Then the man can go home and live in peace. It's a promise I made."

"Which was not yours to give," Gaius said irritably.

"Perhaps, but the man contributed greatly to my being here and alive." Marcus took another sip of the wine, his face thoughtful as he nodded to himself, then toward Jessa. "In fact, at the last, he's likely the reason we're both alive. I've no idea what he's worth where he is, but I'll give you five hundred *denarii*, which is quite good for something you haven't really got."

"Sounds like a bargain." Elena spoke for the first time, her features tight with suppressed amusement. "When you bought the two of us," she placed an arm around Coira's shoulder, "you paid less. For me, anyway."

"You were battle booty, stank like a goat, and totally untrained," Gaius grunted, his annoyance fed by the feeling of being outflanked by both his son *and* his—his—his own mutinous slave! "And you're still not trained enough to get a decent price," he added with a growl.

"And speaking of being trained, there's a man called Crispus I want to see. I wonder if he's still alive?"

"Decanus? One of the Batavi infantry cohorts?" Gaius frowned, knowing full well who Crispus was, but his son wasn't the only one who could be obtuse.

"A centurio, with the Twentieth." Marcus's features suddenly split in a huge grin as he looked first at the two women, then back to his father. "I can't wait to see the old fox's face when he discovers the new horse he's saddled with. You see, I'm going to complete my tour of duty."

"That's nonsense," Gaius said, his mind flitting over the effect such a move would have on the boy's career. His own ambitions had been interminably delayed due to his brother's imprudence, and he was damned if that was going to happen to his son. "Once back in Rome, you'll be hailed as a—"

"Father, at this point there's nothing else I want to do," Marcus said firmly, and glanced at Jessa, his eyes growing suddenly soft. "I think it's best for both of us, really."

"I'd like to go with you," Rhun said as he raised one arm, halting the small column of cavalry that rode behind. "I'd feel more comfortable."

"No." Marcus shook his head. "It's got to be just me. Alone."

"Then you'll leave the child with me?"

"Almost alone, then." Marcus glanced down at his daughter, who straddled the saddle in front of him as if sitting on his lap. "She's probably safer out here than any of us."

"You want the other horse, then?"

"No, we'll walk back," Marcus said, and kicked his own mount in the belly, urging it forward. "We should be within earshot, so just stay here and relax. I'd keep the pickets out, though."

The cluster of huts should have been just over the next rise, and for a moment Marcus thought he had judged it wrong; the tattered, reed-covered rooftops were nowhere to be seen, nor were the crude, mud-covered walls. But as he drew near, his nostrils caught the all too familiar smell of burnt wood and abandonment. Perhaps his coming here was a mistake after all—not because of any danger, but because Urs, like all the others, had likely gone.

The weather was fair, though, and Marcus reasoned they could still enjoy the day, even if it did all come to nothing. He dismounted, hobbled the horse, and lifted his daughter from the saddle. A bulging leather packsack came next, and he pulled out a large square cloth and spread it on the grass near the giant fir tree. Jessa eagerly started filling it with plates and mugs, while her father peered anxiously into the dim forest and along the steep trail that led west, into the hills.

It was well over an hour before an arrow thudded into the fir tree, well away from where Marcus and Jessa sprawled on the grass. The sound startled them both and Jessa looked to her father, her eyes wide with fright.

"Shh, rabbit," Marcus whispered, "be still. It's only a friend."

Urs called out a few moments later, without showing himself. "The Roman cavalry. Why are they there?"

Marcus sat up on his knees and turned to face the forest, even though there was nothing to be seen of the big slave. "To protect me from the likes of you."

"You think you need that?"

"Urs, a Roman would be a fool to venture here by himself." Marcus rose to his feet, arms apart as a sign of goodwill. "I neither want to die nor spend another winter with Galgar. Those men back there will do you no ill, I swear. But they'll also keep me out of Galgar's hands."

"You have what I want?"

Marcus bent down and fumbled in the bag, retrieving a copper wafer etched with writing. He held it where it could be seen, turning it so the sun glinted on the shiny surface. "All you have to do is tell me, and I'll leave it in the burrow and be gone. Otherwise, join us to accept my thanks, and bid farewell to me and my daughter."

Jessa ran to Urs the moment he ambled from the trees and he picked her up, swinging her around as she giggled in delight. Marcus watched with a huge smile on his face, and when the slave was finished, simply held out the copper sheet.

"This is it?"

"A bit late, but yes. Believe me, I would rather have given it when the three years were up."

Urs took the copper square and placed it casually in the pack that swung from his shoulder, then sat down at the edge of the picnic cloth and crossed his legs. His eyes took in the food arranged on the surface of the cloth, coming to rest on a clay pot filled with garum. "You still eating that rubbish?" he complained.

"No, I use it to wash my armpits." Marcus chuckled, surprisingly pleased at the slave's banter.

Urs leaned forward, twitching his nose. "Then keep doing it. You'll smell far better than I remember."

"Da doesn't smell," Jessa said loyally, and sat comfortably down at his side, staring up at his bearded face. A small hand reached up and tugged at the long strands. "You've got white hairs in your beard."

"That's because he's growing old," Marcus jibed.

"No it's not, little one," Urs said seriously. "It's because the gods give people a white hair for every good deed they do. That's why my hair is turning white, and your da's is all black."

"You've done a lot of good deeds," Jessa said, equally serious, and both men laughed.

"She believes it, too. And she's quite right, you know." Marcus passed an earthenware jug to the slave. "Here, try this. It's a half-decent vintage."

Urs's initial wariness eased as they ate. The talk ranged from their journey across Gaul, which seemed to be a hundred years ago, to Marcus's safe arrival in the Roman camp under the guard of Agricola's auxiliaries. Only then did the talk turn serious, when Marcus asked the slave if he knew what Galgar planned to do.

"I have friends among his people," Urs growled, his face suddenly taut. "It's not a good thing you ask of me."

"Then let *me* tell *you* what the Romans are doing," Marcus replied, convinced his words were reasonable, even though they rang of treachery. "Agricola's boats will be arriving soon, packed with supplies and replacements. In the meantime, he plans on building a huge fortress above the Tava. A fortress of stone. And Urs, you know that when they build of stone, they mean to stay. It won't be finished this summer, just the walls, but that will be enough to serve as a base. A base for a campaign that will march all the way up the east coast, destroying everything in its way. Do you know why Agricola is doing that?"

Urs thought the question over. "To make Galgar's piss boil, I suppose, and get him to fight in the open."

"Just so! And let me tell you what I think Galgar *is* already doing," Marcus said, carefully watching the slave's thoughtful grey eyes. "His piss is already hot because he didn't destroy the Ninth. He thought he cut it close, though, which makes him think he can actually do it next time—which is pig swill, for next time Agricola's army will be united. But Galgar doesn't believe that makes a difference, and he's already starting to gather the tribes. He thinks numbers will solve the problem, which is also pig swill. Is that about it?"

Urs didn't answer the question, but sat brooding. Jessa seemed to sense the big man's tenseness, and turned instead to a pair of ladybugs. They seemed to be fighting as they clung together on a single blade of grass.

"Myself, I would guess that's about it," Marcus persisted.

"If you know the answer, why ask the question?" Urs shrugged, and pushed onto his knees. "I've told you more than once that what these people do is none of my concern."

"And I suppose it's none of mine, either." Marcus shrugged in turn. "It's just that over the past few years, there are some of them I've come to know well. Not the savages who crawl about these hills," he waved a hand toward the forest in dismissal, "but those who've been with us in this together, you and I, from the beginning."

Urs paused, his interest caught. "Such as … ?"

Marcus grimaced as if embarrassed. "A few of the women. Some were kind. Very kind. And the men—some of them, too. Those stupid twins, for example, and their irritating humour. The old cripple with one arm; what's his name … ?"

"Balor."

"Balor! And there are others. To be candid, I don't want to see them die." Marcus realized the words were true, and included another name unmentioned: the one man other than Urs who had managed, for whatever reason, to keep him alive. He grunted his amusement. "Including that bumbling oaf called Cethen. What he ever saw in that bitch Morallta besides tits and tail, I don't know. The woman's vicious."

Urs grinned and shook his head. "Some would say that's more than enough."

"She'll be the death of him, if he doesn't go home. It's not his fight, you know. Nor is it a fight of the others'. And Urs, the reason I ask what Galgar is doing," Marcus pushed onto his knees as well, and placed one hand on the slave's shoulder, "is because someone should talk him out of it. Submit to Rome, as the rest of the province has done. It's the only sane thing left for them to do."

For a moment both men were silent, then they rose to their feet and stood staring at each other. Urs broke the silence. "Galgar will do nothing but plow onward, taking his own course." He cocked his head to one side, grinning at his next words. "In fact, he's now plowing Morallta. They feed off each other. Between them, they think they're invincible."

"No! What happened to Cethen? Did Galgar kill him?" Marcus blurted, surprisingly disturbed by the thought.

"Just the opposite. Cethen almost killed Galgar." Urs laughed out loud. "Snuck up on him from behind when he was playing the double-backed beast. The story is, he let Galgar go, but only if he promised he'd take Morallta off his hands. Honest," he added when he saw Marcus's look of disbelief.

"Then other than saving my skin, that's the first sensible thing I've seen him do," Marcus said, and impulsively thrust one arm toward Urs, hand extended. "Look, my friend, we should go, for your sake. If you see Cethen, wish him well. Tell him his son and daughter are also well. In fact," he smiled, "his daughter is very well, to the point that she scares me."

"I'll tell him." Urs grinned and briefly clasped Marcus's wrist. "May the gods be kind."

"And to you, too." Marcus beckoned to Jessa, feeling strangely reluctant to leave. Taking her hand, he stood ready to return down the trail, then paused as another thought struck him. "Oh, and if you find it appropriate, tell him his wife is also doing well. I'd say she's moderately happy."

"Moderately?"

"You know how women are."

Marcus grunted as he set his daughter in the crook of one arm and, after a final wave, started walking back down the hill. He'd hardly gone more than ten steps when the expected question came.

"Aren't you forgetting something?"

He turned to find Urs standing with his arms spread, his head bent toward the horse and the leather pack set alongside the trunk of the fir tree. An enormous, unexpected surge of pleasure filled Marcus's chest.

"It's a long way home, Urs," he said, trying with some success to sound indifferent, "but one horse should get you there. There's money in the pack, and a few supplies. Oh, and there's a pass from the legate of the Ninth—that's what the scroll is for. For my sake, if nothing else, use the damned thing."

Rhun ordered the troop to mount up when he saw Marcus walking down the trail, the girl Jessa perched on his shoulders. Riders were sent to call in the pickets, and the dark silence of the forest quickly filled with the murmur of voices and the soft creak of leather harness. Rhun waited patiently, for the pair were chatting, and seemed in no hurry.

In a way he was envious of the two as his eyes followed their aimless wandering down the well-worn track. His own son was at Eboracum with his mother, and he had not seen either for three months. In fairness, the legate had been decent about it. Every few months over the past winter he'd found his name posted in orders to go there, usually when a large escort was needed for one of the slow-moving supply trains. But he still missed the boy, and of course Aelia, too; and more so, the longer he stayed in this contrary land.

Yet perhaps that trace of envy was not warranted, when he thought on it. The man would likely have to part with the child if he returned to the Twentieth, a decision that had surprised everyone. From what he'd seen, he guessed the legate had expected his son to bolt for Rome at the first opportunity.

There had been a major change in the spoiled tribune from the Praetorians; his own sister, Coira, was perhaps more astonished than anyone. And it was Coira most of all who offered the opinion that, if indeed the change was sincere, it would prove only temporary. She offered no reasons, though he suspected them. He would have to ask Aelia next time he saw her...

Chapter XXVII

Mons Graupius, A.D. 83

The legions were terribly under strength. The new fortress at *Pinnatis* could not be left half complete and unmanned, and a dozen other forts strung all the way back to Eboracum needed their garrisons. That, along with a half-dozen cohorts seconded to Germania by order of Domitian, had eroded the army's numbers far more than any enemy. The Twentieth, the strongest of the three, was down to almost half its authorized strength, and the Second and the Ninth could raise less than three thousand regular troops between them. Where more than fifteen thousand might, under ideal conditions, fill the rolls, the three legions together could muster less than six thousand.

Agricola, after much soul searching, decided to combine all three under one command before continuing his march. He already held the reins of the Twentieth, sitting back of an empty saddle, for the legion's legate had never been replaced. The man's tour of duty had expired the previous year, and the governor found no need to ratify the appointment of another. The Second was now also leaderless, and the Ninth, already light in numbers, was a shadow of itself. The decision to combine all three was sensible, and pronounced final as Agricola and Gaius inspected progress on the new fortress.

Only one man of legate rank remained with the army: Gaius Sabinius Trebonius. Who spoke only three words as the governor mulled his problem, voicing each thought as it came to mind. There was much to distract Gaius as he listened, for thousands of men toiled on the stone walls, while more cut blocks in the quarries.

"The combined force will, of course, number no more than a single legion. It will be commanded as such." Agricola frowned as his mind ran over the numbers. "We'll reduce each of the three into their own cohorts first. The Ninth will provide only two cohorts, each at full strength. Many of your men are nursing cuts and burns; they're best left here to secure Pinnatis."

Gaius nodded agreement, mentally working the arithmetic. Almost half his remaining strength, including the sick and wounded, would be left behind. Was he going to remain with them? No, he wouldn't tolerate that. And as to the Second Adiutrix...

"The Second came here with only five cohorts," Agricola continued, his lip curling in disgust. "Now we can't even muster four! We'll take three and leave the rest here in reserve, which leaves the Twentieth."

He again frowned, counting off the unseen units on his fingers. "They can make up the other five, including the first cohort. Though no, that's not going to work..." His brow furrowed deeper as his mind worked the figures. "The first cohort needs ten centuries, not six, and I'm short there. That one will have to be made up from all three . The Second can send on maybe two hundred troops to make up the difference. They've got them. You can talk to the primus there, a man called Vettius. Tell him I need mainly service support. Though if there's any such men to spare in the Ninth, we can use those too."

Gaius nodded again as Agricola reined in his horse. The governor bit his lip as if lost in thought, and Gaius wondered if his own role in this new army was on the man's mind. They had now been together for more than five years, both having extended their tours of duty. He'd done so for obvious reasons: Marcus. But as to Agricola, Gaius often wondered. The man was heading toward six years in Britannia, which was double the normal tour.

Earlier that summer, he'd lost a son born just the year before. The tragedy seemed to spur the man on, however, setting his mind more firmly to the task at hand—which had to be more than just a sense of duty. Was it an obsession to subjugate the entire province, from one end to the other? Or was it simply convenient for the emperor Domitian to keep the man as far from Rome as he could? Vespasian had known the value of that, and practised it quite successfully, though history had more than once proven that strategy to be a two-edged sword.

Gaius watched from the corner of his eye, vainly trying to read Agricola's face; giving up, he sighed and gazed once more about the camp. Nearly all the auxiliary infantry were working alongside the soldiers, plus the camp's slaves and hundreds of barbarian prisoners, each shackled to another. Almost six thousand feet of wall was nearing completion, which meant the fortress would be closed in before the march north. It had to be.

"There'll be twice as many auxiliary troops marching with us," Agricola finally said, as if talking to himself. "The legion itself will be held in reserve. I want the auxiliaries to do the fighting. Which means someone will have to take a firm grip on them, for they're a mixed lot."

Again the governor lapsed into silence, while Gaius silently cursed. He did not want to be responsible for any mixed force of auxiliaries, never mind that the number was double that of a full legion. There would be a score or more commanders to deal with, hardly any he knew, and that part of the army was not the compact, well-organized, well-drilled force that was a legion. In many ways, the auxiliaries were a separate army. They were good, yes, but they...well, they were just not a legion.

"That's going to keep any man occupied, even with good staff officers. So that's where I'm going to have to devote *my* time, Gaius. This jaunt isn't just about marching up the coast, killing barbarians. It's about forcing a major battle that will set them in their place for years." Agricola pursed his lips, clearly taking for granted that only his expertise would carry the day; a fact that Gaius readily conceded was true. The man's record was better than his own, or that of anyone else he knew, for that matter. Yet he still hadn't said—

"You looking to see this out?" Agricola asked, the words catching him by surprise. "Your son is back. You're more than two years overextended. You have affairs in Rome that likely need tending. I suppose you'll be wanting to go home."

Gaius's mood shifted. Was he being dismissed, no longer needed, cast aside with his excuses already offered? But Agricola's features were sincere, and it dawned on him that the man was actually looking for assurance that he would stay. "Not at all," he said emphatically.

"Good. Excellent." Agricola leaned back in the saddle as if suddenly at ease. "Then you'll continue on as legate of this mongrel legion we're going to form, and I wish you the best of it. Your man Titus will remain here in camp; the poor bugger can't move anyway. So the Twentieth's primus will be your first spear. Fellow's name is Crispus. You'll like him."

Gaius nodded his agreement and, apparently satisfied, Agricola soon turned to more mundane matters. The arrangement was a good one, Gaius thought. He would have a full strength legion at his command for the first time, which was a prize not to be discounted; few legates of late, including Agricola himself, had enjoyed that luxury. And added to that was the satisfaction and relief of retaining the governor's confidence, though there had been absolutely no need to think it was ever in doubt.

Only later, when Gaius pondered the logistics, did he find it irksome to be given command of a legion that was to be held in reserve.

Agricola began his march north in August, following a broad, shallow valley that angled gently down to the eastern coast. There he again joined with the fleet that kept pace on the choppy waters of the *Germanicus* sea. Sometimes the small armada trailed the army, but more often than not it preceded. The weather, for the most part, was clement; and the governor, for the most part, was cautious. Mounted patrols rode ahead, behind, and to the sides of the tight columns.

Long before the army gained the coast, Rhun grew disheartened by Agricola's ruthless progress. It wasn't that he sympathized with the violent, savage people who dwelt in the windswept hills and the shallow valley. The issue was the governor's order to burn, kill, and destroy everything in the army's path; everything, that is, except what was worth saving for Rome. That meant looting goods that had value— which were few; and taking captives that would serve as useful slaves— which were many. These, to his distress, were mostly wild, distraught women and terrified children.

Hovels, barns, lodges, pens, anything that might burn—all were torched. A trail of grey smoke and black, acrid rings of charcoal and ash marked the passage of the army; all of it littered with the bodies and bones of men who'd been slow to flee. What was left of the prior year's harvest was taken and, had it been ripe rather than the green, the current year's would have been burned. Instead Agricola saw that it was crushed, ridden down by the cavalry; or, if the army paused, reaped and fed as fodder. Which was the way of war and Rhun realized as much, for he'd seen it before, north of the Rhenus. Yet here, somehow, it was different.

After the attack that had almost destroyed the Ninth, there were many whose piss still boiled, which was natural. And it was certainly necessary to punish those who had done it, if for no other reason than to ensure they didn't do it again. And simple revenge was also justified, for revenge was simple justice. Yet despite the logic of it all, the whole thing began to gnaw on his spirit.

A spirit that wasn't lifted by finally being replaced as commander of his own cavalry regiment. Rhun had started to enjoy the rank, temporary though it was. The new praefectus, an *equestrian* called Sextus Sertorius, was not a bad man; he was competent enough and definitely familiar with command, possessing none of Livius's cautious dithering. The man had gone out of his way to make Rhun feel comfortable, a further mark in the man's favour.

While the change had at first felt like a demotion, particularly in the imagined loss of image, it had its compensations. The truth of it was, returning to second-in-command meant a return to an ideal balance of freedom and responsibility that he would have envied as a decurio. So when his mother asked why he moped like a beaten pup, he could offer no clear reason.

Cian, basic as ever, readily supplied probable cause. "He's got the same problem we all have. Nothing to be found up here but randy thoughts and a few scrawny sheep. Things get backed up so bad inside, they eventually flood the brain." He airily waved one hand as if the matter was of no concern. "Happens to all of us, if the pressure isn't let go. I suspect if it builds long enough, a man's skull could—"

"Cethen, would you please shut up," Elena cried, shaking her head. "That's your answer to everything. And it's my firstborn you're talking about. I'd rather not discuss ... "

Cian and Rhun reined in their horses, surprise on their faces at the mention of Cethen's name. Elena stopped too, her face first showing bafflement until her mind played over her words.

"Don't have to ask where your mind was," Cian crowed.

Elena's face darkened and, as if determined to change the subject, she motioned to where dark billows of smoke blew from a nearby gully. Several bodies were scattered where the land fell away, funnelling downward to a small fishing village that clung like lichen to the rocky shore. Every building was on fire, from the crudest of huts set farther back on the slopes to the sheds, cutting tables, nets, and a rough wooden dock set level with the sea. At least a hundred soldiers could be seen through the scudding smoke, most simply watching as the windswept flames spent themselves.

"That's what makes Rhun feel like his heart's hitched to a plow," Elena snapped, and pointed farther inland to where a ragged group of tribesmen, mostly women and children, were being herded in line by more soldiers. "And that! I once stood in a column like that, with my own daughter."

"Everyone does it," Cian muttered. "Venutius was taking Selgovae women long before their husbands were suddenly our best friends. And they were doing the same, if they could lay hands on us. Naw, Rhun's problem's the same as mine. All he needs—"

"All he needs is to get this damn campaign over and done with," Rhun muttered, deciding his mother was likely correct. Certainly his uncle's answer to all things was not. The cause of his foul mood was more the daily orders group with its petty bitching, followed by endless riding, raiding, scouting, patrolling, killing, and burning. A man's duty didn't leave a single moment to remember soft limbs, softer breasts, brown eyes, raven hair, and a pale, pliant belly that—

Bollocks! Maybe they were both right, Rhun decided, but his mother's slip of the tongue grabbed at him. "You wondering about Da?" he asked.

"Sure, I think about him once or twice," Elena murmured, and turned her eyes westward to the dark, undulating horizon that was now constant. "Just wondering if he's still alive."

"Told you. He's a survivor," Rhun said, and glanced over at Cian. "Just like his brother. Only one's careful, the other's just got the gods on his side. How's your back, by the way?"

"I could do without the gods, thank you!" Cian muttered, and flexed his shoulders. The skin had remained tender, but with a lot of grease and padding, it moved reasonably well. "I just got confused who the enemy was. Show me the real one. Galgar."

Rhun glanced at his uncle, wondering if he really meant the words. The challenge was a common one, as everyone waited for Galgar to accept battle. Every man was confident of Rome's invincibility and Cian, with his bluster, was simply voicing his conviction. If anyone was going to die, it would be the next man, not him. Unlike Luga, who for as long as anyone could remember had voiced the opinion that the next skirmish would be his last. Rhun, as superstitious as the next man, wondered if it was the big man's own talisman to say so.

"The navy, late again," Rhun muttered, shading his eyes with one hand, though there was no sun. The first ships of the fleet were rounding the spit of land that sheltered the hapless village, sailing smartly through the chop on a favouring wind, their oars shipped.

"I'm surprised they're late. There are slaves to be boarded," Elena said snidely, "and time is money."

Marcus also grew despondent as Agricola's army marched farther north. The relentless advance had picked up once the army reached the coast, for there was little resistance. Only four temporary camps were built, all an easy day's march apart. And at each one the army waited before moving on. But the enemy, a heavy, phantomlike presence in the western hills, would not be tempted into battle.

The coast now belonged to the Taexali a wild, hardy people, different from Galgar's only in that many depended on the sea. Both tribes had united in a common goal: survive together long enough to rid the land of Rome. Differences could wait as, almost to a man, they fled inland ahead of the Romans, intent on joining forces with Galgar's growing army.

They set the camp close by the sea and the fleet lay offshore, bobbing at anchor in a small, windblown bay. The burnt ruin of yet another small village sat at the centre, nestled at the foot of a sharply sloped valley. All that remained, other than ashes, was the wooden deck that capped the village's rough stone pier, which was as busy as it had ever been, piled high with sacks of grain and the tools of war. Wagons and mules moved steadily back and forth between the pier and the camp, resupplying the ever-hungry army.

"He's going to need every last bit of what they're carrying if he breaks from the coast and marches inland," Marcus observed conversationally.

Coira turned, surprised. Like others with a small space of time on their hands, she had come to see the fleet at anchor in the bay below. The day had for once turned pleasant. A fresh breeze, warmed by the sun, blew gently off the sea, which was an agreeable blue rather than the ever-present expanse of grey chop. She had been enjoying the solitude, and was particularly irked to find Marcus intruding. "No doubt," she replied, her voice deliberately flat.

"I hear the man's patience with Galgar is wearing thin." Seemingly oblivious to her icy tone, Marcus stepped up beside her, his gaze on the jumble of ships spread across the bay.

"Who, Agricola or Gaius?" Coira asked, though she knew exactly who he meant.

"Agricola, though I imagine both grow tired of the killing."

"No doubt," Coira said again, almost sneering. "A total waste of warm, working bodies. Though I hear that the males are more or less useless as slaves for the first generation. They won't tame, they won't train, and they don't fight worth a damn in the arenas. However," she turned her head to look directly at him, "unlike their women, I hear they willingly fuck."

Marcus lowered his eyes and stared down at his feet for a moment; then, as if the effort was a chore, he raised them until they again met hers. "I'm sorry. There are things we do that we regret. Especially when we're young, and ... and ... "

Coira interrupted as he struggled for the right words. "And as stiff-pricked as a goat, but with less conscience. No doubt Rhun was just as

345

horny, but he didn't go twisting the arms of every skivvy in the kin, just for a quick hump! If it hadn't been for my mother and, and—"

"And my father," Marcus finished as Coira faltered in anger. "Look, I am sorry. Truly. But you were a slave, and in Rome, well, things are different. And your people do it, too. I've seen as much over here. Even so, as I said, there are things we live to regret."

"No doubt!" Coira cried angrily, annoyed that all she seemed able to do was repeat the same two words. "And now you're ridden with guilt. A changed man. A father. The honourable protector of his poor, helpless little girl. You'll have me in tears next. But don't worry, I'll be sure they don't fall on your new Roman armour. Changed? In a pig's hind end!"

Marcus stepped back, his expression shocked. He spread his hands helplessly and for a moment bent his head as if unsure what to say. Then he looked Coira in the eye, and when he spoke his voice was hard. "I'm sorry. And perhaps what you say is true. But there is one thing that I will not accept: don't you ever taunt me with my daughter! That girl needs me. And ... " Marcus bit his lip as if reluctant to say more, then said as he turned on his heel and strode away, "and I need her!"

Coira stood dumbfounded, staring at his back. An odd feeling swept through her, dousing her anger; a dark sense of something that could only be shame. For a moment she was speechless, then she gulped and called his name. When Marcus continued on as if deaf, she shouted it. He hesitated, then turned, his expression impatient.

"I, I ... " Coira stuttered, briefly wondering why she'd called out. She uttered the first thought that came to mind. "How is the little girl?"

"She's fine."

Coira knew where his daughter was, but asked anyway.

"With one of the camp women, back at Pinnatis." Marcus stood uneasily, as if unsure whether to linger or depart.

Coira took a step forward, her mind uncertain. She didn't like the youth. No, he was a man now, and she didn't like the man, either! Yet there was something written on his face that puzzled her. Then, as she thought what next to say, it struck her what it was. Marcus had the looked of a trapped rabbit: vulnerable.

"With one of the camp women? Is that good?"

"She's not what you may think. Her name's Julia, the camp praefectus's woman. Jessa's with her. She'll be safe."

Coira grinned. "Who, the woman or Jessa?"

Marcus frowned, then seemed to decide the words held no malice, and smiled. "You may have a point."

"Her mother; I was wondering ... "

"Whose mother, Jessa's or Julia's?" Marcus shot back, but this time the rejoinder did not come with a smile. In fact, he looked annoyed.

He didn't like that, Coira thought, and wondered why. She murmured Jessa's name, and promptly had her answer.

"She was the same size as you," Marcus said curtly, and again turned to go.

"I was going to ask what she was like, arsehole, not how big she was!" Coira cried in exasperation, and experienced an odd sense of relief when he again stopped, his head cocked to one side as he mulled his answer.

"She was a great, fat bitch of a woman with a face like a horse's hind end. And she stank as bad as a pig," Marcus growled, and dropped his eyes to the ground as if shamed. "It was horrible. Two of them held me down while the woman had her way, and when it was over, I cried for days."

"Now you *are* being an arsehole," Coira said.

"And aresholes put up with a lot of shit," Marcus muttered, then just as quickly he relented. "If a man is called a jackass often enough, then he begins to bray. Do you really want to know?"

"Know what?" Coira asked, the words tumbling out even as she understood.

"About Jessa's mother."

"I wouldn't ask if I wasn't interested. The girl seems quite bright. There's a lot hidden behind those enormous brown eyes of hers. Was her mother the same?"

Marcus paused, his features thoughtful, and Coira had the feeling he was going to walk away again. Then he spoke, and she was shocked to see his eyes water and his gaze lose focus. She stared at his lean features, thinner now that the thick black tribal moustaches were gone, and found they were—what? Interesting. There was character there, where once there had been only the spoiled petulance of indulgence. Had Marcus been one of her own kind, someone other than a Roman fop, she might even have found them appealing …

※

Marcus's thoughts had not turned to Fiona for a long, long time, and when they had, it was to push them further back in his mind, to be deliberately ignored as he tended the woman's daughter. His daughter. Jessa.

"She wasn't a bad woman," he began, his voice tight to check his emotions. "And in a way, she was a warrior. A fighter. True to her own people. She had dark brown hair and green-flecked eyes that flashed when she was angry. We'd hardly met when she tried to kill me. You'd have enjoyed seeing that."

Marcus smiled at the memory, hardly aware that his eyes had filled and threatened to spill over. No, Fiona had not been a bad woman at all …

Chapter XXVIII

Mons Graupius, A.D. 83

Cian was the first Roman to locate Galgar's great army, and his brother sat idly by and watched from the depths of a shaggy stand of spruce trees. Its discovery was probably inevitable, Cethen mused, but it was ironic that his brother did the discovering. It was yet another gesture by the gods as they played their eternal games. Whatever the reason, Galgar would be pissed, Cethen thought as he watched other riders emerge one by one from the trees. Though Cian had yet to stumble on the larger part of Galgar's army, he rationalized; and even if he did, he still had to get back ... *If there's a wager to be made, though, you put it on the man with the mindless luck.*

The Roman army had suddenly abandoned the coastline, cautiously angling inland to cross the great bulge of land that topped the coast north of the Bodotria estuary. Its commander would be frustrated, as Galgar intended. His soldiers had marched away from one coast and were moving toward yet another, but had still to force battle. The Roman's impatience would be boiling. His great fleet had already rounded the bulge, sailing west into the larger estuary, where it obviously intended to meet with the army it supplied. Yet, other than the odd skirmish and the ruthless looting and destruction, Galgar had not given them a glimpse of his army.

"If he had a grain of sense, he'd leave the Romans marching up and down till they run out of food and patience. Waiting to catch them with their shields down is dreaming," Cethen muttered, squinting at his brother on the far side of the ravine. There had to be at least two, maybe three squadrons over there. Which meant there were about—he shook his head and turned to Borba. "How many you think there are?"

"Fifty to sixty," the twin replied, and grinned.

"Yeah, that's what I thought. See the man in front? You've got the eyes. Who do you think it looks like?"

Borba didn't bother to look again. "It's Cian."

"Yeah, that's what I figured," Cethen murmured, his attention again on the line of horsemen riding along the ridge. "There's only— what, nine of us?"

There was a pause, and a female voice spoke up—Ficra. "Hey, he's right!"

Borba chuckled. "So what do you want to do, charge across and send them running?"

"Just thinking out loud. If he keeps going, in a mile or two he's going to run into Galgar." Cethen nodded to where the ravine fell away to form a broad valley. "But if he sees us, maybe they'll take off."

"Good plan," Borba said sarcastically. "We ride out and yell. They panic and bugger off."

"There's no need for that," Cethen growled, irritated. "What would we do if a bunch of Romans popped out of the trees, a mile from Eboracum? It would be boots to the belly, and bugger the balls. We'd be out of there faster than—"

"There's no need to fight, boys," Ficra slipped up beside Cethen and squeezed his rear to gain attention. "Look there, farther along the ridge."

A rider raced through the trees at a breakneck gallop, heading straight toward the Roman patrol. Cethen turned his eyes farther down the valley, expecting to find pursuit. For the moment, at least, there was none.

The trooper reined in alongside Cian, pointing excitedly back down the valley, jabbing a finger to make his point. The man's loud voice echoed faintly across the ravine, the words indistinct. Cian heard them, though, and acted quickly, barking an order that had each man wheeling his horse, a ragged movement that, for the moment, looked chaotic. Then, just as quickly, the column straightened out and rode back the way it had come.

Cethen kneed his horse forward, forcing it through the prickly branches of the spruce trees until it was out in the open. He yelled at the top of his voice, "Cian!"

His brother, now bringing up the rear, pulled back on the reins and stared across the ravine. A grin appeared, and he waved. Cethen returned the gesture, then turned his horse until Cian saw his back. Raising his left arm vertical and the other to a forty-five degree angle, he stabbed back and forward with the right, offering the safest route back. When he turned again, his brother was already on his way, one hand held high in a gesture of thanks.

"Aiding the enemy," Borba murmured as he rode out of the trees, and clucked in annoyance as he brushed spruce needles from his tunic. "Castration's just the start of what they do for that."

"Fight it out with Ficra, then; she doesn't believe in that sort of thing," Cethen said, smiling as his brother vanished into the trees. "Anyway, who's going to tell?"

Which was true, Cethen knew, for everyone there that day was Brigante. They held more loyalty to each other than to Galgar, and there was certainly no love lost where the Caledoni's warriors were concerned. And as to Morallta, if one thing was certain, nobody knew where her mind lay these days. So, when a great horde of horsemen came charging up the valley not long after and Cethen simply pointed farther up the ravine, nobody except Borba said a word.

"To tell the truth, I can't think of anything worse than having your balls hacked off, but if there is, I'm sure Galgar will find it," the twin mused. "The gods help you, though, if he asks Morallta for advice."

"She's been whittling at them for years," Cethen muttered, his eyes following the riders as they forced their mounts up the side of the ravine. "And as I said, who's going to tell?"

"Galgar was hoping to hold off until the Romans had marched through the mountains, and joined up with their ships—when they least expect it."

"Use your head—the Roman patrols aren't going to let that happen. Cian had already found Galgar's army, and you saw it. If it wasn't him, it would have been someone else. All I did was help save my brother's hare-brained butt." Cethen pulled on the reins, turning the chestnut into the trees. "Besides, and I've said it before, I'm getting fed up with all this. The sooner the bones are tossed, the better."

Agricola sat with his elbows on the table, saying nothing. The fingers of both hands were entwined and his chin rested on both thumbs, giving the appearance of a man lost in thought. Only his eyes moved, darting from once face to another as each man who felt bold enough offered his opinion. Rhun, the most junior ranker there, was certainly not one of them. And Gaius, who sat to Agricola's right, followed the governor's lead and remained silent.

The meeting, which was more a forum than an orders group, was attended by the cohort commanders; with a full legion and eleven thousand auxiliary troops, almost fifty men packed the command tent. And more than a few wanted to make themselves heard.

The last to speak before Agricola finally stirred himself was a man called *Aulus Atticus*, the commander of one of the Batavi infantry cohorts, and a man known for his boldness. Or, as Rhun watched him offer a half-dozen impassioned reasons to strike Galgar's army without delay, perhaps also known for his rashness. Certainly the governor seemed unimpressed, for his jaw stiffened then slowly relaxed, as if stifling a yawn. When he finally spoke, his words came as a shock.

"Rhun, you haven't offered an opinion. You debriefed the decurios who saw Galgar's army. What's he going to do?"

Rhun flushed self-consciously, though he might have expected the question. The only reason he was at the meeting was because it was his decurios who had found Galgar. That was the way he had it figured, anyway—or was it because he was a barbarian himself? Not that it made a difference; he had no idea what Galgar would do.

Certainly, if *he* was in the man's position, he'd do something. He'd have to! There was no choice, for the man's army now faced the prospect of being attacked itself. Cian's scout had managed only a glimpse of it before being seen, but it was huge, scattered across an enormous valley as far as the eye could see.

That was the way of it, and the way it had to be. The tribes' logistics were not well-organized to begin with; certainly not as efficient as

Rome's. Nor did Galgar's people neighbour well—the more so the greater the time spent together. He would have to cope with their conceit and their temper, constantly juggling the pride of countless chieftains just to keep them speaking to each other. The answer was to spread them out. But now the man would have to draw them together, gather them in, talk to them, just as Agricola was doing now with his commanders, only their task was tenfold. And when that happened, they wouldn't sit still for more than a moment.

As Rhun thought on it, he realized that Galgar was probably being pressured to attack even as they spoke. Immediately. Just like Agricola was being pressured. In fact, when he thought more on it, Galgar's chiefs had likely been straining on their leashes for weeks. Maybe months. Now his army was discovered, he would have no choice; the man would have to—

"He'll gather his men and march," Rhun said firmly, suddenly aware his silence was growing painful. "He knows where *we* are, always has. And now we know where he is, his chiefs will leave him no choice. I can't see them waiting. His people lack the patience. Cian poked his spear in a nest of wasps; and like wasps, Galgar's people will swarm and attack."

A low muttering spread through the tent, some men nodding their heads, others voicing disagreement. Agricola turned and spoke quietly to Gaius, who simply nodded.

Raising a hand for silence, the governor rose to his feet. "We're dug in here," he said, his voice curt. "I see no reason to leave. We'll let Galgar come to us. In the meantime, I want to take a closer look at the place where we'll defeat the man. Join me if you wish."

Less than a mile from camp the trees, thin before the ramparts, vanished altogether, leaving a wide, open plain. The area had been cleared by barbarian herders, for the droppings that dotted its length showed its use was pasture. All that remained of the crofters' hovels was the familiar scattering of black ash. An enormous hill, almost a mountain, rose sharply on the far edge of the plain; several other hills, all smaller, flanked either side. Grassland covered the lower slopes, but the peaks bore a thick cover of trees. The foliage was already speckled with autumn gold.

"I don't like those hills," Gaius murmured as his eyes took in the open plain and the sharp rise behind, "especially the big one. An uphill fight is exactly that—an uphill fight."

"I'm hoping Galgar thinks the same way, but its deceptive," Agricola said confidently. "If we hold our lines back here, there's ample room to keep the battle down on the plain. Only their reserve will remain on the hill, where we can see it. It will be a large one, anxiously pushing down on those doing the fighting. It should prove obstructive for them. You know how they are—all numbers and little order. I just hope Galgar doesn't do anything clever for a change ... "

Agricola's voice faded as three horsemen rode from the trees high up on the main slope. They reined in and sat staring, until one beckoned casually over his shoulder. More riders emerged from the forest in what appeared to be an endless column. As the lead horses filed from the trees, they turned and formed two long, even ranks behind. A chorus of voices rang out as the governor's auxiliary escort deployed in similar formation.

"Going to chase them off?" Gaius asked, quickly counting the barbarian riders. There were enough to form almost three full squadrons, which meant the escort itself was outnumbered.

"Too evenly matched," Agricola muttered, then smiled. "Unless we all help them out, and I pay my cohort commanders to lead, not fight. What—what are they doing now?"

One of the three riders had turned his horse to face the two ranks and lowered his spear, pointing it directly ahead. The two before him, one in either rank, lowered their weapons as if to acknowledge, then raised them again. As one, the barbarians promptly reined their animals sideways, the front rank to the left, and the rear rank to the right.

"Rhun!" Gaius turned in the saddle, eyes searching for his son-in-law. "What are the buggers doing?"

Rhun urged his own mount forward until it was alongside, his eyes on the performance taking place on the hill—for that was what it was, a performance. The man in front raised his spear and shouted, and each rider kneed his horse in the belly. The animals sprang forward as if one, moving quickly, at a fast canter.

"They're showing off," Rhun said; he was sure of it.

The front rank angled downhill, curving around in a large but perfect circle; the rear rank, with the same precision, did the same riding uphill. As they passed before the lone horseman a second time, however, the two riders who had been marked by the spear broke away to form a smaller, tighter second circle inside the first. When they again approached the single horseman it was in four ranks, half riding in opposite directions.

There was no need to order a halt as the riders closed. The lead man in each rank simply reined in alongside the rear horse of the other. When it was done the riders turned as one, forming four perfect ranks. The leader raised his spear, as did the others, and three times a roar of triumph echoed faintly down the slope.

"That's doing it the hard way," Gaius said dryly.

"It looks good, though," Rhun said, feeling oddly defensive. "And it wasn't done badly."

The leader turned his horse sideways and pulled back on the reins. The animal reared back, forelegs pawing the air as it fought for balance.

"Exhibitionist," Gaius snorted.

"Probably trying to impress the offspring," Agricola said, and turned to Rhun. "Think it's your father?"

"I don't think so." *Not with those antics,* Rhun thought. Though you could never be sure. Yesterday his da was showing Cian the way home. Today only the gods knew where he was.

"But it could be, don't you think?" Agricola suggested. "Why don't you see if he's disposed to talk? You might find something of interest."

Rhun doubted it was his da. If he were to set his own odds, they would be on Morallta. But if in fact it was his da, then this might be his last chance ever… "I'll go see," he murmured, and urged his horse forward.

"Stop halfway and wait, lad," Agricola said. "That's an order."

"Show him your horse can do the same," a voice called from behind. It sounded suspiciously like his own commander, Sextus.

Rhun grinned and waved with his free hand, then pulled hard on the reins. It was a showy gesture, one that Aelia would have laughed at in scorn; and his horse would not have left her disappointed. Poised to run, the animal was confused. Instead of rearing it fell back on its haunches, then, as if afraid of tumbling, lurched sideways, skittering wildly as it tried to regain its footing. One of its forelegs went down, and Rhun toppled helplessly over its neck.

Comments such as "Show them how, Rhun" and "What's you next trick?" drummed in his ears as he hobbled over and retrieved his shield and weapons. He remounted, his face hot, thankful that the axe-headed horse chose to remain still. This time, instead of the histrionics, he simply slapped the animal's rump, then held it to a canter. Shouts of encouragement—or perhaps they were jeers—followed him across the plain.

Rhun brought the horse to a halt at what seemed about the halfway mark, and sat waiting. The response was not long in coming. Only one rider sat ahead of the four ranks now, and Rhun knew it was not his father. As if to show exactly who it was, Morallta briefly removed her helmet and shook her head. A mass of auburn hair fell about her shoulders. Then, shield and spears slung in the same passive mode as Rhun, she lashed her horse to a headlong gallop.

Rhun remained impassive as animal and rider bore recklessly down, clucking soothingly to his own mount as he felt it grow nervous. At the last possible moment, Morallta pulled savagely back on the reins, her horse almost on its rump as it slid to a halt in a cloud of grit and dust. It bounced back, only to dance nervously sideways about four or five paces away. It was a Roman animal, its blood hot and its eyes rolling. Its rider balanced calmly in the saddle, studying Rhun with amusement.

"Perhaps I should offer riding lessons," she suggested derisively.

"Perhaps," Rhun retorted. "What manner of ride did you have in mind?" The words came out without thought; he was irritated, both by his fall and her contempt.

But the woman didn't seem offended, rather the opposite. She laughed, and jibed back, "So, the pup comes not to find his father, but to replace him?"

"Of course not, Morallta, I came to find out how you fare. You look well."

And she had worn well, Rhun realized. Her face was tanned and healthy, her features retaining the hard, aloof beauty he remembered from the trek to the Cumbrian hills. The tresses that burst from under the helmet were rich and almost silken, with not a trace of grey. For a woman who had to be, what? Well into her thirties? She looked damned good.

"You lie," Morallta snapped. "At least about why you are here. You came to make sure it was not your father. And, I suppose, to snoop."

Rhun ignored the comment and pushed elsewhere, for he was more than curious on another matter. "And my half-brother. He does well?"

"He flourishes," Morallta said, her face softening and her voice for the first time sincere. "He will be here alongside me, pushing the Romans back into the sea. The lad's only eleven, but sits a horse as if he were part of it. His skill with a weapon is far beyond his years."

"He'll be fighting?" Rhun asked incredulously.

"He'll have the smell of it," Morallta said, raising her chin in a tight, sneering smile, "and he'll also learn. He'll learn much."

"I wish him good health, then, and perhaps you might tell him that," Rhun said. He had one more question. "My father—you were right. I had to make sure it was not him out here."

Morallta grunted her amusement. "You hold your disappointment well."

Rhun shrugged. "So how does he fare?"

Morallta stared at him, her eyes thoughtful as she considered her reply. When it came, it was short and to the point. "He's dead."

Rhun sat stunned, for the moment unable absorb her words; then, finally, he repeated them. "He's dead?"

"As a granite slab."

"W-what happened?" Rhun asked numbly.

"His heart stopped beating," Morallta said coldly. "That usually does it."

"But it was only—" Rhun promptly fell silent. He'd been about to protest that only yesterday his da had been alive, for Cian had told him as much. Yet his uncle had also told him how the two had met, and what had happened. Had his father's help been discovered? Had they killed him? Rhun carefully phrased his question. "When did he die?"

Morallta ignored it. Her horse skittered again, but she adjusted easily in the saddle. When the animal was once again still, she reached back and tapped one spear, half pulling it from its sling. "I don't suppose you'd be interested … ?"

Rhun gulped, his mind screaming a half-dozen reasons why not, most of them valid. Topping the list was she was a woman, and had been his da's—his da's what? Wife, lover, mother of his child? In the true meaning of the word, the woman could be considered his own stepmother! He said as much as he declined the offer.

"Ha!" Morallta laughed, a loud, humourless bray. "The pup suggests he plow his stepmother, but finds no honour in fighting her!"

"You know I jested," Rhun said, aware the reply sounded weak. "You've heard far worse."

Morallta shook her head as if disgusted, then suddenly fell silent, her teeth biting softly on her lower lip as she sat studying him. It struck Rhun that the woman was weighing the odds on forcing the challenge, and his jaw tightened. Wrong as such a fight might be, he decided it would not hang long in the balance; if one them was left dead in the dirt, it would not be him. He slowly eased himself upright in the saddle, casually squaring his shoulders. While his left hand firmed its grip on his shield, he allowed the other to slip slowly across to the shaft of his spear.

Morallta nodded to herself, and her lip disappeared altogether. With a quick flip of the reins she turned her horse sideways, and raised her feet. "I'll look for you, Rhun," she cried, and slammed both heels into the animal's belly. The horse leapt forward and, eyes rolling, pounded its way back up the hill.

Rhun released his breath in a sigh, and for a moment sat silent. Thank the gods she was his da's problem. Though was she, any longer? Was his da still alive? The woman had dropped two nuggets of information on him. The first, that Galgar would fight them right here, seemed to have slipped out, and was likely true; and if so, the man was probably already on the move. That would now be easy to prove—not like the second poisonous barb. Was his da really dead?

Yesterday he wasn't, that was certain. He'd been seen. But, from what Cian had told him, some coward with cause to bury a blade might have looked to his father's back.

Chapter XXVJJJJ

Mons Graupius, A.D. 83

All fighting was not limited to the battlefield, Elena decided as they settled down in Gaius's tent for the final meal of the day. Coira was there, as was Marcus, and Gaius was on his way; only her boys were missing. Rhun was likely messing with his own cohort, and as for Tuis, in the letter she'd received only yesterday, he'd reported that everything was well: his health, his schooling, and his welfare. She just hoped that its arrival on the eve of a major battle was not an omen.

At least Coira and Marcus no longer seemed to be at each other's throats, which puzzled her. She would have to ask her daughter why. The girl's hostility seemed to have vanished as if by magic. Perhaps it had been replaced by annoyance with Gaius which, as far as Elena was concerned, was justified. He usually let the girl have her own way—which in itself was an annoyance to Elena—but this time he had firmly denied Coira's request to ride with Rhun. When she started to argue, he'd curtly reminded her of her position, something he normally avoided. That alone told Elena that he too was in a foul mood.

She knew the cause: Agricola's battle plan. He'd kept his strategy very basic—use the auxiliaries to do the fighting and hold Gaius's mongrel legion in reserve. Gaius had known ahead of time, of course, but now that reality was at hand, the brooding had set in. And the man complained about moody women!

Elena, as her daughter had done, had pushed him to let her ride with Rhun's cohort. Unlike Coira, however, she knew that was not going to happen. Starting high and settling low was the way she usually handled Gaius, only this time it didn't work. She'd hoped a compromise would allow her to accompany Agricola's staff officers, where she could fade into the background and quietly watch the fighting. She knew Marcus would also be positioned with those same officers to gain experience, along with several other junior tribunes. Gaius had denied her even that, and let slip his reason when he gave his terse answer: if he wasn't going to be there, then he'd be damned if his woman was.

That doubly nettled Elena, for not only was that not true, but calling her his woman prickled hard against her skin. Of course Gaius would be with Agricola, and the man knew it! He'd be there when it all began, and would not move back to his legion unless there was a crisis. After all, his precious command wasn't positioned so far behind the auxiliary force that it couldn't help at any time. Gaius would ride back and forth at will. No, it was because his legion had been tasked as a reserve force only that irked him, and he was taking it out on her.

Romans! Elena bent her head in disgust. If she was honest with herself, it was easy to understand Gaius's annoyance, for she could not comprehend why winning a fight using only foreign troops was a major feat of generalship. It was just the opposite—a bare-faced humiliation. Your own people didn't spill a drop of blood, and you considered that a victory? Where was the pride in that? Where was the legion's honour? It was so … so … so un-tribal!

"Here, would you like something to drink?"

Elena looked up and saw Marcus ready to pour, his eyes on hers holding a glint of amusement. *Well, he doesn't have anything picking at his mind,* she decided, and offered up her empty mug, along with her thanks.

Gaius burst into the tent, his eyes avoiding those of the women. "I can't stay long."

He sat down and reached for the food without bothering to remove any armour, which meant he was caught up in the flow of events, Elena decided, and wanted to appear so. She was pondering on whether it was worth pestering him again when Rhun stumbled through the tent flap, looking slightly bewildered.

"Sit down and eat, lad, sit down." Gaius, his mouth full, motioned to one of the folding chairs. "Rhun just rode in and delivered his report to Agricola. I thought you might like to hear it from his own mouth."

Rhun nodded to his mother and sister, and made straight for the table. He stood with one foot on the bench seat, picking at the food rather than taking a platter. "Nothing to tell that's not expected," he mumbled through a full mouth. "Galgar's vanguard is now about five miles away. The first of them should be here by dusk. They'll keep moving to be in place by morning. I'll tell you this," he turned his gaze on them all, one by one, "I've never seen so many men gathered in one place before."

Gaius waved his hand, dismissing the threat. "The pilus rode out too. Sextus took most of his regiment, just in case. Experienced men, both of them. They both put the figure at thirty thousand."

"Thirty thousand?" Elena tried to imagine that many of her own people in one place, and found a reference. Venutius was supposed to have had that many when he was surprised at Stannick by Cerealis. He didn't, not inside the fortress, anyway, but there was supposed to have been close on twenty; she didn't know if that included non-combatants. Yet he'd lost to a force smaller than Agricola's. Of course, the old bugger had been taken by surprise...

Elena shook her head loose of the memory and forced her mind back to what Gaius was saying.

" ...not that many will battle at once. They'll be bunched up with their small shields and those huge swords they like to bash us with, and there won't be a straight rank among them. What are the numbers, two to one? Or, dammit, three if my legion stays out of it. Shit, based on past battles with these people," Gaius gazed benignly about the table, clearly pleased with himself, "those odds are in our favour. It'll be over by midday."

When no one said a word, he rose with a quarter loaf of bread in one hand and an apple in the other. "I have to go. Agricola wants to deploy long before daybreak, so we're in position at sun-up."

"When are you—" Elena began.

"No idea. Could be away all night. Maybe not until it's over."

"What about Coira and I going ... "

Again Gaius stopped her, sighing as if exasperated. "Look, you can do this: one cohort will remain here to protect the camp, the rest of the legion will deploy outside, between the camp and the auxiliaries. You and Coira may join up with the legion's headquarters staff, as long as you keep out of their way. Otherwise, remain here inside the defenses. Is that understood?"

Elena released her breath and kept her temper. "When it's over, then what?"

"Stay where you are, lad." Gaius motioned to Rhun, who had turned to leave. "Get something to eat, and some liquid into your belly before you report back. Sextus's cohort is on the left flank, is it not?"

"Mmm," Rhun mumbled.

"Did you hear that, ladies?" Gaius turned to Elena and Coira. "If you're interested, Rhun will be on the left flank. That's on *our* left, as you're facing the enemy."

"I know where the left effing flank is," Elena burst out, then noticed Gaius's tight grin, and offered one of her own, for she could see he was relenting. "It's on the other side from the right effing flank!"

"Good. So when I say it's safe, you can ride over to the left *effing* flank and see how Rhun fared—if he's not off hunting barbarians."

Gaius lifted the tent flap to leave, but Elena had one more question, for she knew full well where he'd be if the battle was won: down with Agricola, all of them slapping each other's back and saying what a fine job they'd done. "What if you've not returned yet?"

"May the gods have pity! Please!" Gaius again sighed his exasperation, and threw up his hands. "I'll talk to the primus. You can ask him. Crispus will let you know when it's safe."

After he was gone, Elena sat wondering where that left her. She'd go up with the legion, of course, as would Coira. There was nothing to be gained by remaining inside the camp. Of course, there was little to be gained by going outside, either; but at least it would allow them to better follow events, even if it was from a distance.

"It's something, I suppose," Coira said, as if following her mother's thoughts.

"We'll see," Elena murmured. "I know Crispus. He's an easygoing man."

Both Rhun and Marcus hooted their laughter, Rhun spraying half-chewed barley bread, and Marcus commenting, "That's not the primus I know."

Cethen was uneasy, as were Borba, Ligan, Ficra, and the others. Even Dermat, who had shown up as darkness was falling with an even more dour expression than usual, was not happy with Galgar's strategy. Or, as he put it, the lack of it.

"Morallta's ready to wrap a spear around his neck," he muttered as he edged his horse up to where Cethen and Borba lounged around a large fire with the rest of the troop. He was able to find Cethen only because his force of irregular cavalry had been at the forefront of Galgar's huge, sprawling army. "The woman asked me to see if you can do anything."

"Me?" Cethen pointed to his chest as if to make sure. "She's asking for me?"

"The woman's desperate," Dermat said, then added a moment later, "She's got to be."

"Thanks."

"No, not that, I mean she's got to be desperate because of Galgar. I don't think he knows what to do, other than lose his temper. His men are moving onto the field in a single mass, as soon as they get here. They're settling down wherever they please, like cattle! Cethen, his best warriors should be placed in the centre, his cavalry on the flanks, and some sort of reserve set farther up the hill."

"I thought everyone was going to be on the hill. Morallta said so. It gives an advantage," Cethen complained, but climbed to his feet and began tightening the cinch on Gadearg's saddle.

Dermat nodded, and groaned. "This sounds all too familiar."

"We've got them outnumbered," Borba said cheerfully. "I hear Morallta's got it figured at four to one."

"I'd as soon believe Cethen's figuring, as hers," Dermat muttered. "And even if it were true, from what I've seen of these hill men, that hardly makes it even."

Cethen grunted agreement as he swung wearily up onto the

chestnut. Dermat moved off through the evening gloom. Borba shrugged and fell in behind.

The broad hillside at first seemed sparsely populated, but as the pair rode back the way they had come, the dew-dampened slope became more crowded. It took no time to realize why Morallta was in a rage. Anyone should have known better than to simply arrive and set his fat arse down in the first likely spot. Those who arrived first should have at least gone as far as they could in solid ranks, *then* settled down so others could do the same. Galgar's army was still on the move, and as it continued to arrive, its warriors had to pick their way through the thousands already there, some with fires lit and pots bubbling.

He heard Morallta before he saw her, her voice loud and shrill even from a distance, either barking orders or shouting her anger. Oddly enough, Cethen found he wasn't that concerned. His own troop had been talking over how it would be tomorrow, and they were of one accord: the Roman strategy would be to stand where they were and let Galgar come to them. What else would they do? They were outnumbered, and near the safety of their own camp.

For Galgar to attempt any major shift in position as night closed in was pointless. Darkness was a bad time to be placing anything in order, other than the plans on how to do it. First light would leave lots of room to sort out the things that worried Dermat. Cethen had ridden over with him, though, because an unresolved item nagged at his mind, and it was important. It was Bryn, and when his eyes found the boy before they found his mother, he cursed.

The lad had barely eleven years on him, and she had him fitted up like a toy warrior. His horse was small—although it *was* a horse and not a pony—and the animal would be knocked off its feet by the first Roman auxiliary trooper to slam it sideways. The shield was small too, a round buckler, useless against enemy swords; and he doubted the lad could heft the two spears slung across his back, even though they had been shortened. At least, he saw, she'd given him a decent sword: light, and sharpened long at the end like those of the legions and his own riders.

Bryn saw his father and his face lit up in a brilliant smile that warmed the inside of Cethen's chest. Then, just as quickly, the boy's expression turned stern, as if he was remembering who and what he was supposed to be. Cethen dismounted and, hiding his anger, embraced his son anyway, much to the boy's embarrassment.

"Ah, you got here, did you?"

Cethen turned and looked up at Morallta, then glanced past her shoulder. There was no sign of Galgar, but a large group of warriors were arguing about fifty yards away. He would have bet good coin that was where the man could be found. Cethen sighed as he realized that he didn't give a faerie's fart for Galgar, his woman, or their fight. All that concerned him was Bryn.

"What's my son's place in all this tomorrow?"

"I'm trying to help that clod sort out his battle lines." Morallta gestured angrily toward the arguing warriors. "We'll need anyone who's got any sense to help start things moving, and all you can do is carp about—"

"That's a change," Cethen cut in. "You're looking for someone with sense, and you sent for me? Maybe you're coming to yours."

"Are you here to help, or to whine about Bryn getting his share of glory in the battle tomorrow? Get your mind straight on what's important."

Cethen's mouth opened, but for a moment he was speechless. Then his anger surged, and he fought the urge to strike out. Were it not for Bryn, he might have. "Dammit, woman, I don't want him *near* the sodding battle. Look at him. He's a child. The boy doesn't even reach your shoulders! Get him out of—"

"He's going to be under my protection, fool! I'm not stupid. He'll be farther up the hill, watching. And if he does ride, it will be right behind me, when it's all over, and we're ridding ourselves of the last of these—these vermin invaders!"

"It's still a battlefield," Cethen cried, and turned to Bryn. "Look, boy, why don't you come with me? You shouldn't be here. I'll take you—"

"You won't take him anywhere," Morallta shouted, and whirled to face Bryn. "You'll stay right there. And you," she turned back to Cethen, her face contorted with rage, "if you so much as try to take the boy, I'll have Galgar take your hide and nail it to the nearest tree. And you," she pointed to Borba, "you'll then be joining my cavalry, or hanging with him on that tree. Do you understand?"

Borba shrugged, his expression indifferent. "I'd guess you don't want any help, then."

Cethen swung back into the saddle, ignoring them both. He turned to Bryn, wondering what to do. He couldn't push the matter, for he had no doubt Morallta would at least try to make good her threat—which wouldn't do the boy a speck of good. There was, perhaps, something he could do…

"Son, stay far back on the hill, as your mother says. If things go wrong for us, ride even farther. See over there, the big tree?" Cethen pointed up the dark hillside, to a tall pine that loomed at the very edge of the woods. "Wait there. I'll find you." Then he remembered other times, and the absolute mayhem of other battles. Nothing, nothing at all that was planned came close to being certain. "But if that's impossible, if there are riders and men running away on every side, then keep on going. And when you come down the other side, look for a blue or a red ribbon tied to a tree. There'll be more than one. If I haven't found you, then follow them and you'll find me." He half turned and spoke derisively, an eye on Morallta as he echoed her words. "Do you understand?"

Bryn's eyes flicked between his mother and father, mirroring his confusion. Morallta, however, chose not say anything further, and the boy nodded his understanding.

"Go with care then, son, and may the gods protect you," Cethen said quietly, and turned the chestnut back the way he had come.

He was silent on the way back. Borba, sensing his mood, kept his mouth shut. In the distance, where the plain ended, a thin scattering of trees shaded the Roman camp. The glitter of a hundred fires glowed like sparks in the gloom. *I've got one son up here*, Cethen told himself bitterly, *and down there is another—and if I know my daughter, she's there too*. He could have wept at the sorrow of it all. The gods, when they played their games, did so with a perverse humour. If only…

Cethen grunted. If! Those damned words of Elena's haunted him: *Ifs are nothing more than wishes; the gods made life an is!* Another thought occurred, and it surprised him that he hadn't pondered on it before: was she down there too? A little while later he shook his head and tried to stop his brain from thinking. This whole thing felt far too familiar.

Chapter XXX

Mons Graupius, A.D. 83

Agricola addressed his men before the battle, as was expected. It was a rousing speech, Marcus heard later from one of the other tribunes. He certainly read it afterward in Rome, scribed in one of Tacitus's interminable ramblings; he also read the scribbling sycophant's version of Galgar's speech, which was a farce, because there was no way he could have heard what the barbarian leader said, if indeed the fellow spoke at all.

As for Agricola's speech, Marcus was a good hundred yards away at the time, and doubted anyone else *really* heard it, word for word, unless they were within twenty-five feet. And for good reason—less than a quarter-mile away, thirty thousand barbarians were working themselves into a frenzy, while on the Roman side the murmur of creaking leather, clinking metal, and subdued voices was a chorus unto itself.

The barbarians started their offensive not long after, while Agricola was extending his front, afraid of being outflanked by sheer numbers. A large force of chariots and horsemen, numbering in the thousands, rushed forward to test and harry the Roman front. Angling in, one after another they hurled their spears and arrows, then slanted off as others took their place.

Agricola responded with his own archers, but as the morning wore on, each side picking at the other without actually closing, casualties remained light. Both armies seemed unwilling to launch an attack, each preferring to taunt the other into committing. Marcus, perched high in his saddle, watched it all from the centre of the auxiliary infantry lines. As his eyes swept the crowded plain and the front ranks of auxiliaries, he could have been in the emperor's box at the Circus.

The governor had positioned himself even further forward, and stood dismounted close by one of the Batavi cohorts. Which Marcus thought was foolish, for Agricola had insisted his staff officers do the same, and stand alongside the troops to maintain their spirit. The order was sheer bravado, an action that could leave the body of the Roman army headless if the infantry buckled. Still, the rank and file seemed to love it.

Marcus saw a staff officer gesture passionately toward the rear, and the general shook his head, his expression one of annoyance. He decided the staffer was urging him once again to either get on his fool horse or bring the legion forward. For the moment neither seemed relevant, though perhaps it was good to have an intact reserve—should the real fight ever get started. Marcus smiled as he watched the barbarians continue to swoop in, hurl their spears, and roll away in a hail of arrows. Unless one side was willing to commit, the battle could last a week.

When the action did finally begin, it was fast. The five veteran infantry cohorts holding the centre of Agricola's line, three Batavi and two Tungri, were ordered forward with the blast of a dozen *cornui* that echoed across the field, and almost as one, each unit's standards signalled the advance. In parade square order, the ranks stepped forward behind a solid wall of shields.

Marcus had seen it before, but only on the huge practice fields or in mock battles between friendly foes. He knew what might happen, but even so, the effect was extraordinary: the shields may well have been a wall of stone. The hundreds and hundreds of chariots and riders that were careening across the plain in no sort of order were pushed brutally back onto their own ranks of screaming, howling warriors. Those who could move tried to fight, only to ram hopelessly against the wall of shields, their hill ponies balking, shying, and dying in their traces. The barbarian cavalry harrying the centre, the few that did not flee, shared the same fate under a hail of iron-tipped *pili*.

The forward ranks of Galgar's infantry, the great horde of warriors that filled the plain and covered the lower slope of the hillside, rushed forward to engage the auxiliary cohorts. Any chariots or horsemen left behind were crushed between. Marcus shook his head as the barbarian battle line became a confused, vicious mass of horses, carts, and men.

Galgar's front had been packed with his best warriors, men armed with long, well-edged swords, heavy axes, and shields. The weapons crashed down on the Roman shields, slashing and hacking, each man trying to carve an opening in the unwavering wall. The auxiliary took the blows and lashed back, stabbing and thrusting with short, deadly swords honed to an arrow-like sharpness. The smaller barbarian shields bent under those of Rome as the heavy, raised metal bosses thrust viciously forward, taking a man's teeth and crushing his face.

As Agricola's infantry pushed steadily forward, Marcus found himself scanning the barbarian faces, half expecting to find one he recognized. But there were tens of thousands there, and to find one among so many was laughable. Besides, most of the warriors he'd known were mounted. As the thought occurred, he found himself chuckling: the men he knew were better trained, with more sense than to remain trapped between two closing lines. Yet despite the logic, whenever he saw a man still sitting a horse, he found himself looking for Cethen's face or, if there was a flash of red hair, perhaps Borba—or even the woman Morallta.

The advance had not been long begun when Marcus saw it falling victim to its success. The five cohorts, over two thousand soldiers, plowed into the great mass of Galgar's warriors like a giant fist, the barbarians piling up in front as they fell, unable to give way. Men, horses, even chariots were carried along as if on a bow wave, only to be dashed down and thrown up in the wake of the advancing Roman line: the dead, the wounded, even the dazed and unharmed. The massive wedge of infantry was outpacing the other cohorts, fast becoming threatened with envelopment.

Galgar seemed to have seen it, along with the gods knew how many of his reserve, who so far had remained idle, farther up the hill. Marcus watched in awe as they began edging down onto the plain: a seemingly endless, colourful mass of warriors, most pouring down on the Roman left, intent on flanking Agricola's line. Rhun would be there trying to stem the horde, Marcus knew, as were at least four other regiments of cavalry.

A flurry of movement erupted where he'd last seen Agricola, and for a moment Marcus wondered if he'd fallen. But no, several horses had been brought in, and he saw the governor, now mounted, scanning the battle from his saddle. He was surprised to see his father there, right alongside, and he smiled; he should have known! Then he saw the signals hoisted, and a few moments later a pair of dispatch riders also hared off toward the threatened flank, circling behind those units still holding the line. Agricola was taking no chances on his messages.

Four regiments of the cavalry had been ordered forward, and so close were the forward ranks of Galgar's horde, there was barely space to achieve a full gallop. He was too far away to tell which units had gone, but Marcus knew Rhun's had been the one posted farthest out on the flank. That one had the most chance to gain its legs, and it smashed hard into the barbarian right, which turned in panic and ran. Moments later, a thousand more took flight as the other regiments struck, running to the trees and fleeing farther up the hill. In the centre of the plain, however, the core of the barbarian army remained intact.

Marcus found himself closer to Agricola and his staff as the press of bodies moved with the shifting lines. Another dispatch rider, already sitting his horse, leaned over to grasp a message. Marcus heard the verbal confirmation, which would certainly be paraphrased as it was passed on: "Tell the buggers not to stop. Up the hill, then down on the bastards' backs."

The command proved redundant. Even as the man lashed his horse toward the distant flank, all four regiments broke through Galgar's scattered right wing and surged up the side of the hill as a single force. Marcus drew in his breath, almost afraid to watch as horses and riders flowed up the steep slope like a flooding river. His mouth fell open in awe; it was a sight he knew he'd never see again. The lead squadrons wheeled the moment they broke free and gained the advantage; more than fifteen hundred troopers, swinging around like a great, breaking wave and falling on more than ten times their number.

As the Roman cavalry plunged down on the rear of Galgar's army, the tribesmen were hardly aware of the new threat. The carnage was terrible. Marcus, rooted to his saddle as if glued, simply watched. It was over, he knew that; yet far, far more of the enemy remained alive on the slope than Agricola had men.

Most kept fighting, even as others realized what had happened and ran. In the centre of the plain Agricola's troops began taking captives; yet, in the next moment, the same prisoners were slaughtered as the troops, in turn, found themselves surrounded and attacked. The Batavi and Tungri auxiliaries that had started it finally halted the advance at the base of the hill. All cohorts stood stolidly in ranks as the remnants of Galgar's people, those few who had not abandoned the field, continued to throw themselves blindly against the Roman shields. It was a final, futile, frustrating way to die.

Marcus watched, filled with a strange mixture of exultation and sadness, then he turned and looked over his shoulder. His father's makeshift legion stood in full battle order, perhaps a quarter-mile away. Its three standards fluttered bravely in a brisk breeze, and the glittering ranks stood steady, ready—and untouched. He shook his head in disbelief, then kneed his horse forward. His father was still up there with Agricola. He would, no doubt, expect some form of congratulation.

Chapter XXXI

Mons Graupius, A.D. 83

Cethen didn't bother to ask Borba how many of their people remained after the foolish back-and-forth in front of the Roman infantry, charging in and tossing spears at a solid wall of shields. All of them were quick to note that Morallta's people had avoided the same tasking. He'd no idea where the woman was, but he guessed it would be with Galgar, likely arguing.

A loose sort of organization had been established at first light, just as he thought it would. The stronger, better-armed warriors and their chieftains, by their own insistence and persistence, had made sure they made up the vanguard. The trouble was, that was about the end of it, though a good part of Galgar's cavalry *had* been posted on either flank; whether by good planning or lack of space, Cethen had no idea. And when he said as much to Borba, who smiled, he suggested the words might have been spoken by Elena herself. Most of Galgar's riders had the same lack of discipline shown by Venutius's, before the old king began adopting some of Rome's training methods. It was too bad the old bugger had died. He would have made better use of what he had.

Cethen and Borba had led their small force off the field as soon as the Roman infantry began its advance. It was readily apparent that to remain would see them caught between a hammer and an anvil. Falling into column, they rode partway up the slope on Galgar's flank, where they decided to wait for new orders, which seemed unlikely to arrive. C̶ ̶ ̶ ̶ ̶ along the two ranks, Cethen was gratified to see that nearly all had made it back. But when he turned to look down at the battlefield, he was horrified to find the Romans carving their way through Galgar's strongest warriors as if they were of no consequence.

Not long after, a roar echoed down the hill, along with the pounding of running feet. Hundreds upon hundreds of warriors, some wielding axes, some swords, ran past on either side. He glanced over one shoulder and took heart. Thousands of Galgar's men were on the move, pouring down the slopes, working their way past the jam of their own men caught up in front of the Roman infantry. Cethen's chest filled with pride and hope as he saw the threat to the Roman flanks.

Then their cavalry attacked.

"They're not going to stop," Borba muttered as the first of the Roman auxiliary riders crashed into the forefront of Galgar's horde.

"I don't know ..." Cethen murmured moments later, unwilling to concede anything. Both men watched anxiously as the fighting became general. Then the Roman cavalry, following up its momentum far out on the left flank, broke through the weaker resistance there, and fell hard on the rush of tribesmen still pouring down from the higher slopes. Galgar's other warriors on the flank, now trapped farther down the hillside, panicked and began to run. Cethen slumped back in the saddle, glanced at Borba, and cursed.

"You know," the twin said dryly, reining his horse toward the nearest trees, "They've got far more horses than we've got."

"Where are you going?" Cethen shouted in alarm.

"I think it's time we went home, dammit!" Borba cried, his voice for the first time revealing his agitation.

"I'm for that." Ligan whipped his horse alongside in time to hear the words. His shield was gone, and his hand clutched his sword arm; blood seeped through his fingers. He glared at Cethen's hesitation. "I led you off a lost battlefield once to save your hide. I'll not do it again."

"No, I'm with you, but that way." He pointed to the top of the hill, and the tall pine tree that stood out from the others. "I've got to get up there. Bryn. He—"

"I don't give pig shit which way we go, just as long as we go," Ligan shouted as the others began to mill about in alarm. Wincing in pain, he turned his horse and kicked it forward. Cethen and Borba fell in behind. Still in column, the rest of the troop quickly followed.

There was no sign of Bryn by the tree. Cursing Morallta for not leaving the boy there as he'd wanted, Cethen had the rest of the troop halt, and frantically began collecting the red and blue ribbons that most still wore. As he finished, he glanced down the hill and was shocked to see the Roman cavalry, nearly all of it, galloping their way as if intent on pursuit. There were hundreds, perhaps thousands, thundering up the hillside along the same path they had just taken. Why, with all of Galgar's people filling the damned hill, were they pursuing his paltry column of riders?

Cethen could have wept at the idiocy of it, only there was no time. Cursing the gods, he ordered them all to follow him into the trees. As the last man galloped past the pine, he might have glanced backward and seen the Roman cavalry wheel and charge back down the hill.

Elena, with Coira, watched the battle from the safety of the legion's massed ranks. Even though mounted, she'd found the action difficult to follow, for the first of the fighting had taken place on the plain, hardly visible on the far side of the auxiliary infantry lines. She'd seen the final charge by the cavalry regiments clearly, though, for it took place on the slope of the hill. Both women had watched in silence as the great mass of horses and men swept up the steep incline, then poured back down again, scattering most of what remained intact of Galgar's army.

"We don't seem to have lost many," Elena said finally, her mouth dry, as the field began to clear and the cavalry resumed its station. Her eyes had followed only the regiment farthest to the left, where she knew Rhun to be. It was the one that rode farthest up the long slope and, when the regiments wheeled for the second attack, led the charge that fell on the rear of Galgar's struggling army.

"Wasn't it something?" Coira breathed, her cheeks flushed. "Did you ever see the like? So many. The way they went in, all together. It was l¹· ttering rabbits. Then when they—"

here. Sextus is sending riders." Elena, for the moment er, pointed to two troopers who had broken away, racing to where Agricola sat his horse amidst a flurry of dispatch riders, staff officers, and aides. She glimpsed Gaius's crested helmet there, which meant the bugger had spent the entire battle alongside the governor, just as she knew he would.

"They're going for further orders," Coira said, then, as if echoing her mother's thoughts, added, "Gaius hasn't returned, which just leaves Crispus. There's no better time to ask his leave to go see if Rhun is alright. If we don't go now, it'll all be over."

Elena turned and found the legion's primus, standing within a similar gaggle of headquarters staff, all of them congratulating each other. Waiting until it was all over might not be a bad idea. Her daughter was far too impetuous. Nonetheless, she wanted to make certain Rhun was unhurt and, though she couldn't fathom the reason, there was that old, familiar urge to play some part in it all, rather than simply watch.

"Just give it a moment, until Sextus's riders are out of sight," she found herself saying, then added as an afterthought, "And I'll do the talking. Among a few other things, Crispus thinks I'm quite level-headed."

When a victory skin of wine appeared and the officers began tossing back mouthfuls, Elena and Coira approached. After congratulating Crispus and at least a dozen other officers, all in high spirits, she pointed to where Rhun's regiment stood calmly in rank, as if on parade. "I don't think the legate would mind us joining my son for awhile," she said, careful of her phrasing.

His reply, a definite affirmative by anyone's standard, was "Be careful, then," before he turned back to the seemingly more important business at hand.

A small clod of dirt, thrown up by skittish hooves, pinged off Rhun's helmet, and he turned in surprise as two riders reined in alongside. He groaned when he saw who they were. "What are you doing here? We'll be off again soon."

"So what are you doing sitting on your rear, then?" Coira snapped at her brother. "Waiting for help? Well, you've got it."

"We both saw it all. It was quite something," Elena said quickly, and threw her daughter a warning look. "Your sister would much rather have been part of it than sit on her bum. We came to make sure you were alright."

Rhun glanced toward Sextus, but his eyes were assessing the hill, where the infantry fought its way through the last of any real resistance. The praefectus was clearly occupied, probably deciding where best to begin, once given permission. "Well, I'm doing fine, thank you, and I'm happy, very happy, to see you are too." Rhun waved toward the glittering line of legion cohorts. "Now get back where you should be, or Gaius will have your skin flayed. Not to mention mine."

"Actually, we were given permission to join you, now the fighting is mostly over," Elena said.

Rhun eyed her uncertainly, then his gaze fell to the women's armour. Each wore a tunic of mail that covered the upper body, and both were helmeted and fully equipped. "For the time being, then," he sighed, then, leaning forward in the saddle, he asked his mother and sister what they'd been able to see.

Marcus carried the order, when it came; he'd plainly haggled his way into delivering it. After a surprised glance at the two women, he passed the order verbally: gain the hilltops and clear the trees of enemy; fall back should resistance prove heavy and await reinforcement; recall will be one hour before dusk.

Sextus chose to deploy his men in three ranks, to provide depth. The regiment rode up the slope at a steady trot, and at the edge of the forest formed line by squadron. Each troop then advanced into the wood under the command of its decurio, pursuing the elusive crackle of breaking undergrowth and the endless patter of running feet. The fighting was sporadic, and not heavy when it did come, for Galgar's people were on the run.

Rhun, as he often did, attached himself to Cian's squadron. He'd failed miserably in his last attempt at ordering his mother back to where, as he put it, she belonged—words that only served to antagonize. He briefly pondered riding over to Sextus, now somewhere off to his left, but decided that would only aggravate matters. Both women would say they had permission anyway, which, in all fairness, they apparently did.

Rhun knew that would not be a lie, but he did wonder what, exactly, his mother had been told.

Marcus also appealed to the women, but quickly gave up after a withering suggestion from Coira about what he might do with his sword. Cian, who knew Elena all too well, simply raised his eyebrows, and when she grinned and shook her head, said no more. She and Coira did, however, fall back to the rear rank, where they remained under Luga's wing. Marcus, telling Rhun he had nothing better to do, simply fell in alongside Cian. All three rode in the centre of the front rank.

Once they'd crested the hill, the forest broadened and grew denser. There was soon little to be seen of Galgar's people, who had melted into the trees. Even so, Sextus ordered the regiment to continue in a broad, sweeping line.

Halfway down the reverse slope Cian's troop, covering the right flank, edged up against the lip of a narrow ravine. He raised one hand and bellowed the order to halt. Rhun moved up alongside, eyebrows raised in query. Cian stared back with a baffled look then, with a quick shrug, he urged his horse forward and reined in alongside a dying, leafless birch tree. Leaning from the saddle, he carefully removed a red ribbon draped loose across the lower branches.

They crossed the top of yet another rise, where a break in the dense forest revealed a long, narrow valley; the slopes were treed in a manner that reminded Cethen of Brigantia. A stream wandered down the centre and, just as at home, the banks had been cleared back, opening up the rich bottomland to crops. It seemed a fitting place to call a halt, and wait to see if Bryn might find the ribbons and catch up with them. The last of Galgar's fleeing warriors had been seen a good half-hour ago, and besides, there was hardly a ribbon remaining among them.

"I saw a stream over to the right," Cethen said as the troop made its way down the twisted slope, lost from sight in the shadow of thick-trunked trees still heavy with bright autumn foliage. The horses moved silently, hooves muffled by a thick carpet of leaf mulch. "I'll wait there, see if the boy follows. The rest of you go on—and if you're wise, you'll keep going. Ligan, how's the arm?"

"No worse than the spear I took in Cumbria." Ligan grimaced as his horse bunched its hind legs and leapt a fallen log. "Which, as I recall, hurt so damned bad I could have cheerfully died."

"We'll stop and fix it up when we get to that stream," Borba said. "Ficra can do it."

"And I wouldn't stop again until nightfall, if I were you," Cethen suggested, reinforcing his first order. "I'd put as much distance from the Romans as I could. The way I figure," he pointed vaguely to the treetops off to his right, "the sun was over there somewhere, last time I saw it. Which means that valley points straight south. I'd follow it, as far and as quick as I could."

"We'll see," Borba muttered.

The stream Cethen had seen came bubbling down through a small glade, lush with tall, untrodden grass and rich with wildflowers. *At any other time...* Cethen thought wistfully.

Ficra and one of the other riders followed a game trail that led back into the trees, returning to tell them it offered a quick, safe path of escape over the ridge that formed the east rim of the valley. Everyone dismounted and waited while Ficra looked after Ligan's arm, despite Cethen's insistence that they ride on. Ligan's face was pale and pinched from pain and blood loss, but he sat, uncomplaining, as she washed the wound and began her stitching.

"I'll wait with you," Borba murmured, and nodded to Ficra's patient. "Ligan, press on with the rest of them. We'll catch up tomorrow." He looked at Cethen and raised his eyebrows. "You will leave tomorrow, if the boy doesn't show?"

"I'll stay too," Ficra muttered without taking her eyes off her stitching. Several other voices echoed the words, but Cethen didn't answer.

Borba sighed and continued. "There's no point looking for the lad after that, Cethen. The hills are crawling with Romans. They'll be taking slaves or just killing—and if they catch you, I'd wager on the killing. If Bryn's been taken, we'll get him back one day. If he hasn't, well—" He held both hands out, palms open, and shrugged. "Then there's no point in looking anyway."

"How can you say we'll get him back?" Cethen growled. "I lost my wife to the bastards, my two boys and my daughter. And you say we'll get him back later! You're talking with the faerie."

"We're going south, Cethen. Criff could help," Borba suggested, but his face didn't reflect much hope.

"Let's see if the boy shows," Cethen muttered, and turned to Ficra. "You finished yet?"

In the end perhaps two dozen remained, and the others, about three times that number, rode off down the valley, carefully hugging the shelter of the trees. Those who remained left their horses saddled, but eased the cinches, then most of them settled down in the long grass to wait. Some found food in their saddle packs, and a couple more followed the small stream and found some trout they were able to tickle out from under the bank. An argument quickly broke out as to whether or not they should light a fire to cook them, and it all took on a comfortable familiarity. Cethen was called on for a decision and he was about tell the fishers not to be so stupid when the question became moot. One of the men posted as watch at the end of the glade called out that riders were coming.

The first thing Cethen noticed was that Morallta did not have Bryn with her. That could mean only one thing, and his anger flared even before she reined in. The ragged column that trailed behind bunched up, but when it was apparent that nothing more violent than another argument was in store, they rode forward and wearily dismounted. Many promptly flopped onto the ground in exhaustion, but most simply leaned against their saddles and stood watching and waiting.

Cethen assessed their numbers. Morallta had lost most of her command and, unlike his own people, a good many of those who survived carried wounds. Even so, they outnumbered his own people by... "How many you figure there are?" he asked Borba. "Twice our number?"

"Close enough, but they're badly hurt. I'd not push the bitch, though. She looks ready to chew your mail."

Cethen had to agree, but her anger was nothing compared to his own. Why hadn't the woman done as he'd said? Where was the boy? This was all far, far too familiar. He was about to demand what had happened to his son when *she* asked, "Where's Bryn?"

"You ask me?" Cethen shouted. "You had the care of the boy! I told you he had no business on the field. When did you last see him?"

"When I sent him up to the tree *you* told him to go to!"

"You *sent* him? A boy wandering alone on the battlefield? When? After the Romans had broken through? After it was all over?"

"I didn't send him there alone. I'm not a fool," Morallta whirled in the saddle. "Kemoc! Where is that idiot Kemoc?"

It seemed no one knew where Kemoc was; he hadn't been seen since Galgar's line broke, and the Roman cavalry had smashed the attempt to outflank their army. In fact, nobody had seen Kemoc since Morallta had sent him off the field with Bryn. Which meant…

"Your pigheadedness, your stupid fucking pride, has got the boy killed!" Cethen cried, his gut a sudden empty void as he thrust his face into hers. "What sort of a mother are you? You don't deserve to—"

"Enough!" Morallta screamed, spittle spraying Cethen's face. "Shut your rotten gob or I'll shut it for you. Permanently!"

"Try, woman, try," he shouted, and stepped back, one hand reaching for his sword, which was not there. It was slung from his saddle.

Morallta's people began to stir, climbing to their feet and fidgeting with their weapons. Behind him, Cethen sensed his own people doing the same, and he called for caution. "This is between me and her. Personal. There's no need."

"You're damned right it's personal," Morallta snarled, and jerked her sword free of the saddle. She didn't bother with the shield.

As if by magic, Cethen found his own sword in his hand, probably put there by Borba—but maybe not, for it was Ficra who hissed in his ear, "Kill the bitch."

"There's more riders coming," someone yelled, and everyone began moving, ignoring the fight before it had even begun.

Cinches were tightened and tired men and women swung into their saddles, a seemingly confused mass of milling horses and riders that filled the small meadow. Cethen and Morallta slowly eased away from each other, swords angled toward the ground. When a safe distance had grown between them, both looked to the head of the valley.

Cethen cursed. Roman cavalry, about two squadrons, had emerged from the cover of the trees. The woman must have been followed, the careless bitch! And there was no way, he muttered to himself, no way they could fight off the Romans, not in their condition. Morallta's force combined with his gave them perhaps a slight edge in numbers, but in no manner could they possibly triumph. At best, it would be a bloody, bloody standoff.

The two Roman troops shifted smartly into four ranks then halted, their decurios plainly trying to figure out what, exactly, they had come upon.

"This," Morallta breathed, her mouth twisting into a smile, "this has been planned by the gods."

"What?" Cethen turned in shock. Morallta's features were almost sublime. Her eyes, which had looked tired only moments ago when she'd ridden in, were wide and glittering. Her chest heaved with excitement, and her breathing…"No!" Cethen cried. "No, no, no! They're better trained, better mounted, and in better condition. We've no choice but to run."

"You've already run once today," Morallta sneered.

"You weren't far behind," Cethen cried.

"But we fought before we fled."

"And damned little good it did you!"

"Er, the Romans…they're moving forward, you two," Borba interrupted, edging his horse between them. "We should really make up our—"

"We have," Morallta snapped, and swung into her saddle. "We're going to make them wish they'd never come this far. Dermat."

Cethen turned in shock, surprised to see Dermat pulling himself slowly into the saddle at the rear of Morallta's troop. His face was pale and his tunic bloodstained high on the shoulder, just above the area his shield might have covered. He managed a nod and one of his thin, dour smiles. The man was at the end of his leash, Cethen realized, as were at least a dozen others. The poor sod couldn't even resist Morallta, let alone a squadron of Roman horse…

"We'll go in five ranks, not four," Morallta called out, then turned to Cethen. "That's if you can coax any of your people to fight."

Cethen looked up at Borba, who looked back, his face unreadable. It was Ficra who decided, speaking loud enough so that Morallta could hear. "We can't outrun them. Maybe we'll have the joy of seeing them kill the bitch." Then, in a more practical tone, she said, "Personally, if I get through on the first charge, I'm buggering off up the slope and disappearing into the trees. I'd advise anyone else to do the same."

"I'll be right with you, lass," Cethen murmured and turned to his horse as the others, already mounted, began forming line. He grasped the pommel to pull himself upward, but as he leapt forward to swing his leg over the saddle, the fool thing slid sideways, and he found himself falling under the horse's belly. He climbed to his feet cursing, pushed the damned thing back up, and quickly tightened the cinch. A moment later he was in the saddle, turning the animal's head toward Morallta and the troop.

The woman had started without him and the five ranks, in fairly decent order, were moving toward the Roman cavalry at a good, stiff trot. Cursing, he slapped Gadearg's rump, sending the animal into a canter. There was still plenty of time. The Romans were a good way off, their line tight, their decurios still getting their troopers in order, and…

Cethen blinked, unable to believe his eyes. Three—no, four, now five of the lead riders had removed their helmets and slung them on their saddles. One had a blonde shock of hair, and another—

It was the ribbons, it had to be. They'd brought Morallta down on their trail, and now they'd brought…

He dug both heels frantically into the chestnut's belly, forcing the animal into gallop. "Borba, Ficra, stop! Stop her. Stop!" Kicking, lashing, and almost sobbing his frustration, Cethen beat the horse forward as hard as he could.

Borba turned to see what sort of trouble he was in, then Ficra turned too, and finally, in the front rank, Morallta.

"Stop. It's Elena. My wife," Cethen screamed. "Borba, stop her. There's my daughter. My son. Stop the stupid bitch!"

Morallta's lips curled in a cold smile, and she dug her heels in, hard. Calling loudly for the others to follow, her spear raised high and ready, she pushed her horse to a fast gallop. Behind, her own people picked up the pace and followed. Borba looked puzzled for a moment then, as the words seemed to register, he did the same.

Branaught's troop had been to the left of Cian when they found the first of the ribbons. Rhun told his old friend to close off the gap he'd leave, and send word to Sextus that he and Cian had picked up the fresh trail of a party of Galgar's warriors. Branaught nodded, then stared hard at the number of hoofprints that had churned the dirt. Shaking his head reprovingly, he sent only one of his men to Sextus, with orders to tell him that both troops of cavalry were off following the enemy spoor.

Only one person could have set such a trail, Rhun realized, and it could only have been left for Cian and him. The ribbons had been set twice before, and if he didn't follow them a third time, he would regret it for the rest of his life. More so as he recalled Venutius's dying flight, for his da might be hurt: there were traces of blood on the ground. He had no other choice but to follow. Cian and Coira agreed, but all three saw doubt written on Elena's face.

"I'll provide an escort back," Rhun offered. "Or if you wish, you can join up with Sextus."

Elena had paled, lowered her head, and closed her eyes, her knuckles whitening as they gripped the pommel; Rhun thought she was going to faint. He grasped her arm to steady her, but she simply turned to face him, shaking her head slowly. "I'm fine, Rhun, fine," she murmured, and removed his hand. "It's the damned gods, you know. They're playing their games again, I can feel it." She wiped a hand across her forehead and sighed as if in resignation. "The trouble is, they never leave you with a choice." She looked at him, her smile bitter. "You always think you have a choice, you know, but you never do. Not really."

"Mother, if—"

"No, no," Elena said, and flicked her reins. "As I said ... Let's go find him."

The blue and red ribbons were hardly needed, except to confirm that they chased the same quarry. At least a hundred hoofprints had already churned the earth they rode over, leaving an easy trail. And if that wasn't enough, fresh lumps of dung offered further proof. The fact that some of it still steamed as the ground cooled, while other piles did not, told Rhun that not one, but two groups of riders had passed. More than one animal was lame, and the occasional spatter of blood spoke of either men or horses badly hurt—or, most likely, both.

The scout brought word back just before they came upon a long valley that stretched to the south: a large party of barbarian cavalry, grouped together on the valley floor, seemingly resting…a small stream, off to the right…the valley itself could be reached unseen.

Rhun had the two squadrons deploy as soon as they emerged from the trees, two ranks for each squadron, Cian's taking the lead with himself, Elena, and Coira in front, alongside his father's brother. And Marcus, too—it wouldn't hurt if they saw him, as well. The more of them his da's people recognized, the better. They took their helmets off as soon as they began walking their horses forward, making themselves even easier to recognize.

His father's people, understandably, were running around like startled rabbits. That would change, as soon as—Rhun frowned as the riders formed up in five ranks about the same as his own, fourteen or fifteen across. It was neatly done, considering they were tired, beaten, barbarian cavalry. That they would form ranks was to be expected, he supposed when he thought on it. They had to be sure too. But his father would settle that. The bitch had lied about his death. He'd never really believed the woman, but the ribbons had come as a relief. His eyes searched for Cethen. He should be somewhere in front…

Rhun almost reined in when he saw the entire formation break into a trot, but his training held, and kept them all moving forward at a walk. Even so, he called out a warning, for he was still unable to see his da.

"Cethen's not there," Cian muttered.

"I don't see him either," Coira said, and reached for her helmet.

"I don't think he is there," Rhun muttered, then it struck him as if he'd been bludgeoned by an axe: the bitch had tricked him! She'd laid the ribbons, drawn them all in—"Put your helmets on," Rhun cried, fumbling with his own. He was dimly aware the enemy had broken into a gallop, and were racing forward, spears ready. "Coira, Mother, fall back."

"Ready the charge," Cian roared somewhere off to his left; then, "Charge!"

Rhun slammed the helmet onto his head and glanced sideways. Cian hadn't bothered, choosing instead to toss his headgear to one side. His uncle's horse had already leapt to a gallop, and his own, its blood up, followed with no urging. He eased his shield partway across his chest and took a firmer grip on his spear.

Just as he'd thought, the woman was there, her dark copper hair flowing from under her helmet, her mouth open in an unheard scream, and her horse one stride ahead of any other. He wondered, as the gap closed between them, if she herself had been the cause of his father's death.

Morallta was edging her horse over, Rhun realized, as if trying to ensure that their paths met. Which was fine by him, he thought grimly, and edged his own mount over as well, but the horse running alongside wouldn't move. He turned to yell the order to fall back, and realized with a shock that it was his mother. She'd seen the woman too, and her face was just as intent: jaw set, eyes flashing, ears firmly closed to reason, and no helmet! Rhun cursed. He didn't dare push her further; it could be the death of her. Cursing again, he turned his eyes forward bare moments before the two sides crashed together.

The first horse slammed against Rhun's, a small animal that lost its footing; he deflected the man's spear as rider and horse tumbled away. The second rider appeared from nowhere; there was no doubt of his target as he raised a long iron sword. Rhun lunged forward and buried his spear in the man's teeth, but the weapon rammed right through the skull, and wrenched savagely from his grip. Fumbling for his sword, he raced past the third man, flinching from the blow that never came. Then it was on to the fourth, his sword up just in time to parry a vicious swing that left no time to retaliate. Which left only the fifth horse and its rider, which he crashed into head on. The horses squealed in terror and stumbled, his own tumbling forward on buckled legs. Both riders were tossed from the saddle, each rolling helplessly across the spongy carpet of grass.

Rhun lay breathless for a moment as the hooves of a dozen horses thundered past on either side. The body of the other rider lay close by. It stirred and slowly rolled over. Forcing himself to move, Rhun lifted himself on one elbow and looked about in search of his sword. It was several yards away, well out of reach. Grunting with the effort, he stumbled frantically to his feet, just as the other man pushed himself onto one knee. Both stopped in their tracks, wavering unsteadily as they stared at each other in disbelief.

His da broke the silence. "Help me up, son. We've got to stop this shit."

Cethen staggered to his feet, blinking to clear his eyes. Even though Rhun clutched his arm, a Roman trooper charged out of nowhere and he instinctively raised the other arm in defense. The rider reined in at the last moment, yanking savagely on the reins, his horse pawing the ground barely one pace from Cethen's feet. He found himself staring into Cian's face, and for once it was grim.

"What the fuck is going on?" his brother demanded, turning his head toward the havoc behind him. Those auxiliaries who, like Rhun, had fought their way through were wheeling their horses and charging back into the confusion.

"Morallta!" Cethen shouted as he looked about for his horse; the fool animal stood with its head down picking at the grass, a good fifty yards away. "At first we didn't know it was you. Then the bitch did, and she charged anyway. Cian, we've got to ... "

He was talking to himself. His brother had ridden off, head held high as if looking for someone. Cethen swore as he bent down to retrieve his sword and shield from the grass.

"Up here."

He turned and found Rhun towering above him, again mounted, a sword in one hand and the other extended. Cethen passed up his shield first and, on the second attempt, swung up behind with a loud grunt. As he settled behind the saddle and adjusted the shield, he looked over his son's shoulder in search of his daughter and his wife. A horn sounded nearby, three short blasts, then three more, but it hardly registered. Rhun moved his horse into the fray at a slow walk. The horn sounded again, and Cethen saw Cian alongside the man who blew it.

Some of the Romans, those who could, appeared to be disengaging and drifting off to one side.

Bodies seemed to be strewn everywhere, both wounded and dead, and most were not wearing Roman uniforms. A horse came rushing in, then quickly pulled back. He saw Borba. The twin's eyes showed his understanding, and he edged his horse over so that it walked alongside. The horn sounded again, more insistent.

"There—over there," Cethen cried out to Rhun. A moment later, as it all grew more clear, he cursed savagely and slid from the saddle.

Three or four small fights still raged, all on foot, for the Roman troopers who still sat their horses had ridden off to one side and formed once more into even ranks, with swords or spears raised at the ready. There was little enthusiasm left in his or Morallta's people to challenge them. Cethen limped forward, his rage building with every step. "Stop. Stop it, you idiots, stop," he screamed, and his son did too. One by one the fights finished or broke off, until only one remained. Cethen rushed forward, his mouth twisted in anger, then stopped short.

Neither woman looked; neither dared.

Morallta, cold eyes flashing, a twisted smile on her lips, circled Coira, taunting with her sword. His daughter, not knowing better, simply turned in place to face her enemy, rather than circling in turn. In doing so, Cethen knew, the girl was unable to guide events, only follow them. He remembered Morallta's own words from better times: *act, always act, or you can only react!*

His daughter did have skill with a weapon, though, Cethen conceded. As a brief opening appeared in her guard, Morallta lunged like a snake. His heart jumped, but Coira caught the blade high on her shield and swung her own weapon in a tight arc that missed Morallta's legs only because her shield, more by luck than skill, had drooped. Perhaps Coira had planned it that way, but he was damned if he would stand by and find out. His heart couldn't take it.

"It's my fight, not yours," Cethen cried, and shoved his daughter roughly to one side with his shoulder. Morallta instantly lunged, but he deftly turned the blade away from his daughter and stepped in between.

Coira would have darted back but Rhun, one step behind, grabbed his sister and hauled her, kicking and screeching, to one side. Cethen backed away, raised his shield, and hefted his weapon.

"You can stop it now," he muttered, then his eye caught sight of a body sprawled on the ground behind Morallta. It lay on its side with its back toward him, impaled by a spear—a spear with a bright pennant that Cethen recognized as Morallta's. The point had gone clear through and out by the shoulder blade, where it was held fast under the mail armour: a small, obscene hump, as if it had grown there. The long, honey-blond hair left no doubt of who it was.

Cethen screamed, a strangled cry that echoed across the meadow. He lunged forward, wildly swinging his sword again and again, with all the strength of his anger. Morallta retreated a step at a time, warding off each blow as it hammered down on her shield. When he finally spent his rage and stood gasping for breath, she pulled herself erect and began fighting back.

The Roman troopers had all fallen back in answer to a final blast of the horn. Morallta's and Cethen's people slowly began edging forward, forming a large, loose, silent circle within which the two fought. Marcus staggered forward from nowhere, his head streaming blood from a gash over one eye. He pushed his way unsteadily toward Rhun, who stood with his arms clasped tight about his sister, but she no longer struggled.

"Put a stop to this. At once!" Marcus shouted, and pointed to the auxiliary troopers waiting on their horses. "Order them to stop it."

"Then what?" Rhun said without turning his eyes from the fight. "Fifty more people die? And my father lives in shame for the rest of his life? At this moment I doubt he cares much about the outcome, anyway." He nodded to where Elena lay, hidden now, on the far side of the circle; then he began edging in that direction, dragging his sister with him.

Iron clashed. Morallta started forward, her features taut, yet icily calm. It was Cethen who now retreated, stepping backward as the blows fell on his shield, as fast as his tired arm could move it. He could see in her eyes, cold and focused, that she was intent on finishing it. Her sword swung upward and he lifted his shield, but she twisted and arced it down, aiming for his legs. Glimpsing the barest hint of her intention in her eyes, Cethen lowered his shield, but not quite fast enough. The sword caught the lower rim, which took most of the blow, but it slid off, biting into his good leg.

With a sick feeling of despair, Cethen fell back on one knee, but the old wound twisted and the joint buckled. His sword hand struck the ground as he steadied himself, and the weapon slipped from his grip. A groan rose from those watching, and he swore. His mouth went dry as, for the first time, he sensed failure. Yet he wasn't afraid so much as angry—angry that the woman would triumph, that she would be gloating when he was dead, that she—no, he was pissed—totally, thoroughly pissed, and boiling with a wrath that threatened to burst his chest.

The blows had eased. He risked a glance over the rim of his shield. Morallta had cast her own aside. Gripping her sword with both hands, she was moving forward, a hard smile of triumph on her lips. Cethen fumbled for his own sword and found the hilt, and another groan filled his ears. He could tell from the feel he'd grasped the damned thing backward. The weapon lay in his hand like a long, useless dagger.

He swore at the gods and shoved the point in the dirt, trying to turn the grip. As it dug in, he tried one last time to gain his feet, using the sword as a brace. But he lurched forward as the blows again rained down on his shield, with far more force. From the corner of his eye, as he knelt under its battered cover, he saw her lips counting each strike. One, two, three, four, and ...

Cethen sensed more than saw the fifth blow arc out and sideways, intended for his thigh. In a final, desperate move, he slammed the shield against the ground, leaving his head briefly exposed. As the blow crashed against the shield his eyes slid downward to see Morallta's foot, firmly planted in the grass. Jerking the blade free of the dirt, he stabbed down, hard. Then, with a strangled cry, he lurched forward over the hilt. The point dug in, stopped for one terrible heartbeat, then slid through to the sod below.

Morallta screeched and pulled back, falling away as her foot was impaled. Cethen, with a hideous grin of exhaustion, forced the sword deeper, then downward, until the blade lay even with the grass. The chipped edge sliced through the foot, splitting it from ankle to toes.

Morallta scrambled away, tried to stand, and fell sideways. Her lips peeled back in a rictus of hate as she stumbled to her knees. Cethen stumbled forward, determined to lose no advantage. And the woman— give her what was her due, she tried. Her sword swung in another low arc that Cethen took on his shield. Then he lunged forward and buried the tip of his blade in the side of Morallta's neck.

Then, without a second glance, he turned away.

No one tried to stop him as he stumbled toward Elena, his mind numb. Rhun and Coira were there ahead of him, kneeling beside her, Coira with one hand resting on his wife's forehead.

Behind him, as if through a fog, he heard Cian shouting for order. It hardly seemed necessary. Nobody had any fight in them, except maybe the Romans, and there was no point in picking at their arses, even if Cian was in charge. Cethen shook his head. His mind was wandering useless paths. There was his wife, after all these years, and just when he could finally speak to her again, she—

"Be careful, Da. The spear," Coira muttered as he stepped over Elena's legs.

An empty, icy void had already grasped his gut, even before he turned to see her face. The shaft of the spear held his eye, and he followed it up to where it had entered, just under the bone that topped her shoulder. His gaze shifted, finally, to her face, and he was startled to see her staring back, with those soft, familiar, hazel-green eyes that had haunted him for the past...

"Touch that spear, you daft bugger," Elena murmured weakly, "and I'll have your balls."

There was no choice in the matter, of course, there never was. Rhun would send for help, Gaius's people would come, and events would then follow their natural course. Which was just as well, Elena supposed. But when she'd seen Cethen kneeling over her, blubbering like a bairn, old feelings had surged up, sending her mind into a whirl of confusion. For a moment it even seemed to stop the pain. He may have been a daft bugger at times, but he was her daft bugger; had been since they were almost bairns themselves—her first man, her first love.

Yet it was Cian who put the practical stop to any dilemma. Perhaps the gods were bastards, but at least this time there was no choice. "We can't move her," he said emphatically, and knelt by her side, peering at the wound. "The shaft needs to be cut out, and the whole inside has to be mended right. We can try cutting it short, then taking her back, but she could bleed to death. She could die while we're doing it."

"Cheerful bugger, aren't you?" Elena whispered.

"*We* can look after her," Cethen said, his voice suddenly hopeful. "There are women who are good at this sort of thing. We might find a druid who could ... " Cethen fell silent as everyone glared at him.

"We'll camp here, send a half-dozen troopers back." Rhun looked up at the sky. "It won't be dark for a few hours. We've got the surgeons from three legions in camp. Surely one of them can come out."

"Of course they will," Marcus said, unconsciously wiping the flow of blood away from his eye. "Father will see to it. After all, Elena is his—" He broke off, his mind catching up with his mouth. "I'll go back too, speed things up."

"Then what about my people? And Morallta's? If the Romans come here in force ... " Cethen stood and looked about the meadow, his face the embodiment of indecision.

Elena carefully moved her head, her eyes following his gaze. Branaught held both troops of auxiliaries over by the stream. Cethen's people had grouped over by the forest's edge, at the side of the valley. Several graves had been started, and she could see at least one of the women busy patching up the wounded.

"As far as I'm concerned, we had one bitch of a fight, we won it, but the enemy escaped into the forest," Rhun suggested, and called out, "Any of you have any problem with that?"

Nobody did, except Cethen. "*I'm* not going," he said stubbornly, and looked down at Elena, repeating the words. "I'm not going. Not now."

"Da," Rhun protested, "Gaius will be coming with surgeons, and a larger escort. I'd wager on it."

"So? He owes me."

"Don't be stupid," Cian began, but Coira cut in.

"Dammit, Da, use your head. If they find you here, they'll take you as a—"

"Listen, all of you," Marcus interrupted, his voice almost a shout. "This man can't stay here. Really. Neither can his people. Be practical, there's—"

"My people aren't staying. They're going. It's only me who's not."

"Da ..."

"What about Bryn, Da? What happened to ... "

Elena winced as another spasm of pain rolled through her shoulder. When it had passed, she sighed, rolled her eyes, and breathed one word under her breath: "Shi-it!"

Epilogue

Eboracum, A.D. 96

It was a large fire, built from a huge pile of logs that before they were torched had been the size of a poor man's hovel. The flames lit the night with great orange tongues, topped by clouds of glittering sparks that crackled as they drifted out over the Abus and died. Well over a hundred had gathered around the enormous blaze, sitting well back from the intense heat. Most were well-wishers from Cian and Branaught's auxiliary squadrons, and those who had women had brought them along. There were even some men there who had been with Cian at Vetera, who'd made it down from the northern forts on one excuse or another. It was an occasion not to be missed.

By the time Samhain had arrived, it seemed that everyone had cause to celebrate. The late summer weather had lingered on through October, for once offering more time than needed for the harvest. The small town slowly building around the fortress had prospered, along with its fair share of Britons, and their gods had given reason to be grateful, as had Rome's. And there had been the festival itself, of course. Many of Cian's men still nursed aching heads from the prior week, when the last day of the month had come and gone.

Samhain was quickly followed by other festivities, the first marking the end of the current governor's three-year tour of service: Gaius Sabinius Trebonius was going back to Rome. It was said the man had asked for an extension, citing as precedent the late Gnaeus Julius Agricola, who had served Britannia as governor for six years. But

393

Domitian had refused; probably, the cynics said, because the current governor posed no threat by his return. And the incoming governor, a man called *Metilius Nepos*, would be in want of his own preferment.

So the governor's son, Marcus Sabinius, current legate of the Ninth Hispana, organized a send-off that would doubtless be repeated by the legates of the other two legions in Britannia, and the commanders of every fort and outpost between Eboracum and Rome as he journeyed home. It was all cause for more aching heads, though, for every man not on duty was required to attend—an order that was no hardship, for the governor himself paid for the food and drink.

There had been the usual pomp and puff to go through first: a parade of all ranks in full dress uniform: crests and decorations, armour polished like silver, shields freshly painted, and weapons honed fit for shaving. When the honours were presented, Cian was given his official release, his Roman citizenship, and a land grant of forty *heredia* just downriver from his old farm.

Where, two days later, the great fire was lit to celebrate his retirement.

The release fell three years short of Cian's twenty-five-year service period, as did Luga's, who received a smaller tract of land alongside. But both men were now in their fifties, and the bones did not flex as they once did when a stiff frost covered the ground on a cool, crisp morning. Not that theirs was a medical discharge, for both men, considering the battering they'd taken over the years, were not in bad health. It was just that each was about ten years older than others with their length of service and, as Cian had put it more than once, "Life's too short for this shit." The word was out, though, that the governor's woman had a lot to do with it, for an early release without cause was unusual; but then, governors could do nearly anything they wanted.

The flames settled as the night darkened, yet nobody saw fit to stoke the fire. Instead, everyone drew close as the logs burned down and crumbled into a pile of glowing coals that continued to crackle and spit. Cian called across the fire to Criff, who simply smiled and nodded, then ambled over. Easing himself down on the grass, he crossed his legs and bent forward, making a show of tuning his harp. The children—a score or more including Cian's young son Ur—settled around the bard, pushing and shoving for the better places.

When Criff, head cocked to one side, strummed his fingers across the strings and finally nodded his satisfaction, the talk died and the night fell silent. He turned to Cian, who sat perched on an enormous log beside his woman Deirdre, and asked what the first song should be.

Cian grinned, his mind floating in an alcoholic haze that spawned more goodwill than he'd felt in a long time—for both the men crowded about the fire and the woman who sat next to him. "Something fitting, Criff, for today I'm a free man."

"Ah, but not for long," Criff quipped with a quick wink at Deirdre, then his deep voice broke into the familiar "The Marriage of Skolan Sharvae." Others joined in as the bard sang the refrain, and the riverbank soon boomed with a chorus of voices that echoed lustily across the cool, drifting waters of the Abus.

Criff interspersed stories amidst his songs, and he was a master. Most were droll and bawdy, for this was a night to tell them; but some were of lost love, and others of fights and battles that, for the most part, had been won. One, which proved a great source of amusement, told of a man named Keenan who launched an attack on several Tungri cavalrymen, only to be knocked senseless at the very start. Criff gave a wildly exaggerated account of what happened to the poor fellow in his witless state, ending only when the hero found himself back in Venutius's camp, slung backward on his horse with half his gear missing.

Everyone knew it was the story of Cian and his brother Cethen, when the new fort had been built at Isurium twenty-five years ago— which only served to make the telling that much better. As the laughter died, someone threw a few more logs on the fire, and a great cloud of orange sparks burst skyward. Criff, turning once more to tuning his harp, glanced around the sea of faces lit by the fire's glow. "Anyone else have a tale to tell? A song to sing?" he asked, and smiled. "I'm always looking for one."

At first nobody seemed willing, for Criff's performance was too skillful to follow. But then Luga lumbered to his feet, his great bulk weaving as he raised both hands to silence the loud chorus of groans that followed. "Hey, I really do got a story," he protested and, when the hooting and shouting died down, added, "and it's a good one!"

"Sit down."

"Criff, how about another song?" another voice called out.

"Hey, I said I'm always looking for a good tale. Does it have a name?" Criff asked, and motioned for the big man to continue.

Luga stood frowning, then his bearded face suddenly split in a huge grin. "No, it's not got a name, but it's real interesting. It's about that legate that damn-near killed Cian. You can turn it into a real good story, Criff. You're good at that."

"Luga, that's enough," Cian drawled and leaned forward, vaguely sensing that Luga was walking into a bog. "Sit down."

A clamour of protest rose from the same people who, moments before, had been trying to get the big man to shut up. Luga grinned and bowed unsteadily, beer slopping from his mug as the hand holding it swooped low across his huge belly. "Hey Cian, it's only a story. I didn't say it was true," he said, offering a wink to the crowd along with a loud, comfortable belch.

"If it's only a story, then …" Criff encouraged.

"Luga!" Cian warned.

"You're not the only free man here," Luga growled. "I'm not in your troop anymore, arsehole."

"Ah, you stupid clod," Cian mumbled and rose unsteadily from the log.

Deirdre pulled him down again as others around the fire began to chant, "Fight, fight, fight."

"It's about time they settled it, before they die of old age," someone called.

Criff appeared intrigued. He raised a hand, and the shouting died. "As I said, if it's only a story …"

"Which it is," Luga said self-righteously, glancing askance at Cian.

Cian groaned, leaned back on the log, and buried his face in Deirdre's shoulder as Luga began to speak.

"The legate were asleep, fast asleep," the big man began in a low voice, squatting on his heels after draining the beer mug and tossing it to one side. "His snoring sounded like a sick cow. And the three strange men, who as I said are all make-believe, figured if that weren't going to wake nobody, then nothing would."

"Who was it, really? You and Branaught?"

"I told you, it's just a story!" Luga said firmly, then turned toward the speaker and leered. "And Pisear wasn't there, either."

"Agh, you dumb ox. Shut up!" a voice that could only belong to Pisear cried from the other side of the circle.

"You shut up," another shouted, then, "So how did they get in?"

Luga snorted. "That were the easy part. They slid in under the back. There were three guards, but the silly buggers just stood in front bitching at each other. No patrolling round the tent or nothing. And if there were anyone else inside, then they had their heads down deeper than the legate."

Luga paused as if to be certain his audience listened, and seemed reassured when a voice called out, "So what happened?"

"So one man stood over him with a knife, just in case he woke. And I—" He stopped short and looked furtively about the fire, then explained, "When I say *I*, it's only because it's me telling the story, you understand? It wasn't really me." A mutter of agreement seemed to satisfy him, and he continued. "So I knelt down so I could cover his gob if he woke up. Then Bran—no, oops, it were Brok. I'll call the third man Brok for lack of any other name—he went looking for the legate's sword, and that was when everything started to go wrong."

"What happened?" Cian asked, for Luga had never gone into any great detail about what went on that night. It hadn't seemed right to ask a man how he committed a murder, whether it was justified or not.

"Cian, it were as black as death in there. Bran—I mean Brok—he fumbled around in the dark, making a bugger of a row. After a while he started to panic. He were so nervous, I don't think he could have found his arsehole with all five fingers. The more he looked for the stupid sword, the more he couldn't find it. The legate didn't wake, but you could see he were getting ready to."

Luga looked around for his beer mug, and seemed puzzled when it wasn't nearby. "Where's...?"

"Luga, get to the point," Cian growled, losing patience. "Did you—"

"I'm getting there," Luga hissed, sounding just as impatient. "Brok finally bumped into a big chest, and decided the sword had to be inside.

So the fool lifts the lid, starts poking around, and moves something, for there's a right bugger of a clang."

"That woke him up?" This time Criff asked the question.

"No, no, he just kind of moved and grunted, but kept on snoring." Luga took a deep breath, rubbed his nose on the back of one hand, and sighed. "It were the lid falling on Bran's head and him yelping that woke the bugger."

"Brok!"

"Yeah, Brok."

"Stupid, half-witted ... " Cian mumbled under his breath.

"So Pisear's not taking chances, is he? Sticks the knife in, right in his middle, under the ribs."

"I wasn't there!" Pisear called from the far side of the fire. "I wasn't, I swear it. For shit's sake, Luga, if you're going to tell a story, tell it right."

"Oh, yeah, that's right," Luga mumbled, for the first time looking unsure. "I was just using that as a name. I'll use Crom instead. Yeah. *Crom* sticks him with the knife."

"Did he die quiet?"

"No, not really. He sort of yelped before I got my hand over his gob, and we were all fit to shit waiting for someone to notice. The legate sort of stiffened and twitched for a bit, then after a while just went limp. But nothing happened, so nobody could have heard."

"That just might be why you're still here," Cian muttered sarcastically, then his mind, which wasn't at its peak, realized something was amiss. "They said he fell on his sword. But you said Pis—Crom stuck him with a knife. They would have known the difference."

"No, they wouldn't," Luga said, sounding almost petulant.

Everyone waited, and when nothing more was forthcoming, Cian sighed and asked, "Why wouldn't they, Luga?"

"Because he were lying there with a stab cut in his chest, and *I*," Luga sniffed as he emphasized the word, "I figured we could shove a sword in it, and it would be like he'd done it himself."

"So you did find the sword, then?"

"No."

"Tell me you didn't brain one of the guards and take his," Cian sighed.

"We didn't brain one of the guards and take his," Luga said, and when he saw the look on Cian's face, he added, "Honest. We didn't. Bra—Brok snuck out again and stole one from the armouries."

"Idiot! He could have got caught. Why didn't he just steal one from some Roman's tent? It would have been easier."

Luga looked pained. "Then the poor sod would be short his sword, wouldn't he?"

"So what? Let *him* steal another."

Luga ignored the comment, and plunged on. "Anyway, when this man I'm calling Brok got back, we took the legate and set him on his knees, with me holding him up. Pisear slid the—"

"Crom, you stupid pig!" Pisear roared.

"Yeah, Crom. Crom slid the tip of the sword in until it were snug in the knife wound, and Brok set the hilt on the ground."

"And you, the person who's making up the story, pushed him forward," Cian finished, though there was something that still bothered him, and he couldn't place it.

"Yeah, and that was the real funny part. When he tumbled over, he let go the biggest fart you ever heard. We thought it would bring everyone running, but it didn't." Luga chuckled and nudged Criff's shoulder, making him almost drop the harp. "Bran said it was because they were so used to hearing officers fart, they didn't pay no attention."

Cian snapped his fingers as what was wrong finally struck him. "The blood! Why didn't they figure something out from the blood?"

"Huh?"

"The blood," Cian growled. "If he was stabbed when he was on his back, then the blood would have spread all over his chest, and three ends to sideways. If he'd fallen on his fool sword, the blood would have seeped down over his crotch. Why didn't they notice?"

"'Cause there was no need." Luga shook his huge head.

"No need?"

"No! *Anyone* would know that was a problem. So we set his knees on the grass as you'd expect, *then* laid him out backward. You know, like as if he'd decided to push it in instead, then flipped back with the pain."

Cian sat straighter for a better look at Luga, impressed by the big man's thinking. "You thought of that?"

Luga hesitated, then had the grace to look sheepish. "Naw, Bra—Brok did."

"And that's it?" Criff ran his fingers along the harp strings, the only sound to be heard except the crackle of burning logs.

"Isn't it enough?" Cian muttered, then decided he should at least play along with Luga's drunken travesty. Yet what would the fool say if this slipped out and the great oaf was questioned? "Luga, you dumb ox, the whole thing's made up, isn't it?"

"Doesn't matter," Criff interrupted. "It's the tale that talks, and this one speaks well. I think I'll call it *The Death of the Legate of*—oh shit!"

"That's a stupid sort of ... " Cian began, then saw that Criff was staring, open-jawed, somewhere over his shoulder. He whirled around and muttered the same word as he clambered to his feet.

Gaius appeared out the darkness, and with him Marcus and his daughter, Jessa. The men wore cloaks draped loose about their shoulders to fight the night chill, but were otherwise dressed the same as those about the fire: a warm tunic, leggings, and no weapon. Gaius carried a leather dispatch pouch: a round, sealed tube with a braided lanyard tied at either end so that it might be slung around the neck.

Jessa walked ahead of them both, her small, awkward figure caught by the glow of the dying fire. An impish smile lit her face. "Elena asked me to give you this before she left. Rhun sent it from Judaea." She stopped in front of Cian and handed him a gold chain. Dangling from it, like a pendant, was the deer antler carving of a man on a horse. The charred leg had been cleaned and repaired with a smooth inlay of matching enamel, and small rubies dotted each eye. "It's pretty, don't you think?"

"Er, yeah, it is. Very pretty," Cian mumbled, which was true. The gift, under any other circumstance, would have brought tears to his eyes, but—how much had been heard? The legate and Marcus, he saw, were both leading horses by the reins. The buggers had walked up—no, snuck up—before stepping into the glow cast by the flames. Though they'd probably only been trying to surprise him. The proof, he saw, was that each of the horses carried an *amphora* tied behind the saddle. He returned his attention to Marcus's daughter. "Er, thanks, Jess. Give Elena my thanks, too. I'll have to write Rhun. It's, er, long overdue."

"Then you might tell him about *The Death of the Legate of Oh Shit,*" Jessa whispered, and raised her eyebrows. "Luga tells quite a story."

"Damn!"

The silence that followed was broken only by the popping of burning wood, and the soft footsteps of Gaius and Marcus as they neared the fire, straining under the weight of the heavy clay amphorae. Every eye was on the two Romans, waiting to see which way the reed bent.

"Sorry to hear about your mother, Criff," Gaius murmured, breathing hard with effort as he passed by the bard. "She was a great woman."

"Er, thank you, sir," he replied, edging to one side to allow them room to pass.

"I doubt this is needed," Gaius said as he leaned the vessel he carried against the log where Cian sat with Deirdre, "but consider it a gift from Elena and me."

"And this one," Marcus pretended to gasp for breath as he set the second amphora beside the first, "is from me. And I suppose Jessa, too. Though truth be known, both came from legion stores. I tell you, Cian, you have no idea what it means to be a legate."

"Yeah, I suppose ... "

"Oh, and there's this." Gaius handed the leather case to Cian. "As you know, I'm gone in another few days. You might make use of this later."

"What is it, sir?" Cian stared down at the tube, puzzled.

"It's for your brother," Gaius said, and sat down on the log, motioning for Cian to do the same. "If he gets any sense into that thick skull of his, he can use that to return here and live. I would also add that when it comes to what a man's able to do," he bowed his head to Marcus as if in deference, "you have no idea what it means to be a governor, either. Or, for that matter, to live under the same roof as Elena."

"Elena?"

Gaius ignored the implied question. Just how much Elena had contributed to his decision was none of the man's concern; and he, himself, wasn't even sure. The woman had departed for Rome several weeks ago, but not before certain arrangements had been settled to the satisfaction of both. Before she and Gaius left the province for good, Elena wanted to make sure that Cethen and his family would not run afoul of the next Roman administration, and he could understand that. He, too, found the idea held a certain appeal.

The man lived somewhere in the great hills that lay on the far side of Stannick. Gaius knew that much, and he also realized the fool likely didn't wish to return anyway. Yet if he did, the fellow was now far from being a threat—of any kind. Not only did the man have his own woman, there was also a child—two of them, in fact, one by her and another by the red-haired woman he'd killed. Elena, in fairness, always passed along what she heard. Most of the time.

No, any problem concerning Cethen Lamh-fada, if there had ever been one, no longer existed. More than one pardon had been issued by governors, and in the scheme of things, this one had been minor.

But now there was this! Gaius glanced up at Luga, standing off to one side like a hound that had mistakenly bitten its master. The man's tale was obviously the truth, and yet---

Dealing with it would delay his journey home by the gods knew how long…and what did Catus's death matter, anyway? The only man who might be concerned was Agricola, who'd been dead these two years. Elena herself would put a practical point to it: what good would dragging it all up do, anyway? In fact—and Gaius unconsciously grinned—he could hear her words: *They did you a favour, Gaius, accept it as a gift!* or *After what he did to Cian, the man deserved it!*

Someone, Gaius thought it was Deirdre, passed him a mug of some sort of dark liquid. He sighed. He supposed he would let it go, but first he'd make the big oaf's heart beat a little harder. Gaius took took a long pull on the drink—an excellent flat ale—and climbed to his feet. "That's quite a story you tell there, Luga. So, tell me: is it really myth, or the truth?"

Luga's eyes bulged. His mouth worked like that of a dying fish, but no words came out. Before they did and the big fellow said something that couldn't be ignored, Gaius spoke again.

"Let me see, the tale was about the fate of a certain legate, and the way things might have been. So…" He paused and peered around at the silent circle of faces. Without exception, they all looked very uncomfortable. Lowering his voice in the same manner as Criff when beginning a tale, he said, "Does anyone want to hear a story called *The Death of the Legate of Lindum*?"

Cian gasped and looked across the fire at Luga with an expression of shock and disbelief; the big man's face mirrored his former commander's. Gaius knew that most had heard the rumours. The story had followed him for more than twenty years, growing until it was legend; yet like most legends, only a kernel of it was true. Judging by the faces lit by the glow of the flames, it was clear that most took the legend as fact. The murmur of surprise was almost a rumble.

Gaius cut it short before anyone could say yes. "So nobody does, huh?" He sat down, pretending disappointment, then smiled. He was going home anyway, and there was nothing like leaving a reputation behind; it would give Nepos something to live up to. "Then how about this one? *The Tribune's Swim in the Abus.*"

Gaius felt the tension ease. He too relaxed as he began the tale of his ordeal when marking out the fortress at Eboracum, an ordeal that ended with Cethen Lamh-fada pulling him from the Abus. That had been twenty-five years ago, and at the time he could have cheerfully killed the man. Yet now, what did it matter? His eye briefly caught that of his granddaughter as she settled down alongside Criff, ready to listen to the story. She shook her head as if in despair. He knew both Elena and Coira had told the story a hundred times.

"Criff," Jessa whispered.

The bard glanced sideways, amused. "What is it, little one?"

"The name is Jessa, dammit, not little one."

"Sorry. Jessa."

"Have you heard this story before?"

"Uh-huh."

"Are you going to make it into a song or something?"

"You mean something like 'Lamh-fada Pulls a Fish from the Abus'?" Criff chuckled. "Child, I've been singing that one for as long as I can remember."

"And don't call me child, either..."

Appendix J

A Brief Description of the Roman Legions, Late First Century A.D.

A Roman legion did not march alone. It normally had auxiliary units attached, both infantry and cavalry, that might as much as double its numbers. To some extent these units were organized on lines similar to the legion, especially the infantry, but there were differences. The following briefly details the strength and organization of a legion such as the Ninth Hispana, as well as an auxiliary cavalry regiment and an auxiliary infantry battalion. In order to make the story flow, the modern equivalents have been used for certain elements of the armies rather than the lengthy, unfamiliar name (such as *squad* instead of *contubernia(e)*; or a *troop* or *squadron* instead of a *turma(e)*).

THE LEGION

Each *legio(n)* was made up of ten *cohort(e)s*, which were officially 480 strong, except for the most senior cohort—the first cohort—which had 800 men. There appears to be some debate about the reason for the extra-large first cohort. Based on modern army needs, I have adopted the position that those extra numbers were likely service support or specialist soldiers, much like a modern service battalion. In total, the basic legion strength was 5,250 men, though 4,000 seems to have been its normal garrison strength, perhaps dipping as low as 3,000 after hard campaigning.

The legion was commanded by a *legatus legionis* (*legate*), who was of senatorial rank. He was assisted by mainly ex-rankers, the most senior being the *primus pilus* (definition: the first spear, a rank that might be compared to a supercharged regimental sergeant major, and in many ways equivalent in power to that of the legate himself) and the *praefectus castrorum* (a senior ex-ranker who remained in charge of the base when the legion was in the field). Each cohort (except the senior cohort) consisted of six *centuriae* (companies) of 80 men. It was commanded by a *centurio(n)*, who was assisted by a second-in-command (*optio*), the latter word being a general term. A regular cohort was normally commanded by a senior centurio, and the larger first cohort by the primus pilus himself, though a military tribune might also command.

Each company of 80 men was made up of ten 8-man *contubernia* (squads). The leader, or "squaddie," was called a *decanus*.

The legion strength also included six *tribunes* of varying seniority and career paths, including one of senatorial rank beginning the military portion of his career; four 30-man cavalry *turmae* used primarily for general duties; the artillery, which was dispersed amongst the cohorts; and a complement of musicians.

AUXILIARY CAVALRY

Cavalry cohorts (regiments) were called *alae,* and were normally of two sizes, though each regiment was made up of 30-man *turmae* (troops or squadrons). A cohort of 16 troops was an *ala quingenariam,* and one of 24 troops was an *ala milliaria.* The cohorts were commanded by a *praefectus alae,* the position normally being the career peak of an officer of the equestrian order. His second-in-command was called an *optio.* The troopers themselves were each commanded by a *decurio,* and his second-in-command was also called an *optio.* There were also musicians and other supernumeraries, all of them fighting in the ranks.

AUXILIARY INFANTRY

The auxiliary infantry were grouped in units called *cohorts,* which were of two sizes: a *cohors quingenaria* of six companies (*centuriae*), totalling 480 men, and a *cohors milliaria* of ten companies totalling 800 men. The makeup of the companies, or *centuriae,* was the same as in a legion.

The *cohors quingenaria* was usually commanded by a *praefectus cohortis*. However, if honoured with the designation *civium Romanorum*, which effectively gave the unit the status of a legion, the cohort might be commanded by a *tribunus* or senior tribune. The larger *cohors milliaria* were also, normally, commanded by a *tribunus*.

COMBINED AUXILIARY UNITS

The auxiliary cohorts regularly consisted of combined units of both cavalry and infantry, which might vary in mix, but with the same general grouping of companies (*centuriae*) and squadrons (*turmae*). This was particularly useful and common in the garrisoning of the forts and outposts such as those established by Agricola. Such units were referred to as *Cohors Equitata*.

Imperial Rome kept a standing army of around 250,000 men. It was largely funded by the people it was either conquering, plundering, or protecting, the description likely determined by which side you were on. A small and easily understood softcover book, *The Armies and Enemies of Imperial Rome*, by Philip Barker (Wargames Research Group, ISBN 0950029963), provides a very quick and readable reference for not only the Roman forces but, as the title indicates, those of her enemies. A more detailed but still easily readable book is *The Complete Roman Army*, by Adrian Goldsworthy (Thomas & Hudson Ltd., ISBN 0500051240).

Appendix II

Glossary

Note: Other than the Silures (see below), the territories of the various tribes can be found on the map of northern England and southern Scotland at the front of the book.

Ala(e): cavalry cohorts (regiments); each regiment was made up of 30-man *turmae* (troops or squadrons). See further details under Appendix I, auxiliary cavalry.

Amphora(e): large ceramic urn-shaped wine vessel with two ears (carrying handles). What is particularly unusual about them is that the bottom was pointed, rather than having a flat base. At the time of this story, the vessels had the typical narrow neck with a narrower rather than bulbous "belly." Essentially a huge wine jug, the contents were standardized for the bulk of shipments at around six gallons, or twenty-four litres.

Aulus Atticus: This officer is mentioned here because he is the only casualty that Tacitus listed by name in the battle at Mons Graupius. See Appendix IV, trivia, for that description of the battle, where Aulus's cohort, along with others, outpaced the advance, which seems to have cost him his life.

Beltane: the celebration of life, fertility, and the spring season (crops would have already been planted); traditionally thought to be celebrated on the first day of May.

cornui: see below, included under *tuba.*

cunnies: a slight anglicizing of a Latin obscenity referring to a woman's private parts.

decanus (plural decani): the leader of one of the ten 8-man infantry sections that made up a *contubernia,* or what a modern army might call a squad, or a section.

decurio: the leader of one of the sixteen cavalry *turmae* that make up a basic cavalry regiment. In terms of nineteenth-century cavalry units, these might be equated with a squadron or a troop.

denarius (plural, denarii): in terms of today's value, this coin would purchase around US$20 of bread. At the time of the book, it was also a day's pay, before deductions, for the common soldier. See **quadran** below for its standing in the Roman monetary system.

equestrian: also referred to as "equites," or knights. It was an order of citizenship that ranked below senatorial status (see below), whose members often followed a mixed career in the military, civil service, and trade and commerce. This career was often carried out (like those of senatorial rank) in an orderly, progressive pattern. As to the military, command of an auxiliary cohort was probably the peak of an equestrian's career.

garum: this was a garnish, or thin sauce, that was probably used by Romans as liberally as North Americans apply ketchup. It was a strong, pungent seasoning made from fish parts. One of the simpler recipes is as follows:
Take the entrails of tunny fish and its gills, juice, and blood, and add sufficient salt. Leave it in a vessel for two months at most, then pierce the side of the vessel and the garum, called Haimation

(presumably the name of this particular recipe), will flow out.

Horrible as this recipe may sound, the general effect of the various types of garum was something resembling the taste of an anchovy paste.

heredia (singular, heredium): A Roman unit of measurement, equivalent to approximately four acres.

honour price: a little difficult to describe in today's terms, but it was an assessment of a man's worth in terms of his dignity (face), or present weight in the community; it was also directly related to his material worth. In this way a prosperous man might ascend considerably in rank, but the honour price fluctuated according to his fortunes. This was particularly important when considering compensation for wrongs that were committed, and where redress was awarded.

hypocaust: translation: heat from below. The Romans had central heating in their buildings, though it was expensive and labour intensive and therefore probably found only in public buildings and the properties of the wealthy. The hypocaust refers to the spaces under the raised floors or in the hollow of the walls that trapped and vented heat from a furnace fed by manual labour.

kin: the kin could, in some ways, best be described as a smaller unit or related individuals within the actual tuath (see below). It was a very extended family, and in the instance of the *Eboracvm* books it is primarily applied to the Eburii, led by the minor chieftain Cethen Lamh-fada. It would include anyone who is closely and even loosely related (second and third cousins, adoptees, etc.).

legate (legatus legionis): the commander of a legion, a man of senatorial rank. See further details in Appendix I, The Roman Army.

lorica: Roman upper body armour of the type made from leather or metal sections fastened together.

medicus (plural medici): the fortress doctor, also a field surgeon, who was quite highly skilled when compared, for example, to mid-nineteenth-century physicians. The legion's medicus would be the senior man in a hospital that was usually a building of four wings enclosing a courtyard. There would likely be a large room at the entrance and, in a full-sized fortress, more than five dozen small wards, each accommodating four to eight patients. The entire structure might approach 60,000 square feet, and could technically house almost 10% of the legion. The medicus likely ranked on the same level with a fairly senior centurio (*medicus ordinarius*), and many apparently came from the Hellenistic provinces.

Nepos, Publius Metilius: Publius Nepos actually did become governor of the province of Britannia in A.D. 96. The governors for the previous seven (approximate) years seem to be unknown. As such, Gaius Sabinius Trebonius could very well have been one of them.

optio: this seems to be a general rank assigned to the second-in-command of most designated appointments. For example, a praefectus commanding a cavalry *alae* (regiment), or the decurio commanding one of the *turmae* (squadrons or troops) that made up that regiment would each have a second-in-command called an *optio*.

pilus (correct word for the weapon itself is actually pilum; plural, pili): a type of spear, and one of two main weapon types used by the foot soldier (sword and spear). This particular heavy spear was historically unusual in its construction. The shaft, as might be expected, was of wood, but shorter than most. This was because the tip, instead of being the normal sharp, pointed head about six to eight inches long, had a small barb on the tip of a long, thin iron rod that comprised up to a third of the weapon's length. It was used in the legion ranks primarily as a throwing weapon that, if it didn't kill or wound, caught and stuck in the enemy shield, rendering his defence difficult. (Note: *pilus* in Latin means "hair," and is today the name of a hairlike appendage found on many bacteria.) There were three other types of spears in general use: the *hasta*, a more traditional spear about six feet long, and phased out for the most part sometime during the early Empire; the *contus*, a longer standard spear used mainly by the cavalry (really a lance), would likely have been the type used by Rhun; and the *veluti*, which is the javelin referred to in Rhun's night charge: a lighter, dart-like spear, with more than one being carried by troops such as auxiliary cavalry to be thrown or perhaps used in close-quarters melees.

praefectus castrorum: translation: prefect of the camp. A senior, and usually older, experienced ex-ranker and ex-centurio who had command of the camp or fort(ress) when the legion was in the field.

Praetorian Gate (porta praetoria), et al: the main gate leading into the fortress. In the instance of Eboracum, it was from the south. Using the same fortress as a bearing, the others were as follows: north: *porta pecumana*; west: *porta principalis dextra*; east: *porta principalis sinistra*. "Principalis" was used because these gates opened onto the main street leading east and west, known as the *via principalis*

Praetorian Guard: the unique and in many ways privileged legion that was, in fact, an effective fighting force that at various times was actively used in the field, usually only when necessary. It was the emperor's personal guard (a double-edged sword), and was stationed outside the walls of Rome, with only one cohort deployed at any one time as the palace guard. Its members were paid significantly more than a regular legion.

primus pilus: translation: first spear. The senior centurio of the legion who was usually assigned the first cohort. He had powers (particularly over the discipline, operations, and training of the men) that rivalled that of the legate. The position was filled by a man drawn from the ranks.

procurator: a powerful administrative position in a Roman province held by a man of equestrian rank. He was responsible for the finances, taxation, control of imperial property, and census. He also acted as a "check" to the governor's authority, in that he reported independently to the emperor himself. An example would have been the procurator Julius Classicianus, a man primarily responsible for the recalling of Seutonius due to his brutal reprisals following Boudicca's rebellion (an uprising that was largely a reaction to a former procurator's greed and ruthlessness).

pteruges: on a legion soldier's uniform, the leather straps that dangle vertically over the lower portion, or skirt, of his tunic. At the time of this book, the rank and file likely had a fairly narrow set that only protected the groin area.

puls (or pulmentus): a cereal gruel or porridge, prepared from barley or spelt wheat that was roasted, pounded, and cooked with water in a cauldron. (Possible ancestor of the word porridge?) The mix is similar to the modern Italian polenta.

quadran: the lowest denomination of Roman money. In ascending value: 1,600 quadrans = 1 as; 400 as = 1 dupondius; 200 dupondius = 1 sestertius; 100 sestertii = 1 quinarius; 50 quinarii = 1 denarius; 25 denarii = 1 quinarius aureus (gold); 2 quinarii aureus = 1 aurei; the word *talent* (from the Greek) was used for dealing with large amounts of money, and 1 talent was equivalent to 6,000 denarii.

Samhain: the Celtic festival that marks the end of the harvest season, which is taken to be the final day of October.

senatorial rank: this rank essentially described the privileged few who belonged to the senate. (The senate itself, and membership therein, changed throughout the Republic and into the times of Imperial Rome, and even a basic overview would require several pages. It might, however, be in some ways likened to a Roman House of Lords, with rankings that could determine whether the individual even had the right to speak).

sestertius (**or sesterce, plural sestertii**): a larger coin than the denarius but of brass or bronze and of lesser value. See **quadran** above for comments on relative value.

Silures: a tribe that occupied the southern part of present-day Wales.

sinistra: see the description of the various fortress gates above, under *porta praetoria, et al.* The translation to English is: of the left hand.

stola: much like the men's long toga; a rectangular cloth draped around a woman's body to form a long, flowing garment.

tribunal: a permanent platform that served as a podium, situated at one corner of the cross hall that spanned the headquarters building (*principia*) of a fort or fortress. It was the first room entered once the walled-in forecourt was crossed. It was used for issuing orders, punishment, receiving visitors, and other general HQ duties, including smaller parades. The rear of the hall was lined with rooms, the central one being a shrine (*aedes*) for the standards, a statue of the emperor, and likely several altars. Below it was the unit's treasury, and on either side were administrative offices.

tuath: a word that originally meant "people," but which acquired a territorial connotation. In population and extent it was fairly small, and normally conformed to an area with natural topographical boundaries. Depending on size, it could have its own aristocratic structure that might even extend to a king, nobles (chieftains), and common freemen. The Brigante tribe itself was quite scattered, occupying Lancashire, most of Yorkshire and, on the west coast, extended perhaps as far south as the Mersey.

tuba and cornu(i): two wind/brass instruments that were essentially horns. The former was a long, straight instrument flared at the end like a modern trumpet. The latter was also a long, thin horn, but bent almost in a huge circle, curving away from the mouth in a downward arc that turned under the elbow, then came back over the top of the head; it was braced across the centre by a decorated tube.

turmae: troops or squadrons; see Appendix I: A Brief Description of the Roman Legions.

via praetoria, via principalis: the road immediately inside the primary gate (*Praetoria*) that led directly up to, and stopped in front of, the headquarters building. This building, in turn, sat on the main street leading east and west, called the *via principalis*. The *principalis* was also the site of the commander's residence, usually alongside the legion headquarters.

Appendix III

Place Names and Detail

Abus: History appears to have left no Roman name for the river at York, which is now called the Ouse. The river flows down to the North Sea, where it runs into the River Humber, and then the Humber Estuary. It is known that the Romans called the Humber the *Abus*. Since the river Ouse flows uninterrupted all the way from York, I believe it is reasonable to speculate that the Romans may have referred to it as the Abus along the entire distance. Eboracum was, after all, still on the tidal reach; there is no really dramatic site where the Ouse, the larger river, is tapped into by the River Trent to become the Humber; and, as to the derivatives—dare it be pointed out that the *-us* on the end of Abus sounds very much like "Ouse"?

As to the *Fosse*, the smaller river (which has seen service similar to a canal over the years), it is now called the Foss. I have no idea what the Romans called it. I've simply added an "e" to conform to the spelling of the "Fosse Way," a reference to a main road leading north, which in A.D. 71 terminated on the south bank of the Humber, across from Petuaria (Brough).

Alavana: Watercrook, in Cumbria.

Aquae Sulis: the resort town of Bath.

Bodotria estuary: the Firth of Forth. Edinburgh is sited on its southern shore.

Bremenium: High Rochester, in Northumbria.

Calacum: Burrow on Lonsdale, at the northern tip of Lancashire.

Calcaria: now Tadcaster, about nine miles south-southwest of York, on the river Wharfe. It was the source of much of the sandstone used in the building of York, both in Roman times and later. York's medieval walls were built of this stone and still stand; of particular interest is the fact that they are, for the most part, built on top of the old Roman ramparts. Tadcaster is also the long-time home of the famous John Smith Brewery. A rule of thumb in England: the farther north, the better the beer.

Cataractonium: a Flavian (Vespasian) fort twenty-three miles north of Isurium. It was built on the site of the village reconnoitered by Gaius and Titus in *Eboracvm, the Village*, not long after the time of that story. The present-day town is Catterick, home to an RAF base that sits alongside the A1 North. (Many of the main arterial roads in England are built on top of the old Roman roads).

Camulodunum: now Slack, west Yorkshire, and a Celtic centre at the time of Rome's invasion. Some believe that the site was later the focus of the legendary kingdom of Camelot. It is not to be confused with the settlement of the same name in southern England, now called Colchester.

Derventio: now Malton, east Yorkshire. A base was established here not long before the fortress was built at Eboracum, likely during the initial incursions into Brigante territory before Cerialis began his full-scale subjugation. Derventio was situated either at the extreme southeast of Brigante territory, or the extreme northeast of Parisii territory (it is difficult to ascertain where the two actually overlapped). It would make strategic sense to first establish a sizeable base here in the hillier country above Eboracum, in order to secure the logistics of building there. Based on excavations, original construction was likely a thirty acre camp that provided security in which the Ninth and its auxiliary units, totalling as many as ten thousand men, could shelter when the full-scale assault came. (Not to be confused with Derventio, now known as Papcastle, in Cumbria.)

Deva: the city of Chester, in Cheshire.

Dubris: the port of Dover.

Ebor(acum): the Roman name for the city of York. The origin is the subject of debate. Three theories appear to be the most popular. One is that the name was derived from a man called Eburos who, legend says, fled Troy; though doubtful, it seems even more doubtful that he ever lived at Eboracum. The two others are both alluded to in the book *Eboracvm, the Village.* "Ebor" is apparently similar to, or has connotations with, a Roman word for boar. "Ebur" is a cognate found in the old Irish word *ibhar* or *iuhbar*, which means "yew." As such, its meaning could be extended to "place of the boar" or "place of the yews." This book also introduces the suffix "acum" at this time. The suffix *ium* or *(a)cum* was normally attached to the end of a place name where a civilian settlement had been built up or was attached (e.g., Viroconium, now Wroxeter). Since such settlement did not happen immediately, this suffix was not used in *Eboracvm, the Village,* except in the title.

Galava: Ambleside, Cumbria.

Germanicus Oceanus: the North Sea.

Gesoriacum: the French port of Calais.

Glevum: the city of Gloucester, in Gloucestershire.

Graupius, Mons: the Grampian Mountains, which are southwest of Inverness, below the Moray Firth (I found no Latin name for this huge estuary).

Habitancum: Risingham, Northumbria.

Hibernia: the country, and island, now called Ireland.

Hibernicus Oceanus: the Irish Sea.

Isurium: now the town of Aldborough, about seventeen miles north of York. It was already a substantial Celtic centre before the Romans invaded Brigantia.

Ituna estuary: the Solway Firth, the estuary that separates Cumbria, in England, from the county of Dumfries and Galloway in Scotland, on the west coast.

Lavatris: Bowes, Durham, not far west of Scotch Corner.

Lindum: the present-day city of Lincoln.

Londinium: as it sounds, this is the present-day city of London.

Luguvalium: the city of Carlisle, close by the Scottish border on the west coast of England.

Luna river: the present Lune river in south Cumbria, about forty-five miles long, and slightly changed in spelling to "Latinize" it.

Massalia: the port city of Marseilles.

Moricambe estuary: today's spelling is only slightly different from Morecambe Bay, as it is now called, which sits on the west coast where present-day Cumbria meets Lancashire.

Petuaria: the port of Brough, on the north side of the River Humber (Humber Estuary). It was one of two possible routes for Cerialis's original advance north from Lindum, the other being via *Danum* (Doncaster). It is possible that both were used in a pincer movement. As to the Humber itself (see comments on the River Abus, above), the crossing would have been by ferry.

Pinnatis: the name here is used for the fortress built by Agricola northwest of the Tava, the site now being called Inchtuthil. There is also some thought that the Romans might have named it Victoria. What seems certain is that they did not call it Inchtuthil. That word seems to derive from a translation of the Gaelic, meaning "hillock on the river-meadow." I settled on Pinnatis, which is found in two sources: *Ptolomey's Geography* and the *Ravenna Cosmology*. While it does not refer specifically to this fortress, it is not specific to any other site, and there is a certain logic in the translation of *pinna* as describing a site that *could* vaguely refer to this fortress at Inchtuthil. The fortress's life span proved quite unusual. It was more or less completed, held for at most six years (some references believe as little as two), then was destroyed by the Romans and abandoned ... likely for budget reasons as soldiers were required elsewhere in the empire.

Rhenus river: the river Rhine.

Sabrina river: the river Severn (and estuary) that flows past the port of Bristol.

Stannick: a Celtic centre before the arrival of the Roman invasion, located in Durham, not far from Scotch Corner. It seems to have been fortified, or at least built up and strengthened, after Claudius's invasion. There is conjecture that it was the seat of Venutius, and that at one time Cartimandua may have lived there before the two were divorced. The normal spelling is Stanwick, and I found no Roman name for the stronghold. I have dropped the "w" in the story simply because the "wick" seemed to leave the word too

Anglo(Saxon)fied.

Tava estuary: the Forth of Tay, approximately thirty miles north of Edinburgh.

Tinea river: the river Tyne, which would eventually be the eastern limit of Hadrian's Wall.

Trimontium: Newstead, county of Borders, southern Scotland.

Verteris: now Brough, though not to be confused with Brough in the Humber Estuary. This small town sits on the west slope of the Pennines, approximately twenty miles southeast of Penrith, on the way to Scotch Corner.

Vetera: A large, almost double-sized fortress built at what is now Birten, Germany, just across the border from Holland.

Vindomora: Ebchester, County Durham.

Vinovia: Binchester, County Durham.

Appendix IV

Commentary and Trivia

- Throughout the book *Eboracum* has been spelled with a "u" before the "m". The name on the cover, however, has used a "v": *Eboracvm*. This has been done simply in the interest of "purism," for the Romans employed no "u" in their alphabet. The letter "v" was used instead, to agree with the true Latin. This has, I have to admit, caused a wee bit of confusion.

- There appears to be no conclusive evidence for a settlement at the two rivers where the Eburii lived before the Romans arrived (tribal/kin name *Eburii* invented, though see above under *Ebor*, place names); nor is there any evidence that there was not.

- The use of the Roman numeral VIIII is not an error. Nowadays the number nine is expressed as IX. However, the VIIII usage was common with the Hispana Legio. It has been found stamped on their roofing tiles and chiselled into their monuments and other relics.

- The ambush of the Ninth almost certainly took place in one of three marching camps built a few miles south and southeast of the hill upon which sits the town of Crieff, Scotland. A good deal of the actual battle itself is conjecture. Tacitus was not specific in describing the event; also, he places Agricola as following the

Britons, yet the fighting takes place at night and finishes at the crack of dawn, and this seems to be confusing. Here's what he has to say:

Fearing that their superior numbers and their knowledge of the country might enable them to hem him in, he too (Agricola) distributed his forces into three divisions, and so advanced. This becoming known to the enemy, they suddenly changed their plan, and with their whole force attacked the Ninth Legion, as being the weakest, and cutting down the sentries, who were asleep or panic-stricken, they broke into the camp. And now the battle was raging within the camp itself, when Agricola, who had learnt from his scouts the enemy line of march and kept close on his track, ordered the most active soldiers of his cavalry and infantry to attack the rear of the assailants, while the entire army were shortly to raise a shout. Soon his standards glittered in the light of daybreak. A double peril thus alarmed the Britons, while the courage of the Romans revived; and feeling sure of their safety, they now fought for glory. In their turn they rushed to the attack, and there was a furious conflict within the narrow passages of the gates till the enemy was routed. Both armies did their utmost, the one for the honour of having given aid, the other for that of not having needed support. Had not ...

- The description of the battle at *Mons Graupius* has been essentially taken from the writings of Tacitus. In his writing, he attributes "rousing" speeches to both leaders, which he quotes verbatim. It would seem impossible for him to have known what the leader of the Britons said, if indeed he said anything at all.

Even so, the actual course of battle in the book follows Tacitus's description: the initial probing by chariots and cavalry, the crushing advance by the Batavi and Tungri cohorts and their near-envelopment, the threat of being outflanked, and the clearing of that threat by auxiliary cavalry and their subsequent attack on the rear of Galgar's army. There seems to have been great confusion on the field, including determining just when the battle was over. Prisoners were taken and slaughtered when their captors were counterattacked, and great numbers of Galgar's men did flee the field, though not necessarily in disorder.

Tacitus's numbers of those who fought were placed at 30,000 Britons; 8,000 Roman auxiliary infantry; 3,000 auxiliary cavalry; plus the reserve legion. He does not specify the unit(s) that made up the legion itself, but based on the legions posted in Britain at that time, and their base locations, I have made it a mix of the Ninth Hispana, the Twentieth Valeria Victrix, and the Second Adiutrix. Considering their past battles in Britain, the approximate 2:1 odds against the Romans should not have given them cause for concern.

Tacitus also listed casualties: *About 10,000 of the enemy were slain; and on our side there fell 360 men, and among them Aulus Atticus, the commander of the cohort, whose youthful impetuosity and mettlesome steel had borne him into the midst of the enemy.* I have avoided the mention of numbers in the story because, of course, it is always the victors who seem to write the history.

- Chronology of names for the city of York:

  1.*Ebor(acum)*, see description above under place names.

  2.*Eoforwic* came next. It was named by the Angles (sometime prior to A.D. 627), and may owe some ancestral origins to the Romans, as it was likely pronounced "Evrauc" or "Everwick."

  3.*Jorvik* (pronounced "Yorewick") followed, and this name was in use under the Danish occupation (A.D. 867). It seems to be a slight shift in pronunciation and spelling from Eoforwic. By the end of "Danelaw," which came with the successful invasion of the Northumbrians in A.D. 954, the name appears to have been abbreviated to York.

ISBN 142517363-2